CONTESTED CITY

Contested City

*Citizen Advocacy and Survival
in Modern Baghdad*

ALISSA WALTER

STANFORD UNIVERSITY PRESS
Stanford, California

Stanford University Press
Stanford, California

© 2025 by Alissa Joy Walter. All rights reserved.

No part of this book may be reproduced or transmitted in any form or by any means, electronic or mechanical, including photocopying and recording, or in any information storage or retrieval system, without the prior written permission of Stanford University Press.

Printed in the United States of America on acid-free, archival-quality paper.

ISBN 9781503640580 (cloth)
ISBN 9781503641426 (paperback)
ISBN 9781503641433 (electronic)

Library of Congress Control Number: 2024027964

Library of Congress Cataloging-in-Publication Data available upon request.

Cover design: George Kirkpatrick
Cover art: Map of Baghdad, Shutterstock

For Nodair, Luna, and Koji

CONTENTS

List of Figures ix
Acknowledgments xi
Author's Note xv

Introduction 1

PART I The Making of Modern Baghdad
1 Slums and Subdivisions 23
2 Baghdad Becomes a War Zone 60

PART II Citizen Advocacy and Local Governance
3 The Weaponization of Food Rations 101
4 The Politics of Petitions 132
5 Prostitution and Policing 159

PART III Aftermath of the US Invasion
6 Patchwork Power and Essential Services 187

Conclusion 221

Glossary of Key Arabic Terms 231
Notes 233
Bibliography 285
Index 303

FIGURES

FIGURE 1   Baghdad's Administrative Districts, 2003   5

FIGURE 2   Baʻth Party Organizational Hierarchy in Baghdad   7

FIGURE 3   Map of Baghdad's Historic Districts, 1917   25

FIGURE 4   Photograph of a *Sarifa* Community in Baghdad   29

FIGURE 5   Map of Baghdad *Sarifas*, 1950s   34

FIGURE 6   Photograph of Livestock in a Baghdad *Sarifa*   35

FIGURE 7   Map of Baghdad Bus Routes, 1952   36

FIGURE 8   Doxiadis's Slum Clearance Plan   43

FIGURE 9   Map of Baghdad Bus Routes, 1964   45

FIGURE 10   Map of Professional Neighborhoods, 1965   52

FIGURE 11   Monthly Food Rations Table, January 1991   105

FIGURE 12   Petition Envelope Addressed to the Director General of the Baʻth Party Secretariat, 1997   137

FIGURE 13   Organizational Chart of Baʻth Party Communication   147

FIGURE 14   Organizational Chart of the US–Created Council System, 2003   197

ACKNOWLEDGMENTS

This book would not have been possible without the unwavering support and encouragement of family, mentors, colleagues, librarians and archivists, editors, and—most importantly—Iraqis who shared their insights and stories with me.

I am thankful to many different institutions that provided financial support for this project. My research trips to archives in the United Kingdom, Greece, and France were funded by the Academic Research Institute in Iraq and internal grants from Georgetown University. The Dolores Zohrab Liebmann Fund supported two years of my research in the Iraqi Baʻth Party archives, and a Silas Palmer Research Grant from the Hoover Institution covered my relocation expenses to California. Writing was supported by grants from the American Association of University Women and by the United States Institute of Peace. Three fieldwork trips to Baghdad were funded by the Project on Middle East Political Science, the Arnold and Lois Graves Award for Teaching in the Humanities, and internal grants from Seattle Pacific University. I am grateful for the generosity of these funders, without which this manuscript could not have taken its present form.

I am indebted to many mentors who provided guidance and feedback at many stages of my research, writing, and revisions. Judith Tucker and Joseph Sassoon's scholarship informed my approach to social history, and their encouragement and advice guided me at every step. It was a formative experience to collaborate with Joseph on several research projects, and I am thankful for those opportunities, which helped me grow as a historian. Several other professors at Georgetown University deserve special thanks for their mentorship: Rochelle Davis, Fida Adeley, Sara Scalenghe, John Voll, and Osama Abi-Mershed, among others. At Seattle Pacific University, I'm thankful to many colleagues who supported this work through writing sessions and feedback on early drafts: Becky Hughes, Sara Shaban, Kimberly Segall, and other beloved friends. The Project on Middle East Political Science Junior Scholar Book Development Workshop was a helpful opportunity to refine an earlier version of my manuscript. Over the years, Dina Khoury, Sam Helfont, Lisa Blaydes, David Patel, Marc Lynch, Diane Singerman, Jill Schwedler, Alda Benjamin, Arbella Bet-Shlimon, Wisam Alshaibi, Michael DeGerald, Eckart Woertz, and Achim Rohde provided feedback and encouragement at critical junctures in developing this book. During my visits to Iraq I was grateful to discuss my research with Iraqi academics and with community historians through the Baghdad Cultural Forum. Their questions and insights informed my interpretations of neighborhood histories in Baghdad. There are more people than I can name here, and my appreciation extends to all my colleagues who impacted my work.

The staff and archivists of the collections I visited generously shared their wealth of knowledge and patiently facilitated my research. Haidar Hadi's intimate knowledge of the Baʿth Party records at the Hoover Library and Archives, his years of personal experience with the collection, and his dedication to helping researchers better understand and utilize the archive are unparalleled. Giota Pavlidou's extensive knowledge and expertise with the Constantinos Doxiadis archives in Athens was invaluable in navigating the collection and locating key information about Baghdad's housing projects in the 1950s. I am also thankful to Saad Eskander for facilitating my access to the Iraq National Library and Archives.

My oral history interviews with Iraqis and fieldwork in Iraq would not have been possible without the assistance of friends and research assistants. Saud worked with me for two years to carry out interviews with Baghdadis, connect me with new contacts, and help me interpret my data: his work was absolutely instrumental for this project. Saud also helped oversee a small research team for oral history interviews in Baghdad in 2015–16, and I am thankful to Ilaf and Noor for their work. Saud also took an active role in facilitating my first research trip to Baghdad, and I'm grateful to his family who warmly hosted me during my stays. In addition, Julianna Smith's and Firas's companionship during fieldwork in Baghdad was a gift that I treasure.

My fieldwork trip to Erbil, Iraq, in October 2016 coincided with the start of the battle to retake Mosul from the Islamic State, and I'm indebted to friends and colleagues who assisted me in navigating the unique challenges of that time. I am thankful to Sarah Ali for her advice and to Mélisande Genat for providing initial contacts and hospitality during my trip. My research assistant Hoveen facilitated many wonderfully informative meetings and carried us through long hours of work with his unbounded energy and optimism.

I am grateful to Dr. Ali Taher al-Hammood for his partnership in our research collaboration designing and carrying out structured interviews in Baghdad in 2022–23. It was a tremendous opportunity to learn alongside such a gifted and insightful researcher.

I am thankful to the roughly dozen American civilians and service members who allowed me to interview them about their work on local governance projects in Baghdad after 2003. Joe Rice and Michael Cole were especially generous with their time and in sharing their recollections and records pertaining to their work in Iraq.

At Stanford University Press, I am thankful to Kate Wahl for her strong support for my book, and to Kate and Thane Hale for helping me finalize my manuscript. Their support and advice has been essential in helping make this book a reality. In earlier stages of revisions, my student research assistants, Olivia Heale and Brock Quant, shone by bringing their enthusiasm and indefatigable attention to detail to assist with map data and proofreading. Jenny McCollum did excellent work creating preliminary maps to assist with geospatial analysis of archival data.

My family has been a source of strength and inspiration every step of the way. I'm thankful that my parents, Gary and Nancy, supported my many trips and sojourns to Iraq and other parts of the Middle East. I share my deepest gratitude for my husband, Nodair. He has been a constant companion on this journey, relocating with me several times and patiently enduring my absence during long research trips. His love, playfulness, and care for our family always buoyed my spirits and created the peace of mind necessary to finish this project. This book is dedicated to him and our children.

Finally, the history of Baghdad belongs to Baghdadis. As an outsider, I am thankful beyond words to all those who shared their stories and welcomed me to their city. Eighty-five Iraqis spoke with me or my research teams on the record about their memories and experiences. I cannot thank them by name, but my gratitude is boundless.

I have known Baghdad as a visitor walking through its streets, through blueprints and archival records, and in the fragments of memories and stories retold to me in interviews. Baghdadis know their city's history intimately, narrating stories about their home using all their senses from their lived experiences and from family stories passed down through generations. I think about this living, visceral connection Baghdadis have with their city expressed in the poetic words of memoirist Anwar 'Abd al-Hamid al-Nasiri,

> I was scouring the fragments of my diary about the neighborhood, I heard the voices of my friends and relatives who had died, and my anguish provoked me, smelling the scent of our old house that I loved.... I arrived in the neighborhood before the rooster's crow, and in the dim light my eyes flooded with tears as I recalled the sounds of the roosters blending with the dawn, mixing with the sounds of the mosque's *mu'azzin*, calling us to prayer with the last stars of the night.[1]

The pages that follow paint a portrait of Baghdad, but it only scratches the surface of Baghdad's rich history. This book is an invitation to delve deeper and to listen to Iraqis' stories of their remarkable city. Incomplete as this book is, I hope it can be useful.

AUTHOR'S NOTE

Throughout this book, names of private individuals have been changed to protect personal privacy. In the acknowledgments, I thank some Iraqi friends and colleagues by their first name only for similar privacy reasons. Pseudonyms are marked with asterisks.

I have kept my use of Arabic terms to a minimum to make this book accessible to more readers. Translations from Arabic-language documents and publications to English are my own unless otherwise indicated. For transliterating Arabic terms and place names, I have used a simplified system based on the *International Journal of Middle East Studies*. I have included only the diacritical marks ayn (') and hamza ('). When personal names have a more commonly used version in English, I have used these: Saddam Hussein instead of Saddam Husayn, for example. I also minimized my use of plural nouns in Arabic to reduce confusion for non–Arabic speakers, referring for example to *sarifas* instead of *sara'if*.

While losing some linguistic accuracy, I hope these choices increase reading ease and comprehension for a broader audience.

CONTESTED CITY

Introduction

AHMED* WAS BROKE. IN the 1980s, he worked for the Directorate of Civilian Defense in Baghdad, but his governmental salary was so low that he drove a taxi in the evenings for extra income. Even then, he had to borrow his father's car, since he had no vehicle of his own. His one prized asset was a plot of residential land on the outskirts of Baghdad, a standard benefit given to public-sector employees in Iraq. Still, Ahmed was too poor to build on that land, and the lot sat empty while his family of six crammed themselves into a bedroom in his father's house.

In 1988, Ahmed wrote a simple letter to the Ba'th Party Revolutionary Command Council, the highest authoritative body in Saddam Hussein's Iraq. He requested that the nation's top leaders "help me to build on this plot of land so that I can secure a home for my children." He wrote that his children depended on "the compassion of God, your compassion, and your kindness for them," begging for the leaders to show "fatherly care" for his family.[1]

A senior official reviewed Ahmed's letter. He then contacted the local Ba'th Party officials in Ahmed's district of Baghdad, asking them to verify Ahmed's story and issue a decision on his request. After a brief investigation, Ahmed's local Ba'th Party officials approved his request for financial aid to build a house.[2]

This book explores everyday politics and citizen survival strategies in Baghdad, Iraq, from 1950 to 2011. This chronological span includes halcyon years of oil-funded prosperity from 1950 to 1979, a difficult season of warfare with Iran and Kuwait from 1980 to 1991, thirteen years of devastating economic conditions under UN-imposed international sanctions from 1990 to 2003, and violent upheaval during the US invasion and occupation of Iraq from 2003 to 2011.

Confronting these challenging circumstances over the years, Baghdadi residents pursued a variety of survival strategies to provide for themselves and for their families. Focusing my analysis on survival strategies that required interaction between citizens and the state, I explore how Baghdadis shrewdly negotiated their relationships with regime representatives to secure resources both in times of prosperity and in times of poverty. Drawing on oral history interviews, citizen petitions, and archival research, this book foregrounds the voices and experiences of Baghdadis in proactively negotiating with their government to survive, and even thrive, during periods of war, sanctions, and authoritarian rule.

Everyday Politics in Baghdad's Neighborhoods

This book focuses on state-society relationships as they played out in Baghdad's neighborhoods. Focusing on these micro-level interactions highlights how low-ranking officials and "street-level bureaucrats" are embedded within society, acting as intermediaries between citizens and regime leaders, and blurring the lines between "state" and "society."[3] This lens reveals the fragmentary nature of the state and the often contradictory interests driving different government ministries and party offices.

These neighborhood-level bureaucrats in modern Iraq acted as key decision makers about how resources or punishments would be doled out in their jurisdictions, as seen in Ahmed's case. This localization of governance through neighborhood-based officials worked to "facilitat[e] citizens' access to the state, and inversely, the state's access to citizens."[4] Realizing this, Baghdadis astutely leveraged their relationships with local officials to increase their odds of success. Exploring examples of citizen advocacy illuminates how sub-national governance structures worked in a centralized state.

Though I will occasionally refer to "the regime" for the sake of simplicity, this book's focus on the actions of local bureaucrats illustrates how the Iraqi state was never a unified entity, but a complex, hierarchical bureaucracy with influential actors at every level. Examples in this book will expose moments when various neighborhood-based officials experienced tension about their loyalties to their communities and their obligations to the state's top leadership. In day-to-day matters of governance, then, "the state" does not exist on high, separated from and with a clear view into society, but rather operates within webs of power relations that are embedded in local communities.

This neighborhood-based approach to state-society relations requires an introduction to Baghdad's neighborhoods and how they have been divided and governed over time. In the eighteenth and nineteenth centuries, Baghdad was a provincial city in the Ottoman Empire. During that time, Baghdad's neighborhoods (*mahalla*, pl. *mahallat*) functioned as islands unto themselves: encircled by walls, guarded by gate keepers and night watchmen, and internally regulated by a state-appointed community elder (*mukhtar*).[5] Each neighborhood developed a distinctive identity over time: in the late Ottoman period, Sunni tribes took up residence in western Baghdad, while Christians and Jews tended to live in the eastern half of the city. Guilds, Islamic Courts, and military barracks brought members of the same profession into certain areas of the city, imparting to those neighborhoods an association with those professions.[6] Accordingly, Baghdadis often identified themselves by their neighborhood, developed deep roots within their local communities, and carried with them the reputation of their district.[7]

With the British conquest of Iraq in 1917 during World War I, the city of Baghdad experienced exponential population growth and an almost complete overhaul of its built environment. The British ruled colonial Iraq indirectly, installing a political ally from Saudi Arabia, Faisal bin al-Husayn al-Hashemi, as the new king of Iraq in 1921. The Hashemite royal family, as his dynasty came to be known, worked with the British to transform Baghdad into a modern capital city.

By the 1930s and 1940s, the Ottoman-era reputations of Baghdad's old neighborhoods began to blur as rural-to-urban migration, the construction of new subdivisions in the capital, and the building of new bridges and highways brought new residents to the city and connected Baghdad's different districts more closely to one another. People no longer lived their lives within the small confines of their neighborhood, but could easily travel by bus, train, or car across the city and back for work or school.⁸ However, while western Baghdad was no longer associated with Sunni tribes by the 1950s, for instance, the pattern of dividing Baghdad into distinctive residential quarters overseen by community intermediaries persisted throughout these changes (see chapter 1).

The Hashemite monarchy was violently overthrown by a military officer, 'Abd al-Karim Qasim, in 1958. The 1958 Revolution of Iraq ushered in a ten-year period of political instability: Qasim ruled for just five years before he was overthrown by another military officer, 'Abd al-Salam 'Arif in 1963. After 'Abd al-Salam's untimely death in a plane crash in 1966, his brother 'Abd al-Rahman 'Arif took power. In 1968, the Iraqi Ba'th Party staged yet another coup, and this regime proved to be lasting. The Iraqi Ba'th Party regime was led initially by President Ahmed Hassan al-Bakr and supported by his vice president, Saddam Hussein. Saddam—referred to throughout this book by his first name, following Iraqi convention—took over as president in 1979. The Ba'th Party espoused the values of Arab nationalism and socialism, though Saddam's ideological leanings proved to be flexible and opportunistic, adapting as political and economic conditions changed.⁹ He ruled Iraq until 2003, when the United States invaded and overthrew his regime.

When Ba'thist leaders consolidated their power in Iraq in 1968, they retained this long-standing governance tradition of administering Baghdad through neighborhoods. Under the Ba'th Party system, Baghdad was divided into nine districts (*qada*'), which were in turn divided into eighty-eight large neighborhoods (*hayy*). The term *hayy* best aligns with an urban "neighborhood" in English: this was a mid-sized residential area often bounded by large thoroughfares. These eighty-eight large neighborhoods were further divided into more than four hundred *mahallat*, each the size of just a few city blocks. Lacking more English synonyms, a *mahalla* is also commonly referred to as a "neighborhood," but in its most intimate sense: a cluster of streets and houses that comprise one's most proximate neighbors and local shops where people live out their daily routines. Each of these *mahallat* is assigned a three-digit number that Baghdadis include in their postal address. Even the American invasion of Iraq in 2003 did not alter the practice of governing Baghdad through neighborhoods: the American governing body in Iraq, the Coalition Provisional Authority (CPA), decided to

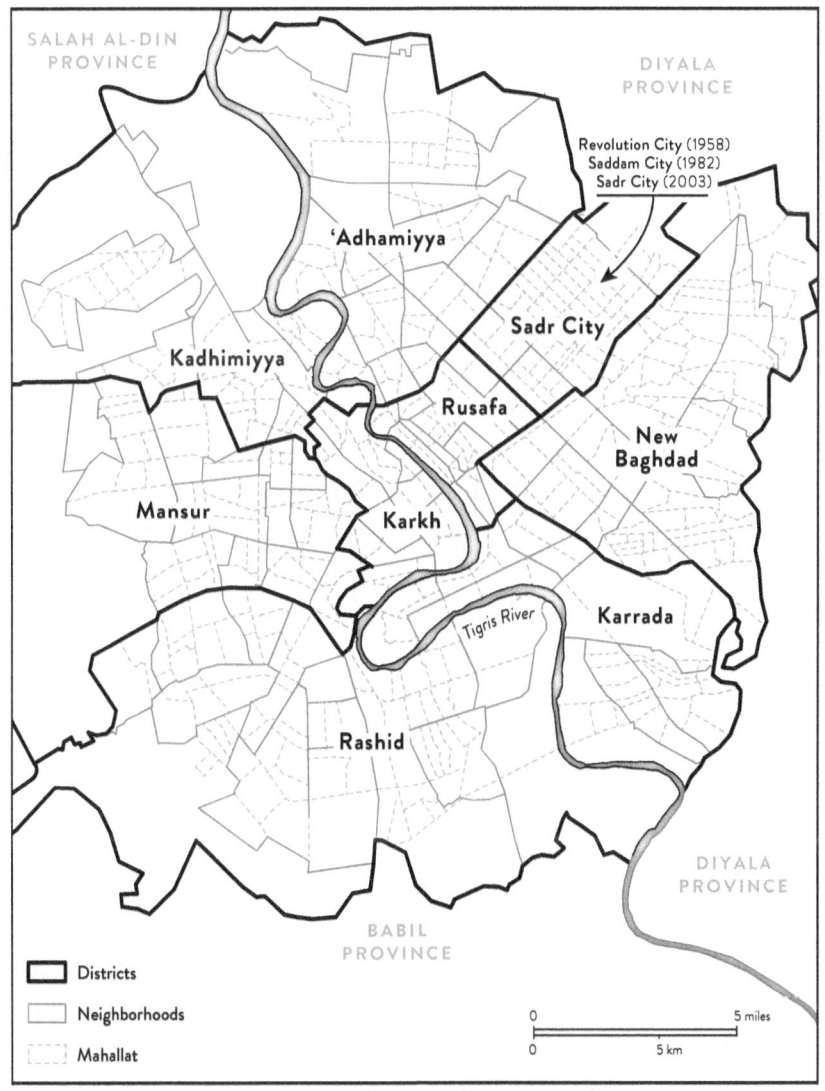

FIGURE 1 Baghdad's administrative districts, 2003.

continue the practice of distributing municipal services through the preexisting administrative framework of Baghdad's eighty-eight neighborhoods and nine districts, though subsequent Iraqi governments have redrawn some municipal borders within the city in recent years.

In the Baghdad context, then, a "neighborhood" is not a loosely defined residential community but a significant administrative unit, with clearly defined borders and official government functions. Each of these geographic units holds personal and bureaucratic layers of meaning for Baghdadi residents. A middle-class Baghdadi man might identify as a resident of the posh Mansur district. When pressed further, he would specify that he lives in the Khadra' neighborhood within the Mansur district, which is home to many white-collar professionals. He might share the personal significance he attaches to his home in Khadra': that he moved to this neighborhood as a child because some housing in this neighborhood was reserved for the police, and his father worked as an officer. On administrative paperwork, his address would clarify that his house is located within *mahalla* 631 in Khadra' neighborhood in the Mansur district in the city of Baghdad.

These formally defined administrative jurisdictions for *mahallat*, large neighborhoods (*hayy*), and districts (*qada'*) formed the backbone for governance and service delivery in modern Iraq. In the era of Ba'th Party rule from 1968 to 2003, each area was overseen by an office of Ba'th Party officials, from the smallest level of a Ba'th Party "cell" (*khaliyya*) at the *mahalla* level all the way to a Ba'th Party "branch" office (*fara'*) at the district level. Neighborhoods, then, formed the basic building blocks of the Ba'th Party apparatus in Baghdad, and, in turn, constituted the most important municipal structure for Baghdadis' daily lives.

There were other local governance systems in place outside of the official Ba'th Party apparatus. Large neighborhoods (*hayy*) were additionally overseen by a government-appointed *mukhtar*, an elder who lived within the neighborhood and who was responsible for assisting the Ba'th Party regime with keeping track of his residents and collaborating in security operations in his area. Over time, the Ba'th Party created various "Popular Committees" to surveil economic activities in each neighborhood, too (see chapter 3). The Baghdad municipality had its own system for dividing the city into large zones for administering public utilities like water, sewage, and electricity.

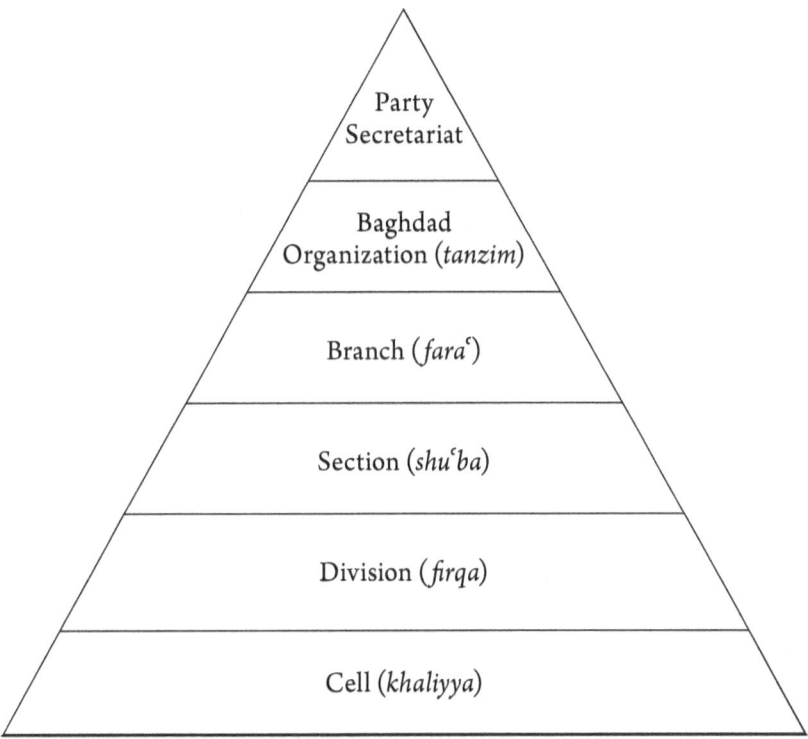

FIGURE 2 Baʿth Party organizational hierarchy in Baghdad.

The result was that Baghdad citizens navigated life within nested levels of locally embedded regime representatives. The *mukhtars*, neighborhood and district Baʿth Party officials, and neighborhood Popular Committees performed various functions simultaneously: monitoring citizens, distributing resources, advocating for or against their residents, and making decisions about local governance concerns in their jurisdictions. The way that Baghdadis navigated their relationships with these neighborhood officials constituted a form of everyday politics that informed the development of the city and shaped the processes of daily governance on the ground.

Many observers of Saddam Hussein's twenty-four-year presidency have emphasized the centrality of Saddam himself in Iraq's day-to-day governance. Decisions were "mostly concentrated in the president's hands and epitomized by lack of consultation," and his decrees were as good as law.[10] It is true that Saddam weighed in on matters both big and small. He personally oversaw seemingly trivial decisions, such as deciding whether or not a Baʿth Party member could divorce his wife.[11] He directed battlefield strategies in Iran and Kuwait, to the point of overriding his generals' advice though he had no military background.[12] Saddam earned some begrudging respect as a dictator who was willing to put in "long hours" at work, who read all the memos that came across his desk, and who held minor bureaucrats to account for mistakes that they made.[13]

Yet the preoccupation with Saddam Hussein's central role in decision-making overlooks the important roles that others, including low-ranking officials, played in Iraq's day-to-day governance. In practical terms, the "face" of the government for residents of Baghdad was not Saddam's mustachioed countenance but a variety of functionaries who worked within their neighborhoods: it was often the neighborhood party officials who ultimately made the decisions that would impact individuals' lives. Focusing on Saddam's centralized power has contributed to a common misconception that party officials and bureaucratic underlings merely received and implemented orders without question or input, and has obscured the more complex reality of local governance in an urban area like Baghdad in which the sheer size of the city required delegation to lower ranking regime representatives. Understanding the active role of street-level bureaucrats also explains how Baghdadi residents were able to take advantage of their proximity to regime representatives to advocate for themselves.

In this book, I will frequently refer to "neighborhood and district Baʿth Party officials" or more simply to "local" officials. This terminology may initially seem imprecise: when I talk about a "neighborhood," do I mean a *mahalla* or a *hayy*? However, this phrasing captures the fact that most internal discussions within the Baʿth Party about citizen concerns moved up and down the party hierarchy between the *firqa*, *shuʿba*, and *faraʿ* offices, where representatives from the *mahalla*, *hayy*, and *qadaʾ* levels would weigh in and issue opinions about decisions pertaining to their jurisdictions. When relevant, I will specify whether it was a *firqa*-level official or a *faraʿ*-level official who advocated for a certain outcome. In most cases, however, internal party communication involved multiple offices from the district level down to the most local *mahalla* level, and the phrase "local officials" helps to capture this. The purpose of my analysis is generally not to distinguish if a *firqa* or *shuʿba* office made a decision but to emphasize how many governance issues were decided by local party officials, rather than by more senior leaders at the national level.

Out of all the communities in Iraq, why focus on the city of Baghdad? The field of urban history in Iraq is a growing but nascent field, and much work remains to be done to understand the evolution of provincial cities, small towns, and rural areas in Iraq's modern history.[14] Restricting the boundaries of this study to the city of Baghdad permits analysis of how state-society relations functioned in postcolonial Iraq in the "best" possible scenario for the government, where the state enjoyed the highest concentration of resources, power, and influence. State ministries, security services, and municipal offices were all based in Baghdad, along with the military base at Camp Rashid and the headquarters for the Popular Army. Saddam's presidential palaces stood as gleaming examples of the power and wealth of his government. In contrast to the semi-autonomous Kurdish zone in the North or the rebellious provinces in the South, Baghdad's population did not mount significant protests against the state during the 1991 *intifada* due in part to the regime's overwhelming presence in and control over the capital city. Studying state-society relations in the capital, then, permits analysis of Saddam's regime at its strongest, while still including a broad ethnic, religious, and socioeconomic sampling of Iraq's population. Here we can see how Saddam's government aspired to rule and the extent to which it was able to act on its ambitions, whereas the North and South of the country were able to blunt the regime's goals to varying degrees.

Citizen Advocacy and Survival

Baghdadis did not simply cower in fear under Saddam's rule, nor did they passively suffer through wars and sanctions. Surveying the survival strategies that ordinary Baghdadis employed during years of authoritarian rule, wars, sanctions, and foreign occupation reveals an array of responses. Some, like Ahmed, were proactive in asking for benefits or entitlements to improve their situation. Others went even further and openly complained to the regime if they felt the government was not taking care of them as it ought to. Many Baghdadis wrote letters directly to Saddam or to other high-ranking officials. In many cases, they received what they asked for (see chapter 4). Exploring citizen agency and survival strategies, including petitions, draws attention to the role that citizens could play in influencing Baʿthist governance.

There were also those who ardently opposed Baʿthist rule. Some broke the law to try to make their fortunes in the black market and through smuggling operations. Still more risked draconian punishments to carry out petty crime to make ends meet (see chapter 5). Some joined the Baʿth Party to gain access to resources; some joined underground resistance movements against the regime.

While scholarship exists on extraordinary resistance efforts by Iraqi opposition groups, such as by the Shiʿi Daʿwa Party or by the Iraqi Communist Party, this book focuses on routine interactions between citizens and regime representatives because the vast majority of Baghdadis did not belong to opposition groups, nor did they even belong to the Baʿth Party. Studies indicate that Baʿth Party membership in Iraq involved no more than 16 percent of the national population.[15] Instead, most Baghdadis were political independents trying to survive the political and economic challenges of their day.

Regular interactions between Baghdad's residents and the Baʿthist regime constituted a routine form of contestation and negotiation in daily life: picking up monthly food rations, writing letters to party representatives about medical expenses, securing housing for one's family. As Ilana Feldman observed in her study of bureaucratic practices in Gaza, "intimate connections with people and place are forged in significant part through regular practices of living," which include "the quotidian formations of place that emerge out of the everyday practices of government services."[16] Appealing to a bureaucrat for more welfare benefits was not a spectacular, headline-grabbing form of contestation with the regime, but it was the most common form of advocacy that Iraqis engaged in, and these efforts have not previously received much scholarly attention.

Consequences of State-Society Relations in Baghdad's Development

Focusing my analysis on the neighborhood level reveals how new geographies of inclusion and exclusion were written and rewritten onto Baghdad's landscape over the course of the last century. The modernization of Baghdad in the twentieth century through state-led development and oil-financed housing created new geographic zones of inclusion and exclusion across the city landscape. New neighborhoods were built to group together pockets of would-be political supporters and public-sector professionals in the city center, while politically troublesome populations were marginalized on the outskirts of the city. An eastern district known successively as *al-ʿAsima*, Revolution City, Saddam City, and, later, Sadr City was the largest and most infamous of these silos. In the twentieth century this district was imagined—and governed—as an undesirable and even deviant area, and the district still struggles with a marginalized status today.

The outbreak of war in 1980, 1990, and 2003, along with the sectarian cleansing of Baghdad's neighborhoods by death squads and militias from 2005 to 2009, altered the city landscape yet again. In short, the physical and imagined landscape of Baghdad has been impacted by the history of the interactions of Baghdadi citizens with their rulers and, after 2003, with occupying forces, militias, and new power brokers. The history of state-society relations in Baghdad is intimately linked to the construction (and destruction) of the physical city over time.

Sources

Work on this book spanned a decade, from 2014 to 2024. I made four trips to Iraq while researching this book and conducted research in libraries and archives in Iraq, Egypt, Greece, France, the United Kingdom, and the United States. Most of my analysis in this book draws from two sources: nearly one hundred interviews, and extensive research in the Iraqi Baʿth Party archives.

Interviews

Oral history interviews were a necessary complement to the top-down perspectives present in the state and party archives that I used for this book. Interviews serve to foreground Iraqis' own perspectives, speak to aspects of their experiences that were not recorded in bureaucratic memos, and contextualize citizens' activities that are discussed in archives.

This book draws on roughly eighty-five interviews with Baghdadis and another dozen with American civilians and soldiers who participated in local governance projects in Iraq after 2003. Following IRB protocols, all Iraqi interviewees have been anonymized in this book to protect their identities, and pseudonyms are indicated with an asterisk. Interviews were conducted in three stages between 2015 and 2023. My first fieldwork trip in Iraq was in the city of Erbil in Iraqi Kurdistan in 2016 because visa restrictions at the time prohibited most US citizens from traveling to Baghdad. In Erbil I met with former residents of Baghdad who had fled to the safer Kurdistan region. The focus of this round of interviews was on food rations and economic survival strategies during sanctions (see chapter 3).

To broaden this sample, I then worked remotely with a team of three Iraqi research assistants to extend these interview questions to two dozen people currently living in Baghdad. Interviewees in Erbil and Baghdad reflected a broad cross-section of Iraq's diversity. Together with my team, we spoke with roughly equal numbers of men and women; with Shiʿa, Sunnis, Christians, and Sabean-Mandeans; former Baʿth Party members, Communists, and political independents; Arabs and Kurds. Most of those we spoke with had lived in Baghdad their entire lives; those I met with in Erbil were filtering their memories of Baghdad through their experiences of displacement.

In 2019 I began a new phase of research focused on Baghdadis' experiences during the US occupation from 2003 to 2011. I initially relied on phone interviews to overcome travel barriers, especially once the COVID-19 pandemic broke out. I spoke with a dozen Iraqi and American interviewees who worked on a local governance project in Baghdad that became the focus of chapter 6. After Iraq changed its visa restrictions in 2021, I made three trips to Baghdad and conducted follow-up interviews with Iraqis who had worked on American-created local councils.

My positionality as a non-Iraqi American citizen could be an asset in certain situations. Sectarian violence in Iraq after 2003 created acrimonious political and social divisions in Iraqi society, and my position as an outsider sometimes made it easier for Iraqis to speak with me about the past. Other times, my positionality as an American citizen could be sensitive, as when inquiring about Iraqis' experiences with occupying US forces. Collaboration with Iraqi researchers was a helpful strategy to overcome these barriers, and I am deeply appreciative for my partnership with sociologist Dr. Ali Taher al-Hammood. Together we embarked on a new round of interviews in 2022 designed to better understand changes in local governance and public services after 2003. We designed structured interview questions that he and his research team carried out with sixty Iraqis in four different areas of Baghdad—Sadr City, 'Adhamiyya, Kadhimiyya, and Fadhil—selected to represent Sunnis and Shi'a with different socioeconomic backgrounds.[17] Interviewees' insights informed my analysis throughout the entire book, and their responses were especially valuable for describing changes in state-society relations after 2003 discussed in chapter 6.

Archives

Years of archival research inform my findings in this book. Diplomatic records from the US National Archives, the British National Archives in Kew, and the French Archives Diplomatiques in Nantes provided outsiders' perspectives on Baghdad's urban development from the 1950s through the 1970s and experiences with the Iran-Iraq War from 1980 to 1988. The architectural plans, photographs, and diaries of urban planner Constantinos Doxiadis in Greece constituted another valuable source of information about Baghdad's urban development in the 1950s.

Many archives in Iraq were destroyed or damaged in 2003 due to looting, fires, and other damage connected to the US invasion and America's failure to protect critical heritage sites in Iraq.[18] The Baghdad municipal archives are reportedly among those files that were destroyed, so I was unable to review these records for my research. However, the Iraq National Library and Archives in Baghdad—though also damaged in 2003—still contains a trove of valuable publications and records about city planning in Baghdad. There I consulted reports by the Baghdad Municipality and Ministry of Planning.

Other sources I used for this book include Ba'th Party newspapers *Al-Thawra* and *Baghdad Observer*. The Cairo University Library and the British Library house dissertations written by Iraqi graduate students in the 1960s and 1970s, which were particularly helpful for illuminating how Baghdad's new housing developments were impacting society. This research is featured in chapter 1.

Much of my analysis in this book draws on my research in digital records from the Iraqi Ba'th Party archives available at the Hoover Institution at Stanford University. To a lesser extent, I also consulted some of the audio recordings seized from Saddam's presidential office that were made available to researchers at the Conflict Records Research Center at the National Defense University in Washington, DC. These expatriated Iraqi archives have generated controversy since their seizure in 2003 and relocation to the United States. My reliance on these records therefore merits further discussion of the practical and ethical considerations of conducting research in these records.[19]

The Conflict Records Research Center made accessible to researchers 200 hours of audio recordings and 52,000 digitized pages of documents taken from Saddam's presidential office.[20] These digital records were originally housed at the National Defense University, where I accessed them. This collection was closed in 2015 due to budget cuts, though the Wilson Center in Washington, DC, is currently in the process of redacting and reopening the collection.[21] The original documents and audio recordings from Saddam's office were part of a vast collection of up to 200 million pages of documents seized by the United States Department of Defense, known as the Harmony Records database. The original audio and paper files were returned from the US Defense Department to the Iraqi government in May 2013.[22]

The Iraqi Ba'th Party archives at the Hoover Institution at Stanford University contain approximately 8 million pages of bureaucratic memos and party personnel files that were originally stored in the headquarters of the Baʿth Party Regional Command near the Republican Palace in the Green Zone. Most of these documents date from the 1980s and 1990s, continuing up to the moment the Baʿthist regime fell in April 2003.

The collection of the Baʿth Party archives now at the Hoover Institution was spearheaded by the Iraq Memory Foundation, led by an Iraqi academic who had been living in exile, Kanan Makiya.[23] These Baʿth Party records were initially stored in Iraq Memory Foundation safe houses in Iraq until the organization successfully appealed in 2005 to relocate the records to the United States, fearing for the safety of the files in the midst of escalating violence in Iraq after 2003.[24] The American Bush administration incorrectly believed these seized records contained documentary evidence about Saddam's crimes against humanity that could provide post hoc justification for the US invasion of Iraq. To this end, the US Department of Defense paid the Iraq Memory Foundation more than $6 million to collect and process the Iraq Baʿth Party archives. (Information about the Department of Defense's contract with the Iraq Memory Foundation was only made public in 2019.)[25] Once the records reached the United States, the US Defense Intelligence Agency completed the process of digitizing the records, a project that the Iraq Memory Foundation staff had begun in Iraq.[26]

In 2008, the Iraq Memory Foundation turned over the files to the Hoover Institution Library and Archives at Stanford University, and the collection was opened to researchers by 2010. As confirmed in a Memorandum of Understanding signed in 2012 between the Hoover Institution and the Iraqi government, the government of Iraq retained legal ownership of these documents, while Hoover claimed only "temporary custody" of these files.[27]

Moving the Baʿth Party archives from Iraq to the United States generated intense controversy; some have described this relocation as "looting" or "theft" of documents that form a significant part of the Iraqi historical heritage. Archivists and academics in Iraq and around the world condemned the expatriation of these archives to the United States.[28]

The return of the original paper documents to Iraq was a repeated point of discussion, negotiation, and controversy for more than ten years. Finally, in August 2020 the Hoover Institution returned the nearly 8 million pages of original paper files of the Iraqi Baʻth Party archives to the custody of the Iraqi government.[29] To date, the Iraqi government has not opened these archives to the public. The Hoover Institution has retained digital photographs of the Iraqi Baʻth Party files and continues to make these available to researchers in its main reading room at Stanford University and through a new annex office in Washington, DC.

I conducted research in the Baʻth Party archives full time for nearly a year at the Hoover Institution; these records form the basis of Part II in this book. I worked primarily in the Baʻth Party Regional Command boxfiles dataset, which consists of bureaucratic memos related to daily governance concerns. This sub-collection contains 2.7 million pages of documents held within 6,420 boxfiles.[30] These are searchable through a rudimentary index originally put together by Iraqi Memory Foundation staff members. Identifying relevant documents is a tedious and time-consuming process: the digital photographs of the Baʻth Party documents are not text-searchable, so one must often spend hours clicking through hundreds of digitized pages of memos before identifying documents noted in the boxfile's metadata or that related to the index's search term. Because of this, it is a nearly impossible task to systematically identify all relevant documents on a particular topic, so the conclusions presented here must be considered preliminary. I was able to hone my searches by focusing my queries on thematic topics in the index (prostitution, rations, crime, petitions, and so forth) and also by searching the names of the different Baʻth Party branches, divisions, and sections associated with Baghdad.

To protect the identities of individuals mentioned in the Iraqi Baʻth Party archives, the Hoover Institution does not allow researchers to make copies of these files, whether digital copies or hardcopy printouts. I found that retyping these files in the original Arabic was the most effective system of note-taking, allowing me to accurately reference the files and to double-check my translations later. This book is based on thousands of pages of records that were painstakingly transcribed in this way.

The Baʻth Party archives provide valuable insights, but working with this collection has limitations and comes with costs. On the one hand, it is one of the few available archives anywhere in the world that offers behind-the-scenes insights into life in a postcolonial authoritarian regime.³¹ On the other hand, the fact that these archives are not censored or redacted can give a false sense that the documents present a complete and accurate picture of Baʿthist governance. As scholars of Iraq have noted, the Baʿth Party documents create an illusion that the Iraqi regime was almost always internally consistent, impartial, and procedural. Historian Dina Khoury wrote that the Baʿth Party archives "represent the party's creation of its own world" that does not necessarily convey a complete and clear picture of reality.³² One example of the somewhat artificial reality presented in the Baʿth Party archives is the near total absence of violence in its pages.³³ Despite the fact that torture, execution, and cruel prison conditions were routine practices in Saddam's Iraq, the Baʿth Party archives rarely refer to such actions. Memos simply mention if someone has been "arrested," rarely with any additional information about their fate in the hands of security forces. Only in exceptional circumstances do Baʿth Party memos admit to the blood spilled in the name of maintaining power.³⁴

There are ethical considerations for researchers using this archive, as well, especially around the notion of consent. To begin, many of the Iraqis identified in the archives did not consent to, and certainly did not have access to, the dossiers collected on them by the Baʿth Party's security services and party officials. Targets of surveillance operations, people named in informants' reports, suspected political opposition group members: none of these people assented to have the details of their lives recorded and filed away in this archive, and many were likely unaware that such files about them existed. The Baʿth Party violated the privacy of Iraqis by monitoring them through secret police. Historian Rebecca Whiting poses an ethical question in response: is the researcher reading these files reenacting this violation of privacy?³⁵

At the most basic level, it is imperative for researchers to safeguard the privacy of civilians named in the records. To protect their identities, I refer to everyone in this book with a pseudonym and remove any identifying details. When referring to archival memos that name civilians, I chose not to divulge the full citation information that would allow someone to find the original file in the Baʿth Party records as a way to further protect their privacy.

One reason I was drawn to focus my attention on citizen petitions in the Baʻth Party archives—the subject of chapter 4—is precisely that these letters were penned voluntarily by Iraqi citizens, in their own voices, framing their own stories. These petition writers expected, and even demanded, that their stories be reviewed by bureaucrats who would file a report about their petition. In other words, these Iraqis knew that their letters would be received and filed away in an archive by bureaucrats. This is a very different situation from that of the atrocity records discussed by Whiting that contain secret surveillance or evidence of human rights violations. While this book does sometimes reference surveillance and security files—chapter 5 focuses on crime and policing—most of my research has sought to highlight the agency of Baghdadis in how they presented themselves to government officials out of their own volition. These Iraqi-penned petitions help to remedy the top-down gaze of regime officials recorded in the Baʻth Party archives.

Another ethical quandary is the issue of researchers' access to the Baʻth Party archives, even after the repatriation of the original files to Iraq in 2020. Because the Iraqi government has not yet chosen to allow Iraqis access to the Baʻth Party archives in their possession, the only accessible copies of this archive are at the Hoover Institution, and visas for Iraqi researchers to come to the United States have been difficult to obtain. Because of the restrictions on making copies of the documents, carrying out research in this collection is a time-intensive process that even American researchers find difficult to afford because of the high costs of living in the Stanford, California, or Washington, DC, areas. My extensive research in these archives was only made possible by competitively securing grant funding, and many grants I received for dissertation research are only available to US citizens. The archives are thus embedded in multiple layers of unequal power dynamics and privilege. Without access to these records in Iraq, Iraqis do not yet have the the opportunity to reclaim their stories and their files, and, with them, their framing of the past. Restoring custody of these records to the Iraqi government was a crucial first step, but it remains important for Iraqi citizens to gain access to their files in the Baʻth Party archives so that they can control their own files and record their own tellings of history.

The ethical dilemmas surrounding the expatriation of the Baʻth Party archives have forced scholars of Iraq to take positions about whether or not to use these materials. Some researchers have chosen to boycott the Baʿth Party archives in protest of their seizure and removal to the United States. However, historians of Iraq like Dina Khoury and Arbella Bet-Shlimon have argued that it is possible to do respectful research in the Baʿth Party archives. As Khoury has insisted, "use of the archive [does not] lend legitimacy to the manner of their acquisition."[36] However, there is an ethical imperative that researchers be intentional about taking approaches that mitigate some of the possible harms that can come from this research. As Bet-Shlimon has argued:

> The alternative [boycotting the archive] is to declare moral superiority by simply avoiding entire classes of research projects. But perhaps considering the limits of this approach will lead scholars to more critical, thoughtful approaches to these problematic archives that think through the archive itself rather than just treating it as a repository of information.[37]

Safeguarding the privacy of Iraqis named in the files and complementing archival records with oral history interviews are two possible approaches for mitigating some of the potential downsides of this archival collection. Bet-Shlimon further encourages historians to weigh the costs and benefits of using these records in considering the impact on the Iraqi people: does bringing these records to light offer something sufficiently valuable to the Iraqis who lived this history, or is it better simply to not research this topic at all?[38] It is possible to write excellent social histories of Iraq without using these controversial Baʿth Party archives. However, there is no alternative source that can replace these records to analyze how the Baʿth Party governed in order to tell the history of state-society relations. Every Iraqi who grew up before 2003 has stories about interactions with the fearsome Iraqi security forces or with intimidating regime representatives in their areas. Consulting these Baʿth Party records provides evidence that documents Iraqis' experiences and reveals the larger bureaucratic systems that were at work behind the scenes that were not always perceptible to citizens on the ground.

I highlight these problematic dynamics of power and privilege associated with the Baʿth Party archives to locate my own positionality in relation to the research presented here. As subaltern scholars have urged, scholars must remain cognizant of the power dynamics inherent in carrying out their research, especially when examining the lives of nonelites, guarding themselves against deigning to "speak for" subalterns in the same way that state officials did, or presenting their research as "objective," without acknowledging their own privilege.[39] I offer my findings from the Baʿth Party archives with humility, recognizing the limitations and problems of these archives. I look forward to the day when Iraqis will gain access to these records to interpret them within their own contexts and lived experiences. I continue to listen to Baghdadis as my authoritative guides in shaping my understanding of their city. My mistakes and shortcomings in writing this history of state-society relations in Baghdad are my own. If any part of my research in the Baʿth Party archives can be useful for Iraqis, I will be glad for it.

Organization of the Book

This book is divided into three parts. Part I, "The Making of Modern Baghdad," focuses on changes to the built environment of the city. Chapter 1 looks at citizen negotiations over housing during the "oil boom" years of 1950–79, and chapter 2 explores the impact of the Iran-Iraq War (1980–88) and the Gulf War (1990–91) on daily life in Baghdad. With the physical context of the city established, Part II, "Citizen Advocacy and Local Governance," shifts the focus to exploring state-society relations *within* Baghdad's different neighborhoods. Drawing on research in the Iraqi Baʿth Party archives and oral history interviews, this part analyzes citizen survival strategies in response to the impact of wars and UN–imposed economic sanctions in the 1980s and 1990s. Chapter 3 approaches food rations as a new point of negotiation between citizens and regime representatives in the 1990s. Chapter 4 examines citizen petitions to explore the possibilities and limitations of personal appeals within the Baʿthist system, and chapter 5 looks at the gendered impact of rising crime rates during the sanctions era. Part III, "Aftermath of the US Invasion," moves forward in time to focus on the impact of the 2003 US war and occupation in transforming everyday politics and state-society relations in Baghdad. Chapter 6 compares the functions of US–created local councils with the efforts by Shiʿi populist cleric Muqtada al-Sadr to provide essential services to the population during a moment of state collapse. The conclusion offers insights into how some patterns of state-society relations established in the twentieth century have evolved since 2003.

PART I

The Making of Modern Baghdad

ONE

Slums and Subdivisions

AT THE TURN OF the twentieth century, Baghdad was a provincial Ottoman city with a population of just 100,000.¹ Although the city boasted a glorious past as the opulent capital of the Abbasid Empire, by 1900 it had slipped in status compared to thriving economic and cultural hubs in the region like Cairo and Damascus.

But as Iraqi memoirist Jamal Haydar wrote, "Baghdad is a city that has been born many times."² The British vaulted Baghdad back onto the world stage in 1920 when they named Baghdad the capital of colonial Iraq, and Baghdad remained the capital when Iraq achieved nominal independence in 1932 under the leadership of the Hashemite monarchy. Iraq's new rulers wanted to revitalize the city to suit its upgraded political status. Over the next few decades, this once-small town bustled with construction: cinemas, riverfront hotels, and a gleaming new train station announced the rebirth of this cosmopolitan city in the modern era.³ But who was meant to benefit from all this new urban development?

This chapter focuses on Iraq's housing policies as an introduction to patterns of state-society relations in the history of modern Baghdad, providing insights into how push-and-pull dynamics between the rulers and the ruled shaped the physical development of the city. Understanding how Baghdad's residents navigated governmental housing policies provides context for later chapters that will further explore dynamics of state-society relations within Baghdad's neighborhoods from the 1980s onward. Here the focus is on Iraq's "oil boom" years in the mid-twentieth century. This period started with Iraq exporting commercial quantities of oil after World War II and ended with the onset of the Iran-Iraq War in 1980, which significantly disrupted Iraq's economy and urban planning initiatives.

State housing policies from 1950 to 1979 were intended to help governmental officials manage politically sensitive populations as the city grew. Two housing policies in particular—one targeting rural migrants, the other targeting a growing cadre of professionals and governmental employees—are key for understanding the political motivations that transformed Baghdad during these pivotal decades. Iraqi governmental housing policies succeeded in creating distinct silos within Baghdad's urban landscape, grouping pockets of political allies close to the halls of power and isolating troublesome populations on the edges of the city where they could be more easily monitored and controlled. Through this process, Baghdad developed new real and imaginary landscapes that demarcated social, political, and economic differences among Baghdadis.

However, Baghdadis themselves were not passive pawns within these governmental housing schemes. A rich body of theoretical and historical literature has demonstrated that modern states frequently attempt to use urban development—with its grid pattern of orthogonal roads, commercial and residential zoning laws, and new building code regulations—to facilitate governmental surveillance of the population.[4] Baghdad, too, was subject to these kinds of top-down development schemes intended, in part, to monitor residents' movements.[5] However, the Iraqi state was not able to guarantee that urban spaces would actually be used in the ways it intended. Residents of Baghdad were able to capitalize on these new housing initiatives to create community networks, subvert government resources to pursue personal and communal interests, appropriate new spaces, and push for new entitlements.

Brief History of Urban Development in Baghdad

In the early twentieth century, the core of Baghdad was divided into two parts, Karkh and Rusafa, split by the Tigris River. The two halves of Baghdad were connected to each other by pontoon bridges prior to the early twentieth century.[6] Each area developed its own distinctive identity under the Ottomans: Rusafa was regarded as the cosmopolitan and sophisticated eastern half, and Karkh was the rough-and-tumble western side populated by recently arrived tribes from the desert.[7]

Two other historic districts near Baghdad, ʿAdhamiyya and Kadhimiyya, host important religious shrines that have attracted Muslim pilgrims for centuries. ʿAdhamiyya is home to the tomb of Sunni scholar Abu Hanifa (d. 767), founder of the eponymous Hanafi school of Sunni legal thought. Kadhimiyya is home to shrines where honored figures in Shiʿi history, Imams Musa ibn Jaʿfar al-Kadhim (d. 799) and Muhammad ibn ʿAli al-Jawad (d. 834), are buried. ʿAdhamiyya and Kadhimiyya existed at

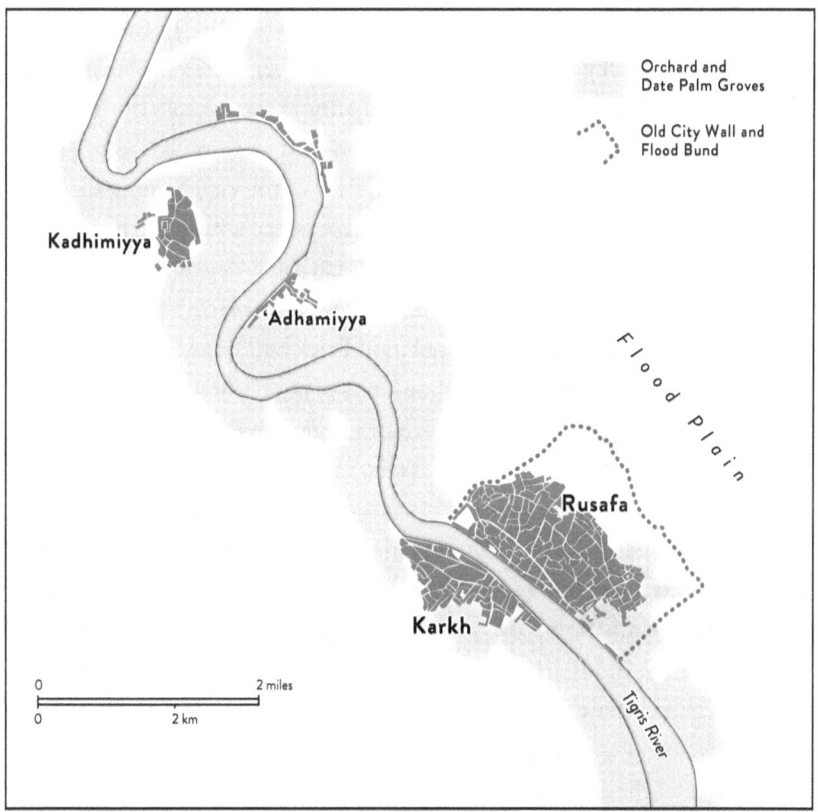

FIGURE 3   Baghdad's historic districts, 1917. Adapted from the map, "Umgebung von Baghdad: Aufgenommen 1916" [Surroundings of Baghdad: Recorded 1916], published in Berlin by the Cartography Department of the Royal Prussian National Survey, 1917.

the turn of the century as suburbs separate from the city center, separated from Karkh and Rusafa by orchards and palm groves.[8] The city expanded far enough by the 1960s to envelop these districts as part of the urban core. However, residents in these districts retained a sense of distinctive identity in part because of their unique histories and roles as shrine districts.[9]

A new era of urbanization came with the British occupation of Iraq during World War I and its installation of the Hashemite royal family. In the 1920s and 1930s, British and Hashemite elites built new "ministries, clubs, train stations, bridges, military hospitals, industrial facilities, and warehouses, along with post-offices and airports ensuring good communication throughout the Empire."[10] The famous al-'Alwiya social club was built in 1924 along a posh stretch of the Tigris by the Abu Nuwas entertainment district, later flanked by some of Baghdad's finest international hotels.[11] In the 1950s, the Hashemite monarchy built new steel bridges to replace the wooden pontoon bridges that had supported foot traffic and animal carts across the Tigris for centuries. New, durable bridges greatly increased the circulation of people and automobile traffic between the two halves of the city, helping to generate a more cohesive and integrated urban experience within Baghdad.[12] The Tharthar dam, built in 1956, protected Baghdad's new development from the Tigris River's flooding. Previously, flooding was a recurring threat that regularly damaged Baghdad's traditional mud-brick buildings. A major flood in Baghdad in 1954, for example, left thousands of people homeless.[13]

From 1950 onward, Baghdad's urban development was funded mostly through oil sales. Oil had been discovered in commercial quantities in 1927, but the two world wars interrupted the development of Iraq's oil fields, and foreign companies originally claimed most of the profits from Iraq's oil production. It was not until the 1950s that Iraq's Hashemite monarchy oversaw the country's transition from a primarily agricultural to a primarily oil-based economy. In 1950, increased global demand and the development of new Iraqi oil fields marked the beginning of Iraq's "oil boom" years. In 1952, a 50/50 revenue-sharing agreement was signed between the Iraq Petroleum Company and the Iraqi government, flooding state coffers with new revenue.[14] Iraq's financial fortunes only improved in the following years: in 1955, the Iraqi government signed a new agreement with oil companies that further increased the government's revenue rate by 17 percent.[15] That year, state oil revenues reached the equivalent of 204.4 million US dollars.[16]

For Hashemite leaders, oil revenues were an opportunity to rapidly modernize, invest in large-scale development and infrastructure projects, and "catch up" with the Western world: another rebirth for the city of Baghdad. King Faisal I had originally committed the Iraqi government in 1927 to the principle of dedicating oil profits for development, but this had only limited impact until oil revenues increased in the 1950s. Once significant oil profits began to flow in, there were renewed calls to use the money for modernization. Dr. Salih Haidar, a top official at the Iraq National Bank, published an article in 1950 calling for public works planning in order to take advantage of the windfall of oil revenues, and Prime Minister Nuri al-Saʿid began to channel funds from the Iraq Petroleum Company into public works projects.[17] This notion was popular with the Hashemites' British backers as well. One British official predicted: "If the oil revenues are spent wisely and well, the country may be transformed, within fifty years, from a poor, backward, semi-feudal state into a prosperous and progressive modern nation."[18]

As a result, the government created the Iraqi Development Board in 1950 to coordinate infrastructure and modernization projects. The board was overseen by the Iraqi prime minister and staffed with representatives from key Iraqi ministries, as well as British and American consultants.[19] Up to 70 percent of Iraq's oil revenues were directed toward the Development Board to fund its projects.

Which kinds of development programs the board would prioritize, and who was meant to benefit from these investments, became a pressing political question that would ultimately divide Baghdad's residents. The politicization of development projects only grew as Iraq's oil income rose: Saddam Hussein oversaw the complete nationalization of Iraq's oil industry between 1972 and 1975, granting the Iraqi government complete control over all of the country's oil revenues at a time when the 1973 embargo by the Organization of Petroleum Exporting Countries (OPEC) was driving oil prices to record heights.[20] At the peak of Iraq's oil revenues in the twentieth century, petroleum sales generated USD 26.3 billion annually.[21] Some Baghdadis would profit handsomely from oil-funded development projects, while others became the object of repressive social engineering efforts.

Baghdad's Housing Crisis

Baghdad's population grew by more than 800 percent in a half-century: from 140,000 in 1904 to 750,000 after World War II to more than 1 million by the mid-1960s. Part of this population growth came from Iraq's educated middle classes who flocked from other provinces to the capital to work in white-collar jobs. But many more newcomers to Baghdad were tenant farmers from the southern ʿAmara region. The South was suffering from poor harvests and abuses by large landlords, conditions that were worsened by ineffective land reform laws and agricultural development efforts under the British and Hashemites.[22] Starting in the 1930s, farmers from the South came to Baghdad seeking new work opportunities. Many lived in reed huts on unclaimed and undesirable land inside and outside the city: along railroad tracks, near drainage ditches, and on the eastern and western outskirts of the city. Some squatters took over lands and buildings left behind in central neighborhoods like Saʿdun and Batawin by the forced displacement of Baghdad's Jewish population in the 1940s and 1950s.[23] Both reed and mud houses were commonly referred to in English as "*sarifas*," and these were derisively viewed as "slums" and "shantytowns" by the Iraqi government and Development Board advisors.

One reason why so many newcomers to Baghdad lived in *sarifas* was the cost of urban housing in the mid-twentieth century. With so many internal migrants, high demand on Baghdad's limited housing stock pushed housing prices out of reach for many.[24] Land speculation by investors drove up the price of residential land in Baghdad tenfold between 1949 and 1955.[25] The result of this intensive urban growth and development was that most lower-class and lower-middle-class families simply could not afford a basic, small house, and it was out of the question for the city's poorer residents.[26]

Modernizing the infrastructure of the city contributed to the housing shortage through demolitions. In a span of three years, from 1954 to 1957, the number of cars registered in Iraq doubled.[27] To address the growing traffic congestion in Baghdad, the Hashemite government ordered large highways and thoroughfares to be built. Previously, Baghdad had only one multi-lane road, Rashid Street, which was built by the Ottomans in the early twentieth century by cutting through a densely populated part of the old city. One scholar recalled that residents had considered the construction of Rashid

FIGURE 4 A *sarifa* community alongside railroad tracks in Baghdad. Photo by Constantinos Doxiadis, 1955. © Constantinos and Emma Doxiadis Foundation. DAA, Iraq Diary, vol. 1, 1955, p. 44 (Doxiadis Archives / file 23873).

Street an "outright atrocity" for the scope of demolition through historic areas it had required.[28] By 1945, several new roads cut through the central districts of Baghdad, like King Ghazi Street (later renamed Kifah Street), Shaykh ʿUmar Street, and ʿAbd al-Muhsin al-Saʿdun Street.[29] Baghdad Municipality and the Development Board worked in collaboration throughout the 1950s to widen more roads and design new highways.[30] Republic (*Jumhuriyya*) Street, built in 1958, repeated the cycle of demolition and displacement of residents.[31] These new roads sliced through the dense alleyways of Rusafa, razing markets and homes and displacing their residents (see Figure 7).[32] In 1955 alone, one thousand households had been made homeless by government-mandated tear-downs, prompting one Iraqi Development Board member to advocate that a priority of the government's new housing initiative should be to rehouse these displaced families.[33]

The combination of home demolitions and rising housing costs forced many Baghdadis to move out of their ancestral neighborhoods. Many Baghdadis began to commute to their jobs, no longer living and working in the same neighborhood, and thereby worsening traffic and unsettling communities, as one Baghdadi memoirist complained.[34] Decades later, Iraqi architect Muhammad Makiya still mourned these roads as "wounds" that "mangled the body of the city."[35]

The private sector did not meet the lower classes' demand for affordable housing. Wealthy Baghdadis built new, modern houses in spacious neighborhoods on Baghdad's western outskirts in areas like Mansur and Harthiyya, but these new neighborhoods added only luxury houses to the city's housing stock.[36] American Embassy officials noted: "Private housing has been booming for several years in Baghdad, to a lesser degree in other cities, but it has been primarily for upper class dwellings. Little has been done about middle class housing and virtually nothing for the lowest income groups, except for a few small workers' housing projects which have been good but have hardly scratched the surface."[37] The movement of the wealthy to new suburbs precipitated a decline in the overall affluence and maintenance of the neighborhoods in the city center. Upwardly mobile Baghdadis rented out their houses in Baghdad's historic districts to the working classes and recently arrived rural migrants, many of whom converted the lower floors to shops and workspaces.[38] Many of these large, Ottoman-era homes began to fall into disrepair as multiple families crammed into one home to afford rent.[39] One researcher found that only 40 percent of houses in Baghdad were assessed to be in "good" condition at that time; the rest, especially those in the old quarters, were in need of demolition or extensive repairs to bring houses up to code in terms of access to electricity and plumbing.[40] Thus, not only was there an overall shortage of available houses in Baghdad, but even much of the existing housing stock was deemed uninhabitable.

Despite the apparent urgency of Baghdad's housing crisis in the early 1950s, neither the Development Board nor the Municipality of Baghdad had undertaken sustained efforts to regulate the growth of Baghdad, implement basic zoning regulations, or devise long-term solutions to informal settlements until 1955, well after the start of the oil boom and the beginning of the Development Board's modernization activities. The Development Board's first five-year plan did not include any housing initiatives. This was despite the fact that the Development Board had "more money than it could use": in 1951, the Development Board's budget was 9 million Iraqi Dinars (ID), but it spent less than half that amount that year.[41] Within Baghdad, only one government-financed housing scheme appears to have been constructed prior to the 1950s: 800 low-cost houses built by the Ministry of Social Affairs.[42] The houses were built with few amenities: there was no indoor plumbing, the streets in front of the houses were still unpaved ten years after construction, and there was often more than one family crowded into the three small bedrooms.[43]

In contrast, the Iraqi government was willing to spend lavish amounts of money to hire star architects from the West to turn Baghdad into a showcase of Iraq's newfound wealth and potential. Major contracts were awarded to architectural celebrities—Walter Gropius to design Baghdad University, Le Corbusier for an Olympic Stadium, Frank Lloyd Wright for an opera house, and Gio Ponti for the Ministry of Development and the Development Board's headquarters—even while there was a major lack of affordable housing.[44] (Because the monarchy was overthrown in 1958, shortly after these contracts were awarded, most of these architectural showpieces were never built.)

By 1955, criticism of the Development Board converged on a single point: not enough was being done to provide housing relief for the middle and lower classes. One Iraqi official ominously warned: "It would be a great tragedy if political disaster were to overtake the country because it had not been able to spend the increased income from oil royalties in a way that pleased the mass of the people."[45] Lord Salter, a British member of the Iraqi Development Board in 1955, urged creation of a public housing scheme that would "allay public discontent" and "provide quick benefits" to the urban poor.[46] In response, the Development Board announced that it would add housing as a new priority for its 1955–60 development plan.

To spearhead its new housing initiative, the Development Board hired the Greek urban planner Constantinos Doxiadis to create a master housing plan for Baghdad and to construct new neighborhoods in the city, along with housing projects in other parts of Iraq. Doxiadis was selected in part because of his emphasis on the social considerations of urban planning, rather than just being a "plain housing engineer."[47] As a Greek citizen, he was also considered a politically neutral choice in the charged Cold War environment.[48]

Though the Hashemite government was slow to begin investing heavily in housing developments in Baghdad, the construction boom that followed dramatically reshaped the entire city. The outskirts of Baghdad had once been in a flood zone and too risky to build on. With the protection of the new Tharthar dam, the Hashemite royal family and Development Board officials saw vast potential in the environs around the old city of Baghdad as a blank canvas on which to develop new neighborhoods with modern housing.[49] By the 1970s, only 7 percent of Baghdad's population still lived in the old quarters of the city, with their narrow alleyways and Ottoman-style houses. Well over 90 percent of Baghdadis lived in districts that were built from the 1940s onward, housed in comfortable subdivisions or in marginalized silos for low-income rural migrants.[50]

The rest of this chapter will explore how political concerns shaped the location, composition, and development of Baghdad's new neighborhoods through a logic of political allegiance. Those deemed by the government to be political threats were forcibly settled on the peripheries of the city in grid-like settlements designed to monitor the movements of the rural poor and to regulate their relationship to the rest of the city. In contrast, the government sought to cultivate the allegiance of middle-class professionals through housing subsidies on desirable land in the city center.[51] In all of these cases, the government sought to maintain the upper hand in controlling where different populations would live, resulting in a curiously unnatural patchwork of homogeneous enclaves across the city.

Slums

> The winter rains transform the whole [*sarifa*] area into a huge swamp and render communication almost impossible. Moreover numerous ditches full of filth, human defication [sic] and garbage are frequently seen all over the area....
>
> The inhabitants of this area are greatly involved in the life of Baghdad and have become an essential element in the functioning and growth since they are the labourers, policemen, street-cleaners ... and guards of Baghdad.
>
> The great lack of health facilities, poor housing and low standards of living in this area breed automatically diseases, delinquency and immorality, & thus are endangering [the] social life and health of Baghdad City.
>
> —URBAN PLANNER CONSTANTINOS DOXIADIS,
> describing *sarifa* settlements in Baghdad in 1958[52]

Large camps of *sarifas* first became noticeable in Baghdad beginning in the 1930s; the largest of them was east of the earthen bund that demarcated the edge of safety against floods.[53] From the 1930s through the 1950s, this eastside *sarifa* settlement was known as "the Capital" (*al-ʿAsima*). This eastern district cycled through a series of externally imposed names over the years: it was called Revolution City by ʿAbd al-Karim Qasim in honor of the 1958 coup that brought him to power, and Saddam rebranded it as Saddam City in 1982. With the overthrow of Saddam's regime in 2003, residents finally had the chance to give it their own name, and this majority-Shiʿa community called themselves Sadr City after the influential al-Sadr family of Shiʿi clerics. In the early twentieth century, though, it was al-ʿAsima, the Capital. The bold name perhaps signals how its newly arrived residents were insisting on their "right to the city," to use Henri LeFebvre's term, by constructing a community to meet their needs and claiming their *sarifa* district as the real capital.[54]

In the mid-1950s, the al-ʿAsima settlement was estimated to be around 3 miles long, about 1 mile wide, and densely populated with as many as 100,000 residents.[55] Three other areas of Baghdad also hosted large *sarifa* communities: Tal Muhammad in Eastern Karrada, Shakriyya in the southwest of the city, and Washash near the northwest district of Kadhimiyya (see Figure 5).[56] These *sarifas* were home to entire families, not just male migrant workers. Men and women resided in Baghdad's *sarifas* in nearly equal numbers, and children under the age of six made up roughly one-quarter of the population.[57]

The *sarifa* settlements were informal and self-supported in the fullest sense: they had no plumbing, no electricity, no paved roads, and no sewers. Rains turned the roads into muddy sinkholes used by the 5,000 water buffalo that resided in al-ʿAsima (see Figure 6).[58] Malaria-infected mosquitos and cholera-causing bacteria multiplied in the stagnant water. Human and animal waste was clearly visible (and smelly) in the ditches, vacant lots, and stagnant pools of water, and garbage was gathered in heaps or burned by residents, since the city did not collect garbage there.[59] The municipality did not invest any essential community services like schools or health clinics in the *sarifa* communities, but it did build police stations, underscoring how Baghdad elites viewed rural migrants as security risks. These police stations were positioned on the top of flood walls where officers were able to monitor the population from on high.[60]

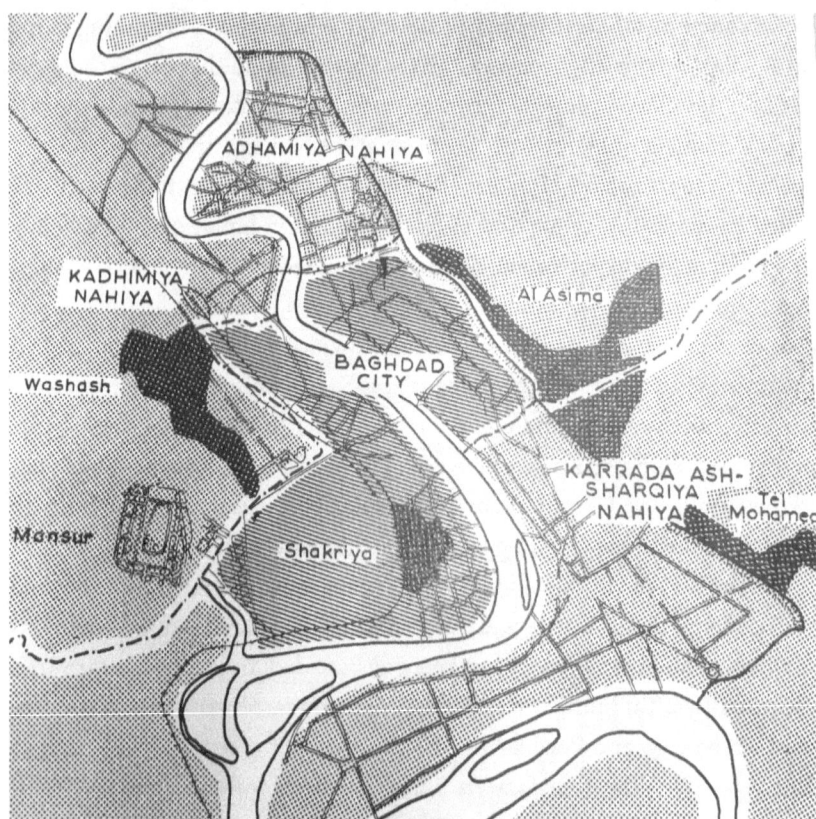

FIGURE 5 Map by Doxiadis Associates indicating in black the areas where large *sarifa* settlements existed in the 1950s. Notably, most official maps at this time did not include these settlements; compare map in Figure 7. © Constantinos and Emma Doxiadis Foundation. DAA, DOX-QBE 1, July 1958, p. 7, Iraq vol. 122 (Doxiadis Archives / file 23996).

Because of their large population, it could be argued that *sarifas* represented the norm within Baghdad, rather than the exception, though they were imagined by the city's urban residents as the uncouth and even dangerous "other."[61] A bus route map from 1952 helps to show how tenuously different parts of Baghdad were integrated in the public imagination in the mid-twentieth century (see Figure 7). On the one hand, this map shows the growth and modernization of Baghdad, now serviced by city buses along the newly built thoroughfares. A new civilian airport appears in western Baghdad, and more railroad lines helped connect Baghdad to other parts of the country. Kadhimiyya is still imagined as somewhat disconnected from the rest of the city, represented not-to-scale with an icon and served by only one bus route. More strikingly, however, *sarifa* settlements are largely erased. The Shakriyya *sarifa* community is blank, depicted as the uninhabited terminus of bus route 21. Informal settlements to the east of the city are completely erased, which can be seen by comparing the maps in Figure 5 and Figure 7. The 1952 bus route map pointedly draws the boundaries of Baghdad Municipality tightly around the Baghdad-Kirkuk railroad on the eastern side of the city, not admitting any of the *sarifa* dwellers of al-'Asima or Tal Muhammad areas living just beyond the tracks. Residents of al-'Asima would have needed to walk into the formally constructed areas of the city to access any public transportation. Maps that only included permanent structures erased tens of thousands of Baghdad residents from the imagined community of the city.

FIGURE 6   A depiction of the livestock that lived alongside residents in al-'Asima on the eastern outskirts of Baghdad. Photo by Constantinos Doxiadis, 1955. © Constantinos and Emma Doxiadis Foundation. DAA, Iraq Diary, vol. 1, 1955, p. 45 (Doxiadis Archives / file 23873).

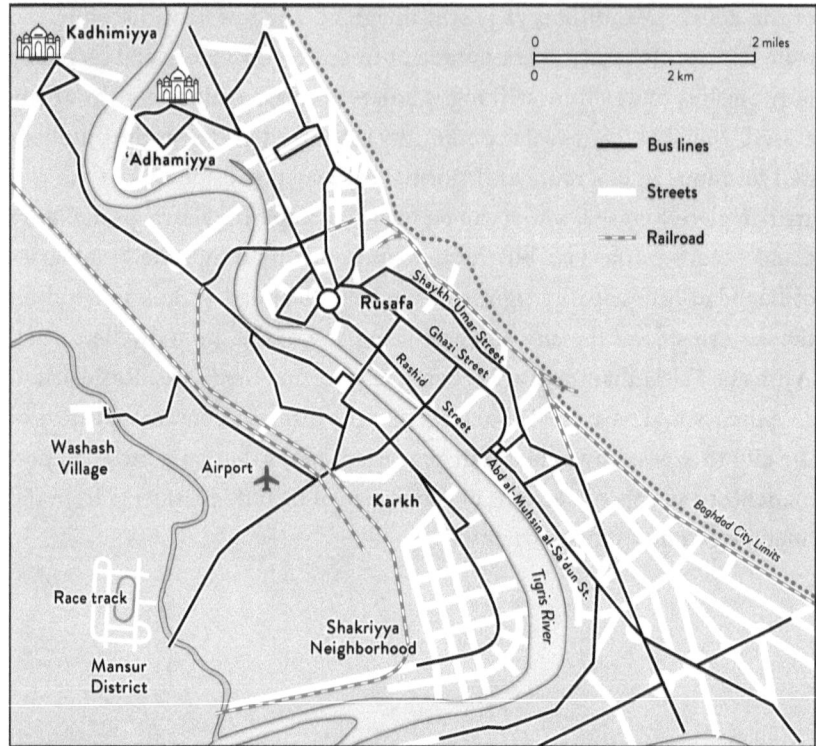

FIGURE 7 Baghdad bus routes, 1952. Adapted from the map, "Baghdad Bus Routes," published by the Iraqi Directorate General of Transport, undated (c. 1952).

Rehousing Sarifa Dwellers: Hashemites (1950-58)

Although the growth of *sarifa* settlements was initially tolerated to some degree, the Hashemite government increasingly saw rural migrants in Baghdad as a political threat that needed to be managed. The 1948 *Wathba* and the 1952 *intifada* mass demonstrations protesting Iraq's close relationship with the United Kingdom underscored the latent political threat that the low-income masses could pose to the monarchy.[62] These protests spurred British and Iraqi officials to try to preempt future unrest through housing and other development projects. A British embassy official cautioned that "one spark would set the country ablaze."[63] In response, the government developed new plans for rehousing the *sarifa* dwellers in the city, but in a way that aimed to neutralize the political threat they posed. However, as the quotation by Doxiadis at the opening of this section indicates, rural migrants were a particularly vexing population for the Iraqi government and the consultants it hired: migrants living in Baghdad's many *sarifa* communities were "essential" for the economic functioning of the capital city, and yet at the same time elites perceived them as "endangering" the metropolis with the crime and disease believed to be emanating from their communities.[64]

In the end, Doxiadis was tasked with demolishing *sarifas* and relocating their residents on the city's outskirts in durable housing. The Development Board called this project "slum clearance," although scholars more recently have referred to such projects as "containment urbanism."[65] Thus, Doxiadis would quarantine Baghdad's recent rural migrants in separated, outlying districts with grid-pattern streets that were easily monitored and controlled. In Baghdad, as in Doxiadis's other projects, new urban infrastructure was used to separate and segregate unwanted rural populations: "Streets were built to identify, isolate, and control certain categories of residents; green spaces were used as boundaries," and rural migrants were rehoused "far from ... the public's gaze."[66]

This marginalization of rural migrants on undesirable land far from the city center was the deliberate outcome of a class-infused worldview, beginning with Hashemite elites: Minister Alawy, chair of the Development Board's subcommittee on housing, argued that "low-cost housing should be built outside of the city. Different classes should not be mixed but classified in categories."[67] When Doxiadis visited an area inside Baghdad where the government had previously demolished *sarifas*, he noted in his work diary: "I am told that the Government has demolished these houses because workers should not live so close to the center of the city. Now, therefore, everybody builds outside of the Band [Bund; the flood walls east of the city]."[68] However, Doxiadis himself also espoused a certain separation of socioeconomic classes: his planned communities separated the rich and poor through strategically building middle-class housing and green spaces as buffers between the two ends of the social spectrum.[69] Thus the forced displacement of rural migrants to the undesirable plains east of the city was by design in accordance with some elites' views about which social classes should live on prime urban land.

The goal of Doxiadis's slum clearance program was therefore to relocate southern rural migrants in a way that would uphold the political and social stability of the city.[70] The primary beneficiary of slum clearance was not imagined to be the rural migrants who would have durable housing, but the government and more affluent residents of the city who would no longer be "threatened" by the *sarifa* dwellers' destabilizing and unregulated presence in the city.

Doxiadis managed to complete construction of a professional neighborhood in western Baghdad to house pharmacists and other professionals. He also began constructing a pilot neighborhood in the late 1950s to rehouse *sarifa* dwellers on the eastern outskirts of the city. However, Doxiadis's plans in Iraq were interrupted by the 1958 Revolution before most of his work could be carried out. Though he did not complete many of his plans in Baghdad, he went on to apply his approach to "slum clearance" in Riyadh and other world cities.

In the end, the work of resettling Baghdad's rural migrants did not take place under the Hashemites and Doxiadis, though they had laid the groundwork for these slum clearance plans. This work was primarily undertaken instead by the postcolonial regimes after 1958, particularly by ʿAbd al-Karim Qasim and then by the Baʿth Party. With each new coup, the real and imagined exclusion of rural migrants from the core of Baghdad was reaffirmed.

Rehousing Sarifa Dwellers: ʿAbd al-Karim Qasim (1958-63)

The rehousing of *sarifa* dwellers in Revolution City is often misattributed to ʿAbd al-Karim Qasim, Iraq's ruler from 1958 to 1963.[71] Qasim was a military officer who led a bloody coup in which the Hashemite royal family and Iraq's long-serving prime minister, Nuri al-Saʿid, were murdered. Qasim was initially supported by the Iraqi Communist Party, and he introduced economic and social programs meant to steer the country toward socialism. This included experiments in rent control, minimum wage, agricultural land distribution, government-set prices for goods, the establishment of peasant unions and other cooperatives, and steps toward nationalizing some foreign companies.[72] Increasing affordable housing was another pillar of his agenda.

Qasim is closely associated in public memory with the rehousing of *sarifa* dwellers in Revolution City in part because many *sarifa* residents politically supported him—so much so that *sarifa* dwellers were dubbed the "sons of Qasim."[73] Large numbers of rural migrants flooded the streets to cheer the downfall of the monarchy during his 1958 coup, and in response, he put his stamp on the largest *sarifa* settlement by renaming al-'Asima as Revolution City.[74] On the first anniversary of the revolution, Qasim gave a speech promising, "On the day when I lay the foundation stone of the villages to be built for the shack dwellers [*sarifas*], I will personally handle a pickaxe and demolish the first shack or two. Flourishing projects will rise in the place of these shacks."[75] Despite these promises, though, the work of replacing reed and mud huts with permanent housing were not implemented on a large scale under Qasim's watch.

Instead—and illustrating a key point of this chapter's argument—he focused his efforts on building new housing for army officers, another group he relied upon to remain in power, and arguably the more politically important when compared to the *sarifa* dwellers. In his five years in power, Qasim broke ground for two neighborhoods for army officers: one in west Baghdad, called Qasim City (after his assassination in 1963, it was renamed Officers' Neighborhood), and another on the east side of the city known as Officers' City.[76] US Embassy officials rightly pointed out that, "while it is the announced intent of [Qasim's administration] to provide adequate housing for all segments of the Iraqi population, housing for government employees, particularly army officers, has received top priority. This can only be construed as a measure to win loyalty to the regime."[77]

Other efforts by Qasim to address Baghdad's acute housing crisis were aimed at lower-middle-class Baghdadis, rather than at the *sarifa* dwellers. He distributed subsidized residential land in Baghdad to various groups of public-sector employees and professional unions, and the fact that 65 percent of these employees were able to build their houses without taking loans from the bank confirms that the beneficiaries of this policy were not the poor, but the professional classes that he hoped to win over as loyal supporters.[78] He also introduced rent control policies that were also aimed to help lower-income workers who rented rooms in individual houses, which effectively lowered rents for most Baghdadis by 15–20 percent.[79] Again, this policy was not intended to benefit *sarifa* dwellers who, as squatters in informal settlements, typically did not pay rent on their homes.[80]

Qasim signaled his support for rural migrants by passing policies encouraging more internal migrants to come to Baghdad. He introduced sweeping agrarian reform laws aimed at dismantling the inequitable land ownership system in southern Iraq, rolled back Hashemite-era restrictions on rural-urban migration, and also granted limited legal protections to the squatters in Baghdad, stipulating that "persons can live on any unwalled and uninhabited piece of ground and can only be moved if the owner builds on the property."[81] Qasim also made a special concession to the distinctive community of Marsh Arabs who lived in Revolution City, many of whom earned their livelihood by raising water buffalo in that district. Recognizing that any rehousing scheme would ruin their distinctive way of life and commitment to animal husbandry, Qasim agreed to set aside a special piece of land for them even farther from the city limits, in an area now known as Fadhiliyya, where they could raise their animals.[82] Thus, instead of increasing durable housing for migrants, Qasim was responsible for the expansion of informal housing in the capital.

Officials in the American Embassy offered their own theory about why Qasim did not act on his promises to rehouse Baghdad's rural migrants: Qasim needed only to distribute a small number of houses to members of the *sarifa* community, which he did with great publicity, in order to inspire hope among the rural migrants that they would one day receive a house of their own. He had enough political loyalty from this population that they gave him the benefit of the doubt and did not object to the slow pace of housing distribution.[83]

Rehousing Sarifa Dwellers: Ba'th Party Rule in 1963

Ultimately, the rehousing of Baghdad's *sarifa* community came not from a leader who championed their cause, but from leaders who—like the Hashemites—feared their political power. Another officers' coup dispatched Qasim in 1963; that new government was briefly led from February to November 1963 by the Ba'th Party. During its ten months in power in 1963, the Ba'th Party orchestrated a brutal crackdown on communists and other political enemies before they were edged out by officer 'Abd al-Salam

ʿArif (r. 1963–66). After ʿAbd al-Salam ʿArif died in a helicopter crash, he was succeeded by his brother ʿAbd al-Rahman ʿArif (r. 1966–68).

The push to rehouse and relocate Baghdad's *sarifa* dwellers took place during the spasm of violence under the Baʿth Party's brief administration from February to November 1963. The Baʿth Party forcibly displaced Baghdad's rural migrant population not as a populist gesture, but in a naked attempt to crush and contain the Iraqi Communist Party.

In the span of their brief ten-month reign in 1963, Baʿth Party militias were responsible for torturing and killing thousands of communists, reportedly even using Baghdad's new train line—constructed as a gleaming example of the city's industrialization and modernity in the 1950s—as a "death train," trapping hundreds of suspected communists inside without food or water as they were transported to a prison in the South of Iraq.[84] The Baʿth Party identified *sarifa* dwellers as supporters of Qasim, whom the Baʿthists had just assassinated, and suspected that large numbers of communist sympathizers lurked within their ranks.

The immediate catalyst for forcibly displacing *sarifa* communities was a communist coup attempt against the Baʿth Party on July 3, 1963. Just four days later, on July 7, an order went out hastily calling for the immediate evacuation of the large *sarifa* on Baghdad's western edge, in an area known as Washash. Some residents from Washash were sent to Revolution City on Baghdad's eastern edge, while others were moved to the Shuʿla neighborhood on the far outskirts of Baghdad's northwest border.[85] Former *sarifa* dwellers were initially given small plots of land and bricks to build their own houses. However, the price of providing building materials grew too costly, so families were instead offered cheap loans to buy materials on their own, with regulations requiring that new houses be built of permanent materials, rather than reeds or mud.[86] Strict regulations sharply limited the size of their new houses, which were grouped into rigid rectangular blocks.

In overseeing the clearing of Baghdad's *sarifa* communities and their forced displacement to the margins of the city, the Baʿth Party ensured that the new durable construction of these neighborhoods would be built according to a logic of surveillance, domination, and control that isolated the rural migrants from the rest of the urban landscape. Within the few short months of Baʿthist rule in 1963, as many as 100,000 *sarifa* dwellers were forcibly relocated to Revolution City or Shuʿla and more than 55,000 reed and mud huts destroyed.[87] The police and army were called in to oversee the evictions and demolitions, which left behind "hills of debris in the very flat areas of Baghdad."[88] Witnessing the demolition of the Washash *sarifa* community, an observer from the British Embassy in Baghdad wrote: "This step was undertaken with no warning or apparent preparation and the presumption is that, while the removal of the sarifas has long been contemplated, the present 'rush' job is to remove a potential source of danger in the event of possible disorders."[89]

In the end, the rapid destruction of *sarifa* camps and the relocation of their residents was the product of political goals. To blatantly underscore the political threat that the Ba'th Party saw in Baghdad's *sarifa* community, Ba'thist leaders hanged two of the communist coup conspirators from gallows in Revolution City as a warning to the population.[90] Revolution City's physical isolation and its unrelenting grid pattern prompted several contemporary observers to detect a logic of security, surveillance, and control in the design. On the city's outskirts, this district could now be "more easily contained" by the military or police than other parts of the city.[91] Demolitions and forced relocations were also meant to appeal to the middle and upper classes as an improvement of "law and order" by decisively dealing with a population viewed as menacing by many other Baghdadis.[92]

The decision to physically relocate the vast majority of Baghdad's rural migrants in a single district separated from the rest of the city had implications for the future development of Revolution City and for the rest of Baghdad. In 1960, the new Army Canal was built as a boundary between desirable and undesirable parts of Baghdad. Originally designed by Doxiadis as a way to bring green vegetation and lushness into the city, the Army Canal ended up serving as an important "psycho-social barrier," separating the population of Revolution City from the rest of the city and contributing to its lack of integration into the imagined community of the city.[93] In the 1960s, highways were built along each side of the canal, emphasizing this line as a boundary between the "real city" of Baghdad and Revolution City as a separate outgrowth.

The exclusion of Revolution City residents from city life was replicated in the production of knowledge about the city: many maps in the 1960s and 1970s did not include Shu'la within the borders of Baghdad, and even some

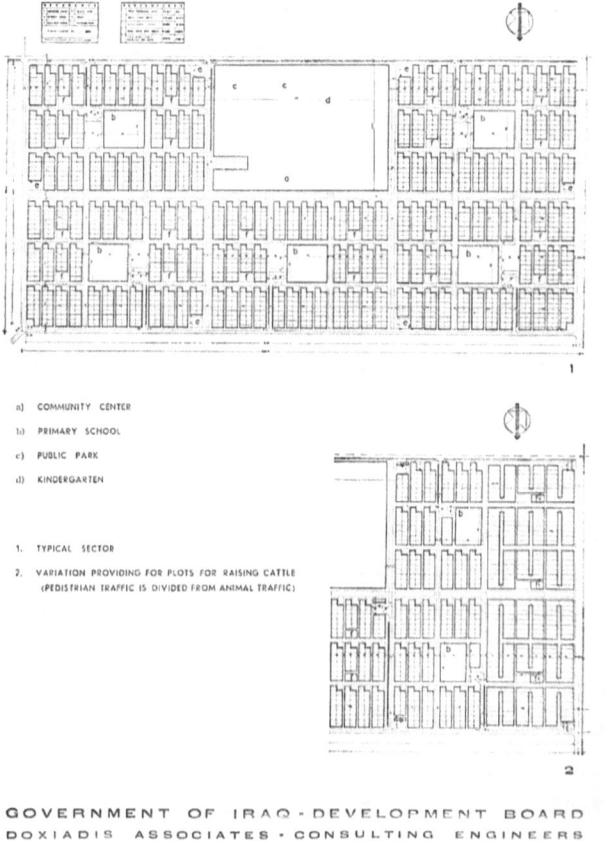

FIGURE 8 Doxiadis's proposed plans for rehousing *sarifa* dwellers in permanent housing. His blueprints influenced the later construction of Revolution City. Though Doxiadis's plans made accommodations for parks, livestock grazing pastures, schools, and community centers, few of these amenities were built for Revolution City residents in the 1960s. © Constantinos and Emma Doxiadis Foundation. DAA, "Eastern Baghdad Development—First Baghdad Slum Clearance Project," October 1958 (Doxiadis Archives / file 28978).

demographic statistical tables for the 1960s did not include Revolution City in statistics about Baghdad city residents.[94]

For example, an updated bus route map from 1964 (see Figure 9) shows how rehoused *sarifa* communities were still largely erased even after the displacement of tens of thousands of residents to Revolution City and Shuʻla. Shuʻla's name appears on the map to the city's northwest side, but the name floats in a blank white space; there is no physical representation of the neighborhood's existence. Revolution City is curiously absent on the east side of the map. Doxidadis's grid-like plan for settling migrants can be seen in the stark rectangular patterns of the Jamila neighborhood to the east of the Army Canal. Revolution City is located adjacent to Jamila, but neither its name nor any physical representation of the district's streets and city blocks appears. Bus route 40, which extends far east of the city, is shown circling around a blank abyss. Had Revolution City been depicted, it would have shown how Line 40 skirted the perimeter of this large district, home to tens of thousands of Baghdad's residents. In contrast, the two new neighborhoods for army officers—Yarmuk in the west and a neighborhood for officers' quarters to the east—both appear on the map with visual details.

Additional neighborhoods built to the east of the Army Canal were also constructed according to a logic of security and surveillance. For example, observers questioned the government's decision in the 1960s to build Baghdad University's student dormitories on the eastern outskirts of the city, requiring students to take a lengthy bus ride to attend their classes. Marooned in a relatively undeveloped area, "politically volatile students could, if necessary, be more easily contained by the army there than in less isolated ... quarters of the city."[95] Similarly, the Baʻth Party later built three prisons and an office for state security on the city's east side, in a neighborhood called Shawra wa Umm Jidr. Loyal Baʻthists were housed around the office for state security, continuing the trend begun in the 1960s to "encircle major urban areas with trusted loyalists and government facilities" as a form of urban control.[96] Students, prisoners, and rural migrants, all imagined by the government and city elites to be politically and socially threatening, were better contained and monitored in grid-like neighborhoods on the city's margins under the watchful surveillance of state security apparatuses.

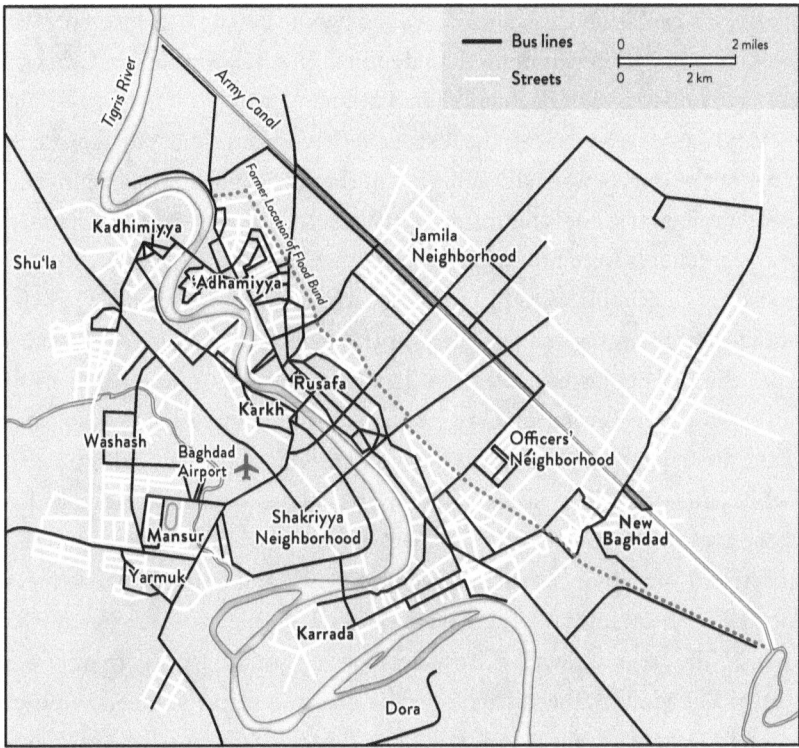

FIGURE 9 Baghdad bus routes, 1964. Adapted from the map, "Baghdad City," published by the Iraqi General Directorate of Transportation (Baghdad: Survey Press, 1964).

Citizen Contestation in Revolution City after 1968

This security-based approach to housing potentially volatile populations on the other side of the Army Canal continued under the 'Arif brothers (1963–68) and then under Ba'th Party rule throughout the remainder of the twentieth century. By the time the Ba'th Party overthrew the 'Arif regime and returned to power in 1968, it was clear that Revolution City had become something of a dumping ground for Baghdad's urban poor, and especially for former rural migrants. More than 85,000 plots of land in Revolution City were distributed by the end of the 1960s, guaranteeing its composition as a dense, large district. The population grew steadily, outpacing governmental efforts (tepid as they were) to provide necessary infrastructure and services: Revolution City housed 353,000 people in 1965 and, just ten years later, its population had more than doubled. In total, Revolution City was home to one-fourth of Baghdad's population by the 1970s.[97]

And yet, despite its size, the district suffered from almost total neglect: most of the streets were still unpaved in the 1970s.[98] There was an insufficient number of schools for former *sarifa* residents: one researcher claimed that 160 schools were promised to have been built in Revolution City, but that only 62 schools were in operation, while another researcher put the number of operating schools there in the 1970s at a mere 24.[99] Statistics from the early 1970s indicated that less than 1 percent of the residents of either Shuʻla or Revolution City graduated from intermediate school, and that illiteracy rates in both areas hovered around 43 percent at this time.[100] Public amenities, like gardens and sports fields, were absent except for those that residents had built for themselves.[101] One library served three-quarters of a million people in Revolution City, and only one cinema was located in the vicinity.[102] There were no post offices anywhere in the district.[103] The ratio of doctors to residents was significantly less than in the rest of Baghdad.[104] The district's public health services suffered in other ways, too: there was no sewage system in those districts for decades after it was first constructed. The gaping pits that Doxiadis had described in 1955, full of excrement, garbage, and rainwater, continued to dot the landscape of Revolution City more than twenty years later.[105] According to Omar Dewachi's history of Iraq's medical system, the Iraqi government only completed Revolution City's sewage system in the 1980s, after discovering that Iraqi communists were hiding subversive literature (or even Communist Party members themselves) in the neighborhood's cesspools to escape detection by the authorities.[106]

Tellingly, the municipality did not skimp on security measures even as it neglected Revolution City's other community needs: six different police stations covered the district, with hundreds of police officers on the payroll, confirming that the government continued to see these residents as a political and social threat.[107]

Resettling the *sarifa* communities on the edges of the city sent the message that these communities did not have the same rights of belonging, or "city-zenship," compared to other populations in Baghdad.[108] But although the *sarifa* dwellers were viewed as disruptive and dangerous by urban planners, politicians, and elites, they were in fact economically integrated into the city and, to a degree, socially integrated, too. According to statistics from 1959, nearly 50 percent of the *sarifa* residents in Baghdad had lived there for more than ten years, and 12 percent had lived there for more than twenty-five years, becoming permanent residents of the city.[109] Residents of the *sarifas* raised water buffalo for milk, and chickens for eggs, and grew vegetables for sale in city markets. Women sometimes took work as domestic servants in the homes of wealthy Baghdadis, in a relationship one researcher called a "spatial symbiosis."[110] Men took on urban occupations as peddlers, construction laborers, and other types of unskilled workers, doormen, and even police officers and soldiers.[111] One survey suggested that as many as 57 percent of Baghdad's industrial workers came from *sarifa* communities.[112]

Despite the violent disruptions and displacements to the original *sarifa* communities by the Baʿth Party in 1963, residents were able to take some actions to rebuild their social networks and to remake the neighborhood on their own terms. The state had distributed housing plots to *sarifa* dwellers at random, meaning that family members who had once lived in proximity to one another were scattered throughout the large urban blocks of Revolution City. But it was common practice for families to illegally swap housing plots with other residents to ensure that they were able to still live close to family. One study showed that, despite the random distribution of plots, more than 50 percent of Revolution City residents lived near relatives, and as a result, certain city blocks became associated with the family or tribal networks concentrated there.[113] In some areas of Revolution City, the names of different tribes reportedly supplanted the number-based street naming system of Revolution City to reflect the kinship identities of the street's residents.[114] Though the district eventually became more diverse, taking in poor residents from other parts of the city, the rebuilding of Revolution City in durable materials like brick and concrete did not prevent the former *sarifa* dwellers from reconstituting aspects of the rural communities they had left.[115]

Residents also took control of critical economic and social functions when the government was unwilling or slow to do so. Residents built coffee shops and mosques for themselves, providing community gathering spots that were not part of the original urban design of the district.[116] There were

222 cafes operating in the late 1970s, testifying to the organic way residents catered to the social needs of their community, as well as to the high unemployment rates that kept the cafes full of working-age men.[117] In another example, the state tried to create durable markets in the form of brick halls with electricity and plumbing. However, an insufficient number had been built to serve the district's needs, so a combination of official private businesses, informal markets, and kiosks proliferated throughout the district. In contrast to the 15 governmental markets, there were 13 large popular markets, 241 privately run bakeries, and 79 butchers that operated in main commercial streets.[118] Observers found the hygienic standards of the popular markets lacking, however, due to their informal nature. One scholar who conducted fieldwork in Revolution City in the 1970s made this observation: "a horribly unhealthy open market has developed, where one can find all kinds of unhygienic cheap foodstuffs such as fish, meat, vegetables, low-grade fruit, sheep, eggs, together with second-hand household tools, etc. Swarms of flies and stagnant pools are found near the squatting sellers who are mainly migrants living in al-Thawrah [Revolution City]. The Directorate General of Health of the capital is little more than a third of a mile away from this primitive and dangerous market!"[119] Here we can begin to see how residents of Revolution City lived between the neglect or insufficient services of the state for many essential community needs, and the over-policing and surveillance of the district on the other. When the state intervened in Revolution City, it was often for policing and not for supplying infrastructure and essential services.

Finally, the government did not have the absolute last word in dictating where and how rural migrants in Baghdad would live; any efforts at "resettling" rural migrants were always incomplete and contested. Rural migration to Baghdad still occurred, but it was often "clandestine" and against official rules meant to control internal migration.[120] Even though it was strictly prohibited after 1965 to build any new *sarifa* or mud hut anywhere in the vicinity of Baghdad, some informal reed dwellings persisted in the city even up through the 1990s (see chapter 5).[121] A Ba'th Party "reverse migration" initiative in 1971 to encourage former *sarifa* dwellers to return to their rural homelands aptly illustrated the regime's antipathy toward the residents of Revolution City, but this program faltered: despite widespread publicity campaigns and the construction of a fledgling community to rehouse any returnees, participants in this experimental agricultural project were disappointed with what the government delivered and ultimately saw their prospects in Baghdad as more promising.¹²² Thus Iraq's rural poor persisted in claiming their right to live in Baghdad and, once arrived in Revolution City, managed to reconstitute their social networks in ways that still referenced their agrarian origins while adapting to city life. In many ways, residents of Revolution City reshaped the physical and social contours of their district, despite the violent coercive power of the Baʻthist regime.

Subdivisions

From the Hashemites in the 1950s to the Baʻth Party in the 1960s, a series of Iraqi government administrations used housing benefits to secure the allegiance of public-sector employees in the capital. As Qasim's ambivalent record in rehousing *sarifa* dwellers illustrated, many Iraqi leaders calculated that using oil funds to shore up support with political allies was at least as important as managing the political threats posed by the urban poor and rural migrants. These new housing benefits to assist middle-class professionals and public-sector workers had important political, social, and economic consequences for how Baghdad developed in the mid-twentieth century.

The trend of building subsidized housing for key political allies began in earnest during the oil boom years of the Hashemite era. The Development Board's first project was to build new housing for Iraqi military officers. This was a politically inspired project aimed at signaling the commitment of the Hashemite monarchy and its British backers to the Iraqi military.¹²³ (The British Embassy also succeeded in securing a lucrative contract for a British firm to build 900 houses for the Iraqi officers, so there were financial motivations as well.)¹²⁴ A few years later, Doxiadis was commissioned to build subsidized housing for middle-class Iraqis, including members of the Doctors' and Pharmacists' Union, in a neighborhood called Western Baghdad.¹²⁵

These early projects in state-constructed houses for middle-class professionals and officers proved to be an expensive and time-consuming enterprise for the government, however. Furthermore, there were moral fears that handing out free housing would lead residents to become lazy or unappreciative, or that the promise of free housing would only worsen the influx of rural migrants to the capital. Doxiadis argued that providing free housing would "infantilize its beneficiaries, turning them into potential troublemakers and agitators."[126] The minister of development shared this viewpoint, stating that making people "pay for their houses," even at highly reduced rates, would help them to "feel that they are the owners."[127] The Iraqi government decided that it would distribute subsidized residential land and offer attractive loans so that public-sector employees and the professional classes could build their own houses at a minimal cost.[128]

The updated law "For Sale of Houses to Workers and Officials," passed in 1955, codified these new requirements that recipients would make regular payments for subsidized residential land that they received as a state benefit, and it set out the rules by which residents could sell, rent out, or bequeath their state-subsidized homes after a certain number of years.[129] This model of distributing residential land for nominal prices, rather than distributing already constructed housing, was continued by all subsequent Iraqi governments, including the Baʿth Party.

After the 1958 Revolution, Qasim's administration continued subsidized housing benefits for public-sector employees, but decentralized the task of distributing land. Rather than have the government distribute residential land to each qualified employee, Qasim tasked labor unions to distribute the land through cooperative housing unions that were organized by and for their members.[130] To support the efforts of these cooperative housing unions, Qasim established a Directorate of Cooperative Unions and a new bank to provide housing loans.[131] By the 1960s, at least ninety different professional organizations had received plots of state-subsidized land for their members.[132]

Cooperative housing societies were responsible for selecting recipients of land parcels from among their professional members by lottery. Recipients of land were required to begin construction on a house on that plot within five years. The recipient paid a low cost for the land itself (ID 60 in 1974, the equivalent then of $202), and they were eligible for loans to cover the costs of building materials and building.[133] This system accounted for the rapid expansion of Baghdad's neighborhoods: by 1967, at least 43,051 plots of residential land in Baghdad were distributed by the government to housing cooperatives, and 28,858 new houses were completed on these plots.¹³⁴ The ʿArif and Baʿthist regimes continued this practice in the 1960s and beyond, recognizing that it would save money and administrative headaches to enlist professional unions to oversee the distribution of land to their members, rather than do it themselves.¹³⁵

Political Impacts of Housing Professionals

Though the decision to delegate responsibility for distributing subsidized land to vocational cooperative unions was primarily the result of expediency, there were important social and political effects of this policy, as well as political motivations behind it. In the short term, distributing residential land was a way of mitigating potentially dangerous critiques that the government was not doing enough to combat Baghdad's housing shortages. This was especially important for a self-styled populist leader like Qasim, who publicly championed the poor but nevertheless still witnessed a period of steep increases in housing prices. By the 1970s, one scholar calculated that 75 percent of Baghdad's population could not afford the $4,500 it cost at the time to build a two-bedroom house.¹³⁶

This method of housing distribution led to the creation of professional enclaves across Baghdad's landscape, clustering professionals of similar backgrounds into readily identifiable silos. Occupations still demarcate many of the city's districts today: Doctors' Neighborhood, Police Neighborhood, Teachers' Neighborhood, Engineers' Neighborhood, Municipalities Neighborhood (for city and federal bureaucrats), and at least three different neighborhoods for military officers (one in ʿAdhamiyya, one in Yarmuk, and one in Zayuna) all carry the names of the intended beneficiaries or the professional cooperative housing unions that were involved in building the original housing development.¹³⁷ Beyond these eponymous neighborhoods, additional plots of land were allocated to certain ministries: land in the Daʿudi neighborhood in western Baghdad was set aside for employees in the Ministry of Agriculture; parts of Workers' Neighborhood in eastern Baghdad were allocated to the Ministry of Finance's housing society; and stretches along the Army Canal Highway corridor were likewise reserved for the employees of various ministries and professional organizations.¹³⁸

In short, the state distribution of land anchored these workers in homogeneous neighborhoods by profession, making them visibly identifiable

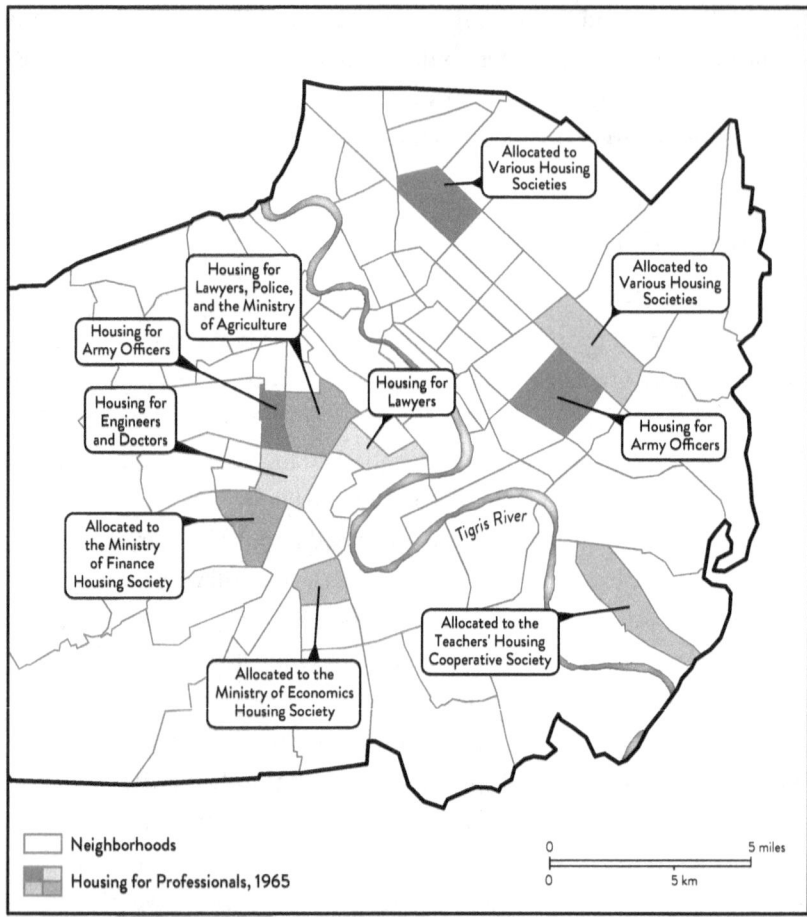

FIGURE 10 Map identifying some of the neighborhoods in Baghdad that were built by 1965 for employees of certain professions. This map was adapted from Gulick, "Baghdad: Portrait of a City," 247.

in the cityscape. A logic of separation and surveillance drove this practice, just as security concerns drove the displacement of *sarifa* dwellers to the city's outskirts. These homogeneous neighborhoods could form reservoirs of support that to be mobilized in times of crisis, and grouping certain populations together made it easier to suppress political threats. For example, one researcher pointed out how "the concentration of the army officers in one community, where they could be easily watched by the government" meant that they could be "more easily contained" if they tried to rise up to overthrow the rulers.[139] The same logic could be applied to the neighborhoods for police officers and secret police agents. If teachers or university professors tried to strike, it would be easy for the regime to surveil or surround Teachers' Neighborhood or University Neighborhood. But the distribution of residential land was intended to neutralize such threats before they began, inculcating loyalty through generous land benefits. As one scholar noted, "the distribution (and conversely, the confiscation) of land within the capital was a way for the regime to consolidate its power, as the loyalty of particular client groups could be cultivated in a manner that simultaneously reaffirmed their dependency."[140]

In contrast to the rural residents who were isolated on the city's margins, Baghdad's professional groups were affirmed by name as important residents who rightfully belonged in the city. Naming districts after the cooperative housing union responsible for their construction reinforced the notion that middle-class professionals had a "right to the city," though it was an illusory right that was permitted to function only in terms dictated by the state.[141] Though public-sector employees and professional classes gained a financially valuable benefit in subsidized houses and residential land, accepting to live in these new subdivisions meant participating in the politicization of the landscape and increasing one's visibility to the state.

Social Impacts of Housing Professionals

Though vocational neighborhoods were created according to political priorities, they had significant social effects by grouping people of similar backgrounds together. Many observers noted the artificiality of these professional groupings in the city landscape. As one scholar wrote: "In its modern development Baghdad provides another peculiar phenomenon, namely the governmental residential suburbs. The government has deliberately created new social segregation. The new social stratification depends on the relative economic and professional status of the occupants. Particular professional groups are housed on particular sites. This is in complete contrast to the naturally developed traditional residential mahallah."[142] These social impacts have reverberated over the decades, even as the original residents of these neighborhoods have moved away or died over the years, ending some of the initial homogeneity. A recent interview with a resident of Baghdad's Police Neighborhood No. 1 in western Baghdad indicates that many current and retired police officers still live there, beneficiaries of these land distribution practices.[143]

New professional neighborhoods had other social impacts in the way new housing designs encouraged by the government were intended to socialize middle-class Baghdadis into the requirements of the modern era, as defined by Iraqi politicians and by Doxiadis. Doxiadis was particularly attentive to the social effects of housing settlements through his formulation of "ekistics," a term he coined to refer to the "science of human settlements."[144] The methods of distributing housing and residential land reinforced a patriarchal, middle-class view of family organization and participation in the labor market. Lotteries to distribute housing and residential land were according to the professional membership of the head of household, a legal designation that went to the father of a nuclear family except in cases of divorce or death.

The houses themselves were also designed to enforce a new trend of residence according to nuclear families, as opposed to extended families—a trend that was meant to signal Baghdad's modernity but also exacerbated the housing crisis, since breaking up extended families into conjugal units required more houses to shelter the same number of individuals. A promotional film for Doxiadis's Western Baghdad housing development, part of which was allocated to members of the Doctors' and Pharmacists' union, showcased how his houses would facilitate a modern, middle-class lifestyle for a nuclear family. In this recorded scene, a married couple and their three children appear clean and happy, living as a nuclear unit rather than with their extended family. The wife tends to the children, rocking her baby in a western-style cradle. The father enjoys free time reading a newspaper in the house's courtyard, while the family enjoys amenities like electric lights and an indoor latrine.[145] Likewise, promotional photos for an experimental housing community in Western Baghdad show a man in a Western-style shirt posing in front of a 1950s tailfin car with rows of clean, newly constructed homes lining the street behind him, indicating the kind of middle-class, Western comforts a homeowner could expect for himself.[146]

The very architecture of Baghdad's new middle-class houses was intended to shift Iraqis' worldview. Master plans by Doxiadis and others were intended to "open up" the city, in part by changing the orientation of houses from a private, interior courtyard by moving the front door and balcony toward the street. As one scholar noted, "symbolically, it was thought that the city and its inhabitants would become more open to the world around them."[147]

Baghdadis did not always accept these Western models of modern, urban life that Doxiadis and others encouraged. Residents of Doxiadis's Western Baghdad settlement and other planned neighborhoods reacted against pedestrian-only zones and opened them for car traffic.[148] Houses that were designed according to Western tastes were altered to continue Iraqi living styles; front porches facing the street were screened off for privacy, while shops built in planned communities to face pedestrian-only zones were rearranged to face street traffic.[149]

Professional housing schemes solidified the notion that receiving residential land was a standard benefit that many Baghdadis could expect and even demand from the state. The categories of beneficiaries expanded over time as later leaders sought to cultivate loyalty among new populations. In addition to continuing to provide residential land to military officers and public-sector employees, Saddam expanded this program in the 1980s to include politically connected friends of the regime and, starting with the Iran-Iraq War (1980–88), families of martyrs. Housing was thus transformed into a new bargaining chip to mediate state-society relations, with the state doling out favors to target populations and Baghdadi residents pressing the state to grant them residential land. There was a dark side to the use of housing as a new state benefit to influence state-society relations: under the Baʿth Party, housing became a coercive tool that was used against enemies. For example, the Baʿth Party later seized homes of suspected Iran sympathizers, opposition group members, and army deserters, and redistributed the homes as gifts to friends. Forced displacement, once used against *sarifa* dwellers, was later used against families that sheltered deserting soldiers.

In sum, a succession of governments from the Hashemite monarchy to the Baʿth Party looked for ways to distribute oil rents to middle-class Baghdadis by providing subsidized housing or residential land. In establishing housing as a new standard benefit for public-sector employees, the state attempted to ensure that the formation of new middle-class neighborhoods was politically advantageous: clustering professional groups together facilitated monitoring and the management of state-society relations, and the state used housing as a new incentive to shore up support. In practice, most Iraqi political leaders leaned away from micro-managing the construction of new professional neighborhoods through top-down urban design and construction, opting instead to allow professionals to build their own houses under the oversight of housing unions. This limited the ability of the state to dictate how Baghdad's landscape would develop and undermined the master plans developed for Baghdad, though it was a trade-off that regimes were willing to make to save money and bureaucratic hassles.

Conclusion

City Plans, Lived Realities

This chapter deliberately moved away from a rich body of academic literature that focuses on the blueprints produced by urban planners and architects to focus instead on how Baghdad's new neighborhoods were actually produced through a negotiation between government leaders and Baghdad's residents. The decision to allow cooperative housing union members to build their own neighborhoods demonstrates the ultimately fictitious aspects of the master plans developed for Baghdad by Minoprio, Spencely, and P. W. MacFarlane in 1956 or by Doxiadis in 1958. As one scholar has written, the impulse behind mid-century urban planning was a desire to construct a modern city according to "rational" or scientific principles, clearly segmenting and labeling each part of the city according to its purpose. "The [Doxiadis] master plan did more than prescribe Baghdad's orderly expansion. Behind the preoccupation with visual order, uniformity, and regularity, was a larger goal to reinvent the old city as an efficient modern capital and make it a symbol and an instrument of modernization. . . . Such a preoccupation with formal clarity was of course typical of high-modernist urbanism, whose grand visions for the rational engineering of social life found fertile ground in the post–World War II era, especially in the postcolonial world."[150] In practice, however, a succession of governments from the Hashemites to the Baʿthists prioritized short-term expediency over meticulous, top-down, and ideologically infused housing plans. Distributing residential land, rather than administering the construction of housing, allowed for more spontaneity and idiosyncrasy in neighborhood development than the master plans indicated on paper. The actual construction of Baghdad's new neighborhoods rarely aligned with the idealized visions and plans produced by urban planners, but instead involved messy interactions between multiple government institutions, housing cooperative unions, individual homeowners, and Iraqi laborers who collectively reshaped Baghdad's landscape in a piecemeal fashion through competing concerns and priorities.[151]

The political objectives that informed the formation of new neighborhoods have rarely been examined in depth: work has only recently begun to understand how "histories of urban space ... inform our understanding of state-society relations in Iraq," and especially for Baghdad.[152] I have argued here that a succession of Iraqi governments transformed housing into a new form of political leverage through the construction of middle-class subdivisions and low-income housing.

However, there were real limitations to the success of these political projects. Revolution City, meant to settle rural migrants and transform them into subdued and productive citizens, was neglected by the municipality and remained a politically hostile area for decades to come. Despite its creation along a rigid grid on the edges of the city, surveillance and monitoring of Revolution City remained difficult for the regime to accomplish. Finally, as later chapters will address, the advent of the Iran-Iraq War severely tested the patriarchal, middle-class vision of a nuclear family supported by one male wage earner that new professional neighborhoods were designed to support.

Real and Imaginary Geographies

The oil boom years of 1950 to 1979 transformed both the physical and imaginary landscape of Baghdad. The physical transformation was apparent to all observers: new highways cut broad swaths through the old city, new middle-class subdivisions sprang up and expanded the city's borders, glistening new hotels lined the Tigris River, and *sarifas* were razed and displaced residents were forced into durable housing on the outskirts of the city. At the same time, an invisible transformation also took place that was no less meaningful, as the social and political significance of Baghdad's neighborhoods and the status and relationship to the state they symbolized changed. New housing projects symbolized these differences: the "rows-on-row of concrete-and-brick cubicles for relocated squatters" in Revolution City stood in stark contrast to the "quite sumptuous two-story houses for army officers in Yarmuk."[153]

All cities have this imaginary geography of significance, which changes with major political and demographic shifts. In the eighteenth and nineteenth centuries, Baghdad was imagined to exist in two socially distinct sectors—Karkh and Rusafa—with the western half of the city populated by rural migrants and desert tribes, in contrast to the urbane population on the eastern side of the city.[154] At that time, Baghdad's old city wall symbolically represented "the most potent dividing line between order and disorder for Baghdad," separating the city from the "rebels" and "tribesmen" who came to "threaten city folk" from the west.[155] These imaginary frontiers had shifted by the 1950s: the city's frightening imaginary frontier zone was located instead to the east, on the far side of the Army Canal where rural migrants built their *sarifas* and mud huts.[156]

It is interesting to observe how the inhabitants of Revolution City were imagined and reimagined as posing different kinds of threats over the second half of the twentieth century: as destabilizing rural migrants in the 1950s, communists in the 1960s, and members of the banned Shiʻi opposition group, the Daʻwa Party, in the 1980s and 1990s. The residents of Revolution City remained a "geographically bounded group," to borrow from Farah al-Nakib's analysis of urbanization in Kuwait City, but the precise nature of the threat posed by the community east of the canal could be redefined according to the politics of the time.[157] Ironically, cutting off Revolution City from the rest of Baghdad reaffirmed and reified this district's contentious and distinct role in Baghdad's political history. Creating a "hierarchy of spaces" for different social groups in Baghdad may have helped to reinforce the loyalty of favored groups, but at the same time it reinforced the oppositional nature of those living on the margins.[158]

Even more broadly, the process of building Baghdad's modern neighborhoods from the 1940s to the 1970s reinforced the importance of the neighborhood (*hayy*) as the city's essential social unit and administrative unit. Neighborhoods were also a key target for governmental surveillance and political manipulation. As I will argue in Part II, the Baʻth Party increasingly relied on neighborhoods and neighborhood-level officials to mobilize support, neutralize threats, and carry out policies. From the 1950s onward, neighborhoods were the scale at which most state-society interactions took place in Baghdad. The delegation of important governance tasks to Baʿth Party officials at the neighborhood level, which I refer to as the "localization of governance," was possible because of how Baghdad's neighborhoods were created from the outset with certain political priorities in mind.

TWO

Baghdad Becomes a War Zone

THOUGH BAGHDAD HAS SUFFERED in the early twenty-first century from a reputation as a war-torn city, armed conflict is a relatively recent development in the context of Baghdad's longer history. From 1950 to 1979 Baghdad was a cosmopolitan metropolis that boasted high-quality schools, excellent health care facilities, an active artistic and literary scene, and oil-financed urban development. This chapter explores how 1980–91 was a significant transitional period in which Baghdad went from being a privileged site of oil-financed modernization to a war zone, focusing on the impacts of the Iran-Iraq War (1980–88) and the Gulf War (1990–91) on the urban landscape and social order of Baghdad.

The Iran-Iraq War brought changes to Baghdad gradually in the 1980s: Baghdadis had eight years to acclimate to the new threats, challenges, and opportunities that came with this protracted conflict. The Iran-Iraq War changed the rhythms of time in the capital, physically altered the city's landscape, and disrupted the previous social order. In contrast to the gradual changes that the Iran-Iraq War brought to Baghdad, the six-week intensive aerial bombardment of Baghdad during the "Desert Storm" phase of the Gulf War in 1991 devastated the city in a short period of time. By the time the Gulf War began, Baghdadis were already socially acclimated to the demands of wartime, but no one was prepared for the physical destruction the Gulf War brought. The pounding waves of bombs that rained down on the city in January and February 1991 wreaked havoc on the physical landscape of the city, and this destruction brought with it new social, temporal, and political effects. Many of these changes to Baghdad's physical spaces, social order, and rhythms of daily life proved to be enduring, reverberating through the remainder of the 1990s and even to the present.

"The modern city is ... a distinct space of routines," according to urban theorists.[1] Henri Lefebvre wrote that the unique personality of an individual city is known by the peculiar combination of "the layout of places and their linkages," "what happens and takes place in the street," and "the *use of time* by inhabitants."[2] As war affected the built spaces, rhythms of time, and everyday social and economic activities of the city, the character of Baghdad itself was fundamentally altered. War is capable of producing such changes because, as historian Sara Pursley noted in her study of mid-century Iraq, the military is uniquely designed to produce new "chronobiopolitical regimes." The military produces new social groups of people who "shar[e] bodily and affective experiences through participation in shared temporal routines."[3] In other words, war and militarization produce new social categories, rhythms of time, and shared experiences of spaces partly because of the very way that militaries are organized and operated.[4]

Dina Khoury has previously laid out these kinds of social, temporal, and spatial changes that the Iran-Iraq and Gulf Wars brought to Iraq in her 2013 book *Iraq in Wartime: Soldiering, Martyrdom, and Remembrance,* which is also based on the Baʿth Party archives.[5] The purpose of this chapter is not to reiterate her insightful findings, though I am clearly indebted to her scholarship. Rather, the goal of this chapter is to more clearly situate Baghdad within the broader historical narrative of war's impact on Iraq, illuminating how the capital was uniquely impacted by the two major wars that Saddam oversaw as president. Only by examining how these wars were experienced by residents of the capital can we understand how Baghdad was transformed from a prosperous metropolis in the late 1970s to a war-weary city with failing infrastructure in the 1990s.

Though militarization affected all parts of Iraq, each of Iraq's late twentieth-century wars impacted the country's regions differently. In the Iran-Iraq War, the Shatt al-ʿArab waterway in southern Iraq was a focal point of fighting.[6] Basra, the closest Iraqi city to the front lines, experienced almost daily shelling from Iran, whose border was less than 20 miles away. The heavy bombardments of Basra deeply traumatized the population and inflicted terrible physical damage on the city. Understandably, studies of the Iran-Iraq War have often focused on how the war was experienced on the front lines in the South.[7] The Kurdish North also features prominently in histories of the Iran-Iraq War because Saddam Hussein launched genocidal attacks on Iraqi Kurds known as the *Anfal* campaign. This attempted ethnic cleansing of the North was framed by Ba'th Party leaders as retaliation for an alliance formed between some Kurdish nationalist groups and Iranian forces, though the decades-long conflict between Iraqi Kurds and the central government had many underlying political and economic causes. Saddam's regime killed an estimated 50,000–100,000 Kurds by poison gas or mass executions, and many more were forcibly displaced from their homes.[8]

Baghdad, in contrast, has been perceived as having been largely insulated from the day-to-day realities of the Iran-Iraq War, and so has received scant attention in retellings of the impact of this war on the country as a whole. However, this viewpoint minimizes the importance of the "War of the Cities" phase of the Iran-Iraq War and overlooks the importance of politically motivated acts of sabotage and terrorism in Baghdad by the Iraqi Shi'i Da'wa Party during these years. This chapter seeks to address some of these oversights in the scholarship.

But just as this chapter aims to add Baghdad back into histories of the Iran-Iraq War, it is also vital to add the Iran-Iraq War into histories of Baghdad. Though the front lines of the Iran-Iraq War were far from the capital, this conflict nonetheless transformed the physical spaces of the city as showpiece architecture and housing development programs in the capital were replaced by bomb shelters and war monuments. The regime created a new wartime repertoire of holidays and rituals that governed civilian life in Baghdad. Wartime economic demands brought Baghdad's women into the workforce in record numbers, and families of martyrs received residential land in the capital as compensation for their losses, impacting the city's social order. These changes left a permanent mark on the social, political, and economic dynamics of the city. Though these dynamics in Baghdad are similar to the impacts of militarization on other communities throughout Iraq, it is impossible to analyze how Baghdadis responded to the hardships of sanctions in the 1990s (the subject of Part II) without understanding this essential wartime experience that the capital's residents shared.

Background to the Iran-Iraq War

Iranian protestors succeeded in pushing the Iranian Shah, Muhammad Reza Pahlavi, from power through months of protests in 1978. Ayatollah Khomeini proclaimed the creation of the new Islamic Republic of Iran in January 1979 and asserted himself as the country's new leader. Khomeini had vowed to export Iran's revolution, which directly threatened Iraq as its neighbor and as a Shi'a-majority country. Saddam believed that it would be a quick and easy task to remove Ayatollah Khomeini from power, especially given Iraq's well-equipped military. Saddam declared war on Iran on September 22, 1980. The cause of the war was formally the contested ownership of the Shatt al-'Arab waterway between the two countries, though Saddam's real goal was to blunt the Ayatollah's expansionist ambitions and to assert Saddam's regional leadership in the Middle East.[9]

Initially, Iraq's military operations went according to plan: Iraqi forces rapidly occupied a large swath of Iranian territory and Saddam's regime "declared it had reached its objectives."[10] Iran refused to surrender, however, and Iraq's hold on conquered territory in Iran proved to be tenuous. Iran regained momentum, recaptured key cities, and put Iraqi forces on the defensive. Iraq was forced to withdraw from all Iranian territory by June 1982. In July 1982, Iranian forces invaded Iraq, and Saddam spent most of the next six years on the defensive. It was not until April 1988 that Iraq had a major victory in recapturing its port city of Faw, regained the offensive momentum, and finally pushed Iran to the negotiating table to sign a ceasefire on August 20, 1988.[11] The outcome of the eight-year war was *status quo ante bellum*: a combined total of 1.5 million Iraqis and Iranians died in a viciously fought war that ended in a stalemate.[12]

Protecting Baghdad from War: 1980–82

Prior to the Iran-Iraq War, French diplomats noted that "the Iraqi people have had no experience with a foreign enemy," and had not previously "experienced the reality" of war themselves.[13] With the outbreak of the Iran-Iraq War, the regime's first instinct was to keep it that way, at least for residents in the capital city of Baghdad.

Saddam was the newly confirmed president of Iraq in 1979 following his internal coup that sent President Ahmed Hassan al-Bakr into early retirement. Saddam began his presidency by continuing an aggressive modernization and development program for Baghdad while simultaneously waging war with Iran. He believed that this approach would help him consolidate popular support for his rule domestically. His approach was summed up in a national motto: "We fight with one hand, and we build with the other."[14] As Saddam explained in a closed-door meeting with advisors, if any noticeable cuts were made in public spending, he feared that "merchants, intermediaries, and ultimately citizens . . . will realize that it is lower than last year and panic will set in."[15] This impulse to protect ordinary citizens from the hardships of war was most pronounced in Baghdad, where the regime concentrated its development and modernization efforts, and tried to ensure an abundance of consumer goods.

New construction in the capital was the most brazen symbol of the regime's commitment to maintaining normalcy during the war. Journalist Patrick Cockburn described the city in 1981, saying that "Baghdad . . . is like a vast building site; its flat skyline interrupted by cranes and half-completed buildings, while the thump of pile-drivers can be heard on almost every street corner."[16] The Saddam International Airport was among the grandest of Baghdad's development projects that came to fruition during the war, opening to travelers in 1982.[17] Two new bridges were completed in Baghdad, along with a new water purification system in the capital's Karkh district.[18] In 1982, construction began on a new expressway in Baghdad.[19] As if to underscore the regime's confidence that the ravages of war would never come to the capital, Saddam commissioned three projects to renovate historic residential quarters of the city. He oversaw the building of attractive low-rise residential buildings and shopping areas in Khulafa' Street, Haifa Street, and the famed Abu Nuwas riverfront corridor.[20] In addition, the regime contracted with French companies to build new housing developments in the Dora, Zafraniyya, and Revolution City districts.[21] The renovation and expansion of Haifa Street in historic central Baghdad in particular was meant to be a showpiece during the Non-Aligned Movement summit that Baghdad planned to host in 1982.[22] These projects clearly articulated the regime's vision that money was best invested in refining and improving Baghdad, rather than saving money to spend on possible postwar reconstruction needs. The assumption seemed to be that the war would be fought on Iranian soil, not Iraqi. Foreign workers, including as many as 1 million Egyptian young men, were recruited to help carry out these ambitious development projects while young Iraqi men waged war.[23]

In addition to the country's investment in new brick-and-mortar construction, Saddam also sought to improve upon and expand many essential services for the population. Four new medical schools were built during the Iran-Iraq War, serving both the troops and the civilian population. Baghdad's Medical City opened a new surgical hospital with more than 500 beds. The government expanded the national health care system into rural areas, helping to improve health outcomes and lower infant mortality rates even in the midst of war.[24]

The regime's initial ability to provide both "guns and butter" and maintain its aggressive urban development plans evidently worked to assuage the anxieties of Baghdadis during the early years of the war. Baghdad's residents appeared to "react with apparent serenity" to the start of the war as development projects continued apace.[25] Cockburn observed at the time: "it is clear that few people in Baghdad are very worried ... [about] Iranian fighter bombers.... The Iraqi government works hard to give the impression that all is business as usual. The airport is open again at night.... The blackout has been largely abandoned in the capital."[26]

There was an international audience for this performance as well as a domestic one: creditors, business partners, and political allies sought assurances that Saddam's regime was strong enough to weather the war with Iran, especially after it became clear that it would not be the quick and painless operation that Saddam had promised. For the first two years of the war, at least, many outside observers were convinced of Iraq's apparent economic miracle at waging war and investing in long-term development simultaneously. One year into the war, a British embassy official stated, "the level of economic activity has been surprisingly unaffected. There have been no signs of cutting back on imports or a slowing down on the development program."[27] The international media picked up this narrative: the *New York Times* ran an article proclaiming, "Despite War Cost, Iraq Pushes Development," and the Iraqi minister of industry boasted in 1981 that the regime had signed contracts worth millions of dinars even after war broke out.[28] Not to be outdone, the mayor of Baghdad announced in 1982 that billions of dinars had been spent on development projects in the capital alone since the start of the war.[29]

However, there were growing signs that the government's attempts to pay for both development projects and military costs were unsustainable. Politically and psychologically, an important shift for the people of Baghdad occurred in 1982 when the Iraqi armed forces went from being on the offensive to being on the defensive and the Iranian military succeeded in seizing some Iraqi territory. As Iraqi researcher Nuri Najm wrote in the 1980s: "Writing about war and peace under the shadow of an ongoing war is different from writing about them in other circumstances. When you are living with war, and especially when the enemy army has the goal of occupying your national homeland, it makes writing about war something that is part of your everyday life, even if you are trying to write about it from a tactical or analytical side. . . . Defensive war affects the people."[30] Though Iranian troops never came within the vicinity of Baghdad, the occupation of Iraqi territory meant that the capital could no longer afford to think of the war as something distant and inconsequential for life at home.

A major economic blow came in April 1982 when Syria cut off Iraq's access to its most important pipeline, severely curtailing its ability to export oil.[31] Iranian attacks on Iraq's oil infrastructure also devastated Iraq economically: Iraq's oil production dropped by nearly 85 percent within the first few months of the war.[32] Without oil income, the regime began to spend through its foreign reserves rapidly, and international investors also began to withdraw from Iraq as the war dragged on.[33]

Saddam began to take out foreign loans, mostly from Gulf countries. In 1982, Iraq was borrowing $1 billion per month from Kuwait and Saudi Arabia to pay for war costs.[34] Iraq transitioned from a rentier state dependent on oil revenues to a rentier state dependent on foreign loans, offered in generous terms by Gulf rulers in exchange for Saddam's military protection against Iranian aggression.[35]

One by one, the regime began to renege on its construction contracts with its international partners. The crowning achievement of all the regime's frantic development work was meant to be Baghdad's hosting of the Non-Aligned Movement summit in 1982, and the government had spent $7 billion on infrastructure in the capital to prepare for this honor.[36] But the regime's dream of insulating Baghdad from war officially came to an end in

August 1982, when the organizers of the Non-Aligned Movement summit decided to move the meeting from Baghdad to India because of the dangers posed by the war. Despite the regime's best efforts to protect Baghdad, it could ignore reality no longer. In November 1982, Saddam announced the start of a new austerity program, slashing expenditures in nearly every part of the national budget that was not related to the war effort.[37]

War Comes to Baghdad: Changes in City Spaces

War brought numerous physical changes to Baghdad's city landscape. Austerity measures introduced in 1982 brought an end to many improvement projects planned for the city's development. Though a few housing projects were completed later in the 1980s, most of the new construction Baghdad saw in the 1980s consisted of new war memorials that became iconic features of the Baghdad skyline. Changes to the landscape were also inflicted by damage from terrorists' bombs and from Iranian missiles.

Terrorism and Sabotage

Though Baghdad did not experience the extensive shelling that cities like Basra did in the South, Baghdad was not immune to wartime violence. One source of attacks came from underground groups that sought to destabilize the government. Between 1982 and 1984, car bombs hit the Baghdad headquarters of the Popular Army, blew out the first two floors of the Ministry of Planning, and killed as many as 100 people in an attack on the Security Directorate and Military Directorate buildings in the capital, to give just a few examples.[38] Official Iraqi state media blamed these attacks on "Iranian agents" and on "terrorism orchestrated by foreign countries."[39] Some who carried out these attacks may have been Iranian citizens, but others were likely affiliated with the Iraqi Daʿwa Party, an outlawed Shiʿi opposition group.

The largest act of terrorism to take place in Baghdad in the 1980s was an assassination attempt on a top Baʿth Party leader, Tariq ʿAziz. According to British diplomatic reports, an unnamed suicide attacker rushed at ʿAziz during his visit to Mustansariyya University in Baghdad on April 1, 1980, throwing a grenade and firing a revolver, ultimately killing himself with one of his own grenades. 'Aziz emerged relatively unscathed with only an injured hand, though two university students standing nearby died during the attack. On April 5, a funeral procession was held for the two slain students. A large bomb went off in the crowd, injuring 200 people and killing 52, constituting one of the worst terrorist attacks to strike Baghdad at the time.[40]

In retaliation for the assassination attempt, and signaling that the regime would no longer tolerate any Shi'i opposition activities, Saddam brazenly executed a top Shi'i religious leader, Grand Ayatollah Muhammad Baqir al-Sadr, and his sister days later.[41] (The Grand Ayatollah's assassination was memorialized by Baghdad's Shi'a residents after 2003 through the renaming of Revolution City as Sadr City.) When this failed to put an end to Da'wa attacks on the capital, the regime intensified its efforts: RCC decree no. 461 in 1980 made membership in the underground Da'wa party punishable by death, and thousands of alleged Da'wa members were thrown in jail in the 1980s.[42] After another suspected Da'wa Party attack in 1983 on the Air Force Intelligence Office and a television station in Baghdad, the regime rounded up seventy members of a prominent Shi'i clerical family associated with the Da'wa Party, the al-Hakim family, and executed six of them.

These periodic car bombings and explosions in Baghdad in the 1980s created a jumpy atmosphere of uncertainty in the capital. Ultimately, however, their effects were described as primarily "psychological, rather than political": neither Saddam nor his regime was in any real danger of falling.[43] Nevertheless, the routinization of terrorist attacks in Baghdad contributed to the transformation of the capital by warfare and violence, a process furthered by the even more imminent threat posed by Iranian aerial bombardments.

Air Raids and Bomb Shelters

In the initial days of the war, Saddam believed that Baghdad was unlikely to be directly affected by battles or air strikes, given its relative distance from the Iranian border and the unlikeliness of an Iranian ground attack on such a faraway, fortified city. Thus, the regime did not initially invest in building bomb shelters in Baghdad as it prepared for war in 1980. Rather, basement-level restaurants and bars were designated as makeshift shelters.⁴⁴ Baghdad's air defense system was also shoddily put together. Civilian defense volunteers and Popular Army fighters were tasked with manning anti-aircraft equipment on rooftops, but reportedly, a "combination of poor training and command and control made fratricide a serious threat to Iraqi pilots."⁴⁵

Though Iran's air power was significantly weaker than Iraq's, surprise air strikes in and around Baghdad in the opening days of the war indicated that the capital was not safe from harm after all. Iranian air strikes nearly disabled an important power plant on the outskirts of Baghdad that resulted in unpredictable and lengthy blackouts in the capital for months after.⁴⁶ The air strikes near Baghdad clearly caught the regime off-guard, but the capital settled back into a state of calm and quiet—save for the occasional car bomb by a Daʿwa Party resistance member—from 1980 until 1983. Then a new phase of the war, known as "War of the Cities," abruptly turned the residents of Baghdad into targets.

Saddam authorized launching Russian-made Scud missiles at Iranian cities in 1983. Initially, the goal was to hurt Iran economically by targeting major oil installations, factories, and infrastructure. By 1984, however, Iraqi air strikes more often hit population centers, purposefully inflicting civilian casualties in the hopes of pushing Iranian leaders to the negotiating table.⁴⁷ Iraqi publications cheered the fact that, by sending bombs "deep into Iran," Khomeini would be forced to recognize the superiority of Iraq's air power.⁴⁸ However, Iran retaliated for each Iraqi sortie into its territory, making Iraqi civilian population centers fair game in this total war.

The term "War of the Cities" refers to mutual air strikes that went on for months at a time until a de facto or explicit agreement between the two sides temporarily ended the strikes on civilian centers. These periods of bombing campaigns on civilians punctuated most of the war, taking place in February 1983, February–March 1984, March–June 1985, September–October 1986, January–February 1987, September–October 1987, and February–April 1988. Iraqi missiles initially could not reach far enough to target Iran's most important cities of Tehran and Qom, so cities like Dezful, Ahwaz, and Abadan were among Iraq's first targets. As Iraq's missile technology improved over the course of the war, however, Iraq was eventually able to hit Tehran, as well as Qom and Isfahan, and focused its later attacks on these major cities.⁴⁹ Iran used artillery heavily against the southern city of Basra, owing to its close proximity to the Iranian border, and launched missiles and bombs at Baghdad, Mosul, Tikrit, and other Iraqi cities and border towns. However, Iran conspicuously avoided targeting the Shi'i holy cities of Najaf and Karbala and its allies in the majority-Kurdish areas in the North.[50]

Iranian civilians bore the brunt of the "War of the Cities" attacks: for example, in February–April 1988 Iraqi missiles killed 1,500 Iranian civilians versus the 300 Iraqi civilians who were slain.[51] Nonetheless, Baghdad was greatly impacted by this new phase of war. Iranian attacks on Baghdad between 1983 and 1988 terrorized the Iraqi capital, habituated ordinary citizens to air raid alarms and air strikes, and altered the city landscape with new bomb shelters—and bomb craters. Interviewees recalled how terrifying the threat of Iranian air strikes could be, especially since they were known to be highly inaccurate: they could land anywhere, including in residential areas. Baghdadis often stayed awake at night listening to the air raid sirens, with a few brave (or foolish) young boys in the family venturing to the roof to see where the missiles were striking.[52]

When Iranian bombs and missiles did strike the capital, confusion and deliberate misinformation from the regime multiplied the psychological impact of the explosions. The Ba'thist regime had a policy of rarely confirming the strikes or their origins, leaving an open question as to whether Iranian missiles caused the damage or whether terrorist bombs were to blame. This pattern was set early in the war: for example, French diplomats were unsure whether the explosion of a munitions depot near the Baghdad airport in 1981 was the result of an Iranian strike or a terrorist attack, and the regime never clarified what happened.[53] Even in the midst of a particularly heavy phase of the "War of the Cities" in 1985, Saddam waited weeks before confirming that the explosions occurring in Baghdad were coming from Iranian missiles rather than terrorist bombs.[54] Furthermore, the main government newspaper, *al-Thawra*, rarely acknowledged any of these attacks at all. Researching copies of *al-Thawra* for the dates of known Iranian air strikes or terrorist attacks reported by foreign embassy officials, one finds almost total silence. This also fits with the regime's policy against publishing casualty statistics from the Iran-Iraq War: it rarely confirmed attacks unless it could leverage these events for sympathetic international press coverage, as it did during the Gulf War.[55]

While Ba'thist newspapers frequently downplayed or misrepresented the threat of Iranian air strikes, their lethal impact was real. During a particularly deadly spate of air strikes in May and June 1985, as many as 200–300 Baghdadis were killed by Iranian missiles.[56] Eyewitnesses reported seeing explosions level houses and bury families in the rubble, and journalists estimated that a "huge explosion" in downtown Baghdad on one occasion caused "hundreds" of injuries.[57] Another explosion caused part of a highway to collapse, and another blast took out the top floors of Iraq's state bank—though officials did not confirm in this instance whether missiles or terrorist bombs were the cause.[58] Internally, Ba'thist bureaucrats were more forthcoming. An internal memo from the Ba'th Party archives clarified that Iranian missiles were to blame for a strike that damaged or destroyed thirty-nine houses near Baghdad's Muthanna airbase, killing fourteen people and wounding another fourteen.[59]

After one large, unmistakable hit by an Iranian missile in Baghdad in September 1986 that killed thirty-four Iraqi civilians, the regime took the opposite of its usual strategy by publishing the names of the victims and staging large public demonstrations declaring revenge for their lives. An Iranian missile strike near a Baghdad elementary school that killed 32 children and wounded 218 more was also publicly commemorated and mourned.[60] This missile strike on the school was also used as the occasion to launch a fertility campaign encouraging women to bear more children to make up for those killed in the war.[61]

Once the regime began to take seriously the threat of Iranian air strikes on Baghdad, the government began to plan for a system of bomb shelters for the capital. The government contracted with Swedish and Finnish companies to build a series of shelters, the first of which was completed in 1984. A group of 750 Baghdad civilian volunteers carried out practice drills in these new bomb shelters for 72-hour periods to ensure that adequate protocols were in place to provide food, water, and medical care. The drills indicated that the existing protocols could use improvement: half of the participants complained there was not enough food, and the lack of tea, coffee, or opportunities to smoke cigarettes left many volunteers with terrible headaches by the end of the three-day experiment.[62]

Though a total count of all the designated and newly built bomb shelters in Baghdad could not be located in the archives, there were at least five major bomb shelters in Baghdad, and each was designed to hold 2,000 people.⁶³ This was obviously inadequate to protect even a small percentage of the 3 million residents who lived in the capital at that time, so most Baghdadis had to make do on their own. One woman from Revolution City recalled regularly hearing air raid sirens while she was on her way to and from school. She would try to take shelter in the doorways of homes and shops as best as she could; she was not aware of any official bomb shelters located near her family's house.⁶⁴

Monuments

Iranian missiles and terrorist bombs were not the only instruments that changed Baghdad's physical landscape. The regime erected several new wartime monuments that rerouted the flow of traffic, created new landmarks by which residents oriented themselves, and indelibly changed Baghdad's skyline. Three grand monuments were erected in honor of the Iran-Iraq War: the Unknown Soldier Monument, the Martyrs' Monument, and the Victory Arches. Unusually, these were commissioned and constructed during the war, at moments when a ceasefire felt as elusive as ever. Constructing victory monuments during the war was a clear attempt by the regime to insist on its own framing of the conflict.

The Unknown Soldier Monument was opened in 1982, the Martyrs' Monument was opened in 1983, and in 1985, Saddam ordered the building of the Victory Arches to honor the "leaders and heroes" who defended the "honor, sovereignty, and dignity of the glorious Arab nation."⁶⁵ Many Iraqis found the Unknown Soldier and Martyrs' Monuments to be genuinely moving tributes to their fallen loved ones. However, the Victory Arches were the most infamous in a series of new wartime construction projects meant to celebrate Saddam himself. The Victory Arches feature two massive arms modeled from Saddam's own body holding curved swords and surrounded by real helmets of Iranian soldiers killed in battle, forming a canopy over one of Baghdad's largest thoroughfares. Since the monument was commissioned and erected long before any actual "victory" had been achieved, the Victory Arches are rather a tribute to Saddam, cast to represent an early Arab Muslim knight battling against Persian enemies.⁶⁶ Likewise, Saddam built himself a new "Victory over Iran" palace. He also commissioned Saddam University in his name (now named *Nahrain*, or "Two Rivers," University) in Baghdad between 1987 and 1988, and built a large clock tower in Baghdad with his portrait on all four sides.[67] These new monuments to Saddam's cult of personality were the natural progression of a process Saddam began upon commencing his tenure as president, which was to reinforce his cult of personality through portraiture and naming practices. Tellingly, Saddam found the financial resources to build these vanity projects even as most development work had halted in the capital.

Yet a slightly different impulse was behind one of Saddam's most memorable efforts to leave his mark on the capital. As mentioned in chapter 1, in 1982 Saddam renamed the former *sarifa* district on the city's eastern edge after himself, from Revolution City to Saddam City.[68] Renaming this district "Saddam City" was a provocative step. Rather than give his name to a neighborhood of Baʻth Party loyalists and regime supporters, Saddam claimed an area that simmered with opposition to his rule. French diplomats described Saddam City as a "Shiʻi neighborhood known for its hostility to power," but the anti-regime undercurrents in that area were not necessarily sectarian in nature: communists, common criminals, Kurdish opposition groups, and the Daʻwa Party all viewed Saddam City as a sanctuary, where the densely populated streets and the district's sheer size made it easier to escape detection.[69] Furthermore, class-based grievances also fueled resentments within this neighborhood for a population that often felt overlooked by the state.[70]

Years later, Saddam reflected on his decision to rename Revolution City after himself, stating, "I am the one who called it Saddam City. I never did that before, as far as instructing anyone to name certain places with specific names, especially since it was very costly. . . . I thought I would give Revolution [City] my name and say, 'This is Saddam City,' in order to generate passion, honesty, and equal treatment among the people. [Even those] who hate it will hesitate to describe it in an inappropriate way."[71] The final sentence hints at what may have inspired the name change: by forcing the area's residents to adopt his name, Saddam hoped to push grumblings and dissent even further underground and to bind the area ever closer to him. Archival evidence demonstrates this in action: when community leaders from Saddam City were hauled up before Saddam to explain crimes in their neighborhood (discussed in chapter 5), they prefaced their comments by saying, "First: it is a great honor that you named the city after your name, we consider that the greatest honor ever."[72]

Renaming Revolution City was just the most visible of Saddam's many efforts in the midst of the Iran-Iraq War to bring this district further under his control. The French Embassy noted that Saddam personally visited the district "several times" during the first month of the war as a show of force against would-be sympathizers with Iran and the Shi'i political opposition groups based there. Saddam continued to make conspicuous visits to that neighborhood several times a year throughout the war.[73]

The regime's most potent fear about this district was the presence of Da'wa Party members who used it as a base to "carry out small-scale operations against the regime" in Baghdad, especially during mandated blackouts in the capital and other vulnerable moments.[74] In contrast to the memorials, clock towers, and the proliferation of portraits of the president, renaming Revolution City was not so much about self-glorification as it was a threat: this district would remain under Saddam's control, or else face the consequences.

War Comes to Baghdad: Social Disruptions

Declaring war against Iran led to a pronounced shift in how the Ba'thist regime governed Iraqi society. As scholars have previously noted, war provided the regime with new motivation to expand the scope of its domestic surveillance, mobilize more citizens into state and party organizations, and bind Iraqis to the regime through a system of rewards and punishments.[75]

New Categories of Citizens

Khoury described in *Iraq in Wartime* how the Ba'th Party militarized Iraqi society by creating new social categories of "inclusion and exclusion" based on one's participation in the war and standing with the regime.[76] This process actually began in the months before Iraq declared war on Iran, as the regime sought to prepare the population to view Iran as its enemy. Saddam had faced a conundrum: how could he justify waging war on another Muslim-majority country? His solution was to frame the conflict as one between Arabs and Persians, tying the current conflict to a long history of pre-Islamic and Islamic-era wars between Arab and Persian empires. (Saddam's preferred name for the Iran-Iraq War, *Qadisiyyat Saddam*, referred to the Battle of Qadisiyya in 637 CE, when Arab Muslim armies defeated forces of the Persian Sasanian Empire.)⁷⁷ To this end, Saddam encouraged students, academics, and journalists to write about the historic enmity between Persians and Arabs, enlisting religious texts, historic sources, and even archaeological artifacts to bolster this interpretation of Iraqi history.⁷⁸

The regime's first move was to exile and dispossess "Persian" Iraqis, whose identification documents prior to World War I belonged to the neighboring Persian state ruled by the Qajar dynasty, not to the Ottoman Empire. The regime used a derisive term, *Shuʿubi*, for these Iraqis who were allegedly of Persian descent. Though many of these families viewed themselves as ethnically Arab or Kurdish, not Persian, and had lived within the modern borders of Iraq with Iraqi citizenship for generations, the regime viewed them suspiciously as crypto-Iranians who could form a fifth column.⁷⁹

A surge in deportations of "Persian" Iraqis took place in April 1980, after the assassination attempt on Tariq ʿAziz, which was blamed on an "Iranian agent."⁸⁰ The crackdown on Daʿwa Party members described above was accompanied by decrees stating that any Iranian citizens in the country would be immediately deported. Later decrees stripped those Iraqis with Persian backgrounds of their Iraqi citizenship and confiscated their assets; houses of deportees were later distributed as gifts to regime insiders.⁸¹ Scholars estimate that hundreds of thousands of people were deported over the course of the war.⁸² Many who were classified as *Shuʿubi* were detained and tortured prior to their deportation.⁸³ Even in the final months of the war, when the threat of an insider attack had lessened, Baʿth Party members were still asked to produce their Iraqi nationality certificate in order to prove that they did not have Persian origins as part of standard vetting protocols in the 1980s.⁸⁴

The social disruption of these deportations was profound. For Baghdad's Shiʿa-majority population, the process was designed to be terrorizing: deportations often occurred without any warning in the middle of the night, and families were prohibited from taking their possessions with them.⁸⁵ Many of the deportees from Baghdad were merchants and shopkeepers, including a large proportion of jewelers, whose valuable goods were confiscated by the regime.⁸⁶ Mixed families were targeted: Iraqi wives of deported "Persian" men were not allowed to accompany their husbands into exile in Iran, and Iraqi men married to "Persian" wives were offered financial rewards for divorcing them.[87] As a result of these deportations, Iraqi citizens were pushed to adopt new conceptualizations of Iraqi nationality, one that sharply distinguished between those with historic roots in the Ottoman Empire or in the Persian Qajar state.

At the same time, the war created new categories of privilege: soldiers, martyrs, and recipients of medals of bravery all gained a new, elevated status that included tangible material benefits in addition to social and political perquisites.[88] The regime started off lavishly rewarding families of "martyrs" (the regime's term for soldiers killed in action) with ample monthly stipends, land and housing benefits, and even gifts of new cars.[89] As the number of martyrs rose and the Iraqi economy constricted, these rewards were scaled back somewhat and less consistently provided. However, this marked a new era in state-society relations in Iraq, as families of martyrs came to expect (and demand) that such rewards be fulfilled.[90]

One function of these rewards, medals, and new social categories was to allow the regime to identify and maintain close ties with Iraqi families that had lost relatives in the war, helping to manage popular discontentment about the war and to quiet criticism.[91] The regime created special committees of neighborhood-level party officials called "Committees for Maintaining Ties to Martyrs' Families," who were instructed to meet regularly with families of martyrs in their jurisdictions. New holidays and party events created during the war (described below) created new opportunities to involve these families in regime functions.[92] Ba'th Party members were also tasked with regularly visiting families affected by Iranian missile strikes in the capital.[93]

In theory, these meetings provided ordinary families with opportunities to share grievances and make requests, which were sometimes successful. However, families of martyrs still frequently reported feeling overlooked and forgotten by the regime despite these efforts. For example, a group of families whose relatives were missing in action wrote to the regime to complain about the insufficiency of the pensions they received and, in general, their feeling that the regime did not care about them. They complained that it took as long as two years to received promised benefits and aid.[94] Families that lost loved ones in Iranian missile strikes also complained about the adequacy of the government's response.[95] While the regime was evidently not always successful in securing the support of soldiers' families, martyrdom benefits became a new and frequent point of transaction between citizens and the government. Saddam tried to translate these benefits into political support for his regime. Those with higher status within the regime could hope for better and more timely benefits: when an intelligence officer's house was destroyed by an Iranian missile, Saddam himself ordered that one of the houses confiscated from a deported "Persian" Iraqi be given to him, and he personally wrote the officer a check to pay for furnishing it.[96]

Consequences of Mass Mobilization

Though the regime tried to turn soldiers and martyrs into venerated social categories through top-down programs and policies, the reality was that mass mobilization set off unintended social and economic disruptions that were keenly felt in the capital. The regime initially tried to limit conscription during the first few months of the conflict as part of its efforts to shield the population from the hardships of war.[97] But by 1981, the regime implemented a national draft, calling up nearly 200,000 conscripts by the end of the war's first year.[98] From there, the Iraqi military grew rapidly: from 200,000 soldiers at the war's beginning to nearly 1 million by its end in 1988.[99] Over the eight years of war, at least 40 percent of the adult male population served in the war.[100]

This conscription was mandatory for young men beginning on their eighteenth birthday, and eventually, conscription was expanded to include men up to age fifty-four.[101] Youths younger than eighteen were encouraged to volunteer before compulsory conscription began, with the promise of "preferred status." Non-Iraqis were invited to join the military, especially the large number of Egyptians who had been recruited to Iraq as laborers.[102] Though conscripts were originally supposed to serve two-year terms, the reality was that most soldiers served for the duration of the war.[103] As Khoury points out, "Almost every Iraqi family had one, often two or three, men serving on the front. It would seem that war, like death, was the great equalizer."[104]

As compulsory conscription into the official armed forces emptied Baghdad homes of adult men, the regime pressured women, teenagers, and older men to volunteer for the Popular Army militia. "We say without hesitation that all Iraqis are prepared—children, the elderly, men, and women, of all different backgrounds and occupations—to fight until they accomplish what they must," Saddam proclaimed in a speech.[105] The Ba'thists had established the Popular Army militia by 1970, and it was originally intended as a small, ideological corps of political supporters who were focused on domestic surveillance. During the Iran-Iraq War, the Popular Army militia became an alternate tool for mass mobilization and its members played prominent roles on the battlefield.[106] Expanding the Popular Army was meant to offset Iran's numerical superiority, as Iran's population of 38 million in 1980 dwarfed Iraq's population of 13 million. The Popular Army was also a coup-proofing measure, as creating two separate fighting forces minimized the chances the military would be able to overthrow Saddam.[107] Finally, it was designed to increase the population's complicity in and support for the war.[108] The Popular Army was often used for propaganda purposes: new recruits were sent off to the front in big public displays in the capital attended by top regime and military officials, and returned home in grand parades capped with reverential displays of loyalty to Saddam.[109]

For these reasons, there was tremendous pressure on a wide range of civilians to volunteer for the Popular Army. Middle-aged and even elderly men, too old for conscription, were urged to enlist: the regime raised the maximum age of Popular Army volunteers to sixty-five, purportedly "in response to popular demand" by an enthusiastic population of retirees.[110] There were even attempts at forcible recruitment: there were reports that the regime conducted surprise raids on young men loitering in Baghdad to force them into enlisting, and volunteer drives at high schools made it more difficult for students to avoid joining.[111] For a brief time, the Ba'th Party forced university students to spend their summers in the Popular Army, but this program was dropped in response to widespread complaints.[112]

Women had been part of the Popular Army since 1976, and they were also allowed to voluntarily enlist in the official Iraqi military, as well.[113] As many as 40,000 women were in the Popular Army, and in 1981, the mayor of Baghdad opened volunteer recruitment centers in Baghdad specifically for women, to encourage still more to enlist.[114] The inclusion of women in Iraq's fighting forces was highlighted in regime propaganda, contrasting the "modern" and "progressive" attitudes of Iraq with rule by religious clerics in Iran.[115] Saddam gave countless speeches during the Iran-Iraq War with titles like "The Party and Women's Freedom," "Women and the Building of a New Society," and "Liberating Women, Family, and Society," all of which highlighted how the Baʿth Party "freed" Iraqi women from oppression.[116]

Due to the regime's heavy-handed recruitment efforts, the Popular Army grew into a massive secondary fighting force, with 400,000 members in 1982 and 650,000 by 1985, rivaling the size of the official armed forces.[117] However, as a fighting force, the Popular Army was a disappointment. Poorly trained for a period of only two months, these often reluctant recruits could not match the martial skills of the increasingly professionalized Iraqi military, and the presence of Popular Army units on the front lines was often to the detriment of the battle's outcome. Scholars have referred to the Popular Army as "hardly more than an armed mob."[118] Though the regime continued to rotate Popular Army units to the front, it was often done to boost the morale of conscripted soldiers as a show of public support, or to provide manual labor for the rear lines.[119] The most effective use of the Popular Army was for domestic political control in tracking down and apprehending deserters.[120]

As a public relations tool, the Popular Army was also less than a success. It was quickly dubbed the "unpopular army." Young men devised various strategies to resist recruitment and conscription: one strategy university students used to delay conscription was to purposefully fail their final exams and then enroll to retake their classes the next year.[121] More ominously for the regime, desertion and absenteeism became serious problems. In December 1983, the regime instituted the death penalty for anyone caught deserting, and later threatened deserters with gruesome corporal punishments, including cutting off ears.[122] However, desertion rates remained high, underscoring the extent to which the population resented conscription demands.

For those civilians unable to serve in the military or the Popular Army, the regime still tried to mobilize them into the war effort by pushing them to make cash donations or do volunteer work for the nation. Students, workers, and farmers were urged to attend "indoctrination rallies" about the importance of the war effort and to volunteer for manual labor projects benefiting military campaigns.[123] Others responded to calls for blood donations, while women were pressured by the state feminist union, the General Federation of Iraqi Women, to donate their gold jewelry for the war.¹²⁴ Jewelry donation drives were particularly onerous, since jewelry given to women during their weddings was considered women's personal property—not shared by their husband—and thus an important source of personal financial security.¹²⁵

Perhaps the greatest secondary impact of the war's mass mobilization was on the women of Baghdad as they were pushed into wage labor.¹²⁶ Women joined the paid workforce in unprecedented numbers: during the Iran-Iraq War female employees held 51 percent of all administrative jobs and constituted 31 percent of the public sector, in total making up 25 percent of the formal labor force in the country.¹²⁷ By one count, women made up 80 percent of certain governmental ministries.¹²⁸ The General Federation of Iraqi Women, the national Ba'th Party women's organization, took advantage of the regime's reliance on female labor to push for new benefits and freedoms, including new rights related to inheritance, marriage, and divorce.¹²⁹ Child care was provided as a state benefit for working women, and the regime invested more resources into increasing the female literacy rate in order to bring still more women into the workforce.¹³⁰

At the same time, the economic burden of running a female-headed household was crushing for some. Soldiers' salaries were low, inflation rates averaged 40–50 percent during the war, and women were often significantly underpaid for their work in the labor force in comparison to men.¹³¹ A Sabean-Mandean family from Baghdad recalled that female relatives from four different families decided to move in together during the Iran-Iraq War because their male family members were all absent—some fought in the war, while others were hiding underground or had been executed because of their affiliation with the Iraqi Communist Party. Only one woman in the family had no children, so she alone was supporting these four families of women and children by working in her family's goldsmith shop, a craft that was practiced by many in the Sabean-Mandean community in Baghdad.¹³² Samar*, a lawyer and women's rights activist who grew up in Saddam City, recalled that her father, who was enlisted in the army during the Iran-Iraq War, was unable to rest whenever he was granted leave. During his few days at home from the front, he would work long hours at a construction job to supplement his meager wages from the army so that he could financially support his wife and seven children.¹³³ While Samar's father was able to help make ends meet with supplemental work, many other families had difficulty surviving financially, facing eviction or hunger.[134]

The consequences of mass mobilization were a hardship for many Baghdadis. French embassy officials noted that "there is no doubt . . . that the population has gained a certain weariness as each family has been tested."[135] Ba'thist authors encouraged the population to practice "patience" and "steadfastness," which form the "essential basis for victory."[136] Saddam particularly urged mothers and wives to remain "steadfast" when communicating with their husbands and sons on the battlefield: "whenever [soldiers] hear encouraging words from a mother or from a wife, they become more and more brave."[137] As the years of the war dragged on, remaining "steadfast" proved to be a greater and greater challenge.

Crime and Class Divisions

In many respects, the lifestyles of the upper, middle, and lower classes began to diverge more sharply during the war. The financial costs of the war, the physical destruction of much of Iraq's oil production and export infrastructure, and government-imposed austerity measures had noticeable effects on daily life in the capital. Rents in Baghdad increased by 200–300 percent over the course of the 1980s.[138] By 1982, staple vegetables in the Iraqi diet like cucumbers and eggplants increased in price by 600 percent, the price of chicken doubled, and by 1984, eggs cost $19 per dozen.[139] Overall, inflation hovered between 40 percent and 50 percent throughout the eight years of war, reducing the value of paychecks and savings. Restrictions and disruptions on imports forced the lower and middle classes to go without amenities that were previously affordable. The difficulty of obtaining spare parts made it increasingly expensive to maintain an air conditioner or a car, pushing these items out of reach for even many middle-class families.[140] Things that were once staples in the capital—including cigarettes, infant formula, and candles (essential for the blackouts that increasingly plagued the city)—were now affordable only for the well-to-do and for those with access to smugglers.[141]

As a result of these austerity measures and economic disruptions, social and political tensions began to flare. Soldiers had to be posted at gas stations to maintain order in the face of petrol shortages.[142] To deflect blame from the regime, Saddam began to speak out against smugglers, hoarders, war profiteers, and black market agents as the causes of these consumer shortages. Black markets flourished during the war, and the regime publicized its efforts to counteract these trends and crack down on any perpetrators. The Ba'th Party established neighborhood-based "Economic Surveillance Committees" to coordinate monitoring of shops and marketplaces for selling smuggled goods or selling at prices above those set by the state.[143] Though a decree by the Revolutionary Command Council in 1984 threatened fifteen years' imprisonment and the confiscation of assets for any shopkeeper who sold goods for higher than set prices or who hoarded goods with the aim of war profiteering, such activities remained a widespread phenomenon in Baghdad during the war.[144] Adding to social tensions in the capital, citizens were pushed to inform on one another if they knew of "illegal economic activity."[145] To add incentive, informants were promised 20 percent of all confiscated goods as a reward for actionable intelligence about hoarding or black market activities.[146] The economic impact of the Iran-Iraq War was an ominous foretaste of the scarcity Baghdadis would experience and the survival methods they would need to endure sanctions in the 1990s (see Part II).

War Comes to Baghdad: Reordering Time

Ba'thist, Islamic, and military rhythms of time reordered patterns of life in the capital city. A new series of Ba'thist holidays and war-related media programming were the first prong of Saddam's strategy to mobilize the country around the war. Saddam also intentionally reoriented life in Iraq around Islamic rhythms of time as a second prong to his governance strategy. Finally, military time became yet another way that rhythms of life in the capital changed. Conscriptions marked a new rite of passage for youth, and furloughs for soldiers became new temporal reference points that restructured life for civilians in the capital as well as for soldiers in the field.

The regime introduced a flurry of new state and party holidays in the 1980s, partly designed to provide distractions from the tragedies and hardships of war.[147] At the same time, they functioned as highly scripted, ritualized occasions for the regime to build and maintain ties with the population while demanding outward displays of loyalty. As historian Aaron Faust argues, despite the artificiality of many of these "celebrations," one can go through the motions of performing rituals of loyalty to the regime only so many times before it starts to take a deeper hold.[148] Examining these holidays provides an opportunity to see how the regime tried to actively cultivate support for Saddam's rule and for the war.[149]

In 1982 a political stunt became the occasion for a new national holiday. In November of that year, Saddam called for a popular referendum of his rule, meant to dispel rumors that the war had left Saddam vulnerable to a possible coup. In response, it was reported that "millions" of Iraqis had turned out in the streets chanting pro-Saddam slogans and declaring their fidelity to the leader.[150] However, British diplomats wryly noted that newspapers published lists of acceptable slogans in advance of these "spontaneous" rallies, and observed party officials rounding up people to attend the parades. They estimated that in Baghdad only "tens of thousands" attended, rather than the millions claimed by the regime.[151] Iraqi officials presented Saddam with oaths of loyalty written in their own blood, which soon became a standard way for any Iraqi citizen to signal fidelity to the regime.[152] This event became known as the *bayʿa*, in reference to a kind of loyalty oath given to Muslim rulers throughout Islamic history, and Saddam's own *bayʿa* event was subsequently commemorated annually on November 14 of each year.[153] This Saddam-centered holiday coincided in 1985 with the Prophet Muhammad's birthday (which rotates a few days every year within the Gregorian calendar since it is celebrated according to the Islamic lunar calendar). French diplomats sardonically noted that this overlap created widespread confusion among party officials about which man should be more celebrated.[154]

Not content with annual celebrations of the 1982 loyalty oath, Saddam made his own birthday an official state holiday in 1983, known as "Saddam Hussein Day" and celebrated on April 28. The French Embassy described these festivities in a tone of mild disbelief: celebrations stretched for two days, and all the main streets in Baghdad were covered in garlands, pictures of the president, and flags. Temporary museum displays commemorating the president's achievements were installed throughout the city in prominent locations. A plaza in the posh district of Mansur displayed sixty enormous portraits of Saddam. Children performed songs, dance recitals, and poetry in honor of the president, and state offices hosted numerous speeches.[155] One Iraqi interviewee recalled that children born on April 28 received an annual gift from the president for the honor of sharing his birthday. Despite the somber realities of war, Baghdad was nevertheless transformed into a "carnival atmosphere," and images of the capital in celebration were broadcast on television throughout the country.[156]

Finally, nearly the entire month of July was devoted to celebrating the Ba'thist regime. State holidays had already included the establishment of the Iraqi republic (July 14) and the anniversary of the Ba'th Party's rise to power (July 17–30), but now expanded in the 1980s to include the anniversary of Saddam's ascension to the presidency (July 16). All three of these commemorations ran together into a month-long series of public events, parades, speeches, and celebrations in praise of Saddam and his regime.[157]

The regime also introduced new holidays to commemorate and honor soldiers and martyrs as a means of controlling the public narrative about the war. The anniversary of the start of the Iran-Iraq War (September 22) was first celebrated in 1981.[158] Martyrs' Day, celebrated on December 1, soon became one of the most important occasions. The program of events for Martyrs' Day eventually came to include dawn prayers in all mosques and churches, a twenty-one-gun salute during evening prayers, media programs about martyrs, and recitations of patriotic poems and speeches in schools and state offices.[159]

Muslim religious holidays took on new cultural and political importance in Iraq during the Iran-Iraq War. As soon as the war began, Saddam began to refashion himself as a pious president. In a highly orchestrated media event, Saddam prayed in public for the first time in a mosque in Baghdad during the first week of the war.[160] Two weeks later, he made a similarly publicized trip to Karbala to pray in a conspicuously Shi'i setting.[161] He then made a pilgrimage to Mecca in 1986 to bolster his own image as a pious leader.[162]

Social life in Baghdad had not been markedly religious in the mid-twentieth century. For example, foreign observers noted that in 1980 and 1981, many Baghdadis did not appear to observe the month-long Ramadan fast, and most restaurants in the capital remained open for the month, suggesting that businesses had plenty of nonfasting customers.[163] In line with

Saddam's shift toward public religiosity, the regime made an abrupt change in 1982 to enforce public observance of the fast: no one was allowed to eat or drink in public during daylight hours.[164] In 1986, the regime went further and banned the sale of alcohol nationwide during the entire month. Bars and nightclubs were likewise ordered to close for the whole month, while restaurants could open after the fast ended at sundown—so long as they did not serve alcohol in the evenings.[165] However, at the same time as the regime was publicly promoting fasting during Ramadan, it specifically forbade public *iftars* (evening meals to break the daytime fast) out of security concerns related to mass gatherings.[166] As historians Samuel Helfont and Dina Khoury have described, Saddam also conspicuously visited Shi'i shrines even as he maintained restrictions on large public commemorations of Shi'i religious holidays.[167] All of these steps were intended to cautiously reinforce Saddam's religious credentials to contradict Khomeini's allegations that the Ba'thist regime was atheistic or that the new Islamic government in Iran was the sole legitimate representative for the world's Shi'a.[168]

By the end of the Iran-Iraq War, public life in Baghdad was newly ordered around an increasingly full slate of state and religious holidays. The regime took an active role in creating a new repertoire of holidays, rituals, and symbols that reorganized the rhythm of life, and tried to appropriate existing holidays and rituals for its own political purposes. Incidentally, while the Ba'thist regime significantly increased the number of holidays celebrated in Iraq, the trend to pack ever more state and religious holidays into the calendar continued after the fall of Saddam. Iraq reportedly recognized 150 days of official holidays as of 2013, more than perhaps any other country in the world.[169] The continuation of this trend after 2003 underscores the point that inventing or recognizing public holidays is an easy way for a government to shore up its popularity in the midst of difficult political or economic circumstances. The Ba'thist regime used this to full effect during the 1980s, using state, party, and religious holidays to assert its own narratives about the war, to attempt to mitigate the influence of political Islam, and to bolster Saddam's cult of personality.

The Interlude: 1988–90

Iran and Iraq signed a ceasefire agreement in the summer of 1988, and for a brief two years from August 1988 to August 1990, Baghdadis hoped to regain a sense of normalcy and return to peacetime. The regime was eager to jumpstart all of the many development and construction projects put on hold by the war. In addition to reconstruction projects in Basra and Faw to repair the damage of the war, Baghdad was set to be a primary recipient of the promised construction boom: the Ministry of Housing and Construction promised the capital a new sports stadium, new housing developments, shopping centers, and infrastructure improvements to its electrical grid, telephone lines, roads, and water treatment systems.[170] Samar remembered this two-year respite between the Iran-Iraq and Gulf Wars as the "best time": young people were finally able to resume their dreams of pursuing careers, education, and marriage without the threat of bombs or conscription.[171]

However, Baghdadis were frequently disappointed by the reality of this postwar period. Soldiers who had cheered the end of the war were stunned to find that the regime kept them at their posts for months and even years after the war's end in an effort to avoid economic and social destabilization from mass demobilization.[172] The Egyptians who had been welcomed by the regime as laborers were unceremoniously pushed out of the country through intimidation and violence to make jobs for returning soldiers.[173] While women were once encouraged to take up paid jobs outside the home, starting in 1985, the regime began to push women to bear children to help replace the soldiers killed in war (see chapter 5), and many women were pressured to leave their jobs.[174]

The bustle of new construction and the government's rosy economic forecasts were undermined from the beginning by the lingering costs of the Iran-Iraq War. Iraq's economy was still hobbled by high inflation rates and billions of dollars in foreign debt. Prices in Baghdad, already stretched beyond the reach of many families during wartime, rose even higher after the war as returning soldiers increased competition for housing, food, and goods. Even the governmental newspaper *al-Thawra*, which normally put a positive spin on the news, admitted that prices in Baghdad had "increased tenfold in a very short period."[175]

Overview of the Gulf War and *Intifada*, 1990-91

Even as Baghdadis began their transitions to peacetime, the regime began to move toward a new war—this time with Kuwait, Iraq's southern neighbor. Saddam blamed Kuwait for committing "economic warfare" against Iraq by artificially depressing oil prices and failing to forgive Iraq's wartime loans.[176] On August 2, 1990, Saddam ordered the Iraqi military and Popular Army to occupy and annex Kuwait. The Iraqi occupation of Kuwait lasted for six months, during which time the regime laid claim to Kuwait's oil wealth as well as to all other resources it could find in the country: medicine, food supplies, and even chandeliers and appliances from Kuwaitis' houses were brought to Iraq.[177]

The news of Saddam's surprise occupation of Kuwait was met with incredulity and weariness by Iraqi civilians and conscripts alike. Diaries of Iraqi soldiers from the Gulf War reveal low morale and a lack of support for the regime's objectives: "We are defending Kuwait, but we don't know whom we're defending it for," one wrote.[178] Another soldier lamented that his conscription into this war was a virtual death sentence: "I used to plan my future wisely and in detail; but this period has passed and everything in my life has been destroyed, and all my planning has disappeared. My life has become nothing but a black piece of cloth."[179]

From August to December 1990, the United States and a broad coalition of more than thirty allies implemented a defensive operation, called "Desert Shield," to protect Saudi Arabia and other Gulf countries from further Iraqi aggression. At the same time, the United Nations imposed stringent international sanctions on Iraq and Iraqi-occupied Kuwait, effectively imposing a near-total blockade against exporting oil or importing consumer goods. This UN–imposed economic embargo remained in place, with some modifications, until April 2003 (see chapter 3).

As men braced themselves to be recalled to duty and women once again prepared to function as heads of households, Baghdadis initially assumed that the capital itself would be shielded from the worst of wartime fighting. This reasoning held during the initial stages of the Iraqi occupation of Kuwait: Iraqi forces entered Kuwait without facing any significant battles, and while Kuwaiti resistance groups targeted Iraqi forces, these skirmishes took place more than 400 miles from Baghdad.

When Saddam refused to withdraw from Kuwait by the January 15, 1991, deadline imposed by UN Resolution no. 678, the United States and its allies launched Desert Storm, carrying out air raids on Iraqi military positions inside Kuwait as well as inside Iraq. War abruptly arrived in Baghdad. While Iraq had enjoyed superior air power over Iran, Baghdadis now faced air strikes from the world's most sophisticated military.[180] Given the compact timeline of the Gulf War—the phase of active warfare with the United States and its coalition lasted only six weeks, from January to February 1991—Baghdad's experience in the Gulf War was very different from its experiences in the Iran-Iraq War. Neither the regime nor Baghdad's residents had time to gradually adapt to the realities of this war with the United States. During the Iran-Iraq War physical damage to the city was limited to sporadic attacks by Iranian missiles or internal opposition groups. During the six weeks of Desert Storm, Baghdad must have appeared to be on the brink of utter annihilation.

From the start of Desert Storm on January 17, 1990, until the cease-fire on February 28, 1991, nearly 60,000 US and coalition bombing sorties targeted Iraqi urban centers, focusing heavily on Baghdad.[181] This caught many Baghdadis by surprise. Iraqi artist Nuha al-Radi, who published the diary she kept while living through the Desert Storm bombardments on Baghdad, wrote in puzzlement once the coalition air strikes began in January 1991: "The one thing that no one bet on was that Baghdad was going to be bombed and hit like this. They [the coalition forces] were supposed to be freeing Kuwait. Maybe they need a map?"[182]

Night and day, air strikes pummeled the capital with the most advanced weaponry in the world; smart bombs blew out bridges, roads, telephone lines, and 90 percent of Baghdad's electrical grid.[183] Though the United States asserted that it was only striking at military targets, Baghdadis noted that many clothing, food, and cement factories were also destroyed, and many houses and shops were heavily damaged.[184]

An estimated 75 percent of Baghdadis lost access to clean water during the Gulf War.[185] When water did enter the pipes in people's homes, the pressure was typically too low to be able to flow into the sinks and toilets. Because of the weeks-long power outages, houses had no working pumps to push the water through the pipes. In interviews with Samar and in Nuha al-Radi's diary, both women recalled needing to haul dozens of buckets of water per day up and down steps from the ground-level pipes to the living quarters.[186]

Without running water in the pipes, toilets ceased operating. Sewage overflowed in homes and blocked up the public sewer system, spilling human waste into the streets.[187] Families with gardens began using their yards as outdoor toilets, an indignity that also contributed to worsening public health conditions.[188] City residents washed their laundry in the Tigris River. As people turned to the river for ever increasing needs—water for washing, laundry, and cooking, as well as for toileting—many became sick.[189] One family I interviewed decided to dig a well in their back yard rather than risk using the polluted river water. As soon as they had completed the twelve-foot-deep well, the war ended, and some drinking water eventually returned to their pipes. Today, they find some dark humor in their late timing, but their story underscores the lengths families went to for clean water in such difficult circumstances.[190]

After enduring six weeks of bombardments in Baghdad and on Iraqi positions in Kuwait, Saddam called for Iraqi troops to withdraw to Iraq on February 26, 1991. It was a hasty, disorderly retreat: soldiers abandoned their stations in Kuwait and fled—on foot, if necessary—on Highway 80 back to the Iraqi border. Thousands of retreating Iraqi soldiers were gunned down by US and coalition forces in an attack remembered as the "highway of death."[191] Photographs of Iraqi army jeeps incinerated while retreating, with their drivers burned to death behind the wheel, were suppressed in many Western media outlets in favor of narratives about the Gulf War as a "clean war."[192]

The surviving Iraqi soldiers limped across the border in a mix of despair and anger. Their grievances were many: weariness of years of conscription, humiliation over their disastrous defeat and chaotic retreat from Kuwait, and opposition to Saddam's regime. Their feelings spilled over into mass protests that began in the southern city of Basra but soon consumed nearly the whole country. The *intifada* protestors took aim at symbols and representatives of the Iraqi state and of the ruling Ba'th Party, torching governmental offices, killing officials, and filling the streets with protestors. In the North, Kurdish protestors rallied around nationalistic cries for autonomy and independence from the government in Baghdad. In the South, Shi'i slogans and iconography quickly dominated the protests, adding a sectarian dimension to the uprising. This uprising—commonly referred to as the *intifada* but officially named by the regime as the "Pages of Treachery and Betrayal"—lasted nearly three weeks until the government was able to crush the southern protests through helicopter gunship attacks and mass arrests. In the Kurdish North, anti-government rebels succeeded in claiming territory for themselves, with the support of the United Nations and the United States, breaking off Kurdistan as a semi-autonomous zone administered by a new Kurdistan Regional Government.[193]

The 1991 *intifada* may have failed to overthrow Saddam, but these mass protests weakened the Baʻth Party internally and revealed the precariousness of Saddam's grip on power in the early 1990s. Many party offices around the country were attacked, and party officials were killed.[194] Baghdad itself was largely insulated from the 1991 mass uprising: the government managed to block most news of the protests from reaching the capital, and the entrenchment of the government and its military and intelligence services in Baghdad enabled Saddam to stamp out any whiff of protest before it had time to gather momentum. Many Baghdadis recalled hearing only vague rumors about the uprisings that had swept the rest of the country, and the rumors themselves were not reassuring to hear: many believed government reports that Iranians were the instigators of violence in the South, for instance, rather than their own compatriots.[195]

Once the American bombs stopped falling and regime forces crushed the last of the 1991 uprising, the city of Baghdad still felt like it was under siege. The food scarcity that many families in Baghdad experienced during the six weeks of Desert Storm turned out to be a new normal for Iraqis for the next decade. Under the terms of the UN economic embargo, there were scant construction materials available to repair the extensive damage to the city. The impact of sanctions on Baghdad will be explored in greater depth in the remainder of the book.

Bomb Shelters and Regime Survival

As Baghdad was pummeled by bombs in 1991, sheer survival was the only real objective for either the regime or Baghdad's terrified residents. Saddam took steps to ensure his personal survival and the survival of his leadership apparatus by using safe houses and bunkers. Saddam's inner circle designated alternative office headquarters for every tier of the Baʿth Party, from top officials down to neighborhood-level party leaders, on the outskirts of the city or in areas far away from any known military sites that were likely to be targeted.[196] In case the Americans knew the exact locations of important state and party offices, Saddam hoped that the majority of the state and party bureaucracy could survive an attack by moving into party youth centers or training institutes instead.[197] Rumors circulated that Saddam had built himself an opulent underground bunker during the Iran-Iraq War that included a swimming pool and chandeliers, and that he would wait out US aerial bombardments there.[198] Important or sensitive technology—including broadcast equipment; parts for electrical, water, and sewage plants; and even wheat processing equipment—was ordered to be stored in safe houses.[199] Sensitive papers were boxed up and stored in bomb shelters. In an effort to maintain some functionality even during war, the Baʿth Party circulated instructions on how party officials were to hand-deliver memos from office to office to overcome the loss of electricity and telephone lines. Above all, Saddam made it clear that he expected all state and party employees to continue carrying out their duties as usual even in the midst of an aerial attack.[200]

To help protect Baghdad's residents, the government conducted evacuation drills in the capital in December 1990, a few weeks before the United States began its bombardments. This drill involved 1.4 million Baghdad residents from in and around the Saddam City neighborhood, the location deliberately chosen for the drill because it was one of the densest areas of the city.[201] According to newspaper reports at the time, the regime also broadcast instructions to Baghdadis about how to protect their homes from air raids, chemical attacks, and even nuclear strikes.[202] In the end, the regime did not carry out any formal evacuations of the capital during the war, but instead encouraged residents to seek shelter with family and relatives living in other provinces.[203] Many Baghdadis did flee to the countryside, correctly guessing that many other parts of Iraq would escape coalition bombings.[204]

Other Baghdadis took advantage of the handful of large bomb shelters that had been built during the Iran-Iraq War. Most of these bomb shelters burrowed deep into the ground, with as many as three subterranean levels filled with bunk beds. They were not known to be comfortable, but many families felt safer sleeping in the shelters at night.[205]

That sense of safety was shattered on February 13, 1991, when a coalition "bunker buster" bomb destroyed an underground bomb shelter in the well-to-do neighborhood of Amiriyya near the Baghdad airport. Approximately 400 people instantly lost their lives, nearly all of them civilians. Entire families were killed. After this horrific tragedy, many families no longer felt safe going to bomb shelters and waited out the coalition air strikes from their homes instead.[206]

A Baghdadi soldier stationed in Kuwait heard the news of this devastating incident in Amiriyya and feared that his family had been killed. The anguish and anger he recorded in his diary no doubt resonated with many Iraqis that day: "The shelter which was bombed in Amriya is near our home.... Yesterday I didn't sleep. Not a wink of sleep. My rage intensified so much that it blinded me.... I swore by God to take revenge [on behalf of] my family—the most horrible kind of revenge. If I survive I will make all the attackers meat for the vultures. By God, I swear that my mind will never find rest until I have revenge for the blood that was shed."[207] Party members and ministry officials immediately scrambled to Amiriyya shelter to assist with pulling bodies from the embers.[208] Lists of victims' names and, when possible, photographs of them from before the attack were compiled.[209] Notably, the regime removed its usual censorship rules for foreign journalists to allow them to report on the Amiriyya shelter, out of a desire to provide damning evidence of the civilian casualties to the world as quickly as possible.[210]

The Amiriyya shelter bombing revealed the weakness of the Baʿth Party regime in this lopsided war. One week after the air strike, anger and complaints mounted: local residents in the Amiriyya area began to complain about the smells of burned materials and decomposing bodies coming from the shelter, as it had taken the government much longer than expected to remove all the remains while besieged by airstrikes. There were fears that the local water supply would be contaminated by the rot. Many of those who had sought safety in the bomb shelter had brought valuables with them; complaints poured in that many of these valuables had been stolen off their bodies by rescue workers.[211] Worse still, residents were outraged that they had seen regime officials removing boxes of governmental papers that had been stored in the deepest levels of the bomb shelter even before they had retrieved all of the victims. Angry rumors circulated, accusing the regime of caring more about its paperwork than it did about the 400 people who had died.[212]

The Amiriyya bombing marked one of Baghdad's lowest points in the twentieth century: the capital was smoldering, infrastructure was destroyed and nonfunctional, families were grieving their loved ones killed on the battlefront or in coalition air strikes, and the regime appeared to be scrambling to maintain any semblance of control.

Holidays and Memorials after the Gulf War

In the aftermath of this humiliating, destructive war, Saddam tried to repeat the same mobilization strategies he had used to consolidate support. Despite experiencing a humiliating defeat, the regime reframed the war and the sanctions period that followed as Saddam defying American imperialism. Holidays like Martyrs' Day became increasingly propagandistic as the regime capitalized on such occasions to prop up Saddam's cult of personality, rather than meaningfully grieve the dead. The anniversary of the Amiriyya shelter bombing, arguably one of the most emotionally charged events in Baghdad related to the Gulf War, became an annual occasion for the regime to issue boilerplate denunciations of "American imperialism."[213]

Likewise, various milestones of Iraq's invasion of Kuwait and the Gulf War were commemorated on an annual basis through state-run media and public rituals and displays. In preparation for the third anniversary of the Gulf War, for example, party officials began to solicit "stories of bravery" from citizens to feature in the media. They were especially interested in highlighting the heroic steadfastness and loyalty to the regime of Baghdadis and residents of central provinces in the midst of the 1991 mass uprising that took place in the aftermath of Iraq's retreat from Kuwait.[214] Nuha was incredulous that the government chose January 17, the anniversary of the start of Desert Storm, for celebrating "Army Day" and handing out awards to veterans.[215] These state commemorations, holidays, and anniversaries had the effect of managing the script of how these events were publicly remembered and discussed, silencing alternative experiences and making clear who the regime cast as the heroes and as the villains in this state version of the war and uprising.

Saddam built new war monuments in the 1990s, as he had also done during the Iran-Iraq War. He built a "Victory over America" palace for himself in the Baghdad presidential complex, and started construction on the Mother of All Battles Mosque ("Mother of All Battles" was Saddam's preferred name for the Gulf War) to memorialize the invasion of Kuwait. These mosques were part of a larger trend of Saddam Islamizing Baghdad public spaces in the 1990s. While Helfont has convincingly argued that the Baʻth Party was devoted to coopting both Sunni and Shiʻi clerics, institutions, and religious rituals, others point to the 1990s as a turning point in the regime persecuting Shiʻa.[216] Khoury has noted that the regime's public commemorations of its victory over the 1991 *intifada* were aimed against the majority-Shiʻa rebels, and that the regime actively sowed distrust between Iraq's Sunnis and Shiʻa from 1991 onward.[217] Likewise, Harith al-Qarawee argues that Saddam's architectural projects and monuments built after the Gulf War promoted Sunni symbols of Islam over Shiʻi ones in reaction to the participation of a large number of Shiʻa in the 1991 *intifada*.[218]

As the regime attempted once again to stamp Baghdad with its own narrative about the war, ordinary Baghdadis went through their own processes of interpreting the meaning of the conflict for their city and for their personal lives. Some of this process is possible to see in the treatment of certain public spaces. For example, the ruins of the Amiriyya shelter were spontaneously memorialized by Baghdad residents who left behind their own messages and symbols of grief and remembrance.[219] Later, the regime turned the Amiriyya shelter into an official state monument, erasing citizens' tributes that had preserved some sense of how this event was popularly remembered.[220] This small example reminds us that, while regime monuments are more easily identifiable, ordinary Iraqis were simultaneously undertaking processes of symbolizing, memorializing, and reinterpreting the city landscape in the aftermath of the war in ways that often undermined or diverged from state narratives.

In the end, the regime's efforts to mobilize popular support in response to the Gulf War fell flat. The devastation of the city was too extreme to ignore, and the invasion of Kuwait was revealed to have been a tragic mistake that dragged Baghdad and the rest of the country into ruin. Under the heavy restrictions of international sanctions, the physical destruction of Baghdad was slow to be repaired.

One vignette from the archives illustrates the difficult position Baghdad's destruction created for poorer Baghdad residents and the regime alike. In 1996, more than five years after the end of the Gulf War, the regime ordered 117 families from the historic Batawin neighborhood in central Baghdad to evacuate their homes, which had been condemned as unlivable as a result of Gulf War bombing and inadequate repairs in the years that followed. Local party officials intervened, pleading with top regime leaders to delay these evictions or first find the families suitable alternative housing. The local officials pointed out that this neighborhood had produced many "martyrs and prisoners of war," hinting that the regime owed these families on some level.[221] The president rejected any calls for delaying these evictions, stating that these families had been given adequate time to repair their houses over the years.[222] As a last-ditch effort, these families—including women, children, and the elderly—took to the streets to protest their evictions, though they shrewdly carried photos of Saddam with them during their demonstration to signal their overall loyalty to the president.

The fact that these families took to the street is shocking in Saddam's Iraq, where security forces usually met public opposition with swift retribution and viewed any efforts at mass mobilization as a threat. Remarkably, these families were not arrested, and local officials met with them to hear their demands. In the end, however, the protests did not lead to any concrete change: the eviction orders remained in force.

This episode reveals a key truth about the ramifications of the Gulf War for state-society relations for years to come: although international sanctions were designed to turn the population against Saddam, this unusual public protest was not necessarily trying to bring down the regime. Instead, these families were asking for the regime's help through financial aid and housing assistance. As later chapters will explore, economic hardships resulting from sanctions and the Gulf War tended to push Iraqis to become more dependent on the state, which in turn strengthened the party and the regime. Despite the regime's loss of popularity in the immediate aftermath of the Gulf War and 1991 *intifada*, Baghdadis were in desperate need of assistance for food, income, and housing. During sanctions, no one but the regime could reliably provide that.

Conclusion

From 1950 to 1979, city residents and government officials interacted with one another in the oil-boom years of plenty, with residents navigating their place in a rapidly modernizing city. City residents jostled to use public housing programs and social welfare programs to their strategic advantage. White-collar bureaucrats secured rights to subsidized land to ensure that their children would have access to all the benefits of education and employment in the chic capital city, while tenant farmers adapted to life in small cinderblock houses in Revolution City on the outskirts of Baghdad, hoping to help their children achieve upward mobility in their new urban lives.

War dashed Baghdadis' hopes that their children's lives would be better than their own. After 1979, the daily life negotiations between Baghdadi residents and government officials became focused on survival in the face of war, sanctions, and Saddam Hussein's dictatorship. The following chapters will explore how Baghdadis pursued a variety of survival strategies—through petitions, food rations, and sex work—to endure the difficulties of the 1980s and 1990s. For the regime's part, they were also in a struggle for political survival, trying to maintain a firm grip on power in the face of a series of challenges: first from Iran, then from UN–imposed international sanctions, then from US air strikes and, in 2003, a ground invasion.

State-society relations in Baghdad have played out in a fragmented physical environment ever since 1979. In the aftermath of the wreckage of the Gulf War bombings, Baghdad resembled a disjointed time capsule. Parts of the city had been frozen in time in 1982, preserving legacies of the once promising construction boom meant to modernize the capital, while others parts of the city were stuck in 1991, preserving the destruction that rained down during Gulf War bombings. Lefebvre wrote that cities are physically marked by rhythms and cycles of time: "time and space are intimately linked and measured in terms of one another."[223] Baghdadis during the Gulf War perceived the stoppage or even apparent "reversal" of time in Baghdad through the physical destruction of its landscape. Nuha described how Baghdadis during Desert Storm were living like "peasants," carrying out many tasks by hand without electricity, and that Baghdad appeared to have gone back to the "stone age" as the effects of the sanctions had set in, echoing the famous threat by US secretary of state James Baker in 1991.[224]

At the time of writing, we can consider how the landscape still bears witness to the many different episodes of violence and upheaval Baghdad has experienced in recent decades: time and space remain inextricably linked. Baghdad's glitzy (and often corrupt) development projects in the 2010s still have to connect to the faltering electrical grid whose problems date back to 1991. The new "1,001 Nights" shopping and restaurant complex fashioned from one of Saddam's former palaces in Baghdad is a short distance from buildings still pock-marked with bullet holes from war and sectarian violence after the 2003 US invasion. As Baghdadis traverse the city today, they move through a landscape that is still marked by these different eras of devastation, punctuated by glimpses of Baghdad's mid-century modernist past or Ottoman heritage and also by recent efforts at renewal.

War brought lasting consequences to Baghdad's built environment and to the city's residents. While the first two chapters of this book focused on changes in the physical landscape of the city, the next three chapters shift the focus to state-society relationships as they played out within the administrative boundaries of Baghdad's neighborhoods and districts from the time of the Iran-Iraq War through the end of the sanctions era. How well Baghdadis could negotiate with neighborhood Baʻth Party officials and leverage the resources available to them would determine how well their families would survive the new challenges ahead.

PART II

Citizen Advocacy and Local Governance

THREE

The Weaponization of Food Rations

WHEN SADDAM HUSSEIN INVADED Kuwait on August 2, 1990, the UN Security Council, with strong backing by the United States, swiftly passed resolution no. 661 to enforce an economic embargo on Iraq. The terms of these sanctions initially prohibited Iraq from selling any oil, which constituted 95 percent of Iraq's export revenues and 65 percent of its GDP.[1] UN-imposed sanctions devastated Iraq's economy and threatened the health and survival of the entire civilian population. Iraq was particularly vulnerable to the economic effects of sanctions because Iraq was a net food importer. Iraq's agricultural sector had been hampered by soil salinity issues in the twentieth century, and by the 1950s, oil revenues were sufficient to pay for food imports instead.[2] By the late 1980s, Iraq was spending $2 billion annually on imported food that provided 70 percent of the country's caloric needs.[3] Severe restrictions on imports under the terms of UN sanctions impacted the availability and affordability of food after 1990.[4] One woman remembered splitting a single egg among six family members by mixing it with some flour and water because the cost of eggs had soared by 1,500 percent in 1991.[5] Food shortages were so dire that rumors circulated about people stealing food from funerals or about families intentionally harming their children so the children could eat free meals at the hospital.[6]

Starvation and malnourishment threatened Iraqis of all social classes, not just the poor. The value of the Iraqi dinar collapsed in the early 1990s because of the impact of sanctions on Iraq's financial system. The devaluation of Iraq's currency wiped out the savings of the middle classes and rendered pensions and fixed public-sector paychecks nearly worthless. Consequently, many white-collar workers were also unable to provide for their families.[7] One interviewee complained that most paychecks at the time could not cover more than 20 percent of total household expenses.[8] Many families reported that they needed to work multiple jobs just to survive, like one interviewed school teacher who sold gas canisters over the summer and gave private lessons in the evenings so he could clothe his children.[9] Some even put their own young children to work: one mother lamented in an interview that her son had to drop out of school to work in a sweets shop to help support the family. The hardest part of the sanctions years, she said, was seeing her son return home with injuries from carrying heavy trays all day.[10]

To prevent widespread hunger (and the food riots that were sure to follow), Saddam's government rapidly implemented a nationwide food rations distribution system.[11] These basic staples provided by the state—flour, rice, sugar, lentils, tea, cooking oil, and soap—were a genuine lifeline for most Iraqis. In the hands of Saddam's regime, however, these humanitarian goods had the potential to be brandished as a powerful new form of leverage to keep dissidents and deserters in line.

The history of food rations in Iraq, then, is a story of contestation between state and society. As seen in earlier chapters, negotiations over resources often took place at the neighborhood level between Baghdadis and the low-ranking regime representatives embedded in their local areas, and this was the case for the food rationing system, too. Local party officials at the neighborhood *firqa* office or at the party branch office (*fara'*) for a large district in Baghdad were often the ones to determine whether a particular family's food rations could be punitively cut off or if, after receiving a punishment, a family's food rations could be restored again. Examining the history of Iraq's food rations program demonstrates how food distribution functioned as a way for the regime to mobilize locally embedded bureaucratic systems to surveil the population and to reestablish control in the aftermath of the 1991 anti-regime uprising. Furthermore, state-society negotiations are a two-way street, and the localization of the food distribution system also provided greater access for citizens to contact regime representatives, including their state-appointed rations agents and officials in their neighborhood *firqa* and district branch party offices. This chapter illustrates how citizens tried to leverage their relationships with neighborhood and district Baʿth Party officials to access resources.

The history of Iraqi food rations can also be read as a story of evolving survival strategies in the sanctions era for citizens and rulers alike. There were high stakes for the success of the food rationing system: food rations were a matter of life and death for many Baghdadis in a rapidly deteriorating economy. This was also a turning point for the political survival of Saddam Hussein and his administration. Reeling from the 1991 *intifada* uprising internally and the external threat of sanctions, Saddam's regime was operating in an unstable political environment with reduced resources and manpower. Delegating the task of running the food rations distribution system to low-ranking, neighborhood-based officials was one survival strategy that Saddam used during the early sanctions years to compensate for the administration's weakened capacity for centralized governance. The decision to weaponize food rations by cutting off food to dissidents and deserters was another strategy to shore up Saddam's grip on power.

Creating the Food Rationing System

The Iraqi government implemented an emergency food distribution system almost immediately after sanctions began in early August 1990.[12] As an initial emergency measure, the government sent around trucks in Baghdad to distribute bread to "thronging crowds."[13] By October, it started to offer rations in a more systematic way, distributing set amounts of food staples to distribution centers around the country on a monthly basis.[14]

The logistics of implementing a nationwide food rationing system were daunting. Rations cards had to be printed and distributed to each family in the country after first verifying their name, their residence, and the validity of the family relationships for each card.[15] Each rations card listed a designated head of household, followed by a list of up to twenty names of all family members connected to that household.[16]

To create these rations cards, the Iraqi government had to carry out an accurate national census while it was also fighting a war in Kuwait and staggering through the meltdown of the domestic economy. The grunt work of creating the rations rosters was entrusted to neighborhood-level Baʿth Party officials at the *firqa* and *shuʿba* levels of Baʿth Party offices (see Figure 2).

In coordination with local police departments, these neighborhood Ba'th Party officials met with each family in their jurisdiction to review their IDs and, later, to cross-check their own rosters against those of other districts in the city to look for duplicates.

Despite the speed with which the rationing system had to be implemented, the party secretariat still took the time to chastise Baghdad party branches for not printing the cards carefully enough: Baghdad's rations cards had been "ruined" by low-quality printing that would also enable them to be easily counterfeited, and, besides that, they "lacked beauty."[17] The Office of the Party Secretariat recommended that they cancel the old cards and start over, conscious of the costs of fraud and the importance of maintaining a professional-looking operation for the population. The lesson here was that the rationing system was meant not only for humanitarian relief, but also to demonstrate the continued competence and efficacy of the government despite the difficult circumstances of the embargo.

It was a constant challenge for the regime to provide consistent amounts of food in each month's rations delivery due to the blockade on imports. The first few months of the rationing system witnessed several adjustments in the proposed amounts of food for each family as the regime tried to calculate what it could sustainably deliver. For example, the first proposal called for 8 kg of flour and 2 kg of rice distributed to each person per month, which was quickly cut to 6 kg of flour and 1.5 kg of rice, and then reduced again. The amounts listed in the accompanying table were characteristic of rations distributions for much of the early 1990s, before supplies improved somewhat after the implementation of the Oil-for-Food Program in 1997.[18]

Rationed goods amounted to approximately 1,000 calories per person per day, which is considerably less than the recommended daily caloric intake for adults. Many Baghdadis recollect that food rations made up anywhere from 50 percent to 90 percent of their food for the month. To supplement their rations, interviewees reported that they spent approximately 70 percent or more of their income purchasing luxuries like eggs, chicken, or fresh fruits and vegetables, since these items were not included in the rations.[19] Some Iraqis recalled how they sometimes received a chicken in their monthly rations during Ramadan, but most low-income Iraqis ate very little meat and relied almost entirely on rationed food.[20] A widowed schoolteacher interviewed by anthropologist Yasmin Husein al-Jawaheri in

Family of One	Family of Two	Family of Three
5 kg flour	10 kg flour	15 kg flour
1 kg rice	2 kg rice	3 kg rice
0.75 kg sugar	1.5 kg sugar	2.25 kg sugar
0.075 kg tea	0.15 kg tea	0.225 kg tea
0.5 kg oil	1 kg oil	1.5 kg oil
0.25 kg beans	0.5 kg beans	0.75 kg beans
3 boxes of infant formula*	6 boxes of infant formula*	9 boxes of infant formula*
1 small packet of powdered soap	1 small packet of powdered soap	2 small packets of powdered soap

*Infant formula was only available to families with young children.

FIGURE 11 Monthly food rations table, January 1991. Ministry of Trade, "Medical Report," July 24, 1999, BRCC 01-2129-0000-0530.

the late 1990s lamented: "We thought we could divert part of our rations to sell on the 'black' market for some cash. We desperately needed to buy candles for lighting and some oil for heating. However, by the last days of every month, we were literally starving. The most painful thing was seeing my child withering away in front of me."[21]

Strategies for Regime Survival

A successful food distribution system was vital to Saddam's regime to ensure the longevity of his grip on power and to pin the blame for Iraqis' suffering on the United Nations and the United States, rather than on his shortcomings.[22] The Iraqi food rationing system is generally regarded as a humanitarian and logistical success, especially in comparison to mass starvation that occurred under Chinese or Soviet food rationing systems.[23] Food rations helped to reduce the prevalence of outright starvation. Politically, Saddam hoped it would also assuage popular discontent.

The Iraqi regime had two main political audiences for its rations system: one was Iraq's international critics, and the other was its domestic audience. Internationally, food rations were important for the Iraqi government's propaganda: food distributions highlighted the continued effectiveness of the government despite the damage it sustained from Desert Storm and from sanctions. In the court of global opinion, the fact that the Iraqi government needed to distribute food to forestall mass starvation highlighted the humanitarian suffering caused by the UN embargo.[24] In light of the mounting international criticism about the humanitarian impact of sanctions on Iraqi civilians, the Iraqi government did win reluctant praise from international monitors for the efficacy of its rationing system. In a recording from a closed-door meeting of top Baʿth Party leaders, Taha Ramadan bragged that "all the international organizations give a positive evaluation of the Iraqi ration card."[25]

Domestically, the government's goal was to use rations to broaden its base of supporters who depended on the government for sustenance and who therefore would not agitate for its downfall. The director general of the party secretariat described the rationing system as a way to "combat the oppositional plans against our great Iraq, which will test our abilities to defeat the conspiracy."[26] Many of the Iraqis interviewed for this book, including those who bitterly opposed Saddam, had positive remarks about the food rationing system. A seventy-year-old retired military officer shared how he held the United Nations primarily responsible for sanctions, not Saddam's regime. "I hate Saddam Hussein immensely. . . . But the economic sanctions were imposed on Saddam, and with him, on the people. Because of the United Nations, the people went hungry."[27] A middle-class man from Harthiyya, a central neighborhood home to many public-sector employees, declared that rations were the only way that Iraqis were able to survive the sanctions. He recalled the system as being "reliable" and "good," which he saw as important because some families relied on rations for "100 percent" of their food.[28]

As an extension of its policy to use food rations to shore up domestic support, the government provided additional rations to reward the loyalty of certain state employees and Baʿth Party officials above a certain rank.[29] This secondary form of rations enabled these privileged few access to rare goods like meat, eggs, tomatoes, and clothing at affordable, fixed prices and at a higher quality than was available to the public.[30] Baʿth Party offices also received monthly rations of tea and sugar for refreshments at work, an additional perquisite so officials could drink tea on the job without diminishing their household's rationed supplies.[31]

The regime also used the food rationing system to increase its surveillance capacities, underscoring how humanitarian systems can simultaneously serve political purposes. The strict requirements that Iraqis register their rations card in their own neighborhood helped the government monitor and limit the movements of Iraqi families.[32] For example, the regime restricted Iraqis from other parts of the country from moving to Baghdad during sanctions years, fearing the destabilizing effects internal migrants would have on the capital.[33] Rations card registration provided a new tool to monitor movement and prevent families from moving their permanent address to Baghdad.

Rations cards could provide other valuable information for the regime, too. Iraqis who had been prisoners of war in Iran during the Iran-Iraq War were viewed suspiciously as potential supporters of Iran. When one former prisoner of war left Iraq without travel authorization, Iraqi intelligence services used his rations card to determine which other family members might have gone with him and which remained in their neighborhood to continue picking up their rationed food.[34] Other populations could also be monitored: foreigners residing in Iraq were eligible to receive rations if they renewed their identity papers monthly. Though it was costly to the regime to feed noncitizens, this option had the advantage of helping the party better monitor their activities.[35]

Maintaining an aura of competence and consistently delivering food rations under the severe restrictions of UN–imposed sanctions was difficult for the regime to accomplish, and it was not always successful. Flour posed a particularly vexing challenge for the government: even today, Iraqis vividly recall the rank smell of the rationed flour that only got worse when the bread baked in the oven.[36] The wheat flour that the government delivered was inexplicably dark in color, and Baghdadis complained that all of their white bread was now "black."[37] The color can be explained in part by the fact that the government often did not have enough white flour to distribute, and so mixed it with brown flour.[38] Many Iraqis complained that the color and smell were really because of dirt or other impurities mixed into the flour, or alleged that the flour was milled from rotten grain.[39]

As unsavory as the flour was, there also simply wasn't enough of it.[40] The government ordered flour mills to operate twenty-four hours a day in order to produce enough for the country, but even this did not keep pace with demand.⁴¹ Periodic flour shortages continued throughout the 1990s due to mechanical breakdowns in the flour mills; spare parts were very difficult to come by under the terms of the sanctions.⁴² With flour in such high demand, black market dealers were known to bribe mill workers and transporters to sell off a portion of the flour, leaving less to distribute to the families.⁴³ Rations agents were also accused of sometimes skimping on the amount of flour they distributed to the families so they could sell the best portions on the black market.⁴⁴

When rations agents in Baghdad experienced shortages in flour, some temporarily closed their distribution centers so as not to contend with disappointed residents. Saddam angrily ordered that any rations agent violating instructions would be punished and have their license canceled immediately.⁴⁵ The political success of the rationing program depended on its reliability. Dangerously for the regime, food shortages called into question the ability of the government to keep its commitment to prevent "hunger and deprivation."⁴⁶ Internally, the party secretariat bluntly referred to the "insufficiency of goods distributed through rations cards to completely meet the needs of families."⁴⁷ The challenges of consistently providing rationed flour to the population underscores the weakened capabilities of the regime in the early 1990s. The political stakes for the food rationing system were high as Saddam sought to use rations to bolster his regime's image that was tarnished in the Gulf War and *intifada*.

Localized Rations Distribution

As a way to compensate for the state's diminished capacities, Saddam delegated the day-to-day operations of the food rations system to low-ranking, neighborhood-based regime representatives, rather than attempting a highly centralized food distribution system like those of China or the Soviet Union in the late twentieth century.

The food rations distribution system was set up so that the Ministry of Trade was responsible for overseeing the entire food rationing system, and it in turn relied on the State Company for Foodstuff Trading and the State Company for Grain Processing to distribute rationed food to major warehouses throughout the country.⁴⁸ Baʻth Party branches ensured that food was successfully transported from these central warehouses to their jurisdictions. The physical distribution of food took place in thousands of small rations centers sprinkled throughout Baghdad and the rest of the country, many of which served only 100 families each.[49]

Within each neighborhood, the responsibility for overseeing the minutiae of the day-to-day aspects of rations distribution fell to Ba'th Party neighborhood committees. In the fall of 1990, Saddam revived the institution of Economic Surveillance Committees, used during the Iran-Iraq War, to meet weekly in each neighborhood and monitor the activities of shopkeepers, rations agents, and market vendors.[50] This committee was usually the first to report the presence of a black market or to identify a corrupt rations agent.

Another neighborhood-based regime initiative to help with food rations was the Popular Committees (*majlis al-sha'b*). Popular Committees had been around since the 1970s as nonelected municipal bodies intended to incorporate local elites into aspects of community regulation.[51] According to one estimate, there were approximately 700 Popular Committees active in Baghdad in the 1990s that worked to offload the everyday tasks of governance from the regime.[52] Prior to the inauguration of the rationing system, Popular Committees in each neighborhood were busy conducting surveillance of their neighborhoods for "immoral" activities on behalf of the government. They interfaced with local police departments, internal security and intelligence organizations, neighborhood Ba'th Party organizations, and various ministries to solve minor disputes and to monitor potential troublemakers.[53]

Popular Committees took on new responsibilities for the food rations system: they were tasked with giving each family a unique ID number for their rations card and with verifying families' information. These committees were responsible for keeping track when new families moved into or out of their district, or investigating if a family claimed to have lost their card.[54] They were also responsible for notifying the regime of any suspected fraud.

Finally, the Ba'thist regime relied on local shopkeepers as part of its strategy for distributing food and monitoring the population. Shopkeepers applied to serve as rations agents who distributed the subsidized food, and they received payment based on the number of families they served. Rations agents converted their family-run grocery stores into food rations distribution centers two days per month and sometimes set aside a spare room in their store to hold the rations.[55] If a rations agent became ill or died, the license typically remained in the family so that the adult children or spouse of an agent might take over the local distribution of rations. There were a limited number of shops that were suitable, and it was more stable for the entire system and for Iraqi citizens to keep the rations where Iraqis were already accustomed to getting their groceries.[56] Using neighborhood grocery stores to distribute food rations is a distinctive characteristic of the Iraqi food rations system and a sign of Saddam's tendency toward decentralized day-to-day governance strategies in the early 1990s; many other countries with rationing systems have used large warehouses and distribution centers.[57] There were advantages to this localized system: distributing rations within each neighborhood increased the ability of the state to monitor rations operations through the work of rations agents and neighborhood committees. The small scale of each rations center made it easier to spot abnormalities, fraud, or mistakes.

Rations agents were a new position in modern Iraqi history, one that occupied a critical intermediary position between the regime and the population it served. Though they became official regime representatives, these were familiar community pillars who interacted daily with their neighbors. The neighborhood basis of distribution made the entire rationing system more personalized as a bureaucratic process; Iraqis knew the key individuals responsible for providing them with food each month. Interviews with Iraqis indicate that most people lived within half a mile of their rations distribution center.[58] Though rations agents were technically considered employees of the Ministry of Trade, the agents did not come from a bureaucratic background. Furthermore, most agents were not members of the Ba'th Party, though they were vetted to ensure their families had good or unobjectionable standing with the regime. Both men and women worked as rations agents, and the Ba'th Party archives indicate that women were well represented among their ranks.

There was room for favoritism in selecting who would become rations agents and how large their jurisdiction would be: an official from the Ministry of Trade was reprimanded for designating his father as a rations agent and assigning him 150 families, whereas other rations agents nearby were assigned only 30–60 families, as a way to make sure his father would receive more payment for his role.⁵⁹ There was also the potential for rations agents themselves to abuse their position. Rations agents sometimes exploited their positions to sell off rations illegally. For example, rations agents in one Baghdad neighborhood were caught distributing spoiled milk and rotten flour in the rations and then selling their fresh food supplies on the black market.⁶⁰ Another rations agent repeatedly stole an elderly woman's rations, and when she complained, he physically attacked her.⁶¹ Rationed infant formula was especially vulnerable to illegal sale because it was the only source of animal protein included in the monthly rations and only given to families with young children.⁶² One father petitioned to receive formula because his disabled adult children could not eat solid food. His petition was denied: only young children were eligible.⁶³ Desperate needs such as these drove a thriving black market for formula. Because of the high price infant formula could fetch on the black market, some families reportedly did not receive their portions because theirs had already been illegally sold by their rations agents for a profit.⁶⁴

Profiteering and corruption earned rations agents a poor reputation. Only two months after the emergency rations were first introduced, the head of the Presidential Diwan called rations agents a "parasitic class" whose greed injured the middle and lower strata of society.⁶⁵ As state employees, the rations agents who engaged in shady dealings threatened to make a mockery of the regime's reputation for competent control.

Saddam responded by announcing harsh new punishments for rations agents and merchants who broke the law. Just one month after sanctions began, Saddam issued new punishments for shopkeepers and rations agents caught selling goods for higher amounts than stipulated, threatening them with fifteen years in prison and the confiscation of their assets.⁶⁶ The Revolutionary Command Council followed up in 1994 with a decree stating that any agents who resold rationed goods would be jailed for one year and their shops and goods would be confiscated.⁶⁷

The regime also went after other kinds of shopkeepers for hoarding, price manipulation, and profiteering. Saddam issued a proclamation that made hoarding a crime punishable by execution:

> For the purpose of . . . causing the economic sanctions to fail . . . and to offer a sufficient amount of food for all citizens on an equal basis, and to eliminate those who are susceptible to bribes, who have weak character,

and who are short-sighted . . . the Revolutionary Command Council has decreed the following:

1) Hoarding food for the purpose of selling it is considered a crime and as an act of sabotage that violates national security.

2) This will be punished by execution, and all movable and immovable assets will be confiscated to all those who commit the crime stipulated above.[68]

On at least one occasion, Saddam carried through with this threat to create a gruesome, cautionary spectacle of violence: Jordanian newspapers reported that in 1992, the regime executed forty-two merchants accused of price manipulations and displayed their corpses in front of their shops.[69]

In reality, however, the regime rarely followed through on its threats of extreme punishments for rations agents and other kinds of shopkeepers. The regime was simply too dependent on local rations agents to keep the emergency food distribution system running; each neighborhood had only a limited number of shopkeepers who were able to take on the additional task of rations distributions, and changing agents threatened to disrupt food delivery to hundreds of families assigned to that center. Thus, these new laws were designed primarily to scare agents into compliance.

Through these new threats, the food rations distribution bureaucracy served not only to surveil the Baghdadi population, but also to surveil the food rations agents themselves through the work of neighborhood Popular Committees and Economic Surveillance Committees.[70] Citizens were also encouraged to inform on corrupt officials through petitions (see chapter 4). Beginning in 1998, the Ministry of Trade introduced a formal process for responding to citizens' complaints against rations agents: it would submit the rations agent to a local referendum with all of the families registered to that agent. If the agent received less than a 50 percent vote of confidence, the agent would lose their job. In one instance, a female rations agent named Ghada* and her husband were accused of embezzling funds from voluntary donations they had collected to rebuild a local school. The neighbors also complained about the husband's "bad behavior" when distributing rations, which may have alluded to sexual harassment of his customers. The Rashid branch in Baghdad recommended canceling Ghada's post, but when she secured 80 percent of the votes in a neighborhood referendum, she was allowed to keep her position.[71]

Thus, a key feature of the Iraqi rationing system was that, though there were centralized aspects, most activity took place on a neighborhood level, and local regime representatives and party officials had considerable responsibilities and leeway in running the rations system. Neighborhood party leaders, Popular Committees, and rations agents all lived in the same communities they served, and these were the individuals responsible for managing lists of recipients and monitoring food distribution: a clear example of the embeddedness of state agents within society.[72] Though party branch officials and the Ministry of Trade were ultimately the ones who would answer to Saddam for the functioning of the system, they were not in touch with the day-to-day operations on the ground. Distributing rations on a neighborhood level placed these low-level state and party officials in an important position as intermediaries. They were expected to act as the eyes and ears of the regime in monitoring the population and enacting its policies. This chapter, however, will also show how these low-level officials could act as important advocates on behalf of their neighbors and the citizens in their small jurisdictions. As historian Dina Khoury observed, "the [party] men and women who managed the lives and deaths of the population within their jurisdiction were proficient in the language of the party, but adept at framing it in local terms and within local constraints."[73] During the hardest years of sanctions in the early 1990s, when the regime's human and material resources were at their lowest, local party members were not just skilled at translating regime policies into their local contexts: top leaders increasingly *expected* neighborhood authorities to shape policies based on their knowledge of local conditions.

Strategies for Citizen Survival
Fraud, Theft, and Black Markets

Crime of all kinds was an increasing problem in the 1990s: black markets, smuggling, and theft were predictable responses to the worsening economic conditions. Prostitution became a growing topic of concern (see chapter 5). The distribution of food rations and the subsidization of certain staples opened the door to new survival strategies for the population, some of which were illegal. The regime acknowledged internally that "a large number of citizens sold their rations" on the black market or engaged in other kinds of rations fraud.[74] In one case, an employee from a state-run cooperative association for consumer goods stole 450 boxes of milk and vegetables and sold them on the black market.[75] Many families were caught registering fictitious or deceased relatives or relatives living abroad on their family rations card, or registering in more than one neighborhood to receive double rations, sometimes with the collusion of a bribed rations agent.[76] One woman in Baghdad was caught collecting rations for three absentee family members for ten years, which meant she had received hundreds of kilograms of extra food. Both the woman and her rations agent were punished.[77] Strikingly, an officer from the elite Republican Guards was among those arrested for selling food rations on the black market. He was caught selling 18 bags of rice, 16 bags of large lentils, and 25 kg of milk out of his car to residents in Saddam City (previously called Revolution City). We can assume from his status as an officer that he was able to sell his surplus because his needs were already met, whereas the residents of Saddam City he was selling to were among the poorest in the city.[78]

The boldness and frequency with which many lower income Baghdadis and even public employees began to flout the law demonstrated a diminished respect for the efficacy and power of the state and an increasing fearlessness about the consequences of breaking the law. 'Izzat Ibrahim al-Duri, vice chair of Iraq's Revolutionary Command Council, saw that the danger of the sanctions was not just the disillusionment and resentment that would grow in a hungry population, but also the visibility of the regime's diminished power and control. In a private meeting with the president's inner circle, he complained: "We have people stealing from each other, an increase in the market prices, tradesmen are out of control, and there are smugglers everywhere. We have been Ba'thist for twenty-three years now; we have never had this many cases of stealing from the government and from citizens. However, when it did happen, we would punish them right away and it would be over with. We have never had corruption to this extent of pervasiveness between our citizens; this is all a result of the sanctions."[79] Officials worked to clamp down on rations fraud, though it took tremendous resources to investigate falsified rations cards to determine which names listed on the cards were real, alive, and present at the listed address. Initially, the Baʿth Party instructed neighborhood surveillance committees to conduct exhaustive investigations to verify and cross-check names on each rations card with the rosters held by the State Company for Foodstuff Trading. In all, these investigations required the cooperation of six different Baʿth Party offices or ministries.[80]

Eventually, this process was streamlined. New protocols were introduced in 1995 that required heads of households to apply in person for a family rations cards at the start of each calendar year, bringing with them all the official identity cards of the family members who would be registered on the same rations ticket.[81] It was a risky moment for anyone daring to present false ID cards. Families caught receiving too many rations had to repay the market value of all of the goods they wrongfully received on behalf of an absentee or deceased family member.[82] To incentivize the party officials to be vigilant, they were offered a reward of 300 dinars for each wrongfully registered person on a rations card that the official caught.[83] This new initiative did seem to help root out rations fraud: beginning in early 1995, citizens were caught registering absentee family members and were made to repay all of the rations they had wrongfully received under their names while they were abroad.[84]

Responding to Collective Punishment

Cracking down on food rations fraud was a persistent headache for the Iraqi government. However, black markets and rations fraud were not the top-priority crimes for the regime: the biggest security concern was targeting Iraqis who were disloyal to the regime and thus posed an internal security threat. Saddam singled out three high-priority types of criminals—deserters from the military, opposition group members, and absentee public-sector employees—and used the withholding of food rations as a new form of punishment against them. Here, I examine how ordinary Iraqis took steps to push back against this weaponization of rations, advocating for themselves and their families to the regime. In the next section, I explore the important function of neighborhood-level authorities in influencing the outcome of these cases.

Desertion from the military and membership in an opposition group were serious crimes that the regime had been actively fighting against for many years by the time sanctions began. These crimes already had stiff punishments: as mentioned in chapter 2, membership in any political party other than the Iraqi Ba'th Party was punishable by execution.[85] Members of the Shi'i Da'wa Party and the Iraqi Communist Party were arrested, assassinated, or driven into hiding in the 1980s. During the Iran-Iraq War, deserters from the battlefield could be executed, while those who failed to show up for duty or return from leave were caught and arrested.[86]

In contrast, absenteeism from public-sector jobs was a new phenomenon in the 1990s that developed because public-sector paychecks had dwindled to an average of two or three dollars per month during sanctions.[87] For such little pay, many workers quit without official permission, worked only sporadically, or simply stopped showing up to work. For example, the educational system faltered throughout the 1990s as an estimated 12,000 teachers simply stopped reporting for work.[88] Absenteeism from public-sector jobs can be seen as an adaptive survival strategy by Baghdadis who could then use their time to try to earn more money through driving a taxi, selling goods, or even begging in the streets.[89] One interviewee from a highly educated and artistic family shared how her father stopped going to work at his prestigious government job in order to make mops during sanctions. Through this menial labor, he hoped to support the family by hand-making goods that could no longer be imported.[90] This kind of absenteeism from public-sector jobs was a serious challenge to the regime's ability to govern and to sustain public services, however. Given Saddam's preoccupation with projecting an image of competence and effective rule in the 1990s, cracking down on public-sector absenteeism became a political priority.

Initially, only *individuals* accused of desertion from the military, membership in an opposition group, or absenteeism from a public-sector job were liable to have their rations cut off. Cutting off rations as a form of punishment of individuals was not a uniquely Iraqi invention; other countries with rationing systems have similarly used rations to punish certain categories of people or to modify behavior. For example, the Soviet Union cut off food rations to absentee factory workers during World War II.[91] But unlike the Soviet example, which was primarily motivated by economic considerations in the context of a total war effort, the Iraqi government's manipulation of rations had a political goal. The temporary exclusion of deserters, opposition members, and absentee public employees from the rations program marked these individuals as disloyal to the regime and therefore outside the reaches of its beneficence.[92] Cutting off rations—rather than, say, a punishment like execution—provided these individuals with opportunities to rectify their standing with the regime, exchanging outward signs of loyalty for restored resources.

As crime continued to worsen throughout the 1990s, Saddam intensified efforts to maintain law and order by resorting to increasingly harsh, punitive measures.[93] This trend of escalating punishments reached a climax in 1994, when the Regional Command Council (RCC) passed new corporal punishments, such as amputations and body mutilation, for crimes like theft and desertion from the military.[94] It was at this point that Saddam decided to introduce a new policy of collective punishment using food rations that cut off entire *families* of those accused of desertion, absenteeism, or membership in an opposition group.[95] Every relative listed on the same rations card as the individual in question would lose rations until the offender turned themselves in, was arrested, or died.[96] Punished families were also sometimes evicted from their houses and forcibly displaced to another province, far from their communities and networks of support.[97]

The goal of this new collective punishment policy was similar to the political objectives in punishing individuals: it stigmatized and punished disloyal families and marginalized them from inclusion in the national distribution of resources. In fact, it was a consistent regime policy to give rewards only to individuals, but to apply punishments to extended families, as Khoury has noted in her research on this period.[98] This policy of collective punishment represented yet another effort by Saddam to refashion Iraqi family structures in order to assert himself as the ultimate patriarch. By coupling the punishment of cut rations to the threat of eviction and displacement, this policy of collective punishment sought to sever social bonds not only within the family, but also within neighborhoods and communities, striving to create social atomization that lessened the likelihood of mass opposition to Saddam's rule. The extent of the regime's efforts to insert itself into the most important pillar of society, the family, illustrates that Saddam believed a certain amount of social destabilization and fragmentation worked in his favor. By trying to turn Iraqis against each other, he might prevent them from joining together to turn against him. The regime did not always succeed in rupturing kinship bonds, of course, but these policies subjected Iraqi families to intense pressure and uncertainty, as those accused of desertion or absenteeism were left to wonder whether their families would disown them and leave them to fend for themselves in Saddam's capricious and cruel justice system.

Letters, petitions, and memos from the Ba'th Party archives illustrate how collective punishment policies put tremendous strain on Iraqi families that were forced to choose between protecting their accused relative and suffering together or betraying that individual in order to restore food rations to the rest of the family. Families of deserters, absentee public employees, or opposition group members who found themselves cut off from rations under this new policy had a bleak array of choices for how to respond.

Simply complaining about the punishment was rarely successful—one had to demonstrate their loyalty to the regime or prove that the punishment was wrongly applied in order to persuade an official to restore rations. A Baghdad resident named 'Abdullah* erupted violently when he discovered his whole family was cut off from their rations because his son was absent from his public-sector job without official permission. 'Abdullah tore up his rations card in anger, shouted at the officials, and threw the scraps of his rations card at them before storming out. In writing up the incident, the local party officials noted that 'Abdullah was an agent of the Ministry of Trade and that his "strange behavior" was "unbecoming" of his position, giving "an impression that he did not respect the government's instructions nor those who carry out their responsibilities." Not only did 'Abdullah and his whole family lose their rations over his son's behavior, but 'Abdullah likely lost his job after his tirade.[99]

Similarly, families rarely succeeded in having their rations restored by trying to distance themselves from other relatives listed on their rations card. Husayn* from Saddam City wrote a petition to the party secretariat to explain that he and his son, who had deserted from the military, were estranged. During one especially heated family fight, "shots were fired," and his son fled the house and never returned. Sometime later, Husayn's son deserted from his position as an army officer, but his family had been out of touch with him ever since their argument and Husayn had no idea where he had gone. Husayn pleaded: "Just sir, I am an old man, I have a big family, and I am too old to work. I do not know the fate of my son, and I am suffering in difficult circumstances," and asked for his rations to be restored. Husayn's local party branch also advocated on his behalf, recommending restoring rations to his family on account of the "difficulties" of his living conditions and the "commitment" of his family to the party. The Ministry of Trade ultimately denied their request, citing strict rules: until Husayn's son was apprehended, his family's rations would not be restored.[100]

Likewise, Nada*, a widow from the ʿAmil neighborhood in southwest Baghdad, tried to distance herself from the possible misdeeds of an estranged relative. After her husband's death, her husband's adult son from a previous marriage had gone abroad to Iran, and regime officials suspected that he had done so to avoid army service. Though Nada's husband was dead and she had no relationship or communication with his adult son whatsoever, they were still listed on the same rations card and their fates, therefore, were linked in the eyes of the regime. She advocated to have her own rations restored and her stepson's name removed from her card. However, the party's decision ultimately would be based on its investigations into the circumstances of her stepson's travels: if he had fled as a deserter, then Nada's whole family would lose their rations regardless of how distant her connection to her stepson might be.[101]

Sometimes families could mount a more persuasive challenge if they could prove that collective punishment had been incorrectly applied to them based on the regime's own rules. One frequent point of confusion among bureaucrats and party officials was whether families should be punished if their family members fled abroad illegally. Unauthorized emigration was widespread during the years of sanctions as Iraqis sought better living conditions elsewhere, and as many as 4 million Iraqis lived abroad by 2003 despite travel bans.[102] Many regime officials incorrectly began to cut off rations to families that had relatives abroad without authorization, though this population was not a stated target of the collective punishment policy (as long as people weren't fleeing abroad just to avoid military service, as in the case of Nada's stepson). The Office of the Party Secretariat was forced to send numerous memos instructing bureaucrats to stop targeting families with relatives abroad for collective punishment through rations, but complaints about this policy being misapplied persisted for years.[103]

For example, a woman named Rana* from the Jihad neighborhood in western Baghdad tersely explained in a petition to the party secretariat that it had erred in cutting off her family's rations. Her rations agent had informed her that her family's rations had been stopped because her son was illegally abroad in Jordan. However, Rana was evidently well informed about regime policies, and even cited relevant decrees according to their exact date and memo number. (In fact, the formatting of her letter closely resembles an official party or governmental document, so it is quite possible that Rana or one of her family members was a Ba'th Party official or state bureaucrat, though she doesn't say so in her letter.) Rana stated that she knew that unauthorized emigration was not a valid reason for cutting off a family's rations. Furthermore, her son was in Jordan with official permission from the government: he had traveled on an Iraqi passport, had already completed his military service in Iraq, and had received permission for his travel from the neighborhood *mukhtar* and local party officials. Rana ended her letter by reminding the party secretariat that she was a good Iraqi citizen who was suffering under sanctions just like everyone else. Wrongfully cutting off her rations was "a moral affront even more than it was a material punishment."[104]

In a similar petition, a woman named Muna* complained that the party had unjustifiably punished her family because her son was studying medicine in Pakistan. She insisted that he was authorized to do so, and further pointed out that his studies were intended to "serve almighty Iraq" once he returned.[105] For both Rana and Muna, their petitions were left up to their local party branch officials to decide, and the outcomes were not recorded in the archives.

Party members could expect some preferential treatment from the regime when it came to this collective punishment policy. A particularly awkward scenario arose for a party member, Samir*, whose son deserted from his post with the police. Even though Samir had a mid-level party rank of "Active Member," rations to his entire family were cut off in accordance with standard policy. Samir wrote two separate petitions insisting that his son had left the house a year earlier and that he had no knowledge of his whereabouts. Samir suggested a compromise solution: that his son's name simply be removed from his rations card, leaving his family's rations otherwise intact. Even though party officials had refused to grant this kind of exception to others, the Office of the Party Secretariat accepted his request, revealing some privileges Ba'thists could hope to enjoy even when their family members contravened regime policy.¹⁰⁶

Families whose relatives truly were guilty of an infraction faced the most difficult decisions, weighing the impossible choice of whether to turn over their own family member or to suffer without rations. Some families ultimately determined that it was better to sacrifice one person to save the rest of the family. One family had their rations cut off after the son, Haidar*, deserted from the army. Even worse, the whole family was subsequently evicted from their home and forced into exile in Diyala province. Haidar's father finally made the excruciating choice to turn over his own son to the authorities. In response, the family's local party branch allowed them to return to their original home a few weeks later with their full rations restored.¹⁰⁷

The archives tell the story of another Baghdad family that made a similarly difficult choice. The entire family's rations had been cut off because one young man, Ibrahim*, had deserted from the army in 1993 and had remained in hiding for two years. Ibrahim's family was already in a difficult financial situation because his father was absent. Perhaps it was the family's poverty that finally pushed Ibrahim's cousin, Amal*, to tell the authorities about his hiding place and have Ibrahim arrested. Her party branch recommended that the rest of the family's rations be restored to reward Amal's loyalty to the regime.¹⁰⁸

Disavowing family members was an excruciating survival strategy, one that many Baghdadi families were forced to consider in the doubly oppressive context of severe international sanctions and Saddam's decision to engage in collective punishment. Saddam's policies that encouraged family members to betray one another were a form of moral and psychological violence on Baghdadi society that threatened to fray the most important kinship bonds that connected Iraqis to one another.

In the cases related here, Baghdadis adopted a variety of strategies to protest and petition when their rations were cut off: pleading for mercy, disowning errant family members, complaining about wrongfully applied policies, or cooperating with the regime. However, none of these strategies was guaranteed to work. Cruelly, this was true even when families chose to cooperate fully with the regime and turned over their own family members to the police. In May 1995, the Rashid party branch in Baghdad forwarded to the party secretariat a list of deserters who had been arrested with the help of their own families. The Rashid branch requested that the party secretariat restore the families' rations because of their cooperation. The party secretariat wrote back to correct the Rashid branch about its mistaken protocols and assumptions: families of deserters would have their rations restored only after a close examination of their cases. Simply writing "cooperated" next to the family's name and address would not suffice.[109]

As the following section explores, one of the most important factors for ensuring a favorable outcome was advocacy by a Baʿth Party official from the family's own neighborhood, highlighting the increasingly influential role that local authorities played in day-to-day governance decisions in sanctions-era Baghdad.

Influence of Local Authorities

Local authorities, including neighborhood *firqa, shuʿba,* and district-level party officials and the government-appointed neighborhood *mukhtar,* played pivotal roles in helping citizens in their jurisdictions to appeal for relief of their punishments or to rectify errors with their rations. In many cases, the decision of whether or not to restore rations to a particular family was left up to neighborhood and district office party leaders, rather than being decided by the Ministry of Trade or another senior official in the regime. This delegation of decision-making authority to local party officials was illustrated in the cases of Rana and Muna, described in the preceding section.

In a few extreme cases, local authorities were even willing to break the law in order to help out a family in need. In June 1995, a neighborhood *mukhtar* heard that the family of a deserter was about to be forced out of their home and exiled to another province as punishment. He was able to warn the family in advance, and they fled to an "unknown location"—likely outside the country—before the police arrived.[110] The fate of that *mukhtar* is unknown, but another *mukhtar* was fired from his post because his own son had deserted from the army and he did not turn his son over to the regime.[111] Interviewees confirmed the high stakes for *mukhtars* who risked contravening official orders. As a fifty-eight-year-old woman from Sadr City explained: "The *mukhtar* was responsible for any problem in the area. He was responsible to report to the regime about young men who didn't report to military service or who fled. If he didn't report that, they would arrest the *mukhtar*."¹¹² *Mukhtars* who were willing to bend the rules behind the backs of the regime faced severe consequences, and accordingly, these cases appear only rarely in the archives.

The most influential form of advocacy took place when lower ranking party officials asked their supervisors for special exceptions to be made for residents in their jurisdictions. Baghdadis understood this and tried to leverage the support of their local officials whenever possible; many petitions included letters of reference from local *mukhtars*, for example, in an effort to influence the outcome of their requests. In June 1995, the Saddam City branch in Baghdad sent the party secretariat five pages listing names of deserters who had been arrested. Next to the name of one family, the Saddam City branch officials wrote, "The family cooperated and we recommend not forcibly displacing them and not cutting their rations." Next to another name, the branch officials noted that the "family is poor," and for that reason alone they recommended not displacing them or cutting their rations.¹¹³ In another case, branch officials advocated for reprieve for a family of a deserter on humanitarian grounds, citing the family's poverty and the fact that they had no real resources to support themselves. Even though this family had also written an appeal to the party secretariat, it was the party branch officials who made the final decision to exempt this family from punishment for humanitarian reasons.¹¹⁴

Pleas to exempt families for humanitarian reasons were not always accepted, however, even with the intervention of local officials. To give a contrasting example: a party member named Mahmud* asked that his family's rations be restored, even though his son had deserted from the army. The local party branch wrote a memo supporting Mahmud's request because he lived in "very difficult circumstances" and was a "party comrade." Despite their advocacy, the Ministry of Trade denied the request with a handwritten note in the margins saying there was "no precedent" for making that kind of exception (though that was not strictly true, as the example of Samir attests).¹¹⁵

One particularly heart-wrenching petition demonstrates that Baghdadis were well aware that their local Baʿth Party officials could play important roles as advocates for their cases. Because this letter encapsulates many of the themes of this chapter, I quote it here in its entirety (removing personal details to protect anonymity):

> My son ʿAmr* volunteered as a soldier at... a military base.... He suffers from diabetes and from a severe mental illness.... I did not know about his desertion [from the military] until I heard about it directly from the commander of his base, because ʿAmr had left our house to some unknown location and I had not seen him since.
>
> Quickly, I informed the top official of our neighborhood Baʿth Party office [*firqa*] that my son had deserted, and he requested that I report my son's whereabouts whenever I learn where he is.... When my son arrived at my house, I reported him, even though he was in an afflicted psychological state at the time. I turned him over to the party. He was held at the... police station... and after two weeks, I learned that he had been transferred... to his military unit at the... base.
>
> They considered him as "arrested" [i.e., they did not treat him as if he had been turned in voluntarily], so I contacted the top official in our neighborhood Baʿth Party office again and requested that he photocopy the document stating that it was I, his father, who turned him in.
>
> I didn't receive a response, so I went to the next highest-ranking Baʿth Party office [*shuʿba*] in my district and explained my request word for word to the administrative director. He informed me that a document had been issued from the party attesting that I, his father, had turned over my son. [He informed me that] the party had decided only to flog him, and that the party would not execute him, cut off his ear, or cut off the family's rations due to the father's cooperation and the fact that he was now back with his unit in good standing. However, the rations are still cut off. This document... was sent to the party secretariat on November 13, 1994. This is what I heard and what I read in the document issued at that time.
>
> After a while, I heard that an investigative committee had been formed [to consider my son's case] and they determined that he had been "arrested" [not voluntarily returned]. They sent him to a military court and there they ruled that he would have his ear cut off on February 19, 1995.... He is still in prison awaiting the sentence.
>
> Here I am submitting the party document that decided he would only be flogged... on account of the fact that it was his father who turned him in.
>
> I have three sons who participated in the Glorious Qadisiyyat Saddam [the Iran-Iraq War]. Of them, one was awarded a medal of bravery, and another was wounded in the Mother of All Battles [the Gulf War] more than once. I plead with you, sir, from the heart of an anguished father, please open a door of hope...[116]

The local *shuʿba* office of the Baʿth Party sent a memo along with his petition that confirmed the father's version of the events and advocated that the family "not be evicted and not have their rations cut off" because the father was "exceptional" in his cooperation with the party.¹¹⁷

This petition illustrates both the possibilities and the limitations of relying on local Baʿth Party officials as intermediaries. On the one hand, ʿAmr's father displayed a savvy shrewdness in how he approached both his local *firqa* and *shuʿba* officials to document his cooperation with the regime. These local authorities responded favorably to his request, advocating for leniency for his family. Their advocacy was influential: the party secretariat agreed with their recommendation and ruled on March 22, 1995, that the family would not face consequences for the son's desertion.¹¹⁸

However, while their appeals on his behalf ultimately provided relief for the father and his remaining children in restoring their rations, the gears of the bureaucracy moved too slowly to spare his deserter son from imprisonment and suffering: the ruling by the party secretariat came four months after the father's local officials documented his cooperation and a month after the son's ear was scheduled to be amputated as punishment. For all the support of his *firqa* and *shuʿba* office, it was likely too late for his son to escape this disfiguring punishment. Local Baʿth Party officials were imperfect advocates, but they were often the only authorities who could meaningfully intervene in the hope of rectifying a dire situation.

In other cases, interference from malicious Baʿth Party officials hurt the chances of Baghdadis' pleas and petitions for help. Local authorities could obstruct justice: a father from the Salam neighborhood of Baghdad, ʿAbd al-ʿAziz*, ran into serious conflicts with his neighborhood party officials. Pointedly, he sent his petition to the party secretariat through the regular mail, rather than through the usual method of bringing petitions to the *firqa* office, to make sure his local party office did not see his letter first. ʿAbd al-ʿAziz's son had previously deserted from the army, but ʿAbd al-ʿAziz had turned him over to the authorities himself and his son had returned to his unit. However, when his son was off the base on official duties one month later, the local party officials wrongfully arrested him as a deserter. ʿAbd al-ʿAziz rushed around in a frenzy to collect documentation from his son's military unit attesting to his regular status to prove that he had not deserted. He tried for days to arrange a meeting with the director of the local party office, but he was repeatedly rebuffed. After five days of frantic efforts, a representative from the party knocked on ʿAbd al-ʿAziz's door and informed him that his son's ear had been cut off as punishment for his alleged desertion, the paperwork from his son's commander evidently having been delayed. In addition, the party was still threatening to evict the family from their home and to cut off their rations. ʿAbd al-ʿAziz wrote his desperate plea to the Office of the Party Secretariat to rectify the situation.[119]

When the office of the party secretariat began an inquiry into the situation, officials from the Baghdad party branch overseeing ʿAbd al-ʿAziz's district defended the Baʿth Party officials in the offices below them. They alleged that the son's paperwork confirming his regular status in the military might have been forged, and they denigrated the father, stating that his testimony was unreliable because he had a "questionable character" and was known for harassing young schoolgirls in the neighborhood.[120] The party secretariat left the final decision about this family's fate up to the office of the party branch—the same office that had maligned ʿAbd al-ʿAziz's reputation. Though the archives do not record the final outcome, it is unlikely that ʿAbd al-ʿAziz or his family received respite from their problems, and his son had already suffered the mutilation of his ear.[121]

The examples given here illustrate the influential role local authorities could play in determining the outcome of individual cases, whether positive or negative. However, lower ranking party officials could be influential advocates on a larger scale, too: they sometimes advocated for changes in the policies themselves. Though these examples of lower ranking officials suggesting policy changes are rare within the larger context of the Baʿth Party archives, their existence has important consequences for understanding how decision-making took place within Iraq's government during the sanctions period.

Earlier scholarship on Saddam's presidency tended to emphasize how he governed by inculcating fear; Saddam would not tolerate dissent or criticism. One scholar asserted that "in Saddam's Iraq there was no way . . . [to] discreetly report some Iraqis' negative views of the president."[122] A 2004 CIA report characterized Saddam's leadership by stating that "subordinates . . . could [not] contradict [Saddam's] goals, power or his judgment."[123] This viewpoint certainly has some basis in truth, as anyone who has seen the chilling televised footage of Saddam purging Baʿth Party members in

July 1979 could attest.[124] However, this is an incomplete view of Saddam, as recent scholarship using the Baʻth Party archives has demonstrated. Even during the final years of his presidency, there were opportunities to offer critical points of view and challenge some existing policies.

Sometimes, for example, local Baʻth Party offices initiated "listening sessions" with residents in their neighborhoods in the 1990s. A few comrades from a Baʻth Party cell held one such listening session in a coffee shop in ʻAdhamiyya in February 1992 to hear how sanctions were affecting locals' lives. On the surface, a listening session is a strange sort of an initiative for an undemocratic regime, and it was almost certainly intended to ferret out useful intelligence for the regime. This provided a "safe" environment for the public to vent their frustrations, rather than waiting for grievances to boil over into public protests. Officials at this meeting took careful notes about the questions and complaints that these Baghdadis raised during the meeting, some of which were quite pointed, and forwarded them to their superiors. For example, residents at this meeting complained loudly about the increased price of food during sanctions and about the poor condition of their streets, which became completely impassable during winter rains. They accused their local rations agent of manipulating prices and skimping on their shares of food.[125] Though these topics were not overtly political, the residents at the meeting strongly implied that the government was not adequately doing its job to take care of them and maintain good order in their neighborhoods.

More extraordinary are cases of local Baʻth Party officials voicing their own criticism of official regime policies and suggesting changes. Rather than harshly rebuking these party officials for insubordination, incredibly, the president sometimes accepted these recommendations and implemented them.

In 1995, local party leaders began to advocate for changes in how, when, and why the regime cut food rations to certain groups. For example, party leaders in Karbala and Babil provinces presented a list of complaints they had received during interviews with citizens in their areas about the logic of collective punishment. The policy of cutting off rations to entire families, they said, unfairly blamed whole groups of people for the errant behavior of one member but did not conversely reward the entire family for the especially good behavior of one person.[126] The desertion of one young man from the army could ruin a family that nevertheless had produced veterans and martyrs who had won medals of distinction and bravery, and other "exceptional children" who were loyal to the regime.[127] Collective punishment threatened to alienate these supporters of the regime and turn them against it. These provincial party leaders called for a change in the regime's use of collective punishment for families of deserters, and recommended that the party adopt a more holistic assessment of whether a given family was "loyal to the party and the revolution" by looking at the actions of all the family members and not just focusing on one bad element.[128] In response, the party secretariat asked those provincial party leaders for a list of specific families that fit this description of having their rations cut despite their otherwise exceptional credentials of loyalty to the party.[129]

Just two months later, in November 1995, party officials from Maysan and Wasit provinces sent a bold list of policy recommendations that further critiqued the implementation of the collective punishment policy. In succinct bullet points, they argued that families should have their rations restored if they met any of the following conditions:

1. If the family was otherwise in good standing with the regime and had demonstrated their loyalty to the party
2. If any immediate family member had received a medal in the Iran-Iraq War or Gulf War
3. If any family member had been martyred in the Iran-Iraq War or Gulf War
4. If any family member had received commendation for fulfilling his or her national duty, whether in the Gulf War or otherwise.[130]

In these recommendations, provincial party leaders in Maysan and Wasit echoed the critiques that other provincial leaders had also made: the policy of collective punishment was alienating families that otherwise outwardly supported the regime.

Remarkably, Saddam began to introduce changes to the rations policy a short while later, in February 1996. At that time, the Office of the President clarified the conditions that could be met in order to restore rations to the families of deserters or absentee employees, to minimize confusion and relax certain rules. For example, if a woman divorced her deserter husband

and maintained custody of her children, she and her children would continue to receive rations. It clarified that presenting the death certificate of a deserter was sufficient for the restoration of rations, that soldiers who went missing in action during the 1991 *intifada* would not be regarded as deserters, and that their families would continue to receive rations.[131]

Then, on June 8, 1996, the policy of collective punishment was abruptly dropped altogether when Saddam issued a decree ordering that rations be restored to all of the families that had been cut off as a form of collective punishment.[132] Rations would still be cut off to individual offenders, as Saddam clarified in a follow-up decree a few days later, but rations would never again be used as a form of collective punishment against entire families for the remainder of the Ba'thist regime.[133] In fact, when some families were collectively cut off from rations later that fall as punishment for their relatives' desertion from the army, the Ministry of Trade scolded the responsible officials for contravening presidential orders.[134]

Why did Saddam abruptly end this policy of collective punishment? From the outside, the most obvious factor is the signing of the Oil-for-Food agreement, which relieved financial pressure on the regime and helped guarantee its survival. The Oil-for-Food agreement was the single most decisive shift in external political factors facing the regime between the imposition of the sanctions in 1990 and the overthrow of the regime in 2003. With the promise of new resources and revenue streams, the regime could return to its usual policy of balancing "sticks" with "carrots" to win over the population with promises of aid and services. It no longer had to resort to an unpopular policy of collective punishment through food rations. The timing is highly suggestive: on May 20, 1996, Iraq signed the Memorandum of Understanding to implement the Oil-for-Food Program according to UN resolution no. 986. Two weeks later, on June 8, 1996, Saddam revoked the policy of collective punishment through rations. The regime could only consider relaxing its restrictions on food rations once it was guaranteed easier access to food imports.

Within the internal documents of the Ba'th Party, however, changes to this policy were framed as the outcome of bottom-up initiatives by both ordinary Iraqi citizens and the lower ranking branch party officials who had advocated for these reforms. Saddam cited three factors in justifying his change in policy. First, he pointed to the results of the national referendum in October 1995, in which Saddam allegedly won 99 percent of the vote, that demonstrated the "love and loyalty" of Iraqis for Saddam.[135] With Iraqis' loyalty confirmed, Saddam argued that he no longer needed to impose such harsh punishments. Second, Saddam cited citizens' complaints about the unfairness of collective punishment. Finally, he pointed to the advocacy of party officials to change the policy, painting himself as a responsive and fair-minded leader.[136] Saddam's memo made no mention of the Oil-for-Food Program. It was a convenient narrative that avoided the less flattering truth that Saddam's political survival was tied to his agreement with the United Nations. His posture also encouraged information to continue traveling up the channels of the Baʿth Party apparatus, which could provide useful intelligence for him.

Conclusion

Domestically, the reputation of the Baʿth Party was severely damaged by its disastrous defeat in Kuwait and by the 1991 uprising that challenged Saddam's control over the country. The United Nations economic embargo, combined with the massive damage inflicted on the country's infrastructure by the US bombing campaign in Baghdad during the Gulf War, threatened the state's ability to keep basic services running in the capital. Though helicopter gunships had worked with brutal efficiency to end open rebellion in southern Iraq, Saddam could not hope to reconsolidate his control over Iraq without providing electricity, clean water, and basic food. Among themselves, Iraq's leaders were frank about the challenges they faced. Al-Duri confessed in a closed-door leadership meeting in December 1991, "We almost lost the Baʿth Party for good; we did not have even a one in a million chance," after the Gulf War and *intifada*. Al-Duri asked Saddam, "Are we not supposed to be fighting the sanctions? Where is our plan? We have to stop this disaster immediately, because the sanctions are killing us. We have to boost the morale of our people and stop the negative results of the sanctions."[137]

In response to these challenges, the Baʿth Party hoped to use food rations to shore up tacit support and increase the dependence of Iraqis on the regime for their physical survival. To a considerable extent, the regime succeeded: these critical food supplies provided the majority of monthly calories for most Iraqi families. At the same time, Saddam was adept at using the rations coercively to reward "good" citizens and to punish disloyal Iraqis and their families. Though this policy of collective punishment was only in place from 1994 to 1996, it illustrates the extent to which Saddam attempted to disrupt social solidarity and kinship bonds by pushing for loyalty to the regime above all else. This collective punishment policy was an effort to prevent Iraqis from rising up again during a period of political and economic weakness for the regime.

The logistical success of the Iraqi rationing system was due to the efficacy and relative reliability of the monthly food distributions, which maintained the appearance of effective state power in the face of sanctions. This was only possible because the regime was able to mobilize existing neighborhood-level institutions, and even grocers, to carry out its work. The heightened role of neighborhood-level officials, including rations agents, *mukhtars*, Popular Committees, and local party offices, enabled the continued functionality of the regime despite the government's weakened state in the early 1990s. But these local authorities were not simply the pawns of the regime: they often decided the outcomes of their residents' requests and even pushed back on the regime's unpopular policy of collective punishment through rations. Looking into the food rationing system in practice demonstrates that the president was not always smoothly directing policies from above; government ministries, local authorities, lower ranking party officials, and even ordinary citizens could influence how policies were interpreted, enforced, and received.

FOUR

The Politics of Petitions

"I AM THE CITIZEN . . ." So begin the thousands of letters that were written by everyday Iraqis to representatives in Saddam's government, beseeching officials for financial assistance or reprieve from punishment: "I am the citizen Hibba," "I am the citizen ʿAlaa," "I am the citizen Salwa." With this formulaic introduction, Iraqis undertook a bold political act by requesting, or sometimes even demanding, resources and resolutions from the regime. Though many would say that people living within a dictatorial system operate as political *subjects*, and not as *citizens* with rights, Baghdadis of all walks of life articulated a strong belief in a social contract in which the government was responsible for Iraqis' basic necessities and for upholding justice.

The purpose of this chapter is to delve more deeply into petitioning as a political act. Focusing here on a sample of letters written by residents of Baghdad from the 1980s until the early 2000s, it becomes possible to hear how Iraqis represented themselves to the government, how they understood their place within the national and local political power structures, what kinds of requests they made, and which ones were granted.[1] Bureaucratic processes for handling petitions changed in the year 2000, which provides a glimpse into the shifting power dynamics within the state and party bureaucracies in the final years of Saddam's regime.

Why Write Petitions?

The period of Saddam's presidency (1979–2003) was marked by chronic instability. In the midst of these hardships that began with the Iran-Iraq War in 1980 and continued under sanctions until 2003, many Iraqis petitioned the government to save them from financial destitution, to provide urgent medical treatment, or to plead the innocence of a relative who was wrongfully accused of a crime. Many Iraqis turned to the government for help during sanctions because they were no longer able to rely on their own means to support themselves and their families.

A letter from a soldier's wife, Fatima*, is one of the many petitions that rose to the attention of Ba'th Party officials in the aftermath of the Iran-Iraq War (1980–88). Though the ceasefire between Iraq and Iran had already been concluded, Fatima's husband was still on active duty—a common, if exasperating, fate for many soldiers in 1988 and 1989 because the regime feared the potentially destabilizing effects of demobilizing its forces too quickly (see chapter 5).[2] Fatima made a plaintive case for Ba'th Party officials to provide financial assistance to ease her family's impoverishment brought on by her husband's absence: "I am the citizen Fatima, mother to ten children under the age of fourteen, with the youngest one just one month old. . . . My husband is completing his military service, and we don't have anyone else to provide for us. . . . We live on his salary of just 87 dinars, and all of it goes to paying the landlord."[3] Her husband had evidently had some kind of dispute with their landlord, and the landlord was now threatening to evict the entire family. She ended her letter with an imploring question—"Where will my children go?"—before asking 'Izzat Ibrahim al-Duri to assist her family "as able."[4] As the vice chair of the Ba'th Party Revolutionary Command Council, al-Duri's ability to help was not in doubt. But why should the nation's top leaders intervene in such a mundane matter?

Her appeal turned out to be a successful strategy, at least this time. The local Baghdad Ba'th Party officials looking into her case agreed that the party would provide her with a monthly cash stipend and guarantee her housing until her husband returned from military service.[5] The responsible officials were even scolded twice by their superiors for their slow response time to her request, showing that the regime took seriously its responsibility to respond to these kinds of petitions.⁶

Though not all petitions were favorably answered—a topic I will return to below—Baghdadis like Fatima could reasonably hope that Baʿth Party officials would provide special assistance to those who asked. One reason why many Baghdadis sent their requests to the country's top leaders was because of the example that Saddam set early in his presidency. He frequently televised his meetings with ordinary citizens, broadcasting his liberal distribution of cash, housing, and even household appliances to people who brought their requests to the president.⁷ One scholar likened a meeting with Saddam to "winning the lottery," since every person who met with the president was sure to receive some kind of gift or assistance.⁸ Saddam well understood the potent political symbolism embedded in this ritual, which echoed the regular Friday meetings held between Ottoman sultans and their subjects.⁹ It was a popular public relations stunt designed to endear Saddam to the population and to cement his cult of personality as the generous patriarch of the country.¹⁰

For example, the archives preserve the story of a well-connected Baʿth Party official, Muhammad*, who was a high-ranking leader of one of the Baʿth Party branches in Baghdad. He had evidently already earned Saddam's favor, because his file noted that he had previously received a house in Baghdad and some agricultural land "as a gift" from the president.¹¹ Muhammad wrote a letter to the Baʿth Party requesting a personal meeting with Saddam, asking to explain his circumstances of "personal suffering" to the leader.¹² Saddam agreed to meet with him. Though we do not know what took place during that meeting, Saddam wrote him afterward to document the outcome: Muhammad received permission and state funding for his wife and daughter to receive medical treatment in the United States, and Saddam additionally gave him a new Oldsmobile car.¹³ For some, it paid to bring requests to the president's attention.

However, the case of Muhammad is perhaps more indicative of how party insiders benefitted from Saddam's largesse. As one party member wrote in his own petition: "I have no connections except God and the party."¹⁴ But the popularity of Saddam's daily meetings with ordinary citizens was based precisely on the fact that even those who did not already enjoy chummy insider status with the president could hope to cash in on his displays of benevolence. A more typical kind of publicity event can be seen in the story of a widow, Layla*, who met with the president in 1991. This meeting took place shortly after her husband was killed defending the regime during the popular uprisings of that year. We can presume that Saddam's decision to meet with her was part of his strategy to reward loyalists. During their meeting, the president promised Layla a house that would be registered in the names of her eight young children to provide them with financial stability for years to come.[15]

Not every letter sent from a citizen to regime officials is a petition: my analysis here focuses on letters that included an explicit request for some kind of aid or assistance. Within the archives, though, Ba'th Party officials also preserved sycophantic letters that had no other stated objective than heaping praises on Saddam Hussein and swearing fidelity to the regime, sometimes in macabre ways. One routine display of commitment to the Ba'thist regime entailed sending oaths of loyalty to Saddam written in the individual's own blood, a ritual that had its origin in the 1982 referendum of Saddam's rule (see chapter 2).[16] Blood oaths became routine performances in Saddam's Iraq from the 1980s onward: a newspaper clipping from 1993 showcased a poet who wrote a love poem to Saddam with his own blood, for example.[17] The officials who received these blood-inked letters dutifully dispatched memos acknowledging their receipt and forwarded them to the president, a seemingly unremarkable event in the day of an Iraqi bureaucrat.[18] Other Baghdadis were more original with their displays of loyalty to the Ba'thist regime: one man offered to donate his internal organs if any party leader needed a transplant, out of his "great love for our party, its historic destiny, and its inspired leader."[19] Another man sent a letter explaining that he had given his own children the names of Saddam's children—'Uday, Qusay, Rana, Raghad, Hala—as a sign of his devotion to his "beloved leader."[20]

Such exaggerated professions of devotion are not unique to the Iraqi context; they are observed in many other authoritarian settings, especially where there is a strong cult of personality around the dictator.[21] Scholars have referred to such acts as "gesture politics" by which citizens signal their political allegiances.[22] Though these letters did not include an explicit request for something from the state, their unstated objective was surely to bolster the individual's standing with the regime.

Who Writes Petitions?

Petitioners represent a peculiar group within society: they are vulnerable enough to have special needs, yet trusting enough in the government to willingly identify themselves to the state. What is striking about this collection of petitions is that we see a broad swath of the population readily approaching the Baʻthist regime with demands and requests; petitioning was not an activity that was safe only for regime insiders or elites. Baghdadi petitioners were an economically diverse group of people: many petitioners referenced their poverty and asked for financial assistance, while others were clearly well off but still required government intervention into some kind of problem. The vast majority of these petitioners were not party members but political independents who nevertheless felt secure enough in their standing with the regime to invite its scrutiny of their lives. Petitioners exhibited a range of educational levels: some of their letters were nicely typed with sophisticated rhetorical flourishes, while others were scrawled by hand and riddled with grammatical errors. Still others were signed with a thumbprint, indicating that the petitioner was illiterate and had someone's help in crafting their letter.[23] Women and men wrote petitions in nearly equal numbers in this archival sample.

A final word of explanation is required about Iraqi petitions, as the word "petition" may bring to mind a widely circulated document with many signatures. Iraqi petitions, in contrast, were privately written documents, signed only by the letter's author in all but a small handful of instances. This tendency for Baghdadis to write individual petitions is not unprecedented: a similar trend existed for petitions written in the Soviet Union, and it is an important indication of how dictatorships actively work to atomize society.[24] Terrified of mass movements, the Baʻthist regime had long sown mistrust between Iraqis by encouraging neighbors and family members to inform on one another, peppering even tight-knit social circles with informants.[25] For this reason, most Baghdadis judged that it was safer to write private, individual letters to the regime rather than risk any appearance of collective mobilization.[26] The exceptions prove the rule: I found only eight petitions that had multiple signatories, with the largest containing only twenty signatures. One group petition was from female medical students working in a military hospital who complained that they were not receiving the same pay and benefits as male medical students there. Another was written by four seamstresses who grumbled about the rising price of sewing machines.[27] Another example, discussed in chapter 5, is a complaint signed by seven neighbors about prostitution in their area.[28] These collective complaints were safe topics about neighborhood or workplace concerns that steered clear of anything that resembled large-scale political organizing.

In sum, petitioning was available to all strata of society, so long as the individuals writing letters were on neutral or positive terms with the regime. For many, fear of Saddam's security apparatus may have outweighed the urgency of their needs, and we can imagine that there were many citizens who did not write petitions because they did not want to invite the attention of this repressive regime into their personal affairs. However, the wide swath of socioeconomic backgrounds represented in this sample shows that a broad segment of Baghdadis expected the regime to help them. As Martin Dimitrov argued in his study of communist countries, citizens only send petitions and complaints to the government when "the public trusts the central government to intervene on its behalf."[29] A large and diverse portion of the public looked to the government to provide for them during difficult times, whether their petition was a desperate act of last resort or an expression of faith in the system.

FIGURE 12   Envelope for a petition addressed to the Director General of the Ba'th Party Secretariat, 1997. Hizb al-Ba'th al-'Arabi al-Ishtiraki in Iraq [Ba'th Arab Socialist Party of Iraq] records, Hoover Institution Library & Archives. *BRCC file number withheld to protect identities.*

The Art of Petitioning a Dictator

> I place our fate between your generous hands. Your will is just, sir . . . you love goodness and to help the poor, the needy, the widows, and the orphans, and God will grant you success.
> — Petition from a widow from the ʿUbaydi neighborhood adjacent to Saddam City[30]

> The party will not be stingy in helping me.
> — Petition from a Baʿth Party member in Ghazaliyya neighborhood, home to many military officers[31]

Dictatorships are characterized in part by their efforts to control the freedom of speech, censor the media, and suppress dissenting voices through surveillance and intimidation.[32] Such practices were the norm in Baʿthist Iraq, where Saddam constrained newspapers, TV stations, and radio channels to broadcast only regime-approved narratives, and where citizens regularly self-censored their speech, fearing denunciation by informants or arrest by secret police.[33] Consequently, observers of Iraq long assumed that ordinary citizens were not permitted to engage in contentious dialogue with the regime; acceptable public speech was believed to be limited to fawning displays of loyalty to Saddam or, at most, to mild criticism about misbehavior by low-ranking officials.[34]

However, an examination of these petitions reveals that Iraqis adopted a variety of tones and postures when communicating with the regime. As the first quotation above shows, many Iraqis did include flowery praise of the leader. At the same time, a significant number of others made bold demands on the regime using the language of rights and entitlements: "the party will not be stingy in helping me."[35] Analyzing the language that Baghdadis used in their petitions gives us a more nuanced understanding of the contours of state-society communication, making clear the boundaries of what was permissible to say and what was not based on one's social position and political standing.

Petitions are both a literary genre and a distinct kind of political performance, with stable norms and scripts that are related to premodern petitioning practices used to beseech sultans.[36] As such, the voices preserved in these petitions are not "natural," but mediated by "prevailing norms, institutions, and power structures."[37] Analyzing the rhetorical strategies of Baghdad petitions reveals how ordinary people presented themselves to the state, and how the regime expected people to perform their roles as citizens.[38] This petition typifies the structure of many letters sent to the Ba'th Party; I have added headings to the original letter to highlight the usual formula used in this collection of petitions.

[Invocation]
In the name of God, the Merciful, the Compassionate

[Address and Blessing]
Mr. President, Leader and Warrior for the Faith, Saddam Hussein (may God protect and preserve him): Warm greetings.
Mr. President, the Commander:

[Exposition]
I am the citizen Zaynab*. Our mother previously provided for our family with a retirement pension from the state that was given to us after the martyrdom of our two brothers, 'Ali* and Akram*, in the Glorious Battle of Qadisiyyat Saddam [the Iran-Iraq War]. However, this pension was cut off when my mother died in 1985. After this, my third brother was also martyred in the Glorious Battle of Qadisiyyat Saddam. He was married and had one daughter. We still had two brothers remaining in military service. One of them was taken prisoner during the Pages of Treachery and Betrayal [intifada] in the North of the country during the month of Ramadan 1991. My fifth brother was released from the army. He now lives with me and our younger sister. He has been without work ever since he was released from the army. There are three of us in the family (one boy and two girls), and we live together without any means of supporting ourselves except for the mercy of God.

[Request and Motivation]
I submit my request for aid to your Excellency and ask for assistance from our father and the father of all Iraqis so that we can have resources to live on, because we have no father and no mother [and no other support] except for the one brother that lives with us, and he is without work and without a salary.
We place all of our hope and trust in your Excellency that you will not abandon a family that has given three martyrs and a prisoner of war and who is without resources and no way of supporting our lives.

[Closing]
    We send you our appreciation and our respect.
    The Citizen Zaynab

[address][39]

Zaynab accomplishes many important objectives required for a successful petition. She fluently appropriates regime jargon to signal her family's sacrifices to the regime and her loyalty to Saddam specifically. She calls Saddam by his full honorific title and invokes the required blessing of protection for his sake, uses regime terminology for Iraqi battles ("The Glorious Qadisiyyat Saddam" for the Iran-Iraq War), and refers to the combat deaths of her brothers as "martyrdom," referencing a legal category designated by the Ba'thist regime.[40] She positions Saddam as a generous patriarch ("our father and the father of all Iraqis") who, given her own orphaned status, she strongly suggests is responsible for her family.[41]

The official who received her petition appeared sympathetic to her case: he underlined in pencil the line in her letter stating that three sons in her family were martyred. He recommended to the Office of the President that Zaynab's family be granted a pension to "combat the difficulties of their life."[42] Though the specific circumstances of Zaynab's family and the high casualties they sustained make her petition unique, the format and formulae used in this petition are nearly identical to many others found in the Iraqi Ba'th Party archives.

Gendered Language

The gendered language in Zaynab's petition is also typical of many of the petitions in the archives, half of which were penned by female petitioners. Many of the women who wrote to the regime were the heads of their households as widows, divorcees, or wives of soldiers who were absent for compulsory military service. Such women were more likely to face financial difficulties, being without a second wage-earner, and therefore they may have been particularly motivated to reach out to the Ba'th Party for help.

In fact, women had some advantages in petitioning. One key criterion that the Ba'th Party used to determine whether a low-income family merited extra financial aid was based on gender. It was government policy that families could be enrolled in a financial assistance program, the Social Solidarity Funds, only if they had no male wage-earners in the family. Many Iraqi women understood this and incorporated gendered pleas to bolster their requests. One woman wrote: "My husband died and left my daughters in my care.... We are in a difficult situation and we are deprived of even the simplest needs for daily life because of our poor situation and *because we are women.*"⁴³ Similarly, a young woman wrote a letter explaining that she was the only child of two elderly parents. Her family was struggling because they had no "breadwinner." By this, she meant no *male* breadwinner, since the petitioner herself was a young adult and presumably able to work.⁴⁴ Both women's petitions were approved.

Though women and men petitioned the regime for all the same kinds of requests and wrote in nearly equal numbers, petitioners tended to frame their requests differently according to the traditional family gender roles idealized by the Baʻth Party in the late 1980s and 1990s. Men utilized patriarchal language by speaking "from the heart of a father" to another (Saddam).⁴⁵ An active duty soldier wrote a letter to al-Duri for financial aid for his two wives and fourteen children while he was away. He wrote that al-Duri was a "tender" and "most praise-worthy father," which is why he should understand this soldier's plight.⁴⁶ In contrast, women often placed themselves under the protection of Saddam's "fatherly sympathy."⁴⁷ One widow wrote in her petition: "for you, your Excellency, are yes, the brother and yes, the father, and yes, the appointed one, after God Almighty."⁴⁸ This patriarchal language fit with Saddam's own cult of personality, which positioned him as a "father of the nation."⁴⁹ These gendered postures that men and women used in their petitions matched the regime's shift in the late 1980s and 1990s toward traditional gender roles, away from the outwardly progressive state feminism the Baʻth Party had championed in the 1970s (see chapter 5).⁵⁰

Supplicants and Citizens

Petitions typically adopted one of two tones toward the regime. Borrowing from Sheila Fitzpatrick's typology of petitions in Soviet Russia, most Iraqi petitioners presented themselves either as a "supplicant" or as a "citizen."⁵¹ Two brief examples illustrate the difference in these rhetorical approaches. The first exemplifies the "supplicant" approach: "All my hope is in God, and then my hope is in your Excellency, that you will not turn me away empty-handed. . . . My husband has abandoned me because my children have an incurable illness. . . . Do not forget me, your Excellency vice-chairman. . . . I ask for sympathy and compassion from God and from your Excellency."⁵²

Supplicants tend to present themselves as downtrodden by circumstances out of their control. Their dominant traits are their destitution and their loyalty; the suffering they experienced was often in spite of their contributions to the glory of the nation and its leader. They typically asked for aid, be it for monthly financial assistance, help with housing, extra food supplies, or a medical procedure they couldn't afford. The petitioner quoted here can be considered a supplicant from the way that she asked for charity based on the difficulties of her personal circumstances. Crucially, she included many flattering phrases and honorifics, even nearly equating the regime official with God ("All my hope is in God, and then my hope is in your Excellency").

In contrast, some Baghdadis wrote their petitions using a "citizen" approach. In this example, a party member chastises the regime for failing to intervene sooner: "I am 'Umar*, a Ba'th Party member with the rank of 'advanced supporter,' and I have written to the party more than once to explain my health situation. I suffer from kidney failure, and I need a kidney transplant surgery because my life is in danger.... I have given enough to the party throughout my career as a comrade, and I have been in the party ranks for nearly twenty-four years.... I request that the party... pay for the surgery, at the very least."[53] "Citizen" petitioners do not ask for charity; they make demands of the regime using the language of rights and entitlements. Rather than showing deference, he strongly implied that the government owed him for his years of service. It was he who, elsewhere in his letter, issued the thinly veiled threat quoted earlier: "the party will not be stingy in helping me."[54]

Both kinds of petitions often included heart-wrenching details, though differently framed: "supplicants" emphasized their misery and helplessness, while "citizens" highlighted the unjust harm caused to them by a wrongfully applied policy. "Supplicants" tended to lavish the addressee with praise; "citizens" tended to dole out expressions of flattery more sparingly, relying on the correctness of their argument rather than their ability to sway the addressee with adulation.

Another remarkable example of a "citizen" approach comes from Sumaya*. Her husband had been murdered by "criminal elements from Iran"—a likely reference to members of the underground Da'wa Party—because he was a leader in charge of a local Ba'th Party office in Baghdad. Suspects were arrested and executed, but Sumaya complained bitterly that the Ba'th Party had not taken care of her family financially after his death. "We have written more than ten requests" to the leadership of her local Ba'th Party branch without receiving a response, she complained, shaming these particular leaders by name. "We demand that my husband be counted as a martyr of the party," she wrote, arguing that she and her children were entitled to party martyrdom benefits. She closed her letter angrily with the question: "Why has no one from the party responded to our demands?"[55] Her forceful petition worked. The party secretariat contacted her local party branch officials to inquire why her husband had not been added to a list of party martyrs. Six months after Sumaya sent her letter to the party secretariat, her local branch officials agreed to provide her family with the financial benefits due to them as the family of a martyr.[56]

'Umar's and Sumaya's bold tone cannot be explained purely on the basis of their party membership, though it may have been a factor. There are numerous examples from the archives of party members adopting a fawning and submissive tone in their letters, and there are just as many examples of non–party members who take the regime to task in their petitions.

In the end, there is no strong evidence that one rhetorical strategy was more effective than another in eliciting a positive response. Rather, analyzing the different rhetorical strategies employed by Iraqis disrupts presumptions about state-society dynamics under Ba'th Party rule. Far from universally exhibiting passive, silent resignation or cowering sycophancy while living in a "republic of fear," Baghdadi petitioners exercised agency when interacting with the regime, making claims to rights and entitlements under the law and entreating the government to do more to provide for poor and vulnerable segments of the population.[57] Fully one-third of all petitions I analyzed took a bolder "citizen" stance in their communication with the regime. Some of these Baghdadis spoke up about the structural violence of international sanctions and, at times, even spoke out against the physical violence and punishments meted out by the regime itself. But even those who presented themselves as "supplicants" engaged in an important political act by pointing out problems with the state medical system, drawing attention to the lack of affordable food during sanctions, or highlighting the inadequacy of government pensions to support a family.

But how effective were petitions as a general strategy for securing help and resources? The next section addresses both the possibilities and limitations of petitions as a vehicle for redress or resources.

The Politics of Petitions

Though authoritarian regimes generally seek to silence dissenting voices, there are important benefits to the regime in allowing some opportunities for citizen-initiated communication with the government. One reason petitions are valuable to authoritarian regimes is that they help leaders gather information about public opinion, subversive political movements, anti-regime rumors, and abuse and corruption by lower ranking officials. Saddam himself was explicit about his goal of using petitions to monitor corruption by lower ranking officials. In fact, Saddam occasionally seemed annoyed that petitions most often contained ordinary requests for money rather than sharing actionable intelligence. In 1980, officials from the British Embassy in Baghdad attended a speech of Saddam's in which the president complained:

> I want you . . . to talk to those people who do not realise the importance of taking up the Head of State's time by calling him on the phone or who have nothing better to do than to come and say, "Sir, I want a house or I want pocket money or I am sick or I want to be transferred"—all demands which are not appropriate. . . . Demands should be confined to those matters in which some injustice has been perpetrated by an official. I am most upset with the demands of those housewives who have no jobs and are on the telephone twenty-four hours a day imagining that it is Saddam Hussein's job to listen to unfair demands. Out of every thousand petitions we receive only two deserve attention.[58]

In 1993, Saddam repeated this point in a sternly worded warning to the officials and ministries that dealt with written petitions: "Ministries and other administrations should deal with the citizens' problems by studying the issues they present according to what the laws instruct, and to fix the problem according to what is permitted within the purview of their ministry. They should not raise the issue with the Office of the President unless it pertains to a matter that relates to the interests of the presidency or pertains to addressing a lower ranking official harming a citizen."⁵⁹ Saddam's annoyance with being called on to make decisions about quotidian requests may be one reason that the vice chair of the RCC, 'Izzat Ibrahim al-Duri, seems to have been designated in the 1990s as the highest office to respond to routine petitions, not the president's office. Baghdadis must have been aware of this, because a significant number of petitions are addressed to al-Duri.

Yet if gathering intelligence on officials' misbehavior was the primary goal of receiving petitions, this strategy produced only limited results for the regime: denunciations of officials constitute a mere 4 percent of the petitions in this archival sample. The regime relied much more heavily on a web of informants to provide intelligence.⁶⁰ Petitions could supply this information, but more rarely.

At the same time, encouraging citizens to report officials who abused their power had the effect of granting ordinary Iraqis a degree of influence in an otherwise constrained political environment. In fact, I argue that any form of petitioning, whether to request aid or denounce wrongdoing, is a political activity. Petitioning is all the more significant when it takes place in an authoritarian regime that has few other licit avenues for dissent, complaints, or pressuring officials to act.⁶¹ Though there were real limits to the power of petitions to influence regime policies, petitioning was one of the few sanctioned forms of political activity that Saddam's regime allowed Iraqis to undertake. If approved, petitions could result in tangible and even life-changing benefits for individual petitioners.

The politics of petitioning was based on an implicit social contract: citizens held the government responsible for providing for their basic necessities, and they furthermore expected some show of response from regime officials to their queries. In exchange, Saddam must have been pleased that petition writers were signaling their dependence on the regime through their requests. Their letters were often filled with expressions of loyalty, and petitions had the potential to provide occasionally useful intelligence.⁶² For this reason, under Saddam it was Ba'th Party policy to respond promptly to all requests received.⁶³

Local Officials and the Outcomes of Petitions: 1980–2000

Though Saddam Hussein welcomed citizen petitions, he never established a centralized office for handling them. This makes Iraq an outlier in comparison to many authoritarian regimes of the twentieth century which typically did establish systematic protocols for handling citizen requests.[64] From 1980 to 2000, there did not even seem to be a clear process for reviewing petitions: petitions passed circuitously between various party offices and government ministries for review. Often, the final decision was left to the local party office in the petitioner's district, which was deemed to be most familiar with the facts of their case. This informal, ill-defined process of reviewing petitions would change abruptly in the year 2000, ushering in significant changes in the way that the Baʻth Party distributed decision-making power in the final years of Saddam's rule.

But for many years, the lack of standardized processes for reviewing petitions appears to have given some advantages to petitioners. In the absence of an established bureaucratic process for handling requests, petitioners were left to strategize about who might be most responsive to their appeals. It's surprising to see such a range of individuals addressed in these petitions for essentially the same kinds of requests: Saddam, al-Duri, the Office of the Baʻth Party Secretariat, specific ministries related to the subject of the petition, and every conceivable local Baʻth Party office, from the smallest neighborhood representative to the party officials overseeing all of Baghdad province. Baghdadis' political intuition did not always pay off: some sympathetic officials championed their cases, while others undermined the requests they received, perhaps as a result of their personal familiarity with the petitioner. The result was that some petitions "spoke louder" than others, whether due to the petitioner's own savvy manipulation of the system or to the intervention of an official into their case. However, the informal petition review process at least created possible openings for personal relationships to influence the outcome more than would have been possible if all petitions were reviewed in more bureaucratic fashion in the same centralized office.

To clarify the many actors within this bureaucratic apparatus, the accompanying figure shows an organizational chart for the state and party actors relevant to the processing of petitions.[65] The entire Baʻth Party apparatus was overseen by Office of the Party Secretariat, through which all party correspondence was funneled. Government ministries were structurally separate from the party's hierarchy, though all ministries were thoroughly infiltrated by Ba'th Party members. Government ministries interfaced with the Ba'th Party hierarchy by way of the party secretariat. All correspondence between levels of the Ba'th Party and government ministries was routed through the party secretariat; party organizations and government ministries were not permitted to communicate with one another directly.[66] In this way, the party secretariat acted as a kind of clearinghouse to oversee all correspondence between the various state bureaucratic offices and the party offices.

The pathways that a petition might take as it was passed between party offices and government ministries up and down the chain of command could vary widely during this time. To take one real-life example: a woman named Amira* wrote a petition requesting to receive a special military pension given to families of martyrs because her son died while serving in the Popular Army. Amira addressed her petition directly to Saddam Hussein,

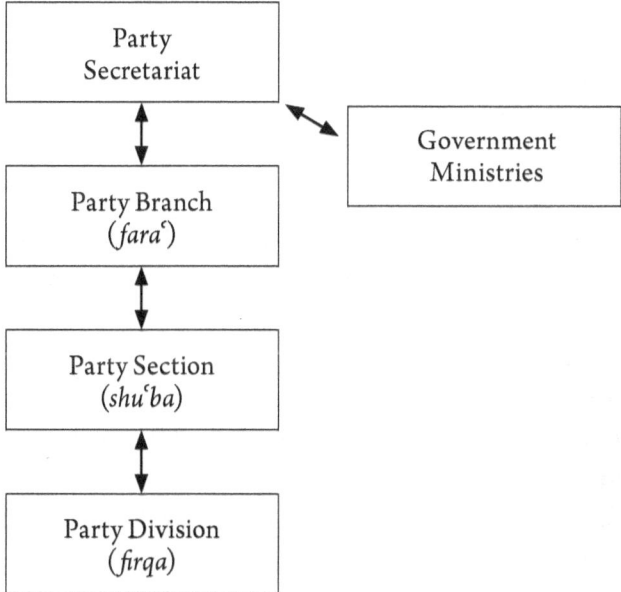

FIGURE 13 Organizational chart of Ba'th Party communication.

but she appears to have actually delivered the letter to a Baʿth Party office in her district of Baghdad. These Baʿth Party district officials provided a cover memo explaining the contents of her request and forwarded her petition to the Office of the Baʿth Party Secretariat, which then sent it on to the Ministry of Defense to confirm details about her son's military service. A general manager in the Ministry of Defense then contacted the Directorate of the Police in Baghdad to confirm the circumstances her son's death. Additional requests for information were sent to the Director General of the Retirement Department to inquire about her son's pension benefits. The Directorate of Police and the Retirement Department eventually issued their findings, which were communicated back to the Office of the Baʿth Party Secretariat, which then forwarded the information to the Baʿth Party branch office where Amira lived. These branch party officials were then responsible for informing Amira of the outcome. In the end, the Directorate of Police disagreed with the proposal to classify her son as a "martyr," because he drowned while on military duty and was not killed by enemy fire. Furthermore, the Retirement Department confirmed that the family was already receiving the correct pension benefits they were due, so Amira's petition was rejected.[67]

In contrast, another woman's petition illustrates the potential for an entirely different bureaucratic response: Hanan* mailed her petition directly to al-Duri, the vice chair of the RCC. She wrote that her husband had abandoned her and her five children, and she could no longer to afford to pay her rent. The Office of the Vice Chair approved Hanan's request immediately and authorized her to be enrolled in a social welfare program, and then wrote a memo that informed the Office of the Baʿth Party Secretariat of its decision without any input whatsoever from other government ministries or from her local Baʿth Party officials.[68]

These two examples serve to illustrate the variety of bureaucratic and party offices involved in responding to requests and the variety of pathways that a request could take: petitioning local Baʿth Party officials at the bottom of the hierarchy, as in the example of Amira, or starting at the top, as in the example of Hanan. Additional examples from the archives illustrate a wide variety of bureaucratic pathways in between.

One striking feature about the early handling of citizen petitions, prior to the formalization of procedures in the year 2000, is the high level of involvement of neighborhood- and district-level Ba'th Party officials. In many cases, Baghdad Ba'th Party offices were involved in receiving requests and implementing the outcome decided upon by government ministries or senior Ba'th Party leaders. In other cases, the party secretariat left decisions about petitions for food rations or granting financial aid up to local *firqa* leaders. The Office of the Party Secretariat frequently asked the *firqa* party office to "issue an opinion" on the subject, given its knowledge of local conditions and area residents.[69] Thus, it was many times neighborhood-based party officials who first received requests, and who then made decisions about the request, and who were finally responsible for implementing the decision. This is consistent with the regime's policy of delegating decision-making responsibilities to neighborhood-level officials during the initial years of sanctions, as was also seen in the food rationing system (see chapter 3).

Baghdadis appeared to be aware of this fact: many of the letters analyzed here were *not* addressed to Saddam or al-Duri, but to their *firqa* or branch officials.[70] Many petitioners asked their neighborhood party officials to advocate for their cases, pleading for financial assistance based on the official's knowledge of their particular family's destitution.[71] Thus, the standing of a petitioner with the local Ba'th Party representatives mattered a great deal in determining whether their request would be granted or not. This could be a blessing or a curse, depending on the petitioner's relationship with local party officials.

In fact, there are many cases of local Ba'th Party officials advocating for the residents in their areas. The empathy party officials displayed at times for the petitioners reminds us of how thin the lines could be that separated low-ranking party officials from the residents living in the neighborhoods they represented. In response to petitions from low-income families, local party officials frequently advocated for leniency and compassion. As party branch officials responsible for a district in southwest Baghdad stated in response to one petition: "We have no objection to restoring rations to the family ... for humanitarian considerations considering that the family lives in a poor state and has no resources."[72] When a group of families were threatened with eviction from government housing, the party branch officials in their district pled for leniency: "out of humanitarian and social considerations for these families, the children, and the elderly, we ask ... that they be allowed to remain in these apartments as long as these conditions [sanctions] on the country continue."⁷³

On rare occasions, local officials took the initiative to respond to petitions themselves without first forwarding the requests up the proper channels to the Office of the Party Secretariat. For example, a woman named Jamila* sent a petition explaining that she had previously received housing assistance from the state as a reward for her husband's military service, but now the assistance had run out, and her family was being threatened with eviction.⁷⁴ Upon receiving her petition, *firqa* party officials assigned to her neighborhood decided to go ahead and pay off the rest of the cost of Jamila's house for her with their own funds.⁷⁵ The party secretariat scolded the *firqa* leaders for this behavior: "Please do not handle these petitions like that in the future because the request went against issued instructions and policies and is the specialty of certain ministries."⁷⁶

Remarkably, this was not the only case of a party *firqa* office offering to buy housing for a constituent. In another example, a retired transit police officer named 'Abd al-Amir* had been renting governmental housing since 1982 that belonged to the state-owned railroad company. His only son had volunteered for the elite Republican Guards, and had been killed during the uprisings of 1991, leaving behind a widow and two children.⁷⁷ (Pointedly, 'Abd al-Amir wrote his letter to Saddam directly, saying his son had been "martyred for you, and for Iraq.")⁷⁸ 'Abd al-Amir wanted to purchase his house, but he had been prevented from doing so because the Ministry of Transportation also laid claim to it as subsidized housing for its employees (see chapter 1). Remarkably, 'Abd al-Amir's local Ba'th Party branch not only advocated for his case, but even offered to purchase the house for him out of recognition for his son's martyrdom.⁷⁹

The details of 'Abd al-Amir's case, combined with the strong support of his local Ba'th Party officials, had all the right ingredients to be persuasive. In fact, his petition even included an unusually detailed memo line that read: "Request for Help for the Family of a Martyr that Has Eight Medals of Bravery."⁸⁰ 'Abd al-Amir's letter made its way up to the Office of the President, but he was ultimately denied: the Office of the President maintained that housing reserved for the Ministry of Transportation could not be used as housing for families of martyrs.⁸¹

Though there were limits to the effectiveness of advocacy by lower ranking party officials, these examples show some of the ways they sometimes tried to take care of local residents. These examples also underscore the fact that petitioners and lower level party officials were often neighbors living in the same jurisdictions who may have had shared elements in their backgrounds. With the dramatic devaluation of public-sector salaries during sanctions in the 1990s, lower ranking officials and ministry employees may have faced similar personal financial difficulties to those writing petitions. Even party members and ministry officials sometimes submitted petitions of their own for extra financial assistance.[82]

In contrast, the influence of local authorities in deciding petitions was bad news for those who did not enjoy good relations with those officials. Mas'ud*, a Baghdadi man with nine family members, sold his house in the Jihad neighborhood in southwest Baghdad to rent a larger house in a new neighborhood located a few miles away. Unfortunately, he started to have disputes with his new landlord, who was a local Ba'th Party official in the neighborhood. This dispute escalated to the point where his landlord threatened to kill him, threw Mas'ud in jail for two days, spread malicious lies about Mas'ud's son deserting from the army, and used his influence within the party to cut off the family's food rations.[83]

When confronted with Mas'ud's allegations, the local party *shu'ba* office defended the official in question, saying he was a "balanced man." They suggested that any dispute between Mas'ud and the party official about the house should be handled by the courts because it was not really a party matter. The Ministry of Defense investigated and determined that, at the very least, no one in Mas'ud's family had deserted the military, and it ordered the full restoration of the family's food rations.[84] Though Ba'th Party leaders did not chastise the *shu'ba* official for abusing his position, the restoration of Mas'ud's rations was an implicit critique of the official's overreach of authority.

Another disturbing example of local Ba'th Party officials taking sides can be seen in the case of Dina*. She wrote a desperate letter to Saddam about domestic violence in her home. Her husband, Fahad*, was a party member home on a short leave from the Popular Army. He had recently threatened her and her children with his army-issued gun.[85] She had gone to her neighborhood *firqa* office to plead for help, and the head of the local party division had agreed to confiscate Fahad's weapons. When he dispatched two party members to go to Fahad to take his guns, they came back empty-handed and uncooperative. Evidently, two neighbors—also Baʻth Party members—took these officials aside and provided an alternative explanation of the altercation, implying that Fahad had not actually threatened his family but that Dina's brothers were actually the instigators of the family dispute.[86] Frantic for help, Dina took her plea directly to Saddam. The president's office ordered an inquiry as to why the two Baʻth Party members had not followed the orders of their *firqa* leader to confiscate Fahad's weapons, but the paper trail in the archives then goes cold, leaving Dina's fate unknown.[87]

Highlighting the influential role of local Baʻth Party officials in determining the outcome of citizen petitions illustrates a larger truth about Iraqi petitioning under the Baʻth Party during these early years: personal connections mattered, to some extent, as did the ability to produce an empathetic response from the official reviewing the petition. Heart-rending details about one's poverty and desperation were likely to elicit special exceptions not only from local officials, but also from the Office of the Vice Chair. Vice Chair al-Duri often personally approved requests to give financial aid to needy petitioners without first consulting with relevant ministries or investigating the veracity of their claims.[88] This is not to suggest that the entire petitioning system was based on personal favors; regime policies were still generally the most important factor for determining petition outcomes. But the informal petitioning review system created openings that citizens and local officials could try to use to their advantage.

People's Day Petitions and New Protocols: 2000-2002

People's Day was a new Baʻth Party holiday commemorating Saddam's 1997 ejection of UN weapons inspectors from Iraq. This act was framed as a reassertion of national sovereignty in the sanctions era.[89] People's Day also coincided with the modest economic recovery after the passage of the Oil-for-Food Program in 1996. With the loosening of restrictions, the state's practice of illegally selling oil and demanding bribes and kickbacks increased in 1997 and reached its peak by 2001.[90] The regime, along with corrupt businessmen closely connected to Saddam, began to enjoy an influx of billions of dollars from licit and illicit earnings.[91] Yet this wealth was not readily distributed to the rest of the population, many of whom suffered from a devastating combination of unemployment, high inflation rates, and the increased costs of food, clothing, and housing. People's Day was one mechanism for the regime to symbolically redistribute wealth and favors to the population, performing gestures of responsiveness in an effort to maintain good will.

People's Day was initially celebrated as a public outreach campaign that included community improvement projects, such as repairing tractors for farmers.[92] By 2000, petitioning became a primary focus of People's Day celebrations, when officials from neighborhood-level *firqa* offices opened their doors to hear the pleas and complaints of residents in their jurisdictions. Internally, party officials referred to People's Day—perhaps with a groan—as the "special day for listening to the complaints of citizens."[93] People's Day was, despite the name, not necessarily limited to one day per year.[94] In addition to celebrations each November, additional People's Day events seems to have taken place during Ramadan, which corresponds to a time-honored tradition of rulers in the Islamic world dispensing charity, receiving petitions, forgiving debts, and granting pardons during the holy month.[95]

During their People's Day interviews with *firqa* party officials, residents filled out short forms with a summary of their problems for which they wanted assistance. The citizen's handwritten form (sometimes accompanied by a more formal written petition the citizen had prepared in advance and brought to the interview) and a brief cover letter written by the neighborhood party official were submitted together up the chain of the Baʻth Party hierarchy to the Office of the Party Secretariat. The Party Secretariat then delegated the task of responding to the petition to the governmental ministry relevant to the topic of the petition.

These new protocols solidified the notion that the neighborhood *firqa* office was the appropriate place to send a petition or lodge a complaint, rather than submitting it directly to Saddam or al-Duri. When an elderly man wrote a petition directly to Saddam in 2002, asking for financial assistance for his "difficult circumstances" (accompanied by two of his original poems praising Saddam's foreign policy), officials called him on the phone to instruct him to meet with his neighborhood *firqa* party officials to discuss his petition instead.[96]

The in-person interviews associated with People's Day lent an even more theatrical air to the process of petitioning, an act that had already required citizens to perform their loyalty and worthiness for assistance within narrow scripts. What was previously only a written performance now, through in-person interviews, added new elements of body language, appearance, and speech, which contained within them all the loaded signals of class, gender, education, and place of origin that petitioners certainly would have tried to manipulate to their advantage to persuade their official audience. Though the idea of presenting petitions through an interview was not a new initiative—Saddam regularly met with ordinary Iraqis to hear their requests—it was rare to be selected to meet with the president. It was much easier to arrange a meeting with a neighborhood representative. Oral petitions were also especially useful for citizens with no or low literacy, which was an increasing problem during the economic crisis of the sanctions years.

The chance to present one's case in person to a party representative evidently struck many Baghdadis as an important opportunity to influence the outcome of their petition, and submitting petitions on People's Day appears to have been reasonably popular based on the number of petitions recorded in the archives. Unfortunately, the Ba'th Party archives did not preserve any interview notes that would provide us a glimpse into how these in-person conversations unfolded and how the performance of petitioning was embodied.

The heightened theatricality of petitioning during People's Day is evidenced in paperwork that petitioners used, however. For example, party officials from the New Baghdad district office gave each petitioner a standardized form for submitting their request with ingratiating language already filled in. The form appeared as follows:

To: The Comrade in Arms, Respected Secretary of the New Baghdad Section
Subject: Interview

I am citizen _____ [blank space for name] living in _____ [blank space for address].

I bring my request to you, along with all of my hope and trust, that you will grant me the opportunity to appear before your generous Excellency to explain my particular issues. I put my fate, and the fate of my family, in your generous hands. I place my hope in God Almighty and then I place my hope in your Excellency because I am suffering from difficult circumstances, and they are: _____

_____[blank space to explain problem]

I wait for help and aid from your Excellency because I see in you the spirit of values, Islamic principles, and noble humanitarianism.[97]

Here the party dictated the very words the citizens had to use in framing their requests, forcing all petitioners to adopt the posture of a "supplicant."

The irony was that, just as neighborhood-level party leaders were becoming even more accessible to their residents through People's Day interviews, the new petitioning protocols introduced in 2000 steadily diminished the influence of these local officials in deciding the outcome of petitions. Rather than issuing their own opinions, *firqa* leaders were expected merely to collect and submit requests up the chain of command without comment. Decision-making shifted toward the bureaucrats in government ministries instead. While government ministry officials had decided the outcome in 32 percent of the petitions submitted prior to People's Day in 2000, their role doubled as they decided the outcome in 67 percent of those submitted in 2000 and onward.

Shifting decision-making from local party officials to government ministries had tangible consequences for Baghdadis. Government ministries used noticeably different criteria for determining outcomes of petitions than had been previously used by local party officials or even by high-ranking leaders like al-Duri. Rather than making decisions based on humanitarian reasons, ministries evaluated petitions based strictly on their eligibility under law.

This brings us back to a key argument in this chapter: that *who* made determinations about petitions was closely related to *how* petitions were decided. Saddam, al-Duri, and party officials benefited from maintaining a public image of paternalistic care for the downtrodden. Bureaucrats working for ministries had no such incentives to make exceptions. Local residents may have been persuasive in their in-person interviews, but their performance was rendered impotent by the new protocols that shifted decision-making to ministries. Thus, through People's Day the regime retained the appearance of responsiveness to the population while steadily diminishing the likelihood that petitioning would result in a special request being granted for the citizen.

This trend toward the blind application of policy is seen clearly in ministries' rejections of petitions for inclusion in the Social Solidarity Fund. Ministry officials were very strict in applying the rules: virtually every family that was already receiving some kind of pension was denied inclusion in the Social Solidarity Fund, no matter how meager that pension was or how dire their financial situation.[98] This usually held true even for female-headed households. For example, a widow's request for financial aid was denied because she received her late husband's pension of 5,000 dinars a month, although this amounted to a paltry $2.50 at the time.[99] Those surviving on pensions were also prohibited from returning to public-sector work as the regime tried to cut costs. For example, one retired employee of the Foreign Ministry asked for the right to return to work because he could not survive and support his family of five on his low pension—shocking even by Iraqi standards—of 65 dinars per month (a mere 3 cents in US currency).[100] His petition was denied because of laws restricting the return of retirees to their jobs.[101]

Similarly strict policies were in place for the many petitions asking for a family member killed in a war to be classified as a "martyr," or to posthumously receive an award or higher party status that would grant the family more benefits and resources. Martyrdom benefits were the second most common topic of the petitions examined here. Many families who lost a soldier on the battlefield or as a prisoner of war struggled to adjust not only to the emotional loss but also to the financial blow of losing a wage-earner. As sanctions devastated the Iraqi economy, many families that had not previously been classified as families of martyrs wrote in to make their case. However, there was considerable confusion within the bureaucracy and among the population about how to classify martyrs and what entitlements families of martyrs were owed, as Khoury documented in her research on wartime conditions in Iraq, and regulations were continually changing.[102] Low-income families often had a particularly difficult time navigating the Iraqi bureaucracy to claim benefits that they were owed, and many families never received much in the way of financial compensation.[103]

Typifying many of the petitions on this theme is the example of a man named Mahdi* who sent a petition on People's Day in which he pointed out that, despite his son "giving his blood to defend the exalted country," he and his wife had never received any martyrdom benefits apart from a measly pension of 1,000 Iraqi dinars per month (50 cents US). Beyond this, Mahdi had seven other children to support who all lived together in a rented apartment that he struggled to pay for. To support his claim, he submitted a photocopy of his son's death certificate. The petition was denied by the Ministry of Defense, which determined that Mahdi's son had merely "died" but was not a "martyr." Though the ministry did not provide additional details or explanation in this case, such determinations were often made when the cause of death was from a car accident, illness, or friendly fire while serving as a conscript, as was also the case with Amira's son, described earlier.[104]

The result of the new People's Day protocols was a steady decline in the percentage of petitions that were approved. Petitions in this sample written between 1986 and 2000 had a 45 percent approval rate. Between 2000 and 2002, approvals fell to 34 percent. One reason for this appears to be that government ministries were much stricter than either local party officials or the president in deciding petitions, denying nearly half of the appeals they received in this sample. People's Day, then, was a misleading campaign: though it purported to increase the regime's responsiveness to popular appeals and requests, the new system appears to have actually resulted in fewer approvals.

Conclusion

This chapter illustrates both the possibilities and the limitations of petitions as a form of political action in Saddam's Iraq. One striking feature of these petitions is that the populations most often overlooked by governments and scholars alike—the poor, the elderly, the ill and disabled, the unemployed, widows, and divorcees—were some of the most insistent and persistent petitioners, demanding help from the regime. Significantly, none of the petitions sent to the regime were anonymous, which is a point of contrast to petitioners in the Soviet Union who omitted their names when writing anything critical of the state.[105] Iraqi petitioners were people who willingly identified themselves and their families to the government, supplying addresses and personal details that were guaranteed to be recorded and filed away. Iraqi petitioners saw the state as the foundation of a welfare system that could benefit their situation, and they therefore sought to draw the attention of officials to their plight. Through petitions, Baghdadis exercised their agency to push the regime to be responsive to the needs of Iraqis who were suffering under the violence and deprivation of sanctions. Petitioning was a survival strategy that many different Baghdadis pursued to their benefit.

But while many Baghdadis exercised their right to contact party representatives and make demands of them, the Baʿthist regime always controlled the outer limits of possible "conversation" that could take place. Political scripts and etiquette informed both the language and content of these petitions. "Supplicants" embraced the role of submissive subject to reinforce the paternalistic power dynamics by which Saddam preferred to govern, hoping this would lead to a favorable outcome. Even those who petitioned as a "citizen" could not level a real challenge at the authorities, however, and always had to defer to Saddam as the ultimate authority in the country.

Despite a decline in approval rates after 2000, petitioning was not a pointless exercise in political theater with predetermined outcomes. Petitions remained an effective method for ordinary Iraqis to push the regime to acknowledge the existence of marginalized members of society and their problems. Though the power of petitions to influence officials appears to have diminished somewhat over time, petitions still could provoke action until the end of Saddam's regime in April 2003. And for those citizens who succeeded in persuading an official to grant them financial aid, housing assistance, funds for a needed surgery, or restoration of their rations, petitions could be a life-saving mechanism. In the face of stringent international sanctions, the collapse of the national economy, spiraling prices, and punitive, authoritarian government, many ordinary Iraqis seized on petitions as an opportunity to speak up for themselves, and in many cases they succeeded in making themselves heard.

FIVE

Prostitution and Policing

SURVIVING THE SOCIAL, ECONOMIC, and political turmoil of the 1990s was a challenge for every Iraqi, albeit in different ways. At the bottom of society, warding off starvation was a top concern for many. After the Iran-Iraq War and Gulf War ended, hundreds of thousands of soldiers returned home. In the midst of sanctions, many veterans were unemployed. The number of female-headed households increased significantly in the 1980s and 1990s because of war widows and rising divorce rates that came with the difficulties of reintegrating veterans to civilian life.[1] As an economic survival strategy, informal and illegal economies sprang up around smuggling, black markets, and prostitution.[2] Crime rose steeply amid the growing poverty and social fragmentation of the sanctions era. Artist Nuha al-Radi chronicled in her diary how thieves began stealing doors from houses, tires and gasoline from parked cars, and even wet laundry off clotheslines to cope with the economic privations of sanctions. A joke circulated in the early 1990s about coffins being stolen from funerals.[3] An Iraqi Air Force officer was caught removing the metal doors from bomb shelters in Baghdad in 1999 and selling the iron on the black market, disrupting notions about the kinds of people likely to be engaged in theft.[4] This rise in crime had important psychological effects, as Baghdadis became more fearful of thieves and common criminals in the streets.

At the very top of society, the political survival of Saddam's regime was at risk: internal rebellion and spiraling crime rates called into question the regime's grip on power and the Ba'th Party's ability to survive the domestic and external challenges of the sanctions era. The 1991 *intifada* fractured any appearance of political stability in the country, as three northern Kurdish provinces broke off in rebellion, thousands of anti-regime protestors were killed or disappeared, Ba'th Party members were attacked and now more isolated within Iraqi society, and the regime heightened its surveillance to sniff out signs of future unrest. The defection of two of Saddam's daughters and their husbands to Jordan in 1995 only heightened Saddam's paranoia about political loyalty and maintaining his rule. Distrust within society and between citizens and the regime surged to new levels.

One way that the rampant economic insecurity, social upheaval, and political distrust of this era manifested itself was through new public discourses about crime. Regime leaders and state media outlets discussed criminal deviance in ways that were coded with gender and class, singling out unemployed men, deserter soldiers, rural migrants, and unattached women as potential criminals. Corollary narratives also discussed victimization in highly gendered ways, contrasting stereotypes about innocent and naïve female victims with the (typically) male criminals seeking to corrupt them.

This chapter explores how elements of state and society worked together to police men and women who were viewed as deviant threats to a patriarchal social order. "Policing" here is meant, on one level, in its literal sense: the work of Iraq's criminal justice system and internal security forces in investigating and punishing alleged criminals. "Policing" in this chapter also refers to the social pressure some Baghdadis exerted on one another to uphold the patriarchal gender norms that Ba'th Party leaders began wholeheartedly encouraging from the Iran-Iraq War onward. As examples in this chapter will reveal, these two forms of policing were often intertwined in practice, as when disapproving neighbors escalated their complaints about prostitutes in their communities to Ba'th Party officials so that the police would investigate.

Focusing on this period of rising crime and changing gender norms draws out the complexity of survival strategies under the conditions of UN–imposed sanctions and Saddam's authoritarian rule. On the one hand, crushing poverty pushed some vulnerable Iraqis into the sex trade as an illicit strategy to earn much-needed income.[5] On the other hand, defying the law risked imprisonment, torture, and execution. The survival strategy that could feed a woman's children could also get her killed by security forces or vigilante neighbors.

As a result of this increased surveillance over sexual activity and gender expressions, all those stigmatized as potential deviants had to navigate life in Baghdad under greater scrutiny, be they single mothers, rural migrants, or unemployed young men. "Respectable" Baghdadis, those unaffected by stigmatizing tropes, also had to navigate delicate social and political pressures in the midst of this social and economic upheaval. The regime pushed Iraqis to inform on suspected criminals or they themselves could be held culpable for allowing deviant behavior to go unchecked in their communities. These tests of citizen loyalty required Baghdadis to weigh maintaining good standing with the regime with betraying their neighbors and severing any remaining sense of social solidarity that had survived the paranoid atmosphere of Saddam's rule.

This chapter analyzes Ba'th Party discourse about gender norms and deviance, and pairs these insights with analysis of criminal investigations into prostitution and sodomy found in the Ba'th Party archives. Through this analysis, a picture emerges about the different costs and consequences of prostitution as a survival strategy during the sanctions era. Certain trends emerge about which criminal populations were viewed as reformable—and, therefore, subject to relatively lighter punishments—and which populations were subjected to more violent reprisal for violating gender norms and laws pertaining to sexual activity. Through this analysis, the social and political consequences of increased state and social surveillance over sexual activities and gender expressions come into clearer view.

Deviant Masculinity

Ten years of war produced profoundly gendered effects on Iraqi society. More than one million men were conscripted to fight in the Iran-Iraq War. These wars "reinforced images of male heroism and superiority," valorizing their military service as an ideal expression of patriotic masculinity.[6] This even led to expressions of smug superiority by some soldiers over civilians, who were "routinely reminded that they were able to live their ordinary lives only because of the heroes defending their honor."[7] The humiliating defeat of Iraqi soldiers in Kuwait, coupled with high unemployment and divorce rates for returning veterans, threatened to emasculate returning soldiers in the eyes of a public that had been socialized to equate masculinity with military victory and with being the head of a household.

Disenchanted veterans also posed a grave political threat to the regime. Many soldiers who had survived the bloodbath of their retreat from Kuwait in February 1991 joined the *intifada* protests in March against the regime (see chapter 2). Veterans' high unemployment rates, greatly exacerbated by the UN imposition of sanctions in 1990, threatened the implicit social contract between the state and the soldiers that promised a bright future for these young men after the wars were over. Saddam promptly worked to neutralize the political threat posed by soldiers by killing and arresting *intifada* rebels, hunting down military deserters, and finding employment for veterans by pushing women out of public-sector jobs. In the aftermath of these wars, the regime tried to delay soldiers' return to civilian life as long as possible by prolonging tours of duty. The result was an eerie absence of men in Baghdad immediately after the Gulf War. Nuha noted in her diary in 1991 that her neighborhood had "nothing but women. Every home has only women. Where are the men, the husbands, brothers and uncles? Could they all be dead?"[8] The regime's efforts to control the rate of veterans' return to Baghdad illustrate how seriously it took the threat that demobilized soldiers posed to the city's stability.

There were many real and imagined risks attached to young men in the volatile period of the early 1990s. Young men—often characterized in the press and in party memos as demobilized soldiers and deserters from the army—were blamed for the increase in crime. State media described young veterans as "wild" and "violent," and prone to causing street fights.[9] As sanctions further eroded Baghdad's economic vitality and social cohesion, the Ba'th Party recorded more and more complaints about young men loitering in public squares, drinking alcohol, smoking, stealing, and generally "acting like thugs."[10] One group of young men were arrested with a list of complaints against them including theft, smuggling, drinking alcohol, desertion from the military, and sodomy (*al-liwat*). This list epitomizes the kinds of lawlessness that Ba'th Party officials complained was plaguing Baghdad because of rebellious young men.[11]

In security reports from the Ba'th Party archives, young men were also associated with illegal black markets. Three brothers were investigated by Baʿth Party officials when one of them was caught in a "stolen valor" crime, pretending to have received medals of bravery when in actuality he had deserted the military. All three young men in this family turned out to be military deserters and were accused of a range of serious crimes, including stealing fuel to sell on the black market, counterfeiting money, using drugs, and forgery. Baʿth Party officials seemed particularly incensed that these men would wear their military uniforms on food rations distribution days or state holidays in an effort to garner more social prestige, and possibly more resources. In response, this family was evicted from their home and likely faced worse punishment beyond that.[12] In another case demonstrating the perceived link between young men and black markets, a group of young men were arrested for selling "indecent" materials on a street corner in the southeastern New Baghdad district—a phenomenon common enough that an exasperated director general of the interior complained he had discussed the issue "many times" with the local police and directorate of security to no avail.[13]

Relatedly, young men were associated with a rise in drug trafficking and drug use in Baghdad. Drug trafficking became a more visible problem in Iraq during the sanctions years, though it had existed in Iraq for decades. By the 1960s, the government created a Narcotics Control Unit to catch the smugglers shipping opium through Iran and Turkey to Iraq.[14] So while drug trafficking and use was not new to Iraq, during the period of the sanctions its visibility increased, and with it, the official response grew harsher. In the 1990s hashish, opium, and unspecified "narcotic pills" were increasingly abused in Baghdad.[15] A Baʿth Party study of "Social Realities in Baghdad" identified the phenomena of youths taking narcotic pills and drinking alcohol as major problems in the capital, especially among military deserters.[16] Several police reports noted that young men arrested for theft, fraud, and other crimes had drugs on them.[17] Publicly, the regime tried to distract from Iraq's small but growing drug problem, as with a 1989 *Baghdad Observer* article that stated: "luckily Iraq is free from both drugs and punks."[18] Internally, Baʿth Party officials identified drug smuggling and addiction as symptoms of the "oppressive sanctions" that created "negative effects" on Iraqi society.[19]

Male Same-Sex Activity

Anxieties about the criminality of unmoored young men were linked to discourses about male same-sex activity. Many of the young men arrested in the cases mentioned above had charges of sodomy added to their cases, playing into Ba'th Party discourse that army deserters were failed men engaged in deviant expressions of masculinity. Negative attitudes toward same-sex activity were not new in the sanctions era: British advisors in the colonial period had complained that same-sex activity was a "prevailing vice" among Iraqi young men.[20] Concerns about masculine deviance, both criminal and sexual, persisted through the Ba'th Party era. For example, historian Achim Rohde analyzed how state newspapers condemned men dressing in women's clothing as a "sexual perversion" and as "morally corrupt" when a group of Egyptian drag performers entertained at a restaurant in Baghdad in the 1990s.[21]

Shortly after the *intifada* uprisings in 1991, Saddam received reports of men in Baghdad's large Saddam City district who were allegedly engaging in homosexual activity and dressing femininely. Outraged, he called a meeting with the district's tribal and community leaders to discuss the issue.[22] This remarkable audio recording from Saddam's presidential office exemplifies gendered anxieties about crime, masculine deviance, and social policing, and thus merits being quoted at length:

> UNNAMED TRIBAL LEADER FROM SADDAM CITY: "Mr. President, the tribal leaders in Saddam City have come to express their loyalty and their faithfulness to you until death.... When the citizens of [Saddam] City noticed the increase of homosexuality and sin, they brought it up to the attention of... the under secretary of the interior affairs.... We came today, Mr. President, asking your forgiveness for any misunderstanding which may have occurred from the people of [Saddam] City.... Mr. President... we know that you are angry with us, and therefore, we beg you. We are your children and you are our father...."
>
> SADDAM: "... Men who dye their hair green and red do not know the values [of Arabism]. It is a shame and sin that you actually allow those people to live. You must slaughter them with your own hands, those kinds of people who dye their hair and wear lipstick like women. I say you must slaughter them and I take responsibility for it."

TRIBAL LEADER: "We are afraid of the outcome from the citizens.... We are afraid that would be a crime."

SADDAM: "I take full responsibility for it and it is not a crime.... I am seeking your help with the issue of those who dye their hair and wear women's clothes. This is shameful for Iraqis and against Islam.... Iraqis are not like that; Iraqis are real men.... I am blaming you if, God forbid, something shameful occurred and nobody is executed—I must blame you."

TRIBAL LEADER: "Sir, there is a more important issue than that ... There is someone from among our citizens, a deserter soldier ... [who] spends his day stealing from homes and hurting people.... This person is an escapee and commits all these horrific crimes. When we make a report at the [police] station ... the case freezes and he is forgotten."

SADDAM: "Enough hurt and pain. He must serve in the army.... Turn him over to the police and say to him 'We have an order from Saddam Hussein that you must arrest this person, or we will report you.'... You should use the same method for the homosexuals.... I know the real honorable men and the shaykhs from the tribes, when they perform their duties right ... they are able to recognize who is a stranger and who is not. More than a police officer, they will actually alert the police to troubled and sinful areas."[23]

This striking exchange illustrates important aspects of how Saddam Hussein perpetuated gendered anxieties about deviant masculinity both in the case of the deserter soldier and in the case of men who were reported to engage in effeminate behaviors and same-sex activities. Interestingly, these two very different kinds of crimes were closely connected in this conversation. Saddam framed both kinds of transgressions as violations of "Arabism" and Iraqi masculinity. Saddam's equation of Arab identity and masculinity is a constant theme in his personal writings: "Arab identity and *rujula* [masculinity] are intimately linked" in Saddam's fiction writing, according to literary scholar Hawraa al-Hassan. Therefore, "effeminate, sexually perverse and cowardly" men cannot be Arab in his novels: they are portrayed as foreigners or ethnic minorities in his writings.[24] Saddam's comments in this recorded conversation that "men who dye their hair green and red do not know the values [of Arabism]" and that "Iraqis are real men" make sense in a context in which Arab masculinity is equated with patriarchal norms. Both deserters and men engaged in same-sex activity violated regime expectations for how men should conduct themselves. Deviant masculinity in all its different forms was punished through community vigilante violence and through state violence. The complicity of community leaders in surveilling and violently enforcing regime edicts can be seen in the role of these community leaders Saddam relied on "even more than a police officer" to monitor their communities and report wrongdoing to security forces.

Though prostitution was not mentioned in this exchange, illicit sexual activity of all kinds became a new fixation within regime discourse about crime and gender. Just as sodomy was framed as a transgressive sexual activity that kept men from fulfilling Ba'thist masculine ideals of heterosexual marriage, prostitution was also framed as a distraction for male clients from their responsibilities toward their wives. Prostitution also threatened patriarchal gender norms through women's sexual activity outside of marriage. For these reasons, gendered narratives about crime tended to link the issues of prostitution and sodomy, and many Iraqi laws included both prostitution and sodomy together in their statutes.

Narratives about Prostitution

In the 1970s and 1980s, Baghdad's red-light districts in Kamaliyya and Batawin were well known, though prostitution was technically illegal.[25] Military officers and officials connected to the Ba'thist regime were known for frequenting high-end brothels and nightclubs in the 1970s and 1980s.[26] 'Uday Hussein, the son of the president, was infamous for his frequent use, and violent abuse, of women and sex workers.[27]

Prostitution became much more prominent in the 1990s, however, as poverty compelled many Iraqis to seek new income for economic survival. The rise of female-headed households through wars and divorce left women and children especially vulnerable to financial destitution. The visible increase in prostitution on the streets or in shabby brothels, rather than in elite nightclubs, garnered attention from national and international observers about the plight of Iraqi women under sanctions.[28]

Popular narratives about prostitution in Iraq at that time focused on deviant femininity and reinforced pernicious stereotypes about the role of rural migrants and ethnic minorities in the commercial sex trade. Divorced women and widowed women, especially those who defied social conventions or lived independently, suffered from stereotypes that they were prone to be immoral, corrupted, and possibly criminals themselves.

Fears about the destabilizing influence of unmarried women is a long-standing trope in Iraqi public discourse: one can find examples throughout the twentieth century of officials decrying how single women were "harmful" to Iraqi society, caused "disturbances," and even prevented the country from reaching its full potential and "economic development" as a modern, sovereign state.[29] These anxieties expressed about single, divorced, widowed, or merely socially unconventional women were amplified in the aftermath of the Iran-Iraq and Gulf Wars, but they were simply the latest iteration of this long-standing trope in Iraqi social discourse.

Discourses about deviant women were also linked to stereotypes about the alleged criminality of the Ghajar ethnic group, who are sometimes referred to as the "Roma of Iraq." They are a quasi-nomadic community that traces its historical ancestry to India.[30] Though Saddam had extended important new rights to the Ghajar, including the right to Iraqi citizenship in 1979, they were often socially marginalized and discriminated against, suffering from stigmatizing stereotypes that associated Ghajar with drinking, dancing, and the sex trade.[31] For example, in 1999 investigators looked into the kidnapping of a young girl by a criminal gang in Baghdad. These investigators initially claimed that the girl was sold by the gang to a Ghajar woman.[32] In a later memo related to the case, the "Ghajar" descriptor was dropped, and she was simply called "the woman accused . . . of practicing pimping [*samsara*]," making it unclear how accurate the term "Ghajar" was in the first place or if it had been used pejoratively to denigrate her.[33]

There were also negative class-based connotations to discourses about the Ghajar as rural migrants destabilizing city life in Baghdad. Many people came from rural areas to the capital in search of work opportunities during sanctions, Ghajar among them, but Ba'th Party leaders viewed internal migrants as a destabilizing force since the city's weakened economy could not absorb so many unemployed residents. As a result, internal migration to Baghdad was banned during the 1990s. Yet clandestine migration from rural zones to Baghdad continued, and the city even began to see the return of *sarifa* huts built on the outskirts of the capital during sanctions.[34] Rural migrants in Baghdad, both male and female, were framed in the 1990s as politically and socially destabilizing populations, even as criminals. The new outcroppings of *sarifa* communities on the city's edges were closely surveilled as suspected sites of illegal sex work, drugs, and alcohol consumption.[35] In my interviews with Iraqis, the Ghajar were associated both with *sarifa* dwellers and with Baghdad's red-light activities, and many urban Baghdadis saw them as a corrupting social force.[36] Ghajar women thus occupied a particularly marginalized position, as they suffered at the intersection of biases pertaining to gender, class, and ethnicity.[37]

Policing Prostitution and Sodomy

These gender- and class-based anxieties about the destabilizing social impacts of loitering young men, rural and Ghajar migrants, and single women were used to support the Baʿth Party's crackdown on prostitution and same-sex activity in the late 1980s and 1990s.

The legality of commercial sex work fluctuated in Iraq over the twentieth century. When the British first colonized Iraq, they initially opted to legalize and regulate prostitution. In Kirkuk, for example, British colonial officials in 1918 set up a system of registering local prostitutes and, if any venereal diseases were detected, quarantining them from the general population.[38] However, the British ended up outlawing prostitution in Iraq shortly after, bowing to domestic pressures to end the legalization of prostitution throughout the British Empire.[39] Iraqi leaders in the 1940s and 1950s followed suit in outlawing prostitution. During a brief coup d'état that put Rashid ʿAli al-Gaylani in power in 1941, he formed a "morality police squad" to go after prostitutes.[40] Red-light areas in the central Maidan district of Baghdad were razed by Hashemite officials in 1951 and in Bab al-Muadhim in 1952–53, pushing the sex trade further to the margins of city life.[41] King Faisal II shored up his commitment to ending prostitution by passing a new law against it in 1956, and ʿAbd al-Karim Qasim reaffirmed its illegality with an updated law in 1958.[42] Yet despite these "tough on crime" gestures, Iraqi leaders may not have routinely enforced harsh punishments on prostitutes themselves. Under Qasim, for example, women convicted of prostitution were sent to "shelters and rehabilitation houses for 'repentant prostitutes,'" a practice continued by the Baʿthists in later decades.[43]

The heightened visibility of prostitution after the Iran-Iraq War, coupled with the regime's worries about the destabilizing influence of returning war veterans, prompted the Baʿth Party to take a harsher stance on commercial sex work. The Baʿth Party passed a law in 1988 that recommitted the government to criminalizing the sex trade. This was the first law to broach the subject in thirty years, inspired by the social upheaval and crime of the postwar era. The 1988 law clarified the legal definitions of prostitution (*bigha'*) pimping (*samsara*), and brothel (*bayt al-daʿara*), all of which were prohibited by law. The 1988 law sentenced pimps and madams to a maximum of seven years in prison, along with the owners and managers of nightclubs, brothels, or hotels where commercial sex work took place. Anyone who forced another person into prostitution was subject to harsher prison sentences, especially if that person was under eighteen years old. Furthermore, those convicted would lose their homes: neighborhood Popular Committees were tasked with evicting and displacing families who were accused of pimping, prostitution, human trafficking, or managing brothels.[44]

Notably, the 1988 law subjected prostitutes themselves to relatively light sentences: they were to be sent to a "reform house" for a period ranging from three months to two years, echoing Qasim's rehabilitation approach. The Ministry of Labor and Social Affairs was responsible for managing "behavioral, cultural, and professional rehabilitation programs" that would enable women to "earn an honorable living."[45] They could be released after meeting one of the following conditions: if they agreed to pay a fine and remain under the care of a husband or other male guardian, if they got married, or if the court decided that they could live an "honorable life."[46]

The 1988 law tended to conceive of prostitutes as female, rather than male, despite the fact that men are technically included within the regime's 1988 definition of prostitution (*al-bigha'*), which was: "fornication [*zina*] or sodomy [*al-luta*] in exchange for money with more than one person."[47] However, the original Arabic text of this law refers to "prostitutes" using female grammatical terms, and the stipulation that a sex worker could be released from a reform house into the custody of a male guardian further confirms that the law was addressing female prostitutes. Though new laws in the late 1980s tended to focus on female deviance related to prostitution, sodomy would become an increasing focus of regime policing and surveillance over the years.

In 1993 the Baʿth Party ratcheted up its punishments for prostitution even further. Law no. 155 stipulated harsher penalties for those who organized and facilitated commercial sex work: instead of a seven-year prison sentence, pimps and madams could now face the death penalty for their crimes, and in 1994, Law no. 118 stipulated that their property would be seized as well.[48] In 2001, Law no. 234 made sodomy and prostitution capital offenses.[49] This law came on the heels of a spate of public executions of dozens of alleged prostitutes, pimps, and madams committed in October 2000 by the *Fidaʾiyyu Saddam* militia overseen by Saddam's son, ʿUday.[50] The mid-1990s thus marked a turning point in the government's approach to punishments for commercial sex work. As mentioned in previous chapters, these anti-prostitution laws aligned with a trend toward increasingly draconian criminal punishments in the early 1990s. Khoury has also pointed to harsh new laws against deserters in the early 1990s as part of the regime's effort to strengthen its grip on society in the midst of sanctions.[51] Cutting off food rations as a form of collective punishment (discussed in chapter 3) also took place around the same time.

The crackdown on prostitution, however, was somewhat distinct from punishments for deserters in that this decision was also informed by new cultural narratives, promoted by the regime, about proper gender roles and expressions. As Rohde documented, the faith campaign of the early 1990s increased the public piety of the regime, leading to the outlawing of alcohol, the closing of bars, and periodic declarations against "excessive makeup," belly dancing, and pornography.[52] So-called "honor killings" against women suspected by their family of engaging in premarital or extramarital sex, even if raped, were briefly legalized by the regime in 1990, and unofficially tolerated to a greater degree than previously throughout the rest of the decade.[53] New punishments against prostitution were therefore guided by two different regime objectives: instilling fear in the population and upholding religiously informed moral visions about women's sexual activities.

The hardening of regime responses to prostitution in the 1990s illustrates some of the ways the Baʿthist government responded to the profound social, political, and economic upheaval of the 1990s through efforts to control women's bodies. Some researchers have argued that the execution of prostitutes and legalization of "honor killings" was Saddam's attempt to show that he was "defending the dignity of the national community" in response to the "shame" of sanctions, positioning Iraqi women as the "repositories of group identity" and as the "guardians of moral order in nationalist projects."[54] Equally it can be said that these new policies and spectacles of violence were meant as a show of force against crime at a time when Saddam's grip on power was threatened by internal unrest and by the external pressures of sanctions.

These new laws and punishments led to a predictable increase in social policing and surveillance of women's movements by security forces. In 1992, for instance, party officials monitored apartments rented out to female university students who had come from other provinces to attend Baghdad University. Local party members had noted that some of the students did not return to their apartments until the early hours of the morning, alleging that "immoral activities" and "amorous liaisons," and possibly even prostitution, were taking place. Interestingly, rather than taking legal action against these students, they recommended that the female student cooperative association appoint older female students with good reputations to act as "guards" to monitor the younger students, indicating that this surveillance was more an expression of moral anxiety about unattached females than an investigation into actual criminal activity.[55] In another case, women who were known to gamble were also placed under police surveillance as suspected prostitutes—these two activities were seen to go hand in hand.[56]

Even older women and respected professionals were subjected to this kind of monitoring. Historian Samuel Helfont has written about a female party member who worked in the Iraqi embassy in Yemen until her husband's death in 1993. After he died, the Baʿth Party ordered her to return to Iraq, uncomfortable with her working in Yemen alone without a male guardian. When she refused to come home (perhaps to avoid the difficulties of life in Iraq under the sanctions), officials accused her of engaging in prostitution in Yemen and of impugning the reputation of Iraq abroad, leading to her being kicked out of the party and fired from her job.[57] However, the woman was not arrested, suggesting that allegations of her work as a prostitute were not credible, but rather an expression of the regime's fears about a single woman occupying this sensitive diplomatic position abroad.

Enforcing Punishments

There are important nuances in how cases of alleged prostitution were handled; exceptions could be made, and the harsh laws described above were not consistently applied. Comparing cases of leniency with cases where harsh punishments were carried out helps reveal the political motivations behind how the Baʿthist regime applied the law.

In 1997, a woman was investigated and found guilty of operating a bar and brothel. Guilty on three counts, she was sentenced to only ten days in jail, evicted from her house, and ordered not to engage in prostitution or pimping again, even though stipulated punishments called for at least seven years' imprisonment and possibly execution for organizing sex work.[58] In a similar example, security forces targeted a large and well-known brothel in 1999. Investigators found that a large number of young men were coming and going from the house day and night, and contributing to "chaos" in the neighborhood and security concerns. They compiled a list of eight men and women known to be working in this establishment, but then ordered each of the accused to be sentenced to only six months in jail, rather than the maximum sentence under the law.[59] In a third example, Baʿth Party branch officials in the Rashid district in southern Baghdad had received reports that a particular apartment housed young female runaways from the countryside who were taught to be prostitutes, suggesting that trafficking was taking place. The police carried out a raid on the building. Instead of runaway girls, they found men with alcohol inside the apartments who subsequently confessed to "prostitution" and "pimping," and there are indications that some of the men may have been engaged in same-sex activities, as well.[60] Despite the severity of the accusations, the detainees received penalties of just six months in prison or a fine, rather than the death penalty stipulated by the 2001 anti-sodomy and anti-prostitution law under which the judge in this case charged them.[61]

So when was capital punishment carried out, and why? Additional examples from the Baʿth Party archives help to clarify the political calculus that informed which punishments were meted out for prostitution cases. In 2001, a group of neighbors wrote to regime officials to complain that an apartment in their building was being used as a brothel. A woman was accused of collaborating with a pimp to operate a prostitution ring that included her two daughters. Residents of the building identified themselves as proud patriots who "upheld Arab values." They also noted that the mother had been arrested previously for prostitution, even appearing on TV for her alleged work in a trafficking gang. Why, they wondered, was the regime tolerating her brazen behavior? Their petition called for "stringent legal action" against all the accused.[62]

From this petition, we learn that officials had evidently chosen to treat this woman leniently during her prior arrest—making a big demonstration through television coverage of their crackdown on criminal gangs, but then doling out only a light prison sentence. In response to this petition, the regime could not afford to appear weak now that people were complaining that it was being lax in enforcing its own laws. Ba'th Party officials acted swiftly: the pimp, the mother, and the two daughters were subsequently arrested and turned over to a court for legal proceedings. A follow-up report by their local Ba'th Party branch stated that the accused were dealt with by the court "in accordance with RCC decree no. 118 from 1994" and that "legal measures were taken," indicating that the accused were likely executed for their crimes according to the punishments stipulated by this law.[63] In this case, the full letter of the law was applied after push-back from Baghdadi residents complaining about rampant criminality in their own communities.

These cases indicate that the regime may have prioritized occasional public spectacles of violence over consistent enforcement of draconian punishments in the cases of petty criminals. These spectacles came whenever there was a risk of the regime looking weak in the face of crime. Scholars previously established this pattern of inconsistent punishments in the case of deserters from the military.[64] Desertion was a much more politically serious crime than prostitution; if military officers and Ba'th Party officials were willing to occasionally look the other way when apprehending deserters, it is not surprising to see that prostitutes were not always punished to the full extent of the law, either. While leaders hoped that passing tough new sentencing laws would deter citizens from sex work, monitoring the activities of pimps and brothels was not an urgent priority for Iraq's security forces.

However, even if an accused prostitute could hope for a light sentence from a judge, social policing by neighbors could pose an even deadlier threat.

Social Policing

The episode of neighbors submitting a petition of complaint underscores the complicity of Baghdadis in enforcing gendered narratives and laws about deviant sexuality and criminality. With the encouragement of the regime, some Baghdadis informed on their neighbors, using their complaints to rein in a disruptive member of their community, to improve their own standing with the regime, or both. In this way, informing can be viewed as a survival strategy, at least when undertaken voluntarily. That Saddam's security forces routinely blackmailed Iraqis into serving as informants is well documented, and it is not always possible to tell from the Baʻth Party archives when neighbors were tipping off regime officials voluntarily or under duress. By encouraging informants and leaning on community leaders to mete out justice, maintain security, and report on any suspicious activity, Saddam was able to uphold the appearance of control and to actually increase the capabilities of the regime during a time of diminished state capacity.[65]

The most marginalized in society were most vulnerable to surveillance and attack by their neighbors. For example, Salafist preachers in Iraq sometimes preached against the immorality of the Ghajar in Friday sermons. In one incident recorded in the Baʻth Party archives, a preacher incited a group to throw a grenade into a "Ghajar party." From the archives, it is unclear how many casualties resulted; Baʻth Party officials reviewing the incident were more concerned about discussing the religious ideology of the preacher than about the harm caused to the Ghajar community in that attack.[66] Social policing and state violence sometimes blurred together to terrible effect to inflict violence on marginalized members of society accused of crimes and deviance. In 1998, three leaders of a local Baʻth Party *firqa* office in Baghdad showed up late one night at the home of a Ghajar family in their neighborhood. They claimed they had been authorized to inspect the house after receiving complaints from neighbors that the thirteen-year-old daughter was working as a prostitute. They had also received reports that the Ghajar father was operating several brothels in the area. Here we see the interplay between social policing and state violence, as the neighbors' complaints evidently emboldened the *firqa* officials to take the investigation into their own hands.

According to a letter of complaint later written by the girl's father, these party officials took her to the *firqa* headquarters, where they beat the girl and forced her to have sex with them.[67] (Given the socially stigmatizing nature of the attack, one is inclined to think that the father's complaint was truthful.) After the father complained, higher ranking Ba'th Party officials investigated. The *firqa* leaders denied wrongdoing and undermined the father's credibility by claiming he was a "bad character" who operated brothels and that he himself was married to four women through an unauthorized, informal tribal marriage practice (*zawaj 'urfi*).[68] Furthermore, they said the father had been making threatening calls to the party members. They admitted to bringing the girl to the *firqa* headquarters, but claimed not to have touched her. Instead, they accused the Ghajar girl of trying to "discredit" the party members by spreading false rumors about her treatment in order to prevent the Ghajar families from being evicted from the area. In the end, it appears that the party members were not punished, though the fate of the Ghajar family is unknown.[69]

This case reveals how vulnerable Ghajar women were to multiple forms of gender-based violence—through accusations by neighbors, assault by security forces, and exploitation in the sex trade. Women with rural, poor, or minority backgrounds were especially vulnerable to accusations of wrongdoing that were socially enforced and subsequently backed up by state violence.

Narratives of Feminine Innocence

The foil to narratives about feminine criminality and masculine deviance was tropes about the innocence of "respectable" Baghdadi women, imagined to be middle-class mothers, wives, and daughters who upheld the patriarchal gender norms being encouraged at this time. Popular narratives in the late 1980s and 1990s emphasized women's vulnerability to victimization and, therefore, their need to protect themselves by staying home, dressing conservatively, and fulfilling domestic roles. Narratives of female victimization tended to uphold class-based notions of middle-class and elite women as innocent and decent, and therefore needing to be especially on guard to protect their safety and their reputations. Indeed, the image of a "respectable Iraqi woman" falling into prostitution was a popular literary trope in Iraq dating back to the 1930s.[70] In the 1990s, state-run newspapers *Babil* and *Thawra* ran editorials and published political cartoons warning women about corruption through movies, makeup, and fashion that could lead them down the road to prostitution.[71] In a meeting between Saddam and government ministers, he argued that women were liable to "deviate" and allow themselves to be "seduced" by men if they wore makeup and fancy clothing.[72]

Scholars Rohde and al-Jawaheri both describe a growing panic in the 1990s about girls being kidnapped in broad daylight by criminal gangs.[73] Rumors and media reports circulated about two women who were "kidnapped, raped, ransomed, burnt with cigarette butts and then dumped naked but alive."[74] Other stories warned women about being kidnapped while stopped at traffic lights.[75] Baghdadi women I interviewed about this period remember being fearful about walking in public and traveling back and forth to school or jobs, worried they might be abducted and sexually assaulted. Many of these rumors centered on ʿUday, who earned a fearsome reputation as a sexual predator who routinely abducted and assaulted women.[76]

Fears about kidnapping and assault encapsulated concerns about the declining efficacy of the state to provide law, order, and security, and about the appropriateness of women in public spaces where they could be vulnerable to attack. These had real consequences for limiting the movement of women through the city of Baghdad, as many began to stay home or limit their socializing to avoid criminal victimization. Relatedly, many more women began to wear *hijab* head coverings and modest ʿ*abaya* robes in an effort to safeguard themselves from attack, as well as in response to the increase in outward signs of piety encouraged by the regime and elements of society during the 1990s.[77] ʿ*Abaya* had the additional benefit of covering up clothing underneath, making it less necessary to buy new outfits at a time when new clothes were unaffordable for many.[78] Regardless of whether women were responding to the regime's faith campaign that encouraged more modest clothing, anti-sanctions propaganda that encouraged less conspicuous consumption, or fears about female victimization that made women dress more cautiously, the combined effect was to increase rates of veiling and also to curtail women's movement throughout the city.

Settling the Men

While "respectable" women were portrayed as easily victimized, they were also regarded as the solution to Baghdad's social instability. Women were called on to solve the problem of male volatility in a variety of ways: leaving the workforce to boost male employment rates, marrying at a young age to stabilize men in domestic roles, and dressing and behaving modestly so as not to be corrupted by perceived male criminal elements like deserter soldiers or Ghajar men.[79] Looking at the way that Baʿth Party rhetoric positioned "respectable" Baghdadi women in a salvific role—stabilizing society through marriage and reproduction—reveals another means by which social policing was intended to complement the regime's state violence against criminals and prostitutes.

In response to male unemployment and the socially destabilizing effects of demobilizing soldiers from the Iran-Iraq and Gulf Wars, Baʿth Party leaders reversed earlier state feminism policies that had encouraged female employment outside the home (see chapter 2).[80] Instead, the regime promoted early marriage and a fertility campaign that were designed to create room for men in the labor market and to anchor society by coupling off unemployed youths. By 1986, the state started cutting paid maternity leave and other state welfare policies that had supported female employment to encourage women to leave their jobs and make room for returning soldiers.[81]

This was not the first time in modern history that the Iraqi government had tried to incentivize early marriage and domestic roles for women: in the 1950s, the government launched a "campaign against singlehood." Methods used by the Baʿth Party in the late 1980s, such as providing prizes for large numbers of children or financial support for young married couples, were first introduced by the Hashemites and their British colonial advisors decades earlier.[82] In retrospect, Saddam's support for state feminism in the 1970s appears as an exceptional trend in Iraq's modern history rather than the norm.

The regime also pushed young couples to wed early, hoping that this would contribute to higher birth rates and that increasing the number of married youths would have a stabilizing effect on society: young women would have a proper and productive sexual outlet within the confines of marriage, and young men would act more responsibly, unlike the youths loitering in the streets and disturbing the peace. Baghdad Baʻth Party officials launched the "Awareness Campaign to Reduce Bride Gifts [*mahr*] and Promote Early Marriage." The campaign recommended actions such as promoting marriages between Baʻth Party members, providing incentive payments for marriage and births, assisting newlyweds with purchasing residential land, and providing favorable loans for furniture purchases. The General Federation of Iraqi Women and neighborhood Popular Committees were mobilized to help promote the message of early marriage, and preachers in the mosques were also encouraged to preach about the benefits of marriage and childbearing in their Friday sermons.[83] Policies promoting marriage had another consequence of creating a modest increase in polygyny rates in Iraq. When a party official in Baghdad wrote to Saddam asking for permission to marry a second, younger wife, he framed his request in terms of the fertility campaign: although his first wife had given birth to six children, she was now too old to conceive again. Saddam approved his request for a second marriage.[84]

Related to its promotion of early marriage, in the 1980s the government encouraged women to bear more children—at least five—through a new national fertility campaign designed to offset the high casualty rates Iraq suffered during the Iran-Iraq War.[85] Saddam gave so many talks about birth rates that his speeches were compiled and published under the title *The Family and Population Growth in Speeches of the Leader President Saddam Hussein*. In one such speech he proclaimed, "Some think that the annual population growth rate in Iraq of 3.2 percent is a high rate and should be decreased. However, we believe that this rate should remain as it is, and if there is a possibility of increasing it, it should be increased."[86]

To encourage women to participate in the fertility campaign, the state began to restrict access to birth control toward the end of the Iran-Iraq War and issued awards to women with large numbers of children.[87] Though some women were able to gain surreptitious access to contraception through personal connections to pharmacists, others found themselves more frequently pregnant with the absence of contraceptives. Birth certificates for babies conceived during the Iran-Iraq War proudly declared these children to be part of the "Qadisiyya army."[88]

The imposition of sanctions in August 1990 ended the fertility campaign. Women were still encouraged to marry early and leave the labor force, but the fertility campaign was dropped as families struggled to afford to care for many children. In an interview recorded by scholar Sarah Persinger, this abrupt shift caused one woman to complain: "[Saddam] interferes in sex between man and woman. 'Now you will have a baby.' . . . 'Now, no babies.' See, he interfered in everything."[89]

With the onset of sanctions, Saddam pushed new gendered visions for the proper way to navigate economic hardships. This vision further committed women to domestic roles. In a closed-door meeting, Saddam described how an exemplary Iraqi man should continue to work, no matter how trifling his paycheck became, serving as the breadwinner for his family. If he was conscripted, he should serve dutifully, rather than desert. He should earn his money licitly, rather than through smuggling or black market deals. Prostitution was also inappropriate for a patriotic Iraqi man: prostitution was antithetical to the successful promotion of marriage and reproduction for young Iraqis that would help stabilize society once more.

The ideal woman living under sanctions had quite a few more expectations to meet: she should stay home with her children, leaving her job to make room for a man. She should sew her family's clothes, rather than spending money on expensive imports. She should find ways to make her rations stretch for the entire month, and never purchase food on the black market. When she does purchase consumer goods, she should try hard to buy locally made products for reasonable prices.[90]

Embedded in these gendered rhetorical admonitions was the assumption that male labor and economic activity was more essential for family survival than female labor. In contrast, female consumption was portrayed as typically frivolous, and, for this reason, it had to be vigilantly monitored by family patriarchs and even by the state. Party and media rhetoric chastised women for purchasing fancy clothes, jewelry, or makeup during sanctions.[91] Saddam lashed out at the idea of elite women dressing luxuriously during sanctions: "If we see a women's suit that's priced over 500 dinars, we will burn the face of the merchant in whose shop we find it. We will burn him totally. . . . Let the wife of the merchant who did not become rich on his own merit, as well as Saddam Hussein's wife, and the wife of the minister, dress in the same way like the wife of the common citizen. Are we not at war? Are we not under siege?"[92] He went on to recommend that women sew their family's clothing as a solution to shortages in the marketplace and to productively engage women's time: "[The merchant] will ... not import suits anymore, but fabric, which we manufacture and sew in Iraq.... Even later, when we start to import, this experience will not go to waste this way, Iraqi women will be busy with something fruitful and fulfill their interests with new priorities in their lives ... namely, good national industry.... Your sister and mine, as well as your mother and so-and-so's mother ... they will all sew their children's clothes."[93]

The new gender roles espoused by the regime and the economic shifts brought about by sanctions impacted middle- and lower-class women differently. Some scholars have argued that middle-class women were among the groups most affected by sanctions. Beginning in the 1990s, one's social class—as determined by educational level, nature of employment, and cultural sophistication—no longer necessarily corresponded with one's level of wealth. As al-Jawaheri found in her survey of Baghdad households in the 1990s, many middle-class men and women fell into poverty as their public-sector jobs, once desirable and prestigious, no longer paid the bills. As "respectable" people with college degrees, however, many felt uncomfortable taking informal jobs as taxi drivers, market vendors, or house cleaners to supplement their income. Women were especially limited by social mores that deemed some work unacceptable, such as retail sector jobs, because they would put the women into contact with strangers. In contrast, women who had always belonged to the lower classes were more accustomed to working in markets or as housekeepers, and there was less of a social stigma with taking on menial jobs.[94] Lower-class women had more opportunities to work outside the home, contribute to the family income, and maintain a level of financial independence. In this way, sanctions had uniquely detrimental effects on middle-class and educated women within the economy and within their own families, as they became "fully dependent on male providers" for financial support.[95]

This illustrates the uniquely challenging role that Baghdad's middle-class women found themselves in. On the one hand, they were being pushed to stay home through fear-mongering narratives about crime and victimization. Simultaneously, they were charged with stabilizing Baghdad society through marriage, reproduction, and homemaking skills. Middle-class women's abilities to earn money were increasingly restricted during the sanctions era, however, and those women who were now divorced or widowed were especially vulnerable. Women who earned income through prostitution were demonized and susceptible to social policing and state violence, however, making survival sex an especially risky choice at this time. Pushed to uphold the patriarchal social order through performing proper femininity, many women were forced to make excruciating choices about whether to fulfill these social norms or pursue illicit forms of income to feed their families.

Conclusion

In analyzing rhetoric and criminal cases related to prostitution and sodomy, state policing and social policing worked together to define and repress transgressive expressions of gender and sexuality that fell outside of the patriarchal norms upheld by the Baʻth Party in the late 1980s and 1990s. However, it is also apparent that social policing and state violence did not apply to all suspected criminals equally. These inconsistent approaches in policing or rehabilitating different populations connect to the question of who had a "right to the city," using urban theorist LeFebvre's phrase.

Returning to themes introduced in chapter 1, this chapter has explored how southern rural migrants, especially Ghajar individuals, continued to be excluded from the imagined community of the city, just as they had been since the early twentieth century. Ghajar men and women were more likely to be harshly penalized through social policing and through the surveillance and actions of state forces. One significant reason for the additional scrutiny and stigmas against them is that they were viewed through the same lens as all rural migrants: outsiders who were not imagined as citizens of Baghdad. Instead, they were believed to destabilize urban society with a purportedly unwholesome way of life. By virtue of their status as a migratory, minority population, they were permanently cast as "outsiders," unable to be reformed and included in respectable society. Rural women who lived at the intersection of marginalized gender, class, and ethnic identities faced the greatest dangers of all.

Men who engaged in sodomy were also viewed as irredeemable to a leader who saw same-sex actions as a perversion and a violation of "Arab masculinity," as seen in his response to the transgressive dress and sexual acts by some men in Saddam City. As residents of Saddam City, these men had already been living on the margins of city life; now their gender expression and sexual activities made their very existence intolerable in Saddam's eyes. Through social and state policing, men transgressing gender and heterosexual norms were violently excluded from the imagined community of the city: Saddam called for their murder. The punishment of execution in the 2001 anti-sodomy law underscores that male same-sex activity was a form of deviance that the state responded to with violence, rather than through efforts to integrate and rehabilitate. The expansion of policing from being a monopoly of the state to falling under the purview of tribal and other community leaders had terrible consequences for marginalized individuals perceived to be deviating from social norms.

In contrast, rehabilitation was a common response to the crimes of loitering, drug-using young men, and also to many female prostitutes. The Baʻth Party regime typically approached prostitution as a temporary condition that could generally be rehabilitated through short prison sentences and through adopting proper feminine roles and behaviors as wife and mother, dressing conservatively, and remaining at home. Likewise, adrift young men were only temporarily destabilized: their condition could be "fixed" through marriage. Criminal young men who used drugs or worked in black markets were not necessarily painted as "outsiders," but as members of Baghdad's community in urgent need of rehabilitation and reform—reform that could happen through marriage and a return to honorable masculine roles.

In this new social order, "respectable" urban Baghdadi women were unquestionably imagined as belonging to the city, now threatened by criminal forces coming from the margins of society. Their bodies were instrumentalized by the regime to reinforce a new social order and to demarcate the boundaries of inclusion and exclusion through their reproductive roles. It would be Baghdadi women who could restore the country's honor by reinforcing traditional gender roles at home, saving men from the shame of unemployment and social dislocation. But because narratives about urban Baghdadi women tended to reinforce their vulnerability, this had the effect of limiting women's movement in the city and emphasizing that public spaces were not safe for them. Public-sector employment was also out of bounds for many women who were fired or discouraged from working in order to give jobs to returning veterans. Though middle-class Baghdadi women were not imagined as a threatening "other" in the same way that rural and Ghajar women were, they also began to lose their "right to the city" because of gendered anxieties about crime.

PART III

Aftermath of the US Invasion

SIX
Patchwork Power and Essential Services

ON MARCH 20, 2003, US troops and their coalition allies invaded Iraq with the purpose of overthrowing Saddam Hussein's regime. US and coalition forces occupied the country with relatively little resistance, and on April 9, 2003, they captured Baghdad. The United States established itself as the occupying authority of the country from April 2003 until July 2004, first under the auspices of the Office of Reconstruction and Humanitarian Assistance (ORHA) and then through the Coalition Provisional Authority (CPA) under the leadership of American ambassador L. Paul Bremer III. Baghdadis had acclimated over decades to the highly bureaucratic systems of the modern Iraqi state. Almost overnight, the state and ruling party system collapsed. With the state went the life-sustaining public utilities on which life in the city depended.

Baghdad's electrical grids, sewage lines, and water plants had been degraded from sanctions in the 1990s and then were torn apart during widespread looting in the wake of the US invasion in 2003. Iraqi public-sector workers initially stayed home during the US invasion in April out of fear or uncertainty, and then many permanently lost their jobs through Bremer's de-Baʿthification order issued on May 16. This order barred any Baʿth Party member above a certain membership rank from any future employment in the public sector, which impacted many career technocrats and government employees who had kept essential services running.

As a result of the invasion, looting, and loss of essential personnel, infrastructure and public services began to fail. Before the war, Baghdad had an average of sixteen to twenty-four hours of electricity per day. In 2008, five years after the war began, Baghdad's average number of hours of electricity per day hovered in the single digits.[1] Food spoiled because of the frequent power cuts. Today, most Baghdadis use private power generators to compensate for the frequent outages that persist in the present, but generators were in short supply in the years immediately following the US invasion.

Fuel of all kinds was in critically short supply: for a country rich in oil and natural gas reserves, gasoline and propane fell to one-fourth of their prewar levels in 2003 due to looting and insurgent attacks on Iraq's oil infrastructure.[2] These shortages worsened nearly every area of life; nearly every Baghdadi interviewed about the post-2003 period for this book mentioned the fuel crisis. Civilians needed gas to boil unclean water, cook their food, and to heat their homes during Baghdad's chilly winters. The shortage of gasoline hindered the movements of civilians and also the work of emergency personnel, since police cars and ambulances were also desperate for fuel.

Water treatment plants also faltered. At the time of the US withdrawal of troops in 2011, only 26 percent of Iraqis had consistently working sewage and sanitation in their homes, and at the time of writing in 2024 more than 30 percent of Iraqis still do not have clean water.[3] Cholera outbreaks have repeatedly struck Baghdad in the years since the US invasion because of sewage contaminating the drinking water supply.[4] Sanitation in Baghdad suffered further because garbage pickup was severely disrupted following the US invasion as garbage trucks were looted in 2003 and many sanitation workers stayed home or lost their jobs. Growing mounds of garbage were more than eyesores: large piles of disease-spreading rot often hid insurgents' improvised explosives or even the bodies of victims slain by criminals, insurgents, or sectarian death squads. In one interview, a middle-aged man described how mortified he was to discover corpses lying in the garbage along the narrow alleyways in his neighborhood in central Baghdad, an area that had been caught in the cross-fire of the sectarian civil war that raged in Baghdad between 2005 and 2009.[5]

Drawing on interviews with sixty Iraqis, and a dozen Americans who worked in Iraq as part of the US occupation, this chapter illuminates how Baghdadis navigated the collapse of essential services and bureaucratic systems in the period of the US occupation from 2003 to 2011, and shows how aspiring new power players in post-Saddam Iraq sought to capitalize on this crisis through meeting Baghdadis' basic needs.⁶

Surviving without Services: Hardships and Opportunities

The collapse of municipal services and infrastructure in the city threatened the health, well-being, and lives of Baghdadis. Baghdadis needed to quickly develop new survival strategies to sustain themselves without being able to turn to state or municipal officials for assistance. The difficulties of sourcing clean water or gasoline multiplied in a rapidly deteriorating security environment, where any movement outside the home could be fatal. A sixty-six-year-old man confessed how debilitating the fear and insecurity of these violent years were even for someone like him, a former soldier: "It was chaos. Every family sat in their own home, afraid to go out. There was an absence of security and a presence of fear and anxiety, and there was no one to help. We had only ourselves," he stated. "The country ended."⁷ Many Baghdadis echoed his sentiment of feeling utterly abandoned with the collapse of the state. One fifty-six-year-old man living in the low-income Fadhil neighborhood in the historic Rusafa district characterized his situation in 2003 this way:

> Services were nonexistent. The streets were full of garbage, and that was true in every part of Baghdad. The *mukhtar* wasn't present.... This was a big crisis period, and the biggest crisis was the absence of the state. There was no one available to fix anything. People had to rely on themselves to make up for the lapses in services.... Electricity was nonexistent and water was scarce.... There was no state, there was no official, there was no *mukhtar*, or tribe, or religious leader. Every person had to take matters into their own hands.⁸

Wealthier areas of Baghdad didn't fare much better. One sixty-two-year-old woman who had grown up in the shaded, tree-lined streets of the upscale district of 'Adhamiyya in northeast Baghdad, stated: "As residents of 'Adhamiyya, we had to rely on ourselves to get what we needed because of the shortages in services. It became everyone for themselves. I didn't turn to anyone then for help then, and I won't now. There is no responsiveness from anyone."⁹

Ruptures in essential services and the collapse of a responsive bureaucracy provided opportunities for emerging power brokers to compete with one another by distributing fuel, repairing broken sewer pipes, or providing security on a localized basis across Baghdad's different neighborhoods. Whoever distributed cooking gas or helped to clear a flooded street could aspire to be, in a functional if not an official way, a kind of local government for a given neighborhood. Militias, religious leaders, tribal shaykhs, nascent political parties, and newly formed local councils vied to be recognized as influential authorities by virtue of their service delivery.

Militias were one of the new power brokers that arose in the violent lawlessness that accompanied the US invasion. For example, long-time residents in Fadhil recalled how their small, working-class community was overrun by "outsiders" in the period following the 2003 US invasion. Displaced Sunni residents flocked to Fadhil fleeing sectarian violence and clashes with Shi'i militias in mixed neighborhoods elsewhere in the city. Armed men from Sunni sectarian militias like *Tawhid wa-l-Jihad*, sometimes referred to as al-Qaeda in Iraq, came to the Fadhil neighborhood ostensibly to protect it from attacks by Shi'i militias. Sunni militias then used the neighborhood to launch their own attacks on neighboring Shi'i districts. The quiet, narrow alleys soon became a front line in the sectarian battles that devastated the city between 2005 and 2009. Upset with these changes, some long-time residents moved elsewhere, but many were trapped by the violence or had nowhere else to go. Without services or protection from a functional state, "the area became closed and chaotic, and it was full of filth. . . . The role of the government was nonexistent," in the words of one resident.[10]

To build up some legitimacy and establish themselves as local authorities in Fadhil, Sunni militia members tried to provide some measure of essential services for the long-term residents and newly displaced Sunni residents of this small district. In the words of one resident: "[Armed groups] provided modest services for residents of the neighborhoods of Fadhil because of the absence of security, the collapse of the state, and the widespread gaps in services that were increasing the needs of the people of the area. . . . Armed groups would try to meet the needs of the people by distributing [fuel] and cleaning out the sewage drains, and things like that."[11] This is just one example of militias providing essential services, like sewage repair, to build up their legitimacy and support within the small neighborhood they controlled.

This often overlooked role of militias in providing essential services is an example of a wider phenomenon in Baghdad in the early 2000s: highly localized competition for legitimacy by aspiring power brokers through service provision. In some neighborhoods it was a prominent family or religious cleric that distributed a small amount of food to nearby residents on a sporadic basis. In other districts, residents were beneficiaries of larger, coordinated efforts at fuel distribution by a rising political party or a militia. Still other neighborhoods reported having no power brokers or service providers to turn to.

In his ethnographic fieldwork in the southern city of Basra in 2003, political scientist David Patel observed how mosques performed an essential function in sharing information during Friday sermons to coordinate residents in the surrounding neighborhood to work together to provide a modicum of order and security. For example, some imams provided instructions during their Friday sermons that residents should only throw their garbage in certain designated areas to minimize the filth and disarray caused by the collapse of sanitation services in the city. Patel observed that imams had a degree of success as local authorities who could successfully disseminate information within the small geographic area around their mosque, but they were only successful with relatively easy requests. As soon as imams requested something more arduous, like asking residents to collect litter from the streets or serve on a security patrol in their neighborhood, these coordination efforts typically failed.[12]

Unfortunately for Baghdadis, these small-scale efforts at volunteer coordination by local mosques or other neighborhood leaders were too limited to meaningfully replace the essential state services they had depended on for electricity, water, sewage, and sanitation. Mitigating the hardships caused by the disruption in the state's essential services would require interventions by larger groups with more funding, organizational capacity, and the aspirations to take on state-like functions.

Of all the different emerging actors in post-Saddam Iraq, this chapter focuses on two who were among the most active in competing for influence through providing essential services. One was an individual, the Shi'i populist cleric Muqtada al-Sadr; the second was the US–created system of local councils. In 2003, Muqtada al-Sadr already enjoyed name recognition within Iraqi society, having been born into one of the most prominent families of Shi'i clerics in Iraq. His father, the Grand Ayatollah Muhammad Sadiq al-Sadr, had gained a large and loyal following of lower income Shi'a through his preaching on populist themes and, later in his life, for his willingness to stand up to Saddam's regime.[13] For his activism, Muhammad Sadiq al-Sadr was assassinated by Saddam's forces in 1999.[14] The memory of the Sadr family was so beloved among Baghdad's poorer Shi'a that residents renamed the Saddam City district (previously Revolution City) as Sadr City in 2003.

Both US–created local councils and Muqtada al-Sadr prioritized service delivery to the neighborhoods within which they operated. Both had access to the initial conditions needed to engage in large-scale service provisions: funding, organizational capacity, and the ambition to establish legitimacy and influence through service provision within the post-Saddam political landscape. Their similarities set them on a collision course as each sought to win the hearts and minds of Iraqis by clearing blocked sewage pipes or by distributing food and medicine in localized areas.

Analyzing the history of their efforts during the years of the US occupation of Iraq (2003–11) underscores how certain dynamics of state-society relations from the Saddam era carried over into post-2003 Iraq. Notably, personalized problem solving between residents and local power brokers—similar to the dynamics of petitioning explored in chapter 4—remained an important expectation that Baghdadi residents had for emerging leaders in the post-Saddam era.

The US-Created Local Council System

In the immediate aftermath of the US invasion, there were few groups with organizational capacity and funding to provide services. Among the few were members of a US–designed local council system established in July 2003. Inside Baghdad, these councils eventually operated at the neighborhood (*hayy*), district (*qada'*), and provincial levels. The provincial councils evolved into powerful bodies within the new Iraqi government, with contested elections, large budgets, and considerable influence within national politics. In contrast, the little-studied neighborhood and district councils have been criticized by Iraqis and outsiders alike for being weak and ineffective.[15] And yet it was the neighborhood and district councils that were principally responsible for acting as local authorities capable of resolving gaps in essential services. In theory these councils were well positioned to act as possible replacements for the localized infrastructure of Baʿth Party *firqa* or *shuʿba* offices and neighborhood bureaucratic processes that had been present under Saddam. Providing services allowed the councils to compete in the political marketplace for influence. As we will see, however, the work of these councils seldomly met Baghdadis' expectations and needs for responsive and effective local governance and service provision.

The idea that neighborhood committees could help step into the power vacuum in 2003 to provide essential services and order was not a uniquely American idea. Iraqi-organized councils sprang up shortly after the US invasion in Basra, for example, and in Baghdad, grassroots neighborhood committees emerged in Shuʿla in western Baghdad and in Sadr City. Interestingly, both Baghdad neighborhoods were originally created to house former *sarifa* dwellers (see chapter 1). Both of these neighborhoods were densely populated with lower income Shiʿa residents, many of whom belonged to families who had migrated from rural areas in southern Iraq half a century earlier. In Sadr City specifically, these new councils in 2003 were an early effort to mobilize the community to support the burgeoning political movement under the leadership of populist cleric Muqtada al-Sadr.[16]

Controversially, Ambassador Bremer ordered that these grassroots councils in Shuʿla, Sadr City, and elsewhere in the country be shut down to make way for officially sanctioned councils that would be organized by the Americans. In particular, Bremer objected to the validity of the grassroots elections that had been carried out to populate these Iraqi-run community councils.[17] Perhaps relatedly, officials within the Coalition Provisional Authority later chose Shuʿla as one of the first test sites for a US-sponsored council system.[18] Shutting down grassroots Iraqi councils would set the new American councils and Sadr on a collision course as direct rivals competing for recognition and legitimacy.

The US Agency for International Development (USAID) officially led the American local governance program as part of Iraq's reconstruction in 2003. Planning for the local governance program was mostly conducted by a USAID contractor, Research Triangle International (RTI), and implementation fell to US Civil Affairs officers and army soldiers. In the Green Zone, representatives of these different groups met at an office called Baghdad Central on the top floor of the Republican Palace. Baghdad Central consulted with a small number of Iraqis. Husam,* an Iraqi exile recently returned from Europe, worked to assist Baghdad Central from 2003 to 2005, until he resigned in protest in response to Ambassador Bremer's policies.[19] Another Iraqi member of Baghdad Central was Faris 'Abd al-Razzaq 'Assam, who had served in the Baghdad municipality under Saddam and was appointed as a deputy mayor of Baghdad by the CPA. In this role, he contributed to setting up the new local council system. Faris was assassinated just six months into his work with Baghdad Central, a fate that would befall many Iraqi council members.[20] His American coworkers deeply respected Faris's work and experienced his death as a "huge setback" that "changed the fate" of the local council program for the worse.[21]

Based on the plans created by RTI, the centerpiece of the local governance program was the creation of powerful *provincial* councils (not neighborhood or district councils) that would act as a counterweight to the central government of Iraq.[22] The George W. Bush administration's interest in local governance came out of an ideological commitment to decentralize political power in Iraq, preventing what some in the CPA called a "dictator ready" centralized political structure.[23]

Apart from the CPA's instructions to decentralize political power in the new Iraqi government, the team at Baghdad Central had little additional information about the previous context of municipal administration, local governance, and state-society relations in Iraq to inform their plans. Denise Dauphinais, a USAID official who worked on the Local Governance Program, recalled "That dearth of information—about how things actually worked on the ground—was pretty astronomical. . . . I asked repeatedly for things like an organizational chart of the Iraqi government and local government structures. Nobody seemed to be able to get any of that."[24] Initial meetings with bureaucrats from the previous regime were taken up with very basic questions. One Civil Affairs officer from Baghdad Central recalled the litany of questions he had as they began their work on local governance:

> When somebody says "I was the governor 20 years ago of this province," what does that mean? Is it "governor" in my terms? When I think of a governor, I think a governor has certain capabilities and powers. You ask them,

"How was the government set up before? How did local governments relate to the national government? What was done? How was the bureaucracy structured? How was the service delivery provided? Who picks up the trash? Who sets that budget?"²⁵

The local governance team at Baghdad Central did not have any answers to these basic questions when they arrived in Baghdad to begin their work. With mere weeks to prepare a local governance proposal to meet the CPA's deadline for their team, all that Baghdad Central had to work with was a two-page concept paper drafted by RTI contractors explaining what a council system might entail. One member of Baghdad Central recalled that, "for two pages, it had a lot of punch," though he was "astounded" that a local governance plan was not yet more developed.²⁶ Colonel P. J. Dermer, a member of the Defense Intelligence Agency who worked in Baghdad Central, recalled their first meetings in response to Bremer's orders to create a council system: "[The Baghdad Central team] sat around and said, 'Okay, how big should it [the council] be? What level are we looking at?' We had to decide that. Hours of meetings and yelling—we had no past script to look on; we had no after-action report from anywhere else. None of us had done this before.... In about two and a half days, I think, we knocked out a plan for the city council, a strategic plan—yelling, pushing, shoving, cussing."²⁷ Officials at Baghdad Central were not even sure how many councils to establish because they did not know how many neighborhoods and districts existed in the city. It appears that the first time the Baghdad Central team saw a map of Baghdad's neighborhood and district municipal boundaries was at a meeting in May 2003, weeks after the US occupation of Iraq began. Ron Johnson, who was in charge of RTI's Local Governance contract with USAID, recalls the moment this way: "we were all asking questions: ... How does Baghdad work? How is it organized?... One of the Iraqis who was the head of the planning department brought out some maps. He laid them out on the table and showed us the geographic organization of the city of Baghdad. And that's where we discovered the notion that Baghdad was organized into ninety-plus neighborhoods."²⁸

At a time when some American advisors were recommending redrawing the Iraqi map into ethno-sectarian zones, the Baghdad Central group decided to stick with borders used in the Baghdad municipal maps they had so recently acquired. US soldiers tasked with establishing the system of neighborhood and district advisory councils were given these instructions: "During your meetings, area residents may tell you that the neighborhood population, name, and/or boundaries, etc. have changed or that some neighborhoods have been combined or split out. *Stick to the maps and representative numbers you were given.* Modifications can be made later, but we have to build the system from a known point. Commander's modifying things on their own now will throw off the entire system."[29] The decision to keep the existing administrative boundaries in Baghdad appears to have been made quickly and for pragmatic reasons. Colonel Dermer remembered a Baghdad Central meeting in which it was decided: "Should we stay with nine districts? Okay, we'll go with nine districts, because the maps were drawn and Iraqis understand that. They identify themselves by those districts. They also identify themselves by neighborhoods. Okay, great. How many neighborhoods were there in each district?"[30] The continuation of neighborhood and district administrative boundaries in the post-2003 era was a significant choice in the longer history of state-society relations in Baghdad. The reification of neighborhood administrative boundaries and the emplacement of councils within them resembled aspects of the bureaucratic structures that Baghdadis were accustomed to from the Baʿthist era. This contributed to expectations among the public that these new councils would serve roles similar to those of Baʿthist-era officials and councils within neighborhoods, though the Americans were largely unaware of what those expectations were.

Council Selections

US-created councils immediately ran into an issue of popular legitimacy. How could committees created by an occupying force be accepted by the public? This issue was compounded by the fact that Bremer adamantly opposed holding direct elections in 2003. This was a deeply controversial position that was critiqued by many Iraqis, including the influential Shiʿi cleric Ayatollah al-Sistani. Despite these protests, Bremer held firm, explaining that elections would likely only produce candidates who were opposed to the United States. "In a situation like this," Bremer explained, "if you start holding elections, the people who are rejectionists tend to win."[31]

Without the ability to hold elections for provincial councils, the team at Baghdad Central needed to find another way to populate the provincial council seats. In response, the Baghdad Central team designed a scaffolded council system over the course of just two or three days of meetings. This pyramidal structure placed the provincial council at the apex. Instead of holding elections, the council system would be populated from the bottom up by holding caucuses in each of Baghdad's eighty-eight neighborhoods. From these neighborhood councils, a small number of council members would be selected to represent their neighborhood in one of the nine district advisory councils to be established across the city of Baghdad (see map in Figure 1). A selection of the district council members would ultimately feed into the Baghdad provincial council, a powerful new political body that was the culmination of the local governance system.[32] This process was then replicated across rural areas in Baghdad province and, ultimately, throughout the country.

The CPA gave Baghdad Central a deadline of just one month in June 2003 to implement these caucuses to populate this pyramid-like coun-

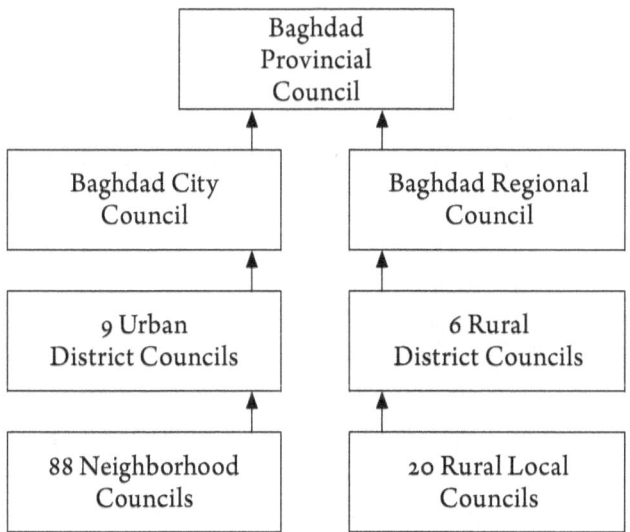

FIGURE 14 Organization of the US–created council system, 2003. The City Council was dissolved in 2005, leaving just three tiers of councils in the city of Baghdad: neighborhood, district, and provincial. My analysis here focuses exclusively on the urban councils, not the rural councils in Baghdad Province.

cil structure within Baghdad province. Over the span of just a few weeks, dozens of caucuses were hastily conducted across Baghdad's different neighborhoods and districts. By July 2003, Baghdad province had 120 new councils and an estimated 1,500 new council members.[33]

While this scaffolded system based on neighborhood caucuses was an expedient solution in the short term, the caucus selection system created significant problems with legitimacy in the long term. The fraught caucus process fell to the US Army to carry out, despite its lack of experience in this kind of work. In running the caucuses, the army relied heavily on the leadership of Colonel Joe Rice, a Civil Affairs officer who was a member of the Baghdad Central group. Deployed as an army reservist, his peacetime job was serving as the mayor of Glendale, Colorado. Glendale had a population of 5,000 residents and a total land area of just 0.6 square miles, and Rice was now responsible for creating a system of more than 100 local government councils to serve a province of more than 5 million people. As one of very few people in CPA headquarters who had experience working in a municipal government, he was viewed by Baghdad Central as one of the best available experts in local governance.[34] He was tasked with training soldiers in how to establish councils. He was also responsible for writing *The Baghdad Citizen Advisory Council Handbook*. This handbook governed how neighborhood and district councils operated until at least 2008, when Iraqi-authored council by-laws were passed.[35]

One striking feature of the US council program was that the American advisors in Baghdad Central did not take into consideration the centuries-old tradition of councils in Arab culture when they designed the structure and roles of these councils. Nor did they build on the more recent bureaucratic legacy of Baʿthist committees that existed in Baghdad's neighborhoods under Saddam's rule. In the eyes of one Iraqi advisor to Baghdad Central, this was a grave error. "When the British came [to colonize Iraq in 1916], they tried to use the way of the country. But the Americans, they tried to use the American way, and that's a big mistake."[36] Rather than follow the existing culture and processes of tribal councils or Baʿthist neighborhood committees based on personalized problem solving, Americans came armed with guides on *Robert's Rules of Order*.

In late May 2003, Rice held workshops to train US soldiers in how to run the caucus selection process. The official CPA terminology for caucuses was "selections" instead of "elections," though it was widely acknowledged that this distinction was lost on most Iraqis, and some US soldiers went ahead and called them "elections" anyway.[37] In some districts, observers recall being pleasantly surprised by large voter turnouts, with some crowds so big that they could fill a local soccer stadium. One caucus was held in an large underground bomb bunker that dated back to the Iran-Iraq War.[38] In other neighborhoods, there were only a few dozen attendees.[39] One Iraqi consultant for Baghdad Central emphasized how afraid Iraqis were to participate in a process that was so clearly associated with the occupying American forces out of fear that insurgents would kill them—a justified fear, given the high rates of assassination and threats that council members faced.[40] Many residents kept their distance because they did not want to be viewed as collaborators with the Americans.[41] The legitimacy of the caucus system depended on having a large turnout, and by most measures, the Americans failed to convince the public that these were adequately democratic processes. A survey conducted in the fall of 2003 found that roughly half of Iraqis did not know that local councils even existed.[42]

Despite low turnouts, officers were still expected to find council nominees who had varied backgrounds in terms of "gender, religion, religious group, income," and so forth despite a total lack of demographic data.[43] This preoccupation with proportional representation mirrored the CPA's decision to use an ethno-sectarian quota system for the interim Iraqi Governing Council. However, there were real, practical challenges with carrying out this task. One American member of Baghdad Central commented, "If we wanted [councils] to be roughly representative of the population, it kind of helps if you know what the population is. How do you know what the population is when you're an American who's been in the country for a month and doesn't speak Arabic?"[44] Beyond that, the ethno-sectarian quotas that were of utmost importance to the CPA were largely irrelevant to Baghdadis in 2003. As one coalition official stated, "representational" is in the eye of the beholder. In working to make the local council system "as representative as possible," he asked, "['Balanced' to] who? Balanced and representative to us? Well, yeah, in one sense, but not to Iraqis."[45]

Roughly six months after the councils were first formed, the CPA ordered a "refreshment" of some councils in order to fine-tune the council membership to more closely adhere to US priorities: they recruited more women onto councils and removed some former Baʿthists who had slipped through vetting during the initial selections. The refreshment process made it clear to everyone involved that the Americans would have a say in the final composition of the council, which cast doubt on the democratic merits of the caucus system. Colonel Dermer stated bluntly: "The difference ... is that in elections the voters actually decide; but in selection there's sometimes large input by us, direction, pushing, cajoling. We would not allow the election to settle the result. We would take the votes, calculate them, and if twenty-seven Sunnis were running an area, we would work it that somebody else, a Shia, for example, got on the council."[46] In some neighborhoods, the notion of carrying out any kind of democratic process was scrapped in the name of expediency: a US military commander in the Ghazaliyya neighborhood in western Baghdad confessed that he "more or less chose the council members" in his area.[47] An Iraqi working for Baghdad Central also recalled the pressure he received from American advisors to include certain influential individuals on local councils without going through the selection process for them.[48]

Iraqis' perceptions of the illegitimacy of the caucus process were not remedied over time. These new councils had no formal processes in place for how to replace the council members through periodic elections or caucuses after their term elapsed. As a result, the same council members who were first selected in 2003 still held their seats on neighborhood and district councils more than fifteen years later, a fact that hindered their legitimacy in comparison to the provincial councils and national parliament that began to hold competitive elections starting in 2005.[49] When neighborhood or district council members quit, moved, or were killed, councils used their own informal method to fill the vacancy, which one American observer derided as an "arbitrary process."[50] No official elections were ever held for the neighborhood and district councils from their creation in 2003 to their dissolution in 2019.

Roles and Responsibilities

From their inception, the purpose and functions of neighborhood and district advisory councils were contested and debated. This was due to competing visions and desires between different stakeholders who interacted with the local councils: the American creators of the council system, the Iraqi women and men who served on the councils, and the expectations and demands of the Baghdadi residents whom these councils ostensibly served.

American advisors in Baghdad Central viewed the creation of neighborhood and district advisory councils as a solution to the problem of not being able to hold elections for the provincial or city councils. "We use[d] the neighborhood council as a mechanism" to create a decentralized political system, according to RTI contractor Ron Johnson. "The endgame was not to create a neighborhood government system with elected council members and so forth and let it go from there."[51] As a result, the newly formed neighborhood and district advisory councils did not have a clear mandate for what roles they would play in mediating state-society relations. Their long-term purpose had to be created and defined after the fact.

In the absence of a clear mandate, neighborhood and district advisory councils persisted in part *because* of the ambiguous mixed messaging that surrounded them: they were initially blank slates onto which different stakeholders could project their hopes. US soldiers who oversaw the caucuses saw themselves as "imparting Democracy 101," in the words of one army officer.[52] New Iraqi council members had their own motives for joining: many approached their work as a way either to build up their influence within the new Iraqi political landscape or to serve their communities. For the American creators in Baghdad Central, the local councils were not meant to be empowered to act on their own, but merely to help communicate issues from their communities to the state. The *Baghdad Citizen Advisory Council Handbook* that was issued to new council members stated the purpose of the local councils:

> [to] promote cooperation and coordination, and to increase communication, among the residents of Baghdad . . . and Coalition civilian and military authorities. The purpose of these interim Advisory Councils is to give Baghdad residents a forum in which to participate in rebuilding their city's infrastructure and institutions. Through these interim Advisory Councils, Baghdad residents will be able to raise and prioritize issues of concern to Coalition and Iraqi authorities, as well as recommend solutions.[53]

In short, the officially stated purpose of these councils was primarily about communication: local councils could field citizen complaints and share those concerns with the CPA (or, later, the Iraqi government), which could then act on the information. In day-to-day activities, the councils also functioned as a liaison between their communities and the US military units assigned to their areas.[54] Pointedly, the councils themselves were not empowered to address residents' complaints: they had no budgets and no authority. They would merely be the messengers and advisors to those who could act.

No legal powers, no budgets of their own, no elections: the local council system was critically undermined even at the moment of conception. Even the Americans who worked with the local councils were stunned that they lasted as long as they did. Lt. Col. Rick Burns, who was a military liaison for the Karrada District Council in 2008, said: "There's no authority. The [Karrada] District Council... they've been meeting since 2003. This is the most amazing thing to me in the world, they continue to meet. They have no power."[55] The International Crisis Group stated the problem bluntly: "Local councils derive their potential legitimacy... from popular acceptance earned by successful delivery of goods and services. To provide services effectively, however, the councils would need to be given real powers, including budget oversight."[56]

Baghdadis had a very different set of expectations for the power and roles of the local councils than the Americans did. Iraqis were accustomed to Ba'thist-era neighborhood Popular Committees and neighborhood authorities like the *mukhtar* and *firqa* Ba'th Party office. These local representatives of the regime had the authority and capacity to reliably provide services and resolve problems within their roles in the Ba'thist system. The weak advisory role that the Americans prescribed for the councils was not what either Iraqi council members or members of the public wanted. Council members expressed their frustrations with their limited purview within the US–designed system, saying: "Okay, great, we appreciate this advisory role... but now give us real authority so we can make those decisions."[57] One council member told a reporter, "I resent my work; it's very frustrating... I hate it." He saw the council's lack of authority as "demeaning, if not insulting."[58] One American in Baghdad Central, who worked with district councils in western Baghdad, recalled that council members would complain to him, saying: "What are we even doing here?... It's like a puppet show."[59]

In response, the council members began to negotiate for more authority and more funding, first with the CPA and later with different Iraqi administrations. Though neighborhood and district advisory councils never won the right to oversee their own budgets, councils initially had access to funds through US military officers. Commanders Emergency Response Program (CERP) funds allowed US brigade commanders to disburse as much as $100,000 without needing authorization from the CPA, and division commanders could do the same with up to $500,000 of reconstruction funds.[60] Councils were also able to partner with other US agencies to access reconstruction funds through grants. After the withdrawal of US forces in 2011, councils worked in coordination with the Baghdad municipality to carry out projects, though getting funding was generally harder in this environment.

Remuneration for council members' work was also a sticking point. The Americans in Baghdad Central were initially staunchly opposed to council members being paid for their work, in line with American models of civic volunteering.[61] Council members, who viewed their positions as jobs and not as volunteer positions, were outraged. Over time, the council members succeeded in negotiating the right to small stipends from the Americans. In late 2003, a stipend (not salary) for district council members was set at $176 per month and at $105 per month for neighborhood council members.[62] These were modest amounts but certainly much more than many Baghdadis were earning at the time: the median income in early 2004 was $144, and unemployment was estimated at 18 percent.[63] Later, Prime Minister Nouri al-Maliki reclassified the local council members as government employees, and by the time the councils were dissolved, neighborhood council members were earning middle-class salaries of $1,200 per month.[64] These negotiations for project financing and salaries are illustrations of how Iraqi council members worked to adapt these US–created institutions to serve their interests, introducing a new chapter of state-society relationships and survival strategies in the post-2003 era.

Competing through Service Provision

Despite their limited powers, the US–created local neighborhood and district advisory councils became players in shaping state-society relations in Baghdad. These councils were organized, had access to US reconstruction funds, and had some security protection from the US military, and this gave them an advantage over most other individuals and groups seeking influence in the new political landscape.

In the years that followed the councils' creation, Baghdadis recalled turning to members of their local neighborhood or district councils for help. One example comes from the Shi'i district Kadhimiyya in northwest Baghdad. Even a prestigious district like Kadhimiyya, famous for its gold jewelry markets in addition to its Shi'i shrines, was facing significant shortages in services after 2003. A sixty-one-year-old shopkeeper from Kadhimiyya recalled the critical role his local council played in resolving issues with essential services and infrastructure: "If I needed help at this time [2003–8], I contacted a member of the local council. We were constantly experiencing problems with sewage, and we would send requests and petitions to the local council."[65] Some councils managed to build up a measure of legitimacy through implementing ambitious projects for their communities. For example, the Sadr City District Council provided free school uniforms to 190,000 schoolchildren in more than 400 schools in the Sadr City area in 2008, one of the last big projects that Samar oversaw in her time as a council member.[66] The Kadhimiyya District Council set up a women's center in 2004 to meet social needs in their community.[67] The neighborhood council for Risala in western Baghdad built a sports field and undertook projects to repair broken infrastructure.[68] The Radwaniyya and Saydiyya Neighborhood Councils on the far southwest outskirts of Baghdad coordinated with the CPA to pave their neighborhoods' dirt roads that flooded and became impassable when it rained, creating jobs by hiring local residents to perform the work.[69] A neighborhood councilwoman whom I interviewed in central Baghdad was proud of her work in creating a new elementary school in her community by soliciting grant funds in coordination with an NGO.[70]

Some Baghdadis assessed the work of neighborhood and district councils as a useful step in the direction of restoring the necessary level of services for the public—or, at least, felt that they were "better than nothing," in the words of one interviewee from 'Adhamiyya, in their efforts to distribute fuel and other resources to the community.[71] This man, a sixty-year-old retiree who had lived in this upscale district his entire life, noted that from 2003 to 2008 the council was only responsive "10–20 percent of the time." He described how much effort it took to petition the local council in those early years to remove heaps of garbage from the street or to address flooding in the roads. However, he praised one councilwoman in particular for her "very excellent work" in recent years in fixing the roads, and he spoke approvingly of how members of the council would tour the neighborhood, giving residents a chance to register complaints. This matches the description of the activities of an interviewed councilwoman in central Baghdad, as well.[72]

To advertise their work, some councils began to publicize their activities online. A photo album from 2011 entitled "Following Up On Citizens' Complaints" and posted on the Risala Neighborhood Council's Facebook page shows photos of a middle-aged man, presumably a council member, behind a desk in a small office decorated sparsely with maps of Baghdad, a certificate from USAID, and some artwork. Ten men of different ages crowd onto the couches in the office, some holding paperwork, all waiting to meet with the council member.[73]

On the whole, interviewees generally offered mixed or negative assessments of councils as having limited effectiveness and responsiveness in the face of the overwhelming needs of the communities they served. In Kadhimiyya, interviewees acknowledged the work of local councils in distributing fuel.[74] Another gave the local councils credit for repaving the streets and fixing potholes.[75] However, these same interviewees acknowledged the limitations of the councils; they might be able to provide fuel or patch potholes, but they were not responsive in solving larger systemic issues, such as electricity outages or security concerns.[76]

As a fifty-three-year-old accountant from the affluent Sunni ʿAdhamiyya district explained, "During this period [2003–8], services were basically gone because the government had no role anymore. State institutions had been destroyed, and there was the occupation and sectarian fighting. Most services went out: electricity, water, along with municipal services like cleaning the streets. With the gas and petrol crisis, people had to provide for themselves with the possibility of only simple assistance from the municipal council."[77] A seventy-year-old man from Fadhil described the council's activities as insufficient in the face of so many urgent needs in the years following the collapse of the state: "Members of the local council had a simple role during that period, and an example of that is that they built sidewalks inside and outside the Fadhil area. . . . The role of the local council was very little, and the people needed a lot in terms of the massive chaos that was happening. There was an absence of anyone effective at that time."[78] Interviewees in Kadhimiyya echoed the same frustrations that councils were not able to provide the entire range of needed services. As a fifty-six-year-old schoolteacher explained: "Members of the local council ... would come to us and knock on our doors as they were doing rounds through the whole neighborhood. They would say 'bring this number and we will give you some oil.' However, in the case of electricity outages, we would call them and call them but we suffered from a lack of responsiveness. But we would persist in contacting them—either us or our neighbors—until they would grant our plea. The council was only helpful in providing petrol, that was it."[79] With limited services and responsiveness, many gave up on the councils as reliable problem solvers for their communities. A woman who was a retired municipal employee living in ʿAdhamiyya complained: "The local council eventually fixed a broken pipe in front of our home, but only after [a friend] documented the issue and pushed them on it. . . . now we just try to solve our problems ourselves."[80]

Bribes and corruption were frequently mentioned in interviews. A forty-five-year-old man living in Sadr City put it this way: "We don't deny that there is a state. [If we have a problem,] we go to the [local] council . . . But they don't solve it." He went on to explain, "The only way anything happens is with a bribe. Bribery has become open in the public sector, unfortunately."[81] Some interviewees shared their perception that members of local councils were "cheaters and get no results."[82] Residents of the New Baghdad district in southeast Baghdad reported that "no one" went to the neighborhood or district councils for help because they were viewed as "corrupt" and "handpicked by Americans."[83] One resident who attended a New Baghdad District Council meeting walked away "disappointed," believing the council members were simply "in it for the bribes."[84] One district council member in Sadr City lamented that the public perceived that council members were taking in huge amounts of money but producing little or no public benefits for their communities.[85] An Iraqi advisor for district councils in western Baghdad concluded that the councils were a "mistake" because of how corruption negatively impacted any development efforts run through the councils, sharing examples of council members soliciting bribes or engaging in kickbacks with contractors selected to build schools in their communities.[86]

Personalized Problem Solving

One reason why councils floundered during the same period when militias gained capital has to do with patterns of state-society dynamics from the late Baʿthist era. As previous chapters have established, personal problems of all kinds—unemployment, medical costs, flooding streets, conflict with a boss or with a neighbor, the death of a wage earner—were often directed toward regime representatives who were embedded in Baghdad's neighborhoods. Depending on the issue, a resident of Baghdad might turn to their *mukhtar* or to their neighborhood rations agent, or submit a petition through their Baʿth Party *firqa* office. Because these actors were official agents within the Baʿthist regime, they were responsible for acting promptly or they would face reprimand.

After the fall of Saddam, Baghdadis continued to seek effective, personalized problem solving from the new actors who emerged to fill the resulting power vacuum. Religious leaders, militia leaders, tribal shaykhs, and members of the new parliament largely continued these same patterns of patronage and personal mediation. It was through personalized problem solving that these actors could increase their social and political clout, proving that they were influential powers within the new post-Saddam Iraq.

In contrast, US advisors to the local council system attempted to dissuade the new neighborhood and district council members from providing personalized problem solving or from giving direct aid to individuals. This partly came from a lack of understanding of how Baghdadis were accustomed to interacting with neighborhood officials, and partly from the fact that the US council system was explicitly modeled on American civic groups where personalized problem solving would have been inappropriate.

Early in the operations of the councils, an American member of Baghdad Central observed that members of the public would show up to council meetings to make what US advisors viewed as unexpected and inappropriate requests. Neighborhood residents would ask their council for personal help: for financial help for their families, mediation to solve a dispute with an employer, or help with child care.[87] From the perspective of this Baghdad Central advisor, these kinds of requests did not align with the purpose of the council as envisioned by its American creators. Personal problem solving would "enmesh" the council in residents' private affairs, whereas the councils were intended by Americans to act as liaisons between the community as a whole and the Baghdad municipality.[88]

However, personalized problem solving is precisely what Baghdadis were accustomed to from their neighborhood and governmental officials in the Saddam era. As discussed in chapter 4, Saddam encouraged petitioning for help with personal problems so that the regime could demonstrate its largesse and use social spending to shore up legitimacy. The CPA was completely unaware of what the dynamics of local governance were like under Saddam, however, so the Americans unwittingly re-created offices of neighborhood officials but gave them very different responsibilities and weaker powers than neighborhood officials had enjoyed under Saddam. Both the Baghdadi public and the Americans who set up the local council system in 2003 were mutually baffled by the expectations of the other for how councils should work.

Of course, Baghdadi council members understood what their communities wanted from them, and many individual council members acted within their personal and professional capacity to provide direct assistance. In the documentary *My Country, My Country*, ʿAdhamiyya District Council member Dr. Riyadh al-Adhadh is shown on many occasions acting as a personal problem solver for residents: slipping money to a destitute mother, helping to personally negotiate the release of a young man who had been kidnapped for ransom, and gathering information from detainees in Abu Ghraib to alert their families to their whereabouts.[89]

In interviews with Baghdadis, praise was often reserved for specific individuals who were uniquely helpful or responsive to their needs, rather than directed to the council as a whole. For example, one woman on the ʿAdhamiyya District Council was praised for being very effective. "No one else but this woman is doing anything in their neighborhood to help."[90] In Fadhil, one specific council member was praised for carrying out an urban beautification project in their neighborhood and creating new parks.[91] Personalized problem solving, rather than leaving time for public comments in town hall meetings run according to *Robert's Rules*, better aligned with what Baghdadis were accustomed to. Not only did it correspond more closely to the kinds of personal problem solving offered by neighborhood officials in the Baʿthist era, but it also was in accordance with a much older and widespread Iraqi custom of turning to family patriarchs, tribal shaykhs, or other respected community elders to intervene to solve an issue. Individual council members could try to provide this expected form of assistance, but because the council system itself was not structured to respond to individual problems, they were at a disadvantage compared to other rival powers who were competing for influence through service provision and personalized problem solving.

Of all the actors vying for legitimacy in the power vacuum after Saddam's fall, the neighborhood and district advisory councils were among the few with the organizational capacity and funding needed to act as service providers in the aftermath of the state's collapse. However, as this section has demonstrated, a key issue limiting their effectiveness was their legitimacy in the eyes of the Iraqi public and their limited mandate within the US–created local council system. Baghdadis had been socialized under the Ba'thist regime to expect that neighborhood representatives of the state should be highly responsive professionals who could solve their individual problems. Iraqis were also suffering from the lack of consistent essential services from the state, and the local councils were only able to provide partial remedies for service outages in their communities.

Of course, any individual or group striving to provide services in the aftermath of the 2003 invasion faced enormous difficulties: the destruction of municipal infrastructure and state offices could not be easily replaced by any council, no matter how well funded or designed. The violence and insecurity of this period took a deadly toll on the work of local councils, too. By 2006, at least 120 council members across Baghdad had been assassinated, nearly one-tenth of all the council members in the city.[92] A Sadr City district councilwoman whom I interviewed remembered the chilling deaths of her colleagues: one councilwoman had been thrown into a car trunk by kidnappers, and her body was later discovered in a heap of garbage. Another council member's body was strung up on a telephone pole as a warning to the neighborhood.[93] Local council members could not provide security to their constituents; they themselves were vulnerable to the rampant violence of the post-2003 period. In contrast, militias could offer the kinds of protection that Baghdadis sought in the violent years of the US occupation and sectarian conflict. Muqtada al-Sadr shrewdly operated both an armed militia and a public services organization, gaining power and influence by effectively providing a range of basic needs.

Muqtada al-Sadr's Bureau

In contrast to the US–created system of neighborhood and district advisory councils, the operations of Shi'i cleric Muqtada al-Sadr demonstrate how service provision could be a successful strategy to establish political legitimacy and influence within the post-Saddam political landscape. By the time of the US invasion, Muqtada was poised to take up his father's mantle of religious populism by preaching against the US occupation while delivering social services to poor Shi'i communities. Though Muqtada has never held office to date, he has been a successful political actor as a prominent opponent of the US occupation and as a rival to other Shi'i political parties in Iraq. His powerful Mahdi Army militia clashed with US forces and with Sunni armed groups during the years of sectarian violence in Baghdad. In the 2018 and 2022 elections, Muqtada led an electoral coalition that won the largest number of seats in parliament. His political supporters, militia fighters, religious followers, and the employees and volunteers who run his social services operations are collectively referred to as "Sadrists."

Muqtada al-Sadr created the Sadr Bureau in 2003 as a social services office to handle resident complaints about public services, food rations, disappeared relatives, property damage, and other pressing issues in the aftermath of the former regime's collapse. Unlike the American council system that lacked stable funding and budgetary powers, the Sadr Bureau had its own coffers from which to draw. Muqtada's funds came partly from tithes and donations, and, increasingly, from his Mahdi Army militia's capture and control of property through its murderous "cleansing" of Sunnis from Baghdad neighborhoods.[94]

Sadr's organizations provided financial aid to needy supporters, ran medical clinics, and responded to individual citizen petitions. These state-like activities helped enhance the reputation of Muqtada's organizations in many low-income, Shi'i segments of the population.[95] For example, Sadrists operated their own internally displaced persons (IDP) camps in the Shi'i neighborhood of Shu'la to house those who had been displaced by Sunni sectarian militias, issuing the displaced residents laminated identification cards as makeshift residency documentation.[96] They successfully diverted electricity from Baghdad's damaged grid to majority-Shi'i neighborhoods.[97] When Sunni militias carried out deadly attacks in Sadrist areas—

such as a series of car bombs in 2006 that killed nearly 200 residents in Sadr City—Sadr was able to swiftly mobilize an effective response: sealing off major roads, establishing security checkpoints, ushering in emergency medical personnel to attend to the wounded, and paying for the funerals of the slain.[98] Sadr also became a major employer of poor, Shi'i youths at a time when jobs were desperately needed: his Mahdi Army militia employed many young men as foot soldiers to carry out violent attacks, kidnappings, and acts of extortion in battleground neighborhoods, and the Sadr Bureau also put many to work providing humanitarian services within Shi'i neighborhoods.[99] The robust array of prompt, effective services offered by the Sadrists prompted one interviewee from Sadr City to proclaim: "There was no state, only the Sadr Bureau."[100]

The Sadr City district may possibly have enjoyed some of the best services in the entire city between 2003 and 2008, when other districts suffered tremendously from an acute shortage of basic life-sustaining provisions. Several interviewees from Sadr City specifically remarked on the Sadr Bureau's successful efforts to distribute petrol and propane to the district at a time when the rest of the city was experiencing severe shortages of fuel: "Every area of Baghdad was suffering from a gas and petrol shortage, but it was available in our area because the Sadr Bureau was providing it."[101] When it came to an electricity outage in the area, one resident recalled that a member of the Mahdi Army came out to repair it "in a way that was almost official," like what a government representative would do.[102] The work of the Sadr Bureau compared favorably to the services provided by US–created local councils. A fifty-eight-year-old woman who lived in Sadr City explained that local councils were hampered by the fact that they needed to coordinate with the municipality to get anything accomplished: "If there was a problem, they would first need to make an appointment with the municipal council, then go to the *mukhtar*, then go back to the municipal council. And nothing would actually get done without paying money [as a bribe]."[103] In contrast, this woman stated, "The most effective leaders at this time were the Sadr Bureau and Mahdi Army" because they did not need to engage in time-consuming interactions with the state in order to provide services directly to the people.[104]

Interviewees described the Sadrists as "controlling" the district or "ruling" the district. For instance, the Mahdi Army took over local policing responsibilities in the areas it controlled. If someone was a victim of theft, interviewees from Sadr City recalled how Sadr's Mahdi Army militia would track down suspects and help to recover the stolen money.[105] Residents remarked on how the Sadrists involved themselves in every matter in the district, big or small, even in family disputes.[106] This is very distinct from how any other state or municipal actors are described anywhere else in the city in the post-2003 era, where a multitude of weak and minimally effective actors operated to provide less-than-satisfactory services. Political scientists have noted that nonstate actors like the Sadrists can use essential services to "establish loyalty and quash alternative power sources," even "undermin[ing] state legitimacy."[107] By many measures, the Sadrists were effective in doing precisely this, acting as spoilers against US claims to authority in Iraq and, later, competing against Iraq's new Shi'i political parties. The effectiveness of Sadr's group in providing for citizens' needs prompted many local residents to see the Sadrists as their effective, if unofficial, government, insisting "[our district] can protect itself better than the government can" because of the Sadrists.[108]

Not every resident of Sadr City personally supported Sadr: some made sure to point out that there were both "good and bad" aspects to the Sadrists' work, including the Mahdi Army's role in sectarian killings. A few Sadr City interviewees were more overtly critical, unhappy at how the Mahdi Army invited US attacks on their district, or complaining about some shortcomings in the services promised by the Sadr Bureau.[109] However, there was remarkable consensus among the interviewees that the Sadr Bureau's services were overall robust, prompt, free, and effective, especially when compared to the rest of the city. That the Sadrists' successes were made possible through violently attacking and displacing Sunnis and other Iraqis who did not align with the Sadrists' worldview disturbed some residents, but not all, in this sample of interviews.

Sadr Bureau and Local Council Rivalries

The similarity between the kinds of humanitarian services offered by the Sadr Bureau and what the US–created neighborhood and district councils sought to offer Baghdadis set the two groups on a collision course. As mentioned earlier, Sadr initially pursued a vision of establishing his own local councils in Basra and in Sadr City in response to the power vacuum that formed in 2003 before Bremer shut them down.[110] In response, Sadr sought to simultaneously undermine and infiltrate the US–established councils in Sadr City and other districts of Baghdad that he controlled.

Sadr's first attempt to take over the Sadr City District Advisory Council happened in mid-2003, while he was first making a name for himself and emerging as an influential leader in Iraq. Clashes were increasing that fall between the Mahdi Army and the US forces stationed in Sadr City. In October 2003, a large group of Sadrists surrounded the Sadr City District Advisory Council and occupied it, taking it over and claiming to be the true representatives of Sadr City's residents.[111] Afraid and unable to return to their council meeting hall, the American-selected council members had to meet off-site, either in private homes or in the secure Green Zone.[112] Several council members are alleged to have switched sides and openly supported the Sadrist movement in the midst of the takeover.[113]

The Sadrists occupying the district council hall proclaimed their grievances about the councils' legitimacy to one of Baghdad Central's top officials, Colonel Dermer, when he came to meet with them. A journalist recounted the exchange, in which a spokesman for the Sadrist protestors claimed that there were "no elections in our neighborhood" and that the council was "not legitimate" because it was "put together by the coalition without the knowledge of the people." The spokesman demanded that the council be disbanded. In response, Dermer defended the caucus selection process and insisted on the power of the CPA to form councils on its own terms: " 'There is no Iraqi law,' shot back Col. Dermer. 'There is only one law in Iraq—it's coalition law.' "[114] The standoff ended through force: US troops retook the council hall and arrested the protestors who refused to leave.[115]

In an odd way, some American observers saw a silver lining in the Sadrist occupation of the Sadr City District Council building in 2003. That Sadr perceived the district council as a threat meant that the council must have achieved some kind of legitimacy and standing in the community. Furthermore, they wondered if the seeds of representative democracy were taking root in Iraq. After all, Sadr did not call for the abolition of a local council; he just wanted his own people to run the council.[116] This interpretation overlooks the fact that Sadr had tried to establish local councils of his own months before, and that councils are a centuries-old tradition within

Arab culture. The Sadrists were not looking to the US–created council system as inspiration, nor are all councils necessarily democratic.

After restoring the Sadr City District Council, the US military fought a series of bitter battles with Sadr's Mahdi Army militia in 2004 in Sadr City and other parts of the city. Although military analysts judge that the Mahdi Army was nearly "routed" by US military forces by the end of 2004, Sadrists were able to maintain their local influence by leaning into their provision of social services within Shi'i neighborhoods through the Sadr Bureau. Militarily, the Mahdi Army shifted its focus from attacking US forces to attacking rival Sunni militias in key battleground neighborhoods as the sectarian conflict worsened. As Sadrists gained territory through the sectarian cleansing neighborhoods, they entrenched themselves in these communities by establishing a "monopoly on service provision" and positioning themselves as "benefactors" of the city's low-income Shi'a through the services of the Sadr Bureau.[117]

By 2004, Sadr City District Council members recalled working out a *modus vivendi* with the Sadrists in their area. As one council member reported at the time: "We have built good relationships with all the parties in Sadr City, including the Sadr Bureau. Before, we had to be scared of them. Now we can go to work, to our house, [to the District Advisory Council] Hall. Most parties show up here and communicate."[118] One US commander even wondered aloud if there was a way to "embrace" the Sadr Bureau without "undermining" the district council, seeing how the Sadr Bureau enjoyed significant legitimacy in the community.[119] The idea of working out some kind of cooperative arrangement with the Sadrists was born out of necessity: it was nearly impossible to get any work done in Sadr City without tacit approval from the Sadrists. As one council member complained, even the district police chief could not carry out evictions or perform other routine police work without first securing approval from the Sadr Bureau. In many cases, the police referred citizens directly to the Sadr Bureau to issue their complaints and receive remedies.[120]

The newfound era of cooperation that developed between the Sadr City District Council and the Sadr Bureau had another explanation—this one more grim. Part of this cooperation was because Sadrists were able to gain more and more footholds within the council itself. When vacancies on the council opened up, Sadrists worked behind the scene to ensure that whoever was appointed to that vacancy would be friendly toward their group. However, vacancies usually only opened up when a council member was assassinated or scared off by threats—as eventually happened to thirty-two of the forty-one original members of the Sadr City District Council.[121] Sadrists were often suspected to be behind these killings and intimidation campaigns. In one case, though, it was a US soldier who killed a Sadr City District Council chair, Muhannad al-Ka'abi, when he objected to being searched entering the district council building where he worked. Muhannad's killing threatened to rupture the already fragile working relationship between Sadr City council members and their American advisors, giving Sadr a bigger opening.[122]

Though the Sadrists and the councils eventually worked out a level of cooperation, this friendliness only took place after the Sadrists had rid the council of most of its political independents.[123] By 2007, the US Embassy estimated that more than two-thirds of the Sadr City District Council members were pro-Sadr.[124] Though Joe Rice recalls that he and others from Baghdad Central were supportive of having Sadrists on the Sadr City District Council, many other Americans did not feel that way.[125] Researcher Mehiyar Kathem found evidence in leaked US State Department memos that the US Embassy hoped to undermine the most fervent Sadrists on the council in support of political moderates and independents.[126]

Despite achieving high levels of infiltration of the Sadr City District Advisory Council, Sadr was evidently still dissatisfied by the presence of the US-created council that still included a handful of political moderates. In 2008, he decided to strike again. Sadr's circumstances that prompted his 2008 attack on the Sadr City District Advisory Council were vastly different from the context of 2003, when Sadr was relatively new to Iraqi politics. The US military and the Mahdi Army had resumed their direct confrontations through a series of battles in 2007 and 2008—part of the US "surge" efforts to gain control of the city. American forces carried out ground raids and bombing campaigns within the densely populated neighborhood of Sadr City in summer and fall 2007, killing dozens of civilians and militia fighters.[127] In the outrage that followed the bombing of civilian areas, Prime Minister Nouri al-Maliki forbade US foot soldiers from entering the Sadr City district from that point onward.[128]

The final showdown between the Mahdi Army and US forces took place in the spring of 2008. During this time the Mahdi Army was facing off not only against the Americans, but also against Prime Minister Nouri al-Maliki, who represented a rival faction of Shiʻi political parties. In spring 2008, Maliki turned on the Sadrists, choosing to empower the rival Shiʻi political parties at the expense of Sadr.[129] While Maliki was focusing his attention on Sadr's strongholds in the southern city of Basra, Sadr directed his forces to mount a surprise attack in Baghdad.[130] Between March 23 and March 25, 2008, Sadr's Mahdi Army effectively took control of all of Sadr City's checkpoints from the Iraqi police—many of whom were sympathetic to Sadr anyway and needed little persuading. With that, Sadr sealed off the district from Iraqi or American military forces and began launching rocket attacks at the Green Zone.[131] Though Maliki told the US military to respond, he still did not allow US soldiers to enter Sadr City on the ground.[132] Even with the US military restricted to the air, Sadr's militia was ultimately unable to hold out against the onslaught. By May 2008, Sadr all but admitted military defeat. The Iraqi Army moved to reclaim control over Sadr City by May 20, and Sadr announced the dissolution of the Mahdi Army militia in June 2008.[133]

In the wake of the Mahdi Army's military defeat in 2008, Muqtada doubled down on his efforts to rebuild his influence and legitimacy through service delivery. He needed to restore his credentials as the sole power broker in the Sadr City district, and in this context, he set his sights once again on the Sadr City District Council as a rival to be completely coopted or eliminated. In December 2008, Sadrists carried out another direct attack on the Sadr City District Council building.

The Sadr City District Council had arguably grown somewhat more influential in 2007 and 2008 as the United States funneled reconstruction aid money through the council as part of the surge strategy to win the "hearts and minds" of Iraqis. Because US troops were not allowed to patrol the district themselves, per Maliki's orders, Americans had to rely on the district council to be the face of US humanitarian aid and development efforts in the area. Other international NGOs also provided grants to the district council to avoid entanglement with other local organizations that might have been coopted by Sadr.[134] Although the Sadrists had infiltrated the district advisory council to a considerable degree, there were still political independents on the council who resisted Sadr's overtures. As Sadr's movement was greatly weakened following his military defeat by the Americans and his political isolation within Maliki's government in May 2008, Sadr could no longer afford to have political independents on the district council stymying his work.

In the summer of 2008, the chair of the Sadr City District Council, 'Abd al-Hassan al-Jibara, had isolated many of his fellow council members. Jibara was known to be pro-Sadrist, but his political affiliation was not the problem. Many council members, even those who were also Sadrists, allegedly complained of his corruption and general ineptitude in his responsibilities as chair. With the encouragement of the US Army officers who advised the council, the council voted to remove Jibara as chair and to replace him with another council member, Hassan Shama, who had served as chair previously. The council was scheduled to issue its vote of no-confidence in Jibara and to vote in Shama on June 24, 2008. While council members, American advisors, and their translators milled around the council building ahead of the vote, Sadrist forces detonated a bomb hidden in the foyer of the district council hall. Twelve people were killed in the bombing. Shama survived unscathed and assumed his responsibilities as the new chair in August 2008, though he was targeted by another unsuccessful assassination attempt in December of that year.[135]

The Sadr City District Council survived the 2008 bombing, but in hindsight, the 2008 bombing of the district council building symbolized a moment in which the fortunes of the district council waned while the influence of Muqtada al-Sadr continued to grow. Muqtada al-Sadr and the Sadr City District Council did not have any more head-to-head violent confrontations, but after the US withdrawal of troops in 2011, Sadr did not need to. It was clear who had won the contest for the hearts and minds of Sadr City's residents. As US forces prepared to withdraw from Iraq, the fortunes of the Sadr City District Advisory Council—and all of the US-created councils in Iraq—continued to decline over the years due to allegations of corruption, ineffective service provision, and perceptions of illegitimacy. Funding for the councils dried up significantly after US troops withdrew, taking their CERP funding with them. In contrast, Muqtada al-Sadr continued to reinvent himself, becoming a major player in national Iraqi politics far beyond the borders of Sadr City, Baghdad. From a low point in 2008, Muqtada al-Sadr demonstrated his astute political skills to advocate political platforms of reform and Iraqi nationalism against other Shi'i political parties. While his political role has taken many forms, he has remained a highly influential and relevant figure to the present. The services provided by the Sadr Bureau helped to cement Sadr's influence and legitimacy as a rising power broker in the immediate aftermath of the US invasion.

Conclusion

> The state was officially dead [after 2003]. There was no authority or executive power. It was a period of ruin and destruction. There were few services, and they were bad. There was the spread of chaos and constant need.
> —Sixty-year-old man from Fadhil[136]

> In this period of destruction and ruin [2003–8], everyone had to rely on themselves. This was the worst time by far.
> —Forty-five-year-old man from Kadhimiyya[137]

> There was chaos.... There was no law, and there was no state.
> —Fifty-five-year-old man from 'Adhamiyya[138]

Across Baghdad, residents of all backgrounds suffered the effects of the sudden collapse of the state in 2003. Uncontrolled looting, battles between occupying soldiers and insurgents, opportunistic violence, and sectarian killings made the streets treacherous. But life inside the home was also increasingly unsustainable as sanitation services, electricity, and water treatment systems faltered. Citizens depended on these essential services that were formerly provided by the state. Even under the strain of sanctions, public services like electricity had been more reliable in the 1990s in Baghdad than they were after 2003. But even as residents of Baghdad suffered, the sudden absence of essential services provided an opportunity for aspiring new power players in Iraq. Distributing fuel to neighborhood residents was a tangible way that nascent power brokers like religious leaders, tribal shaykhs, militias, or council members could try to build up credibility and influence on a localized scale. Few groups had the organizational capacity or funds to provide services consistently or on a large geographic scale: Muqtada al-Sadr's organizations and the US–created local council system were two groups that aspired to city-wide influence through service provision.

Muqtada al-Sadr's Sadr Bureau and Mahdi Army were ultimately more successful in service provision and in building up legitimacy and influence than the US–created local advisory councils, though this came at a steep cost to Baghdadis. Because of the Mahdi Army's bloodletting and seizure of property in Sunni and mixed neighborhoods, the Sadr Bureau amassed substantial resources. This gave Sadr the capacity to deliver services within the Shi'i neighborhoods he controlled, and especially in Sadr City. Sadr was also keenly attuned to the desires and expectations of the Baghdadi public, who had been habituated to expect personalized problem solving for their individual concerns, such as family disputes, health care expenses, or unemployment. In contrast, the US–created council system was structured and advised to provide programmatic services for communities, rather than personalized problem solving, and what it could provide to communities was often less effective and impressive than the work of the Sadrists. Associated with an occupying force, the US–created councils suffered a legitimacy gap that could not be easily overcome.

However, the comparative success of the Sadrists between 2003 and 2011 in providing services to the communities they controlled did not translate into improved conditions for the majority of Baghdadis. Even residents in Sadrist-dominated areas complained about declining services as Muqtada al-Sadr's priorities shifted toward national politics and away from service provision in districts like Sadr City. "The Sadr Bureau became weak" in the period from 2009–19, one resident complained.[139] Over time, residents of Sadr City began to complain about the same ineffective cast of actors present in every other region of the city: politicians, tribal shaykhs, and members of the local council, none of whom was reliably effective or responsive in providing services at the requisite level.[140] At the time of writing governance in Iraq remains a patchwork of competing power brokers and government actors.

Twenty years after the US invasion of Iraq, the services provided by the former regime have not been replaced in a widespread and reliable way, something that numerous interviewees remarked upon. During the fourteen-month period of direct US rule in Iraq, the US Congress pledged more than $18 billion to go toward reconstruction projects.[141] US reconstruction spending increased to $60 billion by the time the United States withdrew its troops in 2011.[142] Additional revenues from Iraqi oil sales were also earmarked to contribute to the reconstruction effort.[143] However, much of this massive influx of aid was embezzled or misspent.

Of the sixty Baghdadis interviewed for this chapter, more than half (35) indicated that the pre-2003 period was the "best" in terms of services and responsive governance in comparison to the 2003–8 and 2009–19 periods. One man in ʻAdhamiyya asserted that the pre-2003 period "remains the best historical period that Iraq experienced in terms of services, and development, and everything that a citizen requires."[144] Even in Sadr City, which had been neglected economically and harshly surveilled by Saddam's security apparatus, some appraised the quality of services under Baʻthist rule positively. An eighty-four-year-old woman from Sadr City stated that pre-2003 was "the best" period for services. Public services were "excellent" and delivered "quickly" to citizens. There was good security, in her recollection. She considered it a comparatively "quiet and stable period when you look back after what happened" after 2003, she stated.[145] Not all Baghdadis agree with her assessment, especially those who were persecuted by Saddam Hussein's security forces. However, the phenomenon of "authoritarian nostalgia" in Iraq today is a testament to the fact that, twenty years after the US invasion and the formation of a new Iraqi government, Iraqis are still suffering from electricity outages, flooded streets, and sewage problems.[146] It remains to be seen whether any Iraqi political actors will finally be able to provide these essential services after decades of strain, neglect, damage, and corruption on Baghdad's infrastructure.

Conclusion

OVER THE COURSE OF six eventful decades from 1950 to 2011, state-society relations in Baghdad evolved as both residents and rulers adapted to changing economic and political circumstances. Through myriad mundane interactions between citizens and bureaucrats, the spaces, rhythms of time, and social networks of the city were transformed, altering the built environment of the city and the relationships between its inhabitants, its rulers, and its physical landscape.

Three key findings emerge from this study of neighborhood-based practices of everyday politics in Baghdad. First is the illumination of how important street-level bureaucrats were for day-to-day governance in modern Iraqi history. Moving away from a focus on national leaders revealed the important responsibilities and decision-making power held by local Ba'th Party leaders, *mukhtars*, rations agents, and neighborhood-based officials. That Baghdadis most often addressed their petitions and appeals to their local *firqa* or *shu'ba* officials—ideally with a letter of endorsement from the neighborhood *mukhtar*, as well—illustrates that city residents were indeed familiar with the roles these intermediary authorities played, and they turned to them to take care of both routine and emergency matters. After 2003, US-created councils and other emerging powerbrokers sought to re-create aspects of neighborhood-based service provision, though with limited success.

A second theme highlighted the possibilities and limitations of citizen advocacy within authoritarian contexts and even now, in an ostensibly democratic system where ethno-sectarian parties have entrenched themselves in systems of patronage. Residents of Baghdad have leveraged their personal relationships with street-level bureaucrats in their neighborhoods to advocate for themselves to acquire resources, solve personal problems, appeal for justice, and more. Foregrounding the agency of Baghdadis in shaping their own history provides a counterbalance to state-centered accounts of Iraq's modern history. Here, Baghdadis are not just the objects of state initiatives but also drivers of change, effective in attenuating the impact of government policies on their lives and advocating for their interests.

A third theme relates to the relevance of Baghdad's neighborhoods as the key administrative units for governance from the Ottoman period to the present. The form, number, and composition of Baghdad's neighborhoods changed dramatically over the years, from small Ottoman enclaves to new silos for professionals and migrants in the 1950s and 1960s, to the sectarian cleansing of Baghdad's neighborhoods in the early 2000s. However, throughout these many periods of change, Baghdadis continued to reconstitute the meaning and identities of their local neighborhoods. The enduring social and administrative significance of Baghdad's neighborhood boundaries are due, in part, to the way that the Baʿth Party relied on neighborhoods as the building block of its entire governing apparatus in Baghdad. These neighborhood and district administrative boundaries survived the US invasion and occupation of Iraq, as the CPA adopted Baʿthist municipal boundaries and endowed them with local councils. Though the councils floundered and the municipality's essential services remain spotty to this day, the underlying administrative structures have remained. That sectarian militias sought to control different neighborhoods of the city is a testament to their importance as geographical markers, strategic positions, sources of revenue, and symbolic codes for social and cultural identities.

Foregrounding the enduring relevance of neighborhood and district divisions in Baghdad's history provides an alternative lens for analyzing Iraqi society that moves way from the problematic reliance on sect as the primary framework for understanding diversity within Baghdad's population. Neighborhoods contain within them layers of identity markers and meaning: socioeconomic wealth, signals of culture and education, vocational profession, ancestral origins, ethnic and religious affiliation, homogeneity or diversity. All of these can be encoded within the identity of a neighborhood. Sect is often deployed as a monolithic marker, but Baghdadis who identify as residents of Sadr City occupy a very different positionality within Baghdad than residents of Kadhimiyya, which is also a Shi'a-majority district. Adopting neighborhoods and districts as an analytical frame can help tie together these various forms of identity markers that Baghdadis inhabit without simplistically reducing communities to a singular demographic trait.

No history is ever a complete telling. This portrait of state-society relations and everyday politics in Baghdad in the second half of the twentieth century and the early years of the twenty-first will undoubtedly be refined through further research. Additional microhistorical and anthropological studies of state-society relations in each of Baghdad's districts will paint a more complete picture of the variations and trends in local governance practices in different parts of the city, delving more deeply into specific neighborhoods.

Another area for future research will be to contextualize the experience of state-society relations in Baghdad in comparison with other Iraqi cities, towns, and rural communities. Piecing together a picture of state-society relations in Baghdad using the vast records of the Ba'th Party archives required the painstaking construction of a mosaic picture with the tiniest fragments of data. Years more of research in these archives would have been required to repeat the process for other cities; there was no straightforward method that allowed for comparative analysis between Baghdad and other cities using the same vast set of records. There are already impressive histories of urban architecture and urban planning for Karbala, Najaf, Erbil, Mosul, and other Iraqi cities by Iraqi scholars, along with some academics in the West.[1] However, more work is needed to analyze the history of governance systems and citizen advocacy in these urban spaces in order to gain a picture of how state-society relations operated in each of these areas.

Likewise, provincial histories and an analysis of rural areas will undoubtedly bring to light a different picture of how locally embedded community leaders and regime representatives functioned in villages and small towns. Historian Arbella Bet-Shlimon has pointed out that "capital cities are often the exclusive points of reference for histories of modern states," calling instead for the study of "political dynamics from the 'peripheries'" to gain a more complete understanding of how areas outside the capital "alternatively cooperate with and resist incorporation into the state."[2] More work is needed to gain this holistic understanding of state-society relations in every part of the country.

Finally, the findings presented here raise the question of how the urban history of Baghdad relates to the experiences of other cities across the globe. Iraq has often been excluded from histories of oil and development in the Gulf States, in part because the damage to Iraq's oil infrastructure during the Iran-Iraq War and prohibitions of oil sales for much of the 1990s put Iraq on a different trajectory than that of nearby oil-exporting states like the United Arab Emirates or Saudi Arabia. Nevertheless, there are compelling similarities in the early history of Iraq's oil-funded modernization schemes and other Gulf states, and further research can help draw out salient points of comparison. Kuwait and Saudi Arabia are two natural starting points for comparison since both experienced construction booms in the 1950s and 1960s, often guided by some of the same urban planners: Constantinos Doxiadis and the Minoprio, Spencely, MacFarlane firm.[3] While the history of Iraq's oil sector diverges sharply from the Gulf in the 1980s, the impact of war and sanctions on Iraq's oil sector in the 1980s and 1990s invites comparison to countries like Nigeria and Iran that also saw disruptions to oil-funded development because of armed conflict and sanctions.

Epilogue: State-Society Relations after 2003

Dynamics of state-society relations forged in the Ba'th Party era continue to have ripple effects in Baghdad today. Personalized problem-solving through the auspices of a *mukhtar* or Ba'th Party *firqa* office in the 1990s informed citizens' expectations even after 2003 that local bureaucrats would fulfill these roles. With the collapse of the state and all essential services in 2003, the need for a competent local authority to solve problems related to sewage or security was dire, though few were able to deliver.

In the competitive marketplace for emerging power brokers in 2003, the practice of personalized problem solving evolved into clientelism. With the establishment of the new Iraqi government in 2005, political power was divided like a pie between ethno-sectarian political parties who each received control of certain government ministries (and their assets) based on census demographics. Since Arab Shiʻa make up the largest community in Iraq, they are granted control of half of the government ministries, including the powerful Ministry of the Interior and Ministry of Oil. Sunni parties control one-quarter of the remaining ministries, including the Ministry of Defense, and Kurdish parties are given 20 percent of government ministries, with the remainder distributed among Iraq's smaller minorities.[4] This ethno-sectarian quota system for sharing power is referred to as the *muhasasa*, or "apportionment" system.[5]

Since the US invasion in 2003, state-society relations in Baghdad have been driven by clientelism. The *muhasasa* power-sharing system incentivized political actors to respond only to their own supporters, rather than to all Iraqi citizens.[6] Baghdadis' survival strategies depend on developing patron-client relationships with actors who are in turn connected to one of the ethno-sectarian political parties that have become entrenched within these apportioned fiefdoms.

The effectiveness of intermediaries depends on their personal relationships and connections to these ethno-sectarian systems of patronage. These kinds of personal connections, or *wasta*, are increasingly needed to secure the basic requirements for a dignified life, like repairing essential services in one's neighborhood and getting hired in a job. Routine interactions between Baghdadis and government officials frequently require bribes, a problem that has worsened dramatically since 2003. Corruption had already been increasing in Iraq during the sanctions years, but it increased significantly in part because of free-flowing reconstruction cash that the United States brought in by the airplane load in the early 2000s.[7] The *muhasasa* system is also an engine for embezzlement, bribes, and kickbacks: state budgets are used as patronage systems to enrich the political supporters of each ethno-sectarian political party that controls a given ministry.[8] As a result, patronage only flows to a small circle of insiders connected to political parties and their affiliated militias; the average Iraqi is not included, except as a payer of bribes if a service is needed.

On October 1, 2019, a massive popular protest movement known as the *Tishrin* (October) protests broke out in Baghdad and spread throughout many parts of the country. The catalyst was the firing of a highly respected anti-terrorism general, Lieutenant General ʻAbd al-Wahhab al-Saʻidi, whose popularity threatened the political elites. Protestors filled the streets in

Baghdad and in cities around the country railing against the *muhasasa* political system. This was blamed as the source of many of Iraq's problems: corruption, failing infrastructure, and chronically high unemployment rates. "We want a country" was the slogan of the protestors, calling for an overhaul of the entire political system.[9] Personalized problem solving, now in the form of party patronage systems, has proven to be an inadequate replacement for functional state systems and essential services.

A Right to the City

The October protests lasted nearly six months until militias and state security forces violently dispersed protestors, killing hundreds of people. Protestors in Baghdad occupied downtown *Tahrir* (Liberation) Square beneath the famous Freedom Monument designed by Iraqi sculptor Jawad Saleem. The symbolic occupation of space by protestors in Baghdad, as well as in other cities throughout Iraq, connects to themes about imagined geographies of inclusion and exclusion from the twentieth century.

Baghdad's urban landscape was violently reconfigured in the early 2000s. Sectarian militias and death squads purged mixed neighborhoods and drove residents to flee to the relative safety of homogeneous Sunni or Shiʻi districts. Christians and other minorities were caught in the cross-fire or targeted, and fled either to Kurdistan or out of the country altogether. As many as 400,000 Baghdadis were displaced.

These demographic changes were reinforced through concrete: hundreds of miles of blast walls were erected by US military forces within the city of Baghdad.[10] One US military unit erected more than 2,000 blast walls in a single week in 2007.[11] These towering concrete walls were designed to hamper the movement of armed groups. Lumbering concrete blast and guard tower walls snaked throughout the city, lining the highways and encircling markets, government buildings, sometimes whole neighborhoods.[12] They constricted the movement of all Baghdadis, cutting off the ordinary and life-giving movement of people traversing the city: people visiting friends and family, customers shopping in their favorite markets, workers and students heading to their labors, and pilgrims traveling to religious shrines. Residents were confined within the walls of their districts or had to endure hours of security screening and congestion when they passed through the heavily armed checkpoints that monitored the few entrances to their neighborhoods. Caecilia Pieri, a scholar of Baghdad's architecture, observed that the blast walls created a "geography of fear," carving the once contiguous fabric of the city into "self-sufficient, separate neighborhoods" and creating new, isolated "centers" and fearsome "peripheries" to be avoided at all costs.[13] Many interviewees called them "open-air prisons." Though most of these blast walls were eventually dismantled, they reinforced the new composition and identities of Baghdad's neighborhoods achieved through years of bloodshed and displacement.[14]

In the context of the forced displacement and sectarian cleansing in Baghdad's recent past, protestors occupying the central Tahrir Square in downtown Baghdad made a strategic and symbolic claim to space at the heart of the city as a space for political demands. Whereas Baghdad's neighborhoods had been violently uprooted and encircled through the logic of sectarian violence and security walls, protestors rerouted traffic and blocked off streets as a manifestation of their calls for a new future for their city. Crucially, protestors represented a diverse array of Baghdad's population, with different socioeconomic and sectarian backgrounds.[15] In this liminal space created by the protests, protestors did not only proclaim their right to the city and demand the services and justice owed to them as citizens. They also symbolically re-created a space in Baghdad's center that "transcended boundaries of class, age, profession and gender" and that was not primarily defined through sectarian logic.[16]

With the violent dispersal of the protestors from Tahrir Square, imagined geographies of inclusion and exclusion remain stubbornly in place. All the while, new, privatized development projects are increasing markers of inequality on Baghdad's landscape in defiance of protestors' demands for an end to corruption. Indeed, the construction of new shopping malls, restaurants, and apartment complexes in and around Baghdad in recent years is not necessarily a sign of a city recovering from harms past but represents the perpetuation of new ones. Since the end of large-scale sectarian fighting in Baghdad in 2009, several new shopping malls and other large development projects have been unveiled, often celebrated as signs of normalcy returning to city life. However, these private enterprises are usually linked to corrupt systems of patronage and embezzlement that have benefited elite networks connected with certain ethno-sectarian political parties and their militias.

Political scientist Omar Sirri has described how private developers have benefited from their corrupt relationships with Iraqi politicians:

> Political and economic elites *legally* appropriate formerly-public lands by "purchasing" property for little or no money—threatening, pressuring, and bribing bureaucrats to change ownership documents in the process. In other cases, businessmen close to politicians are offered sweetheart land-lease rates ... paying a fraction of the value of the land and reaping windfalls in annual profits on whatever they build. Politicians and their parties also benefit from these transactions by way of kickbacks and donations.[17]

These private commercial ventures have taken place with little oversight; Iraqi urban planners I interviewed bemoan how zoning laws and urban planning regulations are quickly set aside for bribes.

The rebuilding of city spaces through unrestrained commercial development reifies inequality in the city, as well-off Baghdadis enjoy shopping for luxury goods in marble-floored malls, while low-income residents suffer the environmental impacts.[18] Baghdad has lost roughly half of its green spaces since 2003.[19] US military forces cut down and bulldozed precious date palms to improve visibility for pilots circling Baghdad's airspace.[20] This recent wave of unregulated commercial construction has further shrunk green space as public gardens have been paved over for development projects.[21] Palm groves in the southern Baghdad district of Dora have been recently cut down to build yet another mall.[22] This environmental destruction has contributed to worsening living conditions for many Baghdadis: trees provide much needed shade and cooling during Baghdad's blistering summers, and they help ameliorate air pollution.

Protestors in Tahrir Square were largely unsuccessful, at least in the short term, in overriding Baghdad's imagined geographies of exclusion with their vision for a more inclusive and responsive government. Instead, the city of Baghdad continues to be remade by the interlinked forces of *muhasasa* patronage and neoliberal development. These new development projects bring back a question from Baghdad's construction boom in the 1950s: who is meant to benefit from all this new development? Religious and ethnic minorities and low-income Baghdadis have found themselves

Conclusion 229

increasingly marginalized within the urban landscape and the imagined community of the city.

Today, Baghdad's city landscape holds many stories in tension, bearing witness to the triumphs and tragedies of recent decades in its streets and squares. On one level, personal traumas remain embedded in the city's neighborhoods, haunting the urban landscape. Driving through Baghdad today, one hears stories about kidnappings that took place in certain intersections, or of snipers who held positions in abandoned apartment buildings alongside main thoroughfares. A seventy-year-old widower from the historic Shi'i district of Kadhimiyya in northwest Baghdad spoke about how seeing corpses floating in the Tigris forever changed his relationship to the river that flows through the center of the city.[23] An Associated Press photographer wrote that, when he passes through the streets of Baghdad today, he will "say a silent prayer for the dead ... on certain residential streets, at a particular restaurant, in a square where minibuses gather," where attacks occurred.[24] Bullet holes still mar the buildings on the prominent Haifa Street promenade, attesting to the violence that took place there.

Baghdad's built environment also speaks to past glories and to the possibility of a brighter future. Baghdadi residents can once again haggle over prices at the famous booksellers' market on Mutanabbi Street, which had been destroyed through a bomb in 2007 and recently rebuilt. The Iraq National Museum reopened after devastating looting in 2003. Abbasid and Ottoman-era monuments stand alongside stunning examples of mid-century modern architecture. And yet it is also true that these proud monuments in the city are themselves still embedded within imagined geographies of inclusion and exclusion, haunted by their associations with corruption or by violence that once occurred at those sites.

The city of Baghdad, like any city, contains a multitude of stories and layers of meaning that speak to the complexities of life that have played out in these spaces over generations. How young Baghdadis and *Tishrin* protestors advocate for themselves to government representatives will continue the process of shaping the city's built landscape and imagined geographies for the next generation.

GLOSSARY OF KEY ARABIC TERMS

al-ʿAsima "the capital," the name given to a large informal settlement on the outskirts of Baghdad in the mid-twentieth century

bayʿa allegiance oath

bayt al-daʿara brothel

bighaʾ prostitution

faraʿ "branch," referring to Baʿth Party offices responsible for one of Baghdad's nine large districts (see Figure 2)

firqa "division," referring to the lowest ranking Baʿth Party office (see Figure 2)

Ghajar an ethnic minority in Iraq

hayy a large neighborhood

intifada uprising, here referring to 1991 protests against Saddam Hussein's regime

khaliyya "cell," the smallest unit in the Baʿth Party organizational structure

al-liwat or **al-luta** sodomy

mahalla (pl. mahallat) small neighborhood

muhasasa "apportionment," referring to the Iraqi governmental system of sharing power according to ethno-sectarian divisions after 2003

mukhtar a government-appointed neighborhood elder

qada' a large residential district

samsara pimping

sarifa a dwelling made from reeds (a traditional housing construction from southern Iraq)

shu'ba "section," referring to the Ba'th Party office above the firqa but lower than the fara' office (see Figure 2)

NOTES

Acknowledgments

1. Anwar 'Abd al-Hamid al-Nasiri, *Suq al-Jadid: Mahalla Mudi'a min al-Janib al-Gharbi bi-Baghdad* [Suq al-Jadid: A Luminous Neighborhood in Western Baghdad] (Baghdad: Dar al-Shu'un al-Thaqafiyya al-'Amma, 1997), 2:9, 11.

Introduction

1. Names of Iraqis have been changed throughout to maintain anonymity. Pseudonyms are indicated with an asterisk. Letter to the vice chairman of the Revolutionary Command Council, November 26, 1988, Ba'th Regional Command Collection (hereafter BRCC), *file number withheld to protect identities.*

2. Baghdad organization to the party secretariat, "Issuing an Opinion," January 25, 1989, *BRCC file number withheld to protect identities.*

3. Joel Migdal, *State in Society: Studying How States and Societies Transform and Constitute One Another* (New York: Cambridge University Press, 2001), 27; Elise Massicard, *Street-Level Governing: Negotiating the State in Urban Turkey* (Stanford: Stanford University Press, 2022), 2.

4. Massicard, *Street-Level Governing*, 4.

5. For more on Ottoman *mukhtars*, see Massicard, *Street-Level Governing*, 25–30.

6. Nicholas Krohley, *The Death of the Mehdi Army* (New York: Oxford University Press, 2015), 184, 186, 191.

7. Dina Khoury, "Violence and Spatial Politics between the Local and Imperial: Baghdad, 1778–1810," in *The Spaces of the Modern City: Imaginaries, Politics, and Everyday Life*, ed. Gyan Prakash and Kevin M. Kruse (Princeton: Princeton University Press, 2008), 188, 194.

8. Krohley, *The Death of the Mehdi Army*, 20; John Gulick, "Baghdad: Portrait of a City in Physical and Cultural Change," *Journal of the American Institute of Planners* 33, no. 4 (1967): 246.

9. For more on the Iraqi Baʻth Party's ideology, see Joseph Sassoon, *Saddam Hussein's Baʻth Party* (New York: Cambridge University Press, 2012); Aaron Faust, *Baʻthification of Iraq: Saddam Hussein's Totalitarianism* (Austin: University of Texas Press, 2015); Sam Helfont, *Compulsion in Religion* (New York: Oxford University Press, 2018).

10. Sassoon, *Saddam Hussein's Baʻth Party*, 172.

11. Head of the Presidential Diwan to the party secretariat, November 11, 1987, BRCC file number withheld to protect identities.

12. Sassoon, *Saddam Hussein's Baʻth Party*, 139.

13. Sassoon, *Saddam Hussein's Baʻth Party*, 171.

14. The workshop "Urban Iraq in the Twentieth Century: Cross-Perspectives," held in Baghdad in October 2022 highlighted recent scholarship and gaps in the literature in both English-language and Arabic-language scholarship. See also Arbella Bet-Shlimon, "Beyond Baghdad: Writing a History from the Iraqi Periphery," in Damluji et al., "Roundtable: Perspectives on Researching Iraq Today," *Arab Studies Journal* 23, no. 1 (2015): 239–41.

15. Faust, *The Baʻthification of Iraq*, 84.

16. Ilana Feldman, *Governing Gaza: Bureaucracy, Authority, and the Work of Rule, 1917–1967* (Durham, NC: Duke University Press, 2008), 157.

17. Additional findings from our research collaboration are published in a co-authored article, "The Politics of Memory in Contemporary Baghdad: A Comparative Neighborhood Study," *International Journal of Middle East Studies* 55, no. 2 (2023): 353–61. Dr. al-Hammood graciously allowed me to use qualitative data from our research collaboration in my book.

18. Ian M. Johnson, "The Impact on Libraries and Archives in Iraq of War and Looting in 2003: A Preliminary Assessment of the Damage and Subsequent Reconstruction Efforts," *International Information and Library Review* 37, no. 3 (2005): 209–71.

19. I published further remarks on the ethics of research in the Baʻth Party archives: "The Repatriation of Iraqi Baʻth Party Archives: Ethical and Practical Considerations," *Journal of Contemporary Iraq and the Arab World* 16, nos. 1–2 (2022): 117–36.

20. "Saddam Hussein Collection," Conflict Records Research Center, https://conflictrecords.wordpress.com/collections/sh/.

21. Michael Brill, "Reintroducing the Saddam Hussein Regime Collection of the Conflict Records Research Center," Wilson Center website, February 27, 2024.

22. Brill, "Reintroducing the Saddam Hussein Regime Collection."

23. Michael Brill, "Setting the Records Straight in Iraq," *War on the Rocks*, warontherocks.com, July 17, 2020.

24. Bruce Montgomery, "Immortality in the Secret Police Files: The Iraq Memory Foundation and the Baath Party Archive," *International Journal of Cultural Property* 18, no. 3 (August 2011): 315–16.

25. Wisam H. Alshaibi, "Weaponizing Iraq's Archives," *MERIP* 291 (Summer 2019).

26. Brill, "Setting the Records Straight in Iraq."

27. State Department Memo from the Secretary of State to the American Embassy in Baghdad, "Negotiating Return of Documents with Iraqi Government," August 8, 2012. Memo released through an FOIA request filed by Wisam Alshaibi and shared with the author.

28. For more on this controversy, see Bruce Montgomery, "US Seizure, Exploitation, and Restitution of Saddam Hussein's Archive of Atrocity," *Journal of American Studies* 48, no. 2 (May 2014): 559–93; Michelle Caswell, "'Thank You Very Much, Now Give Them Back': Cultural Property and the Fight over the Iraqi Baath Party Records," *American Archivist* 74, no. 1 (Spring/Summer 2011): 211–40; Walter, "Ethical and Practical Concerns," 120–23.

29. Michael Gordon, "Baath Party Archives Return to Iraq, With the Secrets They Contain," *Wall Street Journal*, August 31, 2020.

30. Collection Overview, "Register of the Hizb al-Baʿth al-ʿArabi al-Ishtiraki in Iraq," Hoover Institution Library and Archives.

31. East German Stasi records and Guatemalan police records are two notable collections that share some similar attributes to the Baʿth Party archives. See Kristen Weld, *Paper Cadavers: The Archives of Dictatorship in Guatemala* (Durham, NC: Duke University Press, 2014).

32. Khoury, *Iraq in Wartime*, 17.

33. Ann Laura Stoler has noted that many colonial archives have the tendency to erase violence, and arguably this applies to many postcolonial regimes as well: Stoler, *Along the Archival Grain: Epistemic Anxieties and Colonial Common Sense* (Princeton: Princeton University Press, 2009), 33, 160.

34. One major exception is in the correspondence between Saddam Hussein and his appointed governor of Kuwait, his relative ʿAli Hassan al-Majid. Majid included frank depictions of his violent treatment of the Kuwaiti population, often scribbled by hand in the margins. See Joseph Sassoon and Alissa Walter, "The Iraqi Occupation of Kuwait," *Middle East Journal* 71, no. 4 (Fall 2017): 615.

35. Rebecca Abby Whiting, "Living and Dying on Record: 'Atrocity Archives' as Sacred Remains," *Journal of Contemporary Iraq and the Arab World* 16, nos. 1–2 (2022): 141.

36. Khoury, *Iraq in Wartime*, 15.

37. Arbella Bet-Shlimon, "Beyond Conflict: Archives and Ethics in the Middle East," American Historical Association Conference (virtual), January 26, 2021.

38. Bet-Shlimon, "Beyond conflict"; Walter, "Repatriation of Iraqi Baʿth Party Archives," 124–25.

39. Gayatri Chakravorty Spivak, "Subaltern Studies: Deconstructing Historiography," in *Selected Subaltern Studies*, ed. Ranajit Guha and Gayatri Chakravorty Spivak (New York: Oxford University Press, 1988), 8–9.

Chapter 1

1. Caecilia Pieri, "Urbanism in Bagdad before the Planning: A Codification between the Fates of the Arbitrary and Urgent Needs (1920–1950)," *Revista de Crítica y Teoría de la Arquitectura* 1 (2008): 267.

2. Jamal Haydar, *Baghdad: Malamih Madina fi Dhakirat al-Sitinat* [Baghdad: Features of a City in Memories of the 1960s] (Beirut: Al-Markaz al-Thaqafi al-ʿArabi, 2002), 8.

3. Haydar, *Baghdad: Malamih Madina*, 66, 69.

4. See, for example, Timothy Mitchell, *Colonising Egypt* (Berkeley: University of California Press, 1988), 95; Timothy Mitchell, *Rule of Experts* (Berkeley: University of California Press, 2002), 68; James C. Scott, *Seeing Like a State* (New Haven: Yale University Press, 1998), 2; Henri Lefebvre, *Production of Space* (Oxford, UK: Blackwell, 1974), 39.

5. For more on the regulation of bodies through state-building in Iraq, see Omar Dewachi, *Ungovernable Life* (Stanford: Stanford University Press, 2017).

6. Muhammad Makiya, "Al-Mahallat al-Baghdadiyya [Baghdad Neighborhoods]," in *Baghdad*, ed. Muhammad Makiya (London: AlWarrak Publishing, 2005), 271; Caecilia Pieri, "Baghdad Architecture, 1921–1958: Reflections on History as a 'Strategy of Vigilance,'" *Bulletin of the Royal Inter-Faith Studies*, 8, nos. 1–2 (2006): 10.

7. Ahmad Susa, "Rayy Baghdad Qadiman wa Hadithan" [Baghdad Irrigation, Past and Present]," in *Baghdad*, ed. Muhammad Makiya (London: AlWarrak Publishing, 2005), 101; Dina Khoury, "Violence and Spatial Politics between the Local and Imperial: Baghdad, 1778–1810," in *The Spaces of the Modern City: Imaginaries, Politics, and Everyday Life*, ed. Gyan Prakash and Kevin M. Kruse (Princeton: Princeton University Press, 2008), 194.

8. Muhammad Makiya, "Baghdad al-Sitiniyyat [1960s Baghdad]," in *Baghdad*, ed. Muhammad Makiya (London: AlWarrak Publishing, 2005), 97.

9. John Gulick, "Baghdad: Portrait of a City in Physical and Cultural Change," *Journal of the American Institute of Planners* 33, no. 4 (1967): 246.

10. Pieri, "Baghdad Architecture," 9–10.

11. Haydar, *Baghdad: Malamih Madina*, 66, 69.

12. Makiya, "Mahallat Baghdad," 271; Pieri, "Baghdad Architecture," 10.

13. Susa, "Rayy Baghdad," 130–31, 142–45; Pieri, "Urbanism in Bagdad before the Planning," 267; Gulick, "Baghdad: Portrait of a City," 246. This flood is discussed by Dewachi, *Ungovernable Life*, 119; it is also mentioned by Doxiadis: Doxiadis Associates Archives (hereafter DAA), Iraq Reports DOX-QBE, 1–5, July 58–Jan 59, vol. 122, citation number 23996, page number unknown.

14. For more on the history of Iraq's oil industry, see Abbas Alnasrawi, *The Economy of Iraq: Oil, War, Destruction of Development and Prospects, 1950–2010* (Westport, CT: Greenwood Press, 1994); and Arbella Bet-Shlimon, *City of Black Gold: Oil, Ethnicity, and the Making of Modern Kirkuk* (Stanford: Stanford University Press, 2019), 79–88, 165–68.

15. NARA, "Economic Review, Iraq, 1955," American Embassy in Baghdad to Department of State, February 29, 1956, 887.00/1–556, Box 4957, 1955–59 CDF, RG 59.

16. NARA, "Economic Review, Iraq, 1955"; NARA, "Marketing Areas in Iraq," American Embassy in Baghdad to the Department of State, June 29, 1956, 887.00/1–556, Box 4957, 1955–59 CDF, RG 59.

17. TNA, Foreign Office [hereafter, FO] 371/82424, FO to the Baghdad Embassy 15312/16/50, October 21, 1950.

18. TNA, FO 371/104687, economic report, 1953.

19. DAA, Iraq Diary, vol. 1, citation number 23873, p. 3; TNA, FO 371/104687, economic report, 1953; Johan Franzen, "Development vs. Reform: Attempts at Modernisation during the Twilight of British Influence in Iraq, 1946–58," *Journal of Imperial and Commonwealth History* 37, no. 1 (2009): 90.

20. Aziz Alkazaz, "Distribution of National Income in Iraq, with Particular Reference to the Development of Policies Applied by the State," in *Iraq: Power and Society*, ed. Derek Hopwood, Habib Ishow, and Thomas Koszinowski (Reading, UK: Ithaca Press, 1993), 211.

21. Anthony Cordesman and Ahmed Hashim, *Iraq: Sanctions and Beyond* (Washington, DC: CSIS, 1997), 127.

22. Ahmad, "Al-Aathar al-Ijtimaʻiyya lil-Hijra al-Dakhiliyya," 445; Gulick, "Baghdad: Portrait of a City," 248.

23. Gulick, "Baghdad: Portrait of a City," 252.

24. Khattab al-ʻAni, *Jughrafiyyat al-ʻIraq al-Ziraʻiyya* [Iraq's Agricultural Geography] (Cairo: Arab League Press, 1972), 90; Fadil al-Ansari, *Sukkan al-ʻIraq: Dirasa Dimughrafiyya-Jiyughrafiyya Muqarina* [Iraq's Population: A Demographic-Geographic Comparative Study] (Damascus: Maktabat Atlas, 1970), 50; ʻAbd al-Razzaq ʻAbbas Husayn, *Nashaʼat Mudun al-ʻIraq wa Tatawwurha* [Growth and Development of Iraq's Cities], (Baghdad: Maʻhad al-Buhuth wa-l-Dirasat al-ʻIraq, 1973), 77.

25. DAA, Iraq Diary, vol. 1, 1955, citation number 23873, p. 169.

26. Muhammad Hussein Awni, "Urban Case Studies: Baghdad, Iraq: Low Income Dwelling Surveys and a Site and Services Proposal," MA thesis, Massachusetts Institute of Technology, May 1979, 5.

27. NARA, "Questionnaire from the American Automobile on Vehicle Registrations in Iraq," American Embassy in Baghdad to the Department of State, December 15, 1955, 987.6211/4–256, Box 5378, 1955–59 CDF, RG 59; NARA, "Motor Vehicle Registrations, Iraq, 1957," 987.6211/4–256, Box 5378, 1955–59 CDF, RG 59.

28. Gulick, "Baghdad: Portrait of a City," 253.

29. Al-Ashab, "The Urban Geography of Baghdad," 361–62; Makiya, "Al-Mahallat al-Baghdadiyya," 271.

30. Amanat al-Asima, *Nashra Handasa Ijtimaʿiyya Sihiyya* [Social and Health Engineering Report], vol. 1 (1951), 98, accessed from the Iraq National Library and Archives [hereafter INLA].

31. Gulick, "Baghdad: Portrait of a City," 254.

32. DAA, Iraq Diary, vol. 3, 1956, citation number 23875, pp. 143–48. There is a long history of states building new highways through existing neighborhoods to break up undesirable communities. Within Iraq, for example, Arbella Bet-Shlimon has written about how the Iraqi Baʻth Party built highways through Kirkuk's Shorija neighborhood in the 1970s to monitor and disrupt the Kurdish nationalists living there. See Bet-Shlimon, *City of Black Gold*, 177–78.

33. DAA, Iraq Diary, vol. 1, 1955, citation number 23873, pp. 98–99.

34. Fahmi Mahmud Shukri, *Bab al-Shaykh wa-l-Shaykhliyya ʿAbr al-Tarikh* [The Bab al-Shaykh and Shaykhliyya Neighborhoods throughout History] (Amman, 2007), 53–54.

35. Makiya, "Al-Mahallat al-Baghdadiyya," 270.

36. Al-Ashab, "The Urban Geography of Baghdad," 363; NARA, "Recent Major Government Housing Developments," American Embassy in Baghdad to the Department of State, September 14, 1955, 887.00A/9–856, Box 4958, 1955–59 CDF, RG 59.

37. NARA, "Recent Major Government Housing Developments," American Embassy in Baghdad to the Department of State, September 14, 1955, 887.00A/9–856, Box 4958, 1955–59 CDF, RG 59.

38. Pieri, "Baghdad Architecture," 11.

39. Government of Iraq, *Report on the Housing Census of Iraq for 1956* (Baghdad: Ar-Rabita Press, 1956), 11.

40. Saad Salim al-Jassar, "Social Indicators and Housing Policy in Baghdad, Iraq," MA thesis, University of Washington, 1977, 60.

41. TNA, FO 624/209, Memo by M. C. G. Man, September 23, 1952; TNA, FO 371/104687, economic report, 1953.

42. DAA, Iraq Diary, vol. 1, 1955, citation number 23873, pp. 23–24.

43. DAA, Iraq Diary, vol. 1, 1955, citation number 23873, pp. 23–24.

44. Pieri, "Baghdad Architecture, 1921–1958," 13–14; Justin Marozzi, *Baghdad: City of Blood, City of Peace* (New York: Allen Lane, 2014), 320.

45. TNA, FO 624/209, memo from D. J. D. Maitlan, October 11, 1952.

46. TNA, T 236/5138, "Summary of Lord Salter's Report on Iraq," April 1955.

47. TNA, FO 371/104685, Foreign Office, December 9, 1953.

48. Panayiota Pyla, "Back to the Future: Doxiadis's Plans for Baghdad," *Journal of Planning History* 7, no. 1 (February 2008): 6–7.

49. DAA, Iraq Diary, vol. 1, 1955, citation number 23873, p. 176.

50. Awni, "Urban Case Studies," 12.

51. Lefteris Theodosis, "'Containing' Baghdad: Constantinos Doxiadis' Program for a Developing Nation," *Revista de Crítica y Teoría de la Arquitectura* 1 (2008): 168. Workers are the second group listed in the Development Board's housing project. However, the archival sources I consulted for this chapter had relatively little information about worker housing inside Baghdad, so my analysis focuses on the other two categories: rural migrants who lived in *sarifas* and public-sector employees.

52. DAA, Iraq Reports R-QB, 400–433, Jan–Jun 1958, vol. 97, citation number 23976, pp. 4–5.

53. Caecilia Pieri, *Bagdad: Construction d'une Capitale Moderne (1914–1960)* (Beirut: Presses de l'Ifpo, 2015), 192.

54. Henri Lefebvre, "The Right to the City," in *Writings on Cities*, ed. and trans. Eleonore Kofman and Elizabeth Lebas (Malden, MA: Blackwell, 2000), 147–59.

55. DAA, Iraq Reports R-QB, 400–433, Jan–Jun 1958, vol. 97, citation number 23976, p. 2.

56. DAA, Iraq Reports DOX-QBE, 1–5, July 58–Jan 59, vol. 122, citation number 23996, p. 6.

57. DAA, Iraq Reports DOX-QBE, 1–5, July 58–Jan 59, vol. 122, citation number 23996, pp. 6–9.

58. DAA, Iraq Reports R-QB, 400–433, Jan–Jun 1958, vol. 97, citation number 23976, pp. 15–16; DAA, Iraq Reports DOX-QBE, 1–5, July 58–Jan 59, vol. 122, citation number 23996, page number unknown.

59. DAA, Iraq Reports R-QB, 400–433, Jan–Jun 1958, vol. 97, citation number 23976, pp. 4–5.

60. DAA, Iraq Diary, vol. 1, 1955, citation number 23873, pp. 46–47.

61. Interview with H. by the author, Alexandria, VA, July 2015. See also Dewachi, *Ungovernable Life*, 117.

62. Arbella Bet-Shlimon, "State-Society Relations in the Urban Spheres of Baghdad and Kirkuk, 1920–58," in *State and Society in Iraq: Citizenship under Occupation, Dictatorship and Democratisation*, ed. Benjamin Isakhan, Shamiran Mako, and Fadi Dawood (New York: I. B. Tauris, 2017), 88; Jordi Tejel, "'Dangerous Liai-

sons': Abd al-Karim Qasim and the Student Movements of the First Iraqi Republic, 1958–63," in *State and Society in Iraq*, ed. Isakhan, Mako, and Dawood, 138.

63. TNA, FO 624/209, memo from D. J. D. Maitlan, October 11, 1952.

64. DAA, Iraq Reports R-QB, 400–433, Jan–Jun 1958, vol. 97, citation number 23976, pp. 4–5.

65. Pascal Ménoret, "Development, Planning and Urban Unrest in Saudi Arabia," *Muslim World* 101, no. 2 (April 2011): 276; Bet-Shlimon, *City of Black Gold*, 116.

66. Pascal Ménoret, *Joyriding in Riyadh: Oil, Urbanism, and Road Revolt* (New York: Cambridge University Press, 2014), 79.

67. DAA, Iraq Diary, vol. 1, 1955, citation number 23873, p. 26.

68. DAA, Iraq Diary, vol. 1, 1955, citation number 23873, p. 33.

69. Dewachi, *Ungovernable Life*, 116.

70. NARA, "Recent Major Government Housing Developments," American Embassy in Baghdad to Department of State, September 14, 1955, 887.00A/9–856, Box 4958, 1955–59 CDF, RG 59. For more on Doxiadis's plans for Kirkuk, see Bet-Shlimon, *City of Black Gold*, 116.

71. Bakr Mustafa Salim, *Al-Sara'if fi Baghdad* (Baghdad: Shatri, 2005), 36; Haydar, *Baghdad: Malamih Madina*, 35; Marion Farouk-Sluglett and Peter Sluglett, *Iraq since 1958* (New York: I. B. Tauris, 2001), 218–19.

72. Farouk-Sluglett and Sluglett, *Iraq since 1958*, 76–78.

73. NARA, "Support for Qasim among the Lower Classes," American Embassy in Baghdad to State Department, September 17, 1972, 787.00/8–162, Box 2085, 1963–63 CDF, RG 59.

74. Salim, *Al-Sara'if fi Baghdad*, 36; NARA, "Support for Qasim among the Lower Classes," American Embassy in Baghdad to State Department, September 17, 1972, 787.00/8–162, Box 2085, 1963–63 CDF, RG 59.

75. TNA, "Qasim's Inauguration of Housing Projects," July 16, 1959, FO 371/141103.

76. TNA, "Qasim's Inauguration of Housing Projects," July 16, 1959, FO 371/141103; Salim, *Al-Sara'if fi Baghdad*, 35.

77. NARA, "Weekly Economic Review, December 14–18, 1959," No. 51, December 28, 1959, 887.00/1–359, 1955–59 CDF, RG 59.

78. Al-Ashab, "The Urban Geography of Baghdad," 447.

79. NARA, "Rentals Reduced by New Law," American Embassy in Baghdad to Department of State, August 8, 1958, 887.00A/9–856, Box 4958, 1955–59 CDF, RG 59.

80. Pieri, *Construction d'une Capitale Moderne*, 193.

81. NARA, "Support for Qasim among the Lower Classes," American Embassy in Baghdad to State Department, September 17, 1972, 787.00/8–162, Box 2085, 1963–63 CDF, RG 59; NARA, "The Sarifa Population of Baghdad," American Embassy in Baghdad to Department of State, September 24, 1962, 787.00/8–162, Box 2085, 1960–63 CDF, RG 59; Dewachi, *Ungovernable Life*, 121.

82. Nicholas Krohley, *The Death of the Mehdi Army* (New York: Oxford University Press, 2015), 156–57.

83. NARA, "Support for Qasim Among the Lower Classes," American Embassy in Baghdad to the State Department, September 17, 1962, 787.00/8-162, Box 2085, 1963-63 CDF, RG 59.

84. Tareq Ismael, *The Rise and Fall of the Communist Party of Iraq* (New York: Cambridge University Press, 2008), 107; Najm Wali, *Baghdad: Sirat Madina* [Baghdad: Biography of a City] (Beirut: Dar al-Saqi, 2015), 80.

85. Al-Ashab, "The Urban Geography of Baghdad," 441.

86. TNA, FO 371/186800, Memo by S. L. Egerton, British Embassy in Baghdad, December 31, 1965.

87. NARA, "Joint Weekas No. 53," American Embassy in Baghdad to Department of State, August 20, 1963, 1963/11/26 POL 2–1 Joint Weekas IRAQ, Box 3943, POL Iraq, Subj-Numeri c 1963, RG 59; Al-Ashab, "The Urban Geography of Baghdad," 446.

88. Al-Ashab, "The Urban Geography of Baghdad," 441–42.

89. TNA, FO 371/170439, Memo by E. F. G. Maynard, British Embassy in Baghdad, July 13, 1963.

90. NARA, "Execution of Twenty-One of July 3 Plotters," American Embassy in Baghdad to Department of State, August 13, 1963, 1963/12/14 POL 26 Rebellion, Coups, Insurgency 6/1/63, Box 3945, Pol Iraq, Subj-Numeric 1963, RG 59.

91. TNA, FO 371/170439, Memo by E. F. G. Maynard, British Embassy in Baghdad, September 7, 1963; al-Jassar, "Social Indicators and Housing Policy in Baghdad, Iraq," 106; Alansari, "Althawra, Quartier de Bagdad," 12–13; NARA, "Joint Weekas No. 53," American Embassy in Baghdad to Department of State, August 20, 1963, 1963/11/26 POL 2–1 Joint Weekas IRAQ, Box 3943, POL Iraq, Subj-Numeric 1963, RG 59.

92. NARA, "Joint Weekas No. 53," American Embassy in Baghdad to Department of State, August 20, 1963, 1963/11/26 POL 2–1 Joint Weekas IRAQ, Box 3943, POL Iraq, Subj-Numeric 1963, RG 59.

93. For more on the motivations to build the Army Canal, see Besim Selim Hakim, "Co-Op Housing: Baghdad, Iraq," MA thesis, Harvard University, 1971, 22; and Bassim Alansari, "Althawra, Quartier de Bagdad [Al-Thawra, Baghdad District]," PhD diss., École des Hautes Études en Sciences Sociales, 1979, 135–36.

94. Makiya, "Baghdad al-Sitiniyat," 98.

95. Gulick, "Baghdad: Portrait of a City," 250.

96. Krohley, *Death of the Mehdi Army*, 158–59.

97. Awni, "Urban Case Studies," 12, 32.

98. Awni, "Urban Case Studies," 32.

99. Al-Ashab, "The Urban Geography of Baghdad," 453; Alansari, "Althawra, Quartier de Bagdad," 146.

100. Al-Ashab, "The Urban Geography of Baghdad," 449.
101. Al-Ashab, "The Urban Geography of Baghdad," 453.
102. Alansari, "Althawra, Quartier de Bagdad," 150–51.
103. Alansari, "Althawra, Quartier de Bagdad," 153.
104. Alansari, "Althawra, Quartier de Bagdad," 156–60.
105. Al-Ashab, "The Urban Geography of Baghdad," 450–52.
106. Dewachi, *Ungovernable Life*, 124.
107. Dewachi, *Ungovernable Life*, 152.

108. Similar trends toward constructing geographies that reinforce social exclusion can be seen in Beirut's suburbs. See Mona Fawaz, "Neoliberal Urbanity and the Right to the City: A View from Beirut's Periphery," *Development and Change* 40, no. 5 (2009): 828.

109. DAA, Iraq Reports DOX-QBE, 1–5, July 58–Jan 59, vol. 122, citation number 23996, page number unknown.

110. Al-Ashab, "The Urban Geography of Baghdad," 432–33, 438; Dewachi, *Ungovernable Life*, 117.

111. DAA, Iraq Reports R-QB, 400–433, Jan–Jun 1958, vol. 97, citation number 23976, p. 8; DAA, Iraq Reports R-QB, 434–444, Jul–Dec 1958, vol. 127, citation number 24001, p. 85.

112. Gulick, "Baghdad: Portrait of a City," 252.
113. Gulick, "Baghdad: Portrait of a City," 246.

114. Faleh A. Jabar, "Shaykhs and Ideologues: Detribalization and Retribalization in Iraq, 1968–1998," *Middle East Report* 215 (2000): 29.

115. Krohley, *Death of the Mehdi Army*, 29–30.
116. Al-Ashab, "The Urban Geography of Baghdad," 452.
117. Alansari, "Althawra, Quartier de Bagdad," 150–51.
118. Alansari, "Althawra, Quartier de Bagdad," 163–68.
119. Al-Ashab, "The Urban Geography of Baghdad," 445–46.
120. Dewachi, *Ungovernable Life*, 123–24.
121. Al-Ashab, "The Urban Geography of Baghdad," 417, 441–42.

122. Waleed Abbas Hilmi, "Internal Migration and Regional Policy in Iraq," vol. 2, PhD diss., University of Sheffield, 1978, 826.

123. TNA, T 236/5138, British Embassy in Baghdad, May 22, 1953; TNA, FO 371/115797, "Supply of Steel for the Construction of Buildings and Housing for the Iraq Army," November 3, 1955.

124. NARA, "Recent Major Housing Developments—May 1956," May 11, 1956, American Embassy in Baghdad to Department of State, 887.00A/9-856, Box 4958, 1955–59 CDF, RG 59; TNA, FO 371/115797, "Supply of Steel for the Construction of Buildings and Housing for the Iraq Army," November 3, 1955.

125. NARA, "Economic Summary—Iraq—Second Quarter 1956," American Embassy in Baghdad to Department of State, July 31, 1956, 887.00/1-556, Box 4957,

1955–59 CDF, RG 59; DAA, *Report on the Development of Baghdad: A Contribution to the Ideas for the Development of the Capital of Iraq*, Periodical Report no. 2, December 1958, citation number 28978, p. 1.

126. Cited in Ménoret, *Joyriding in Riyadh*, 99.

127. DAA, Iraq Diary, vol. 1, 1955, citation number 23873, pp. 164–65.

128. Bet-Shlimon, *City of Black Gold*, 112.

129. NARA, "Regulation No. 7 of 1955 for Sale of Houses to Workers and Officials," translation provided by American Embassy in Baghdad to Department of State, [1955], 887.00A/9–856, Box 4958, 1955–59 CDF, RG 59.

130. Hakim, "Co-op Housing: Baghdad, Iraq," 31; Al-Ashab, "The Urban Geography of Baghdad," 348, 350.

131. Al-Ashab, "The Urban Geography of Baghdad," 348–49.

132. Gulick, "Baghdad: Portrait of a City," 252.

133. Al-Ashab, "The Urban Geography of Baghdad," 349.

134. Al-Ashab, "The Urban Geography of Baghdad," 348, 350.

135. Hakim, "Co-Op Housing: Baghdad, Iraq," 30.

136. Muhsin K. Chalabi, "Low Income Housing in Iraq," MA thesis, University of New Mexico, 1975, 19.

137. Al-Ashab, "The Urban Geography of Baghdad," 348–49; Krohley, *Death of the Mehdi Army*, 108. There was a premodern precedent for this kind of neighborhood construction in Baghdad: the district of Waziriyya in Baghdad was built by the Hashemites in the 1920s, named after the many ministers (*wazir*) who lived there. See Gulick, "Baghdad: Portrait of a City," 250.

138. Gulick, "Baghdad: Portrait of a City," 247.

139. al-Jassar, "Social Indicators and Housing Policy in Baghdad, Iraq," 106.

140. Krohley, *Death of the Mehdi Army*, 89.

141. Lefebvre, "The Right to the City."

142. Al-Ashab, "The Urban Geography of Baghdad," 8.

143. Interview S.13, Baghdad, August 2016.

144. Pyla, "Back to the Future," 6.

145. DAA, "Housing Program of Iraq," 1958, citation number 29200, page number unknown.

146. *Iraq: A Pictorial Record* (Cologne-Deutz, Germany: In Cooperation with the Iraqi Commissariat of the World Exhibition, Brussels, 1958), 91.

147. Magnus Bernhardsson, "Visions of Iraq: Modernizing the Past in 1950s Baghdad," in *Modernism and the Middle East*, ed. Sandy Isenstadt and Kishwar Rizvi (Seattle: University of Washington Press, 2008), 85.

148. Awni, "Urban Case Studies," 38.

149. DAA, Diary of Iraq, 1956, vol. 9, citation number 23881, p. 379.

150. Pyla, "Back to the Future," 9–10. Many scholars have analyzed the ideological underpinnings behind these master plans for Baghdad. See, for example, Pieri,

Construction d'une Capitale Moderne; Theodosis, "'Containing' Baghdad," 167–72; Pyla, "Back to the Future."

151. Focusing on practice over plans is an approach encouraged by Henri Lefebvre, "Spectral Analysis," in *Writings on Cities*, ed. Eleonore Kofman and Elizabeth Lebas (Malden, MA: Blackwell, 2000), 143.

152. Bet-Shlimon, "State-Society," 50. Dina Khoury has also analyzed the interplay between urban development and state-society relations in Iraq, albeit for an earlier period ("Violence and Spatial Politics," 188). For the post-2003 period, see Mona Damluji, "'Securing Democracy in Iraq': Sectarian Politics and Segregation in Baghdad, 2003–2007," *Traditional Dwellings and Settlements Review* (2010): 71–87.

153. Gulick, "Baghdad: Portrait of a City," 251.

154. Susa, "Rayy Baghdad," 101; Khoury, "Violence and Spatial Politics," 194.

155. Khoury, "Violence and Spatial Politics," 186–87.

156. Alansari, "Althawra, Quartier de Bagdad," 135–36.

157. Farah al-Nakib, "Revisiting *Hadar* and *Badu* in Kuwait: Citizenship, Housing, and the Construction of a Dichotomy," *International Journal of Middle East Studies* 46 (2014): 8.

158. al-Nakib, "Revisiting *Hadar* and *Badu* in Kuwait," 8.

Chapter 2

1. Paraphrased by Gyan Prakash, "Introduction," in *The Spaces of the Modern City: Imaginaries, Politics, and Everyday Life*, ed. Gyan Prakash and Kevin M. Kruse (Princeton: Princeton University Press, 2008), 12.

2. Henri Lefebvre, "Levels of Reality and Analysis," in *Writings on Cities*, ed. and trans. Eleonore Kofman and Elizabeth Lebas (Malden, MA: Blackwell, 2000), 115, emphasis in original.

3. Sara Pursley, *Familiar Futures: Time, Selfhood, and Sovereignty in Iraq* (Stanford: Stanford University Press, 2019), 59.

4. Pursley, *Familiar Futures*, 75.

5. Dina Khoury, *Iraq in Wartime: Soldiering, Martyrdom, and Remembrance* (New York: Cambridge University Press, 2013).

6. Charles Tripp, *A History of Iraq* (New York: Cambridge University Press, 2007), 223–25.

7. Khoury, *Iraq in Wartime*, 110–13; Dewachi, *Ungovernable Life*, 127; Shahram Chubin and Charles Tripp, *Iran and Iraq at War* (Boulder, CO: Westview Press, 1988), 62.

8. Khoury, *Iraq in Wartime*, 115–20; Marion Farouk-Sluglett and Peter Sluglett, *Iraq since 1958* (New York: I. B. Tauris, 2001), 269–70; Tripp, *History of Iraq*, 234–38.

9. Ofra Bengio, "Iraq," in *Middle East Contemporary Survey*, vol. 5: *1980–81*, 579;

Charles Tripp, "The Iran-Iraq War and the Iraqi State," in *Iraq: Power and Society*, ed. Derek Hopwood, Habib Ishow, and Thomas Koszinowski (Reading, UK: Ithaca Press, 1993), 101.

10. Khoury, *Iraq in Wartime*, 29–30.

11. For detailed histories of the Iran-Iraq War, see the following: Khoury, *Iraq in Wartime*; Dilip Hiro, *The Longest War: The Iran-Iraq Military Conflict* (New York: Routledge, 1991); W. Thom Workman, *Social Origins of the Iran-Iraq War*; (Boulder, CO: Lynne Rienner Publishers, 1994); Pierre Razoux, *Iran-Iraq War*, trans. Nicholas Elliott (Cambridge, MA: Belknap Press of Harvard University Press, 2015).

12. Ian Black, "Iran and Iraq Remember War That Cost More Than a Million Lives," *The Guardian*, September 23, 2010.

13. Centre des Archives Diplomatiques de Nantes [hereafter CADN], 54PO/B/5, "The Iraqi Population during the War," October 30, 1980.

14. Dewachi, *Ungovernable Life*, 130.

15. Original source: Conflict Records Research Center [hereafter CRRC], SH-SHTP-A-001–354, Recording of a meeting between Saddam Hussein and Ministers related to the Budget, Circa 1982. Quoted in Williamson Murray and Kevin M. Woods, *The Iran-Iraq War: A Military and Strategic History* (Cambridge, UK: Cambridge University Press, 2014), 188–89.

16. Patrick Cockburn, "Where Guns Fail, Saddam Provides Butter," *Financial Times*, July 16, 1981.

17. CADN 54PO/B/43, "Construction: Public Works—1981," May 1982.

18. "Important Infrastructure Projects Built in Iraq over Past Ten Years," *Baghdad Observer*, January 15, 1990, 2.

19. CADN 54PO/B/5, Political Dispatch, August 11, 1982.

20. Architects Collaborative, *Urban Design Study: Khulafa Development Project* (Cambridge, MA, 1982); Arthur Erickson Architects, *Amanat al Assima: Abu Nawas Conservation/Development Project* (Vancouver: Arthur Erickson Architects, 1981); TNA Foreign and Commonwealth Office (FCO) 8/4697, June 1982.

21. CADN 54PO/B/43, "Construction: Public Works—Year 1981," May 1982.

22. Salah ʿAbd al-Razzaq, "Sharʿa Haifa min al-Turath ila al-Hadatha" [Haifa Street from Heritage to Modernity]," *Al-Zaman*, March 18, 2022.

23. Dewachi, *Ungovernable Life*, 139.

24. Dewachi, *Ungovernable Life*, 129, 137, 138.

25. CADN 54PO/B/5, "The Iraqi Population during the War," October 30, 1980.

26. Cockburn, "Where Guns Fail."

27. TNA, FCO 8/4168, October 13, 1981.

28. Drew Middleton, "Despite War Cost, Iraq Pushes Development," *New York Times*, November 28, 1982; CADN 54PO/B/44, "Economic and Commercial News," June 1981.

29. CADN 54PO/B/5, Political Dispatch, August 11, 1982.

30. Nuri Najm, *Fi al-Harb wa-l-Salam* [In War and Peace] (Baghdad: Dar al-Hurriyya lil-Tibaʿa, 1986), 5.

31. Bengio, "Iraq," in *Middle East Contemporary Survey*, vol. 7: *1982–83*, ed. Colin Legum, Haim Shaked, and Daniel Dishon (New York: Holmes & Meier Publishers, 1985), 588.

32. Bengio, "Iraq," in *Middle East Contemporary Survey*, vol. 5, 597.

33. TNA, FCO 8/4168, October 13, 1981; Cockburn, "Where Guns Fail."

34. Murray and Woods, *Iran-Iraq War*, 188–89.

35. al-Khafaji, "War as a Vehicle," 272–73.

36. CADN 54PO/B/5, "July Political and Religious Celebrations in Iraq," August 8, 1981; CADN 54PO/B/5, Political Dispatch, July 4, 1981; Phebe Marr, *Modern History of Iraq* (Boulder, CO: Westview Press, 1985), 301.

37. Marr, *Modern History of Iraq*, 301.

38. TNA, FCO 8/4697, "Bomb Attack on the Ministry of Planning," August 2, 1982; Ofra Bengio, "Iraq," in *Middle East Contemporary Survey*, vol. 8, *1983–1984*, ed. Haim Shaked and Daniel Dishon (Tel Aviv: Dayan Center for Middle Eastern and African Studies, 1986), 483; Razoux, *The Iran-Iraq War*, 303.

39. Najm, *Al-Harb wa-l-Salam*, 252.

40. TNA, FCO 8/3680, British Embassy in Baghdad, April 7, 1980.

41. Faleh A. Jabar, *The Shiʿite Movement in Iraq* (London: Saqi Books, 2003), 234.

42. Jabar, *The Shiʿite Movement in Iraq*, 233.

43. Bengio, "Iraq," in *Middle East Contemporary Survey*, vol. 8, 483.

44. CADN 54PO/B/5, "The Iraqi Population during the War," October 30, 1980.

45. Murray and Woods, *The Iran-Iraq War*, 105.

46. Murray and Woods, *The Iran-Iraq War*, 105.

47. Razouk, *The Iran-Iraq War*, 327; Murray and Woods, *The Iran-Iraq War*, 318.

48. Najm, *Fi al-Harb wa-l-Salam*, 12.

49. Razoux, *Iran-Iraq War*, 303, 436.

50. Razoux, *Iran-Iraq War*, 326.

51. Ofra Bengio, "Iraq," in *Middle East Contemporary Survey*, vol. 12: *1988*, ed. Ami Ayalon and Haim Shaked (Boulder, CO: Westview Press, 1990), 516.

52. Phone interview with S. by the author, July 8, 2020.

53. CADN 54PO/B/5, "Summary of May 1981," June 2, 1981.

54. CADN 54PO/B/6, "Explosions in Baghdad," April 1985.

55. Bengio, "Iraq," in *Middle East Contemporary Survey*, vol. 7, 566.

56. CADN 54PO/B/6, "Summary of Foreign Policy, May–June 1985," July 13, 1985.

57. "Toll High As Jets Hit Cities in Gulf War," *Associated Press*, March 12, 1985; Judith Miller, "Big Blast Rocks Capital of Iraq; 6th in 2 Weeks," *New York Times*, March 28, 1985.

58. Judy Miller, "Iraq, Iran Vent Frustration on Each Other's Civilians" *New York Times*, April 7, 1985.

59. Saʿd bin Abi Waqas branch to the Baghdad Organization, "Report about the Enemy Missile Strike Incident," June 12, 1985, BRCC 01-2245-0003-0443 to -0446.

60. CADN 54PO/B/6, "Monthly Summary for September," October 13, 1986; "Iranian Missile Killed 32, Baghdad Says," *Associated Press*, October 14, 1987.

61. Dewachi, *Ungovernable Life*, 143.

62. Ministry of Interior to president's office, "Examining the Public Shelters' Capacity," September 16, 1984; BRCC 01-2767-0001-0436; Minister of Interior to president's office, "Shelter Inspection," June 9, 1985, BRCC 01-2767-0001-0391 to -0394.

63. "War in the Gulf: Baghdad Scene; Baghdad Rescuers Search for Life with Little Hope," *Associated Press*, February 14, 1991.

64. Phone interview with S. by the author, July 8, 2020.

65. CADN 54PO/B/5, Dispatch from the French Embassy in Baghdad, August 11, 1982; RCC Decree no. 499, June 11, 1986, BRCC 008-5-3-109; Samir al-Khalil [Kanan Makiya], *The Monument: Art, Vulgarity and Responsibility in Iraq* (Berkeley: University of California Press, 1991), 23.

66. al-Khalil, *The Monument*, 11.

67. Bengio, "Iraq," in *Middle East Contemporary Survey*, vol. 12, 505.

68. CADN 54PO/B/5, Political Dispatch from the French Embassy in Baghdad, July 27, 1982.

69. CADN 54PO/B/6, "Chronology of Events That Took Place in Iraq: February 1983," March 9, 1983; "Social Reality in Baghdad," 1989, BRCC 01-3751-0000-0388 to -0410.

70. CADN 54PO/B/6, "Chronology of Events That Took Place in Iraq: February 1983," March 9, 1983; TNA, FCO 8/3680, May 8, 1980.

71. "Saddam Hussein and Saddam City Tribal Leaders Talk," audio transcript, undated [1991], CRRC SH-SHTP-A-000–891. English translation provided by the CRRC and edited lightly for clarity.

72. "Saddam Hussein and Saddam City Tribal Leaders Talk," audio transcript, undated [1991], CRRC SH-SHTP-A-000–891. English translation provided by the CRRC and edited lightly for clarity.

73. CADN 54PO/B/5, "The Iraqi Population during the War," October 30, 1980.

74. CADN 54PO/B/5, "The Iraqi Population during the War," October 30, 1980.

75. Khoury, *Iraq in Wartime*, 6–7, 50; Joseph Sassoon, *Saddam Hussein's Baʿth Party* (New York: Cambridge University Press, 2012), 146–59.

76. Khoury, *Iraq in Wartime*, 2–3.

77. Eric Davis, *Memories of State* (Berkeley: University of California Press, 2005), 183, 187.

78. ʿAdnan Rashid al-Jabburi, *Al-Wathiqa al-Tarikhiyya fi al-Nizaʿ al-ʿIraqiyya*

al-Iraniyya [Historical Documents in the Iraqi-Iranian Conflict] (Baghdad: Dar al-Shu'un al-Thaqafiyya al-'Amma, 1995), 77, 80, 112.

79. For a fuller account of the regime's shifting rhetoric regarding "Persian" Iraqis, see Davis, *Memories of State*, 184–88.

80. Ali Babakhan, "The Deportation of Shi'is during the Iran-Iraq War: Causes and Consequences," in *Ayatollahs, Sufis and Ideologues*, edited by Faleh Abdul-Jabar (London: Saqi Books, 2002), 193.

81. Babakhan, "Deportation of Shi'is," 200; Murray and Woods, *Iran-Iraq War*, 134. For files related to the distribution of houses confiscated from deported Iraqis, see Party secretariat to Saddam Hussein, October 5, 1988, BRCC 01-3266-0001-0206; Baghdad Organization to party secretariat, "Report," June 29, 1985, BRCC 01-2245-0003-0362,

82. Babakhan, "Deportation of Shi'is," 184.

83. Zahra Ali, *Women and Gender in Iraq: Between Nation-Building and Fragmentation* (New York: Cambridge University Press, 2018), 97–98.

84. Table Evaluating Party Members, undated [1988?], BRCC 037-2-5-0115.

85. Babakhan, "Deportation of Shi'is," 184.

86. TNA, FCO 8/3680, British Embassy in Baghdad, April 1980.

87. Murray and Woods, *Iran-Iraq War*, 133; Ali, *Women and Gender in Iraq*, 97–98.

88. Sassoon, *Saddam Hussein's Ba'th Party*, 157–59.

89. TNA, FCO 8/4126, "Annual Summary of 1980," December 31, 1980; al-Khafaji, "War as a Vehicle," 286–87; Khoury, *Iraq in Wartime*, 167–68, 149–50. Benefits for those wounded or disabled in the war were enumerated in an RCC decree: RCC Decree no. 356, April 26, 1986, BRCC 088-5-3-523.

90. In 1983, the regime introduced a cap on martyrs' benefits: Committee for Maintaining Ties to Families of Martyrs to the Baghdad Organization, "Forwarding Request," May 5, 1986, BRCC 088-5-3-354. See also Khoury, *Iraq in Wartime*, 168–69.

91. Khoury, *Iraq in Wartime*, 69.

92. Committee for Maintaining Ties to Families of Martyrs to the Baghdad Organization, "Forwarding Request," May 5, 1986, BRCC 088-5-3-354.

93. Sa'd bin Abi Waqas branch to Baghdad Organization, "Report about the Enemy Missile Strike Incident," June 12, 1985, *BRCC file number withheld to protect identities*.

94. Baghdad Organization to party secretariat, "Meeting," April 24, 1985, *BRCC file number withheld to protect identities*.

95. Sa'd bin Abi Waqas branch to Baghdad Organization, "Report about the Enemy Missile Strike Incident," June 12, 1985, *BRCC file number withheld to protect identities*.

96. Baghdad Organization to party secretariat, "Assistance," May 14, 1985,

BRCC file number withheld to protect identities; Party secretariat to Saddam Hussein, October 5, 1988, *BRCC file number withheld to protect identities.*

97. Razoux, *The Iran-Iraq War*, 147.

98. Bengio, "Iraq," in *Middle East Contemporary Survey*, vol. 5, 599.

99. Faleh A. Jabar, "The War Generation in Iraq: A Case of Failed Etatist Nationalism," in *Iran, Iraq, and the Legacies of War*, ed. Lawrence G. Potter and Gary G. Sick (New York: Palgrave Macmillan, 2004), 123; Tripp, "The Iran-Iraq War and the Iraqi State," 104; Hiro, *The Longest War*, 132, 195.

100. Achim Rohde, *State-Society Relations in Ba'thist Iraq: Facing Dictatorship* (New York: Routledge, 2010), 43.

101. Hiro, *The Longest War*, 196; CADN 54PO/B/5, dispatches from July 31, August 7, August 11, and September 1982; Bengio, "Iraq," in *Middle East Contemporary Survey*, vol. 8, 474–75.

102. Bengio, "Iraq," in *Middle East Contemporary Survey*, vol. 8, 475.

103. Khoury, *Iraq in Wartime*, 95.

104. Khoury, *Iraq in Wartime*, 95.

105. Quoted in Sabah Sulayman, *Adwa' 'ala al-Harb al-'Iraqiyya al-Iraniyya* [Shedding Light on the the Iraq-Iran War] (Baghdad: al-Maktaba al-Wataniyya bi-Baghdad, 1981), 179.

106. Sassoon, *Saddam Hussein's Ba'th Party*, 146–47; Bengio, "Iraq," in *Middle East Contemporary Survey*, vol. 8, 475.

107. Murray and Woods, *The Iran-Iraq War*, 134.

108. Bengio, "Iraq," in *Middle East Contemporary Survey*, vol. 5, 582; Hiro, *The Longest War*, 89; Khoury, *Iraq in Wartime*, 99.

109. CADN 54PO/B/5, "The Iraqi Popular Army and the General Mobilization against Iran," January 30, 1982; Bengio, "Iraq," in *Middle East Contemporary Survey*, vol. 10, ed. Itamar Rabinovich and Haim Shaked (Tel Aviv: Dayan Center for Middle Eastern and African Studies, 1988), 373.

110. CADN 54PO/B/5, "The Iraqi Population during the War (II)," December 22, 1980.

111. Bengio, "Iraq," in *Middle East Contemporary Survey*, vol. 7, 476.

112. Bengio, "Iraq," in *Middle East Contemporary Survey*, vol. 8, 476; CADN 54PO/B/6, "Mobilization of Iraqi Students," June 29, 1986; CADN 54PO/B/6, "Monthly Summary for September," October 13, 1986; Bengio, "Iraq," in *Middle East Contemporary Survey*, vol. 10, 372–73.

113. Achim Rohde, *State-Society Relations in Ba'thist Iraq: Facing Dictatorship* (New York: Routledge, 2010), 87.

114. CADN 54PO/B/5, Dispatch from the French Embassy in Baghdad, May 9, 1981; al-Hassan, *Women, Writing, and the Iraqi Ba'thist State*, 28; Khoury, *Iraq in Wartime*, 183.

115. 'Abd al-Rahman Sulayman al-Darbandi, *Al-Mar'a al-'Iraqiyya al-Mu'asira*

[The Modern Iraqi Woman], vol. 2 (Baghdad: Wazirat al-Tarbiya wa-l-Ta'lim, 1968), 12.

116. See, for example, Saddam Hussein, "Al-Mar'a wa-l-'A'ila wa Mujtama' al-Thawra" [Women, Family, and the Society of the Revolution], in *Al-Usra wa-l-Numuww al-Sukkani fi Ahadith al-Ra'is al-Qa'id Saddam Hussein* [Family and Population Growth in the Speeches of President Leader Saddam Hussein] (Baghdad: Dar al-Shu'un al-Thaqafiyya al-'Amma, 1988), 44. Saddam originally gave this speech at a conference of the General Federation of Iraqi Women on July 3, 1988.

117. Hiro, *The Longest War*, 89, 132, 195.

118. Murray and Woods, *Iran-Iraq War*, 183.

119. CADN 54PO/B/5, "The Iraqi Popular Army and General Mobilization against Iran," January 30, 1982.

120. Khoury, *Iraq in Wartime*, 100; Murray and Woods, *Iran-Iraq War*, 183–84.

121. Bengio, "Iraq," in *Middle East Contemporary Survey*, vol. 8, 475.

122. Sassoon, *Saddam Hussein's Ba'th Party*, 152–54; Khoury, *Iraq in Wartime*, 154–55; Bengio, "Iraq," in *Middle East Contemporary Survey*, vol. 8, 475.

123. Bengio, "Iraq," in *Middle East Contemporary Survey*, vol. 5, 582; Bengio, "Iraq," in *Middle East Contemporary Survey*, vol. 10, 372.

124. Bengio, "Iraq," in *Middle East Contemporary Survey*, vol. 7, 567; Hawraa al-Hassan, *Women, Writing, and the Iraqi Ba'thist State* (Edinburgh: Edinburgh University Press, 2020), 27.

125. Workman, *Social Origins of the Iran-Iraq War*, 161.

126. Noga Efrati, "Productive or Reproductive? The Roles of Iraqi Women during the Iraq-Iran War," *Middle Eastern Studies* 35, no. 2 (April 1999): 27–44; Ali, *Women and Gender in Iraq*, 101.

127. Hiro, *The Longest War*, 139; Khoury, *Iraq in Wartime*, 34.

128. Dewachi, *Ungovernable Life*, 139.

129. Khoury, *Iraq in Wartime*, 77.

130. Marr, *Modern History of Iraq*, 302.

131. Workman, *The Social Origins of the Iran-Iraq War*, 159–60.

132. Interview with Sabean-Mandean family by the author, Erbil, October 21, 2016.

133. Phone interview with S. by the author, July 8, 2020.

134. Letter from a woman to the Vice President, January 9, 1989, BRCC file number withheld to protect identities.

135. CADN 54PO/B/5, Political Dispatch, December 3, 1982.

136. Sulayman, *Adwa' 'ala al-Harb al-'Iraqiyya al-Iraniyya*, 178.

137. Hussein, "Al-Ummahat wa-l-Sumud" [Mothers and Steadfastness], in *Al-Usra wa-l-Numuww al-Sukkani*, 142. Saddam originally gave this statement on February 19, 1981, when meeting with the mother of a soldier.

138. Bengio, "Iraq," in *Middle East Contemporary Survey*, vol. 5, 582–83, 597;

CADN 54PO/B/5, Dispatch from the French Embassy in Baghdad, April 24, 1982; TNA, FCO 8/3680, December 9, 1980.

139. CADN 54PO/B/70, Dispatch from the French Embassy in Baghdad, February 15, 1982.

140. CADN 54PO/B/70, "Note for the Ambassador," April 19, 1982.

141. Bengio, "Iraq," in *Middle East Contemporary Survey*, vol. 10, 376; CADN 54PO/B/5, "The Iraqi Population during the War (II)," December 22, 1980.

142. Bengio, "Iraq," in *Middle East Contemporary Survey*, vol. 5, 582–83, 597; CADN 54PO/B/5, Dispatch from the French Embassy in Baghdad, April 24, 1982; TNA FCO 8/3680, December 9, 1980.

143. First Deputy to the Prime Minister to party secretariat, "Popular Economic Surveillance," December 19, 1985, BRCC 01-2947-0002-0496.

144. Revolutionary Command Council decree no. 1315, December 17, 1984, BRCC 01-2947-0002-0487.

145. Revolutionary Command Council Decree no. 39, "Popular Economic Surveillance," January 22, 1984, BRCC 01-2947-0002-0045.

146. Revolutionary Command Council Decree no. 97, January 22, 1985, BRCC 01-2947-0002-0484.

147. Bengio, "Iraq," in *Middle East Contemporary Survey*, vol. 7, 566.

148. Aaron Faust, *The Baʿthification of Iraq: Saddam Hussein's Totalitarianism* (Austin: University of Texas Press, 2015), 67.

149. Elie Podeh, *The Politics of National Celebrations in the Arab Middle East* (New York: Cambridge University Press, 2011), 3.

150. Bengio, "Iraq," in *Middle East Contemporary Survey*, vol. 7, 565–66.

151. TNA, FCO 8/4697, "Speech of Saddam Hussein to Iraqi Cabinet, and Popular Demonstrations in Baghdad," November 15, 1982.

152. Bengio, "Iraq," in *Middle East Contemporary Survey*, vol. 7, 565–66.

153. Bengio, "Iraq," in *Middle East Contemporary Survey*, vol. 7, 565–66.

154. CADN 54PO/B/6, "Monthly Summary for October and November," December 8, 1986.

155. CADN 54PO/B/6, "Celebration of Saddam's Birthday," May 5, 1985.

156. CADN 54PO/B/6, "Celebration of Saddam's Birthday," May 5, 1985.

157. CADN 54PO/B/5, Political Dispatch, August 11, 1981.

158. CADN 54PO/B/5, Political Dispatch, August 8, 1981.

159. Party secretariat to Military Office and Leaders of Party Branches, "Celebrating Martyrs' Day," November 7, 1993, BRCC 01-2214-0000-0119.

160. CADN 54PO/B/5, "The Iraqi Population during the War," October 30, 1980.

161. CADN 54PO/B/5, "The Iraqi Population during the War," October 30, 1980.

162. Bengio, "Iraq," in *Middle East Contemporary Survey*, vol. 10, 380.

163. CADN 54PO/B/5, "July Political and Religious Celebrations in Iraq," August 8, 1981; CADN 54PO/B/5, "The Iraqi Population during the War," October 30, 1980.

164. Bengio, "Iraq," in *Middle East Contemporary Survey*, vol. 7, 578.

165. CADN 54PO/B/6, "Monthly Summary from April–May 10," May 17, 1986.

166. Head of Presidential Diwan to All Ministries, "Instructions," April 8, 1988, BRCC 01-3581-0003-0274.

167. Samuel Helfont, *Compulsion in Religion: Saddam Hussein, Islam, and the Roots of Insurgencies in Iraq* (New York: Oxford University Press, 2018), 63–64, 67–68; Khoury, *Iraq in Wartime*, 25, 64.

168. Bengio, "Iraq," in *Middle East Contemporary Survey*, vol. 7, 578.

169. Shukuh Khikhal, "Iraq's One Too Many Holidays," *al-Monitor*, November 16, 2014. http://www.al-monitor.com/pulse/originals/2014/11/iraq-holidays-disrupt-economy.html.

170. Party secretariat to Baghdad Organization, "Suggestion," December 13, 1989, BRCC 001-5-3-0198; "Public Sector Firm to Build 20 Power Sub-Stations, Stadium," *Baghdad Observer*, January 11, 1989, 2; "Baghdad to Mark Arab City Day," *Baghdad Observer*, March 7, 1990, 2; "New Telephone Lines to Be Installed," *Baghdad Observer*, January 29, 1990, 2.

171. Phone interview with S. by the author, July 8, 2020.

172. Phone interview with S. by the author, July 8, 2020.

173. Al-Khafaji suggests that as many as 1,000 Egyptians were murdered by Iraqis who saw Egyptians as "taking Iraqi jobs." See "War as a Vehicle," 275–76.

174. Bengio, "Iraq," in *Middle East Contemporary Survey*, vol. 12, 516–17; Dewachi, *Ungovernable Life*, 143.

175. Cited in Bengio, "Iraq," in *Middle East Contemporary Survey*, vol. 12, 390–91.

176. Majid Khadduri and Edmund Ghareeb, *War in the Gulf, 1990–1991: The Iraq-Kuwait Conflict and Its Implications* (New York: Oxford University Press, 1997), 95.

177. For information about the Iraqi occupation of Kuwait, see Joseph Sassoon and Alissa Walter, "The Iraqi Occupation of Kuwait: New Historical Perspectives," *Middle East Journal* 71, no. 4 (Autumn 2017): 607–28.

178. Kuwait Dataset of the Baʻth Party Archives [hereafer KDS] file 09431, February 8, 1991, p. 10; February 11, 1991, p. 9.

179. KDS file 08223, December 20, 1990, p. 15. For more on the Iraqi occupation of Kuwait, see Joseph Sassoon and Alissa Walter, "The Iraqi Occupation of Kuwait: New Historical Perspectives," *Middle East Journal* 71, no. 4 (2017): 607–28; and Joseph Sassoon and Alissa Walter, "Diaries of Iraqi Soldiers: Views inside Saddam's Army," *International Journal of Contemporary Iraqi Studies* 12, no. 2 (2018): 183–98.

180. Jabar, "The War Generation," 133.

181. "Damage Control—and Real Damage," *New York Times*, February 14, 1991;

James F. Clarity, "War in the Gulf: Baghdad; from TV Reports in Iraq, News an Attack has Begun," *New York Times*, January 17, 1991.

182. Nuha al-Radi, *Baghdad Diaries: A Woman's Chronicle of War and Exile* (New York: Vintage Books, 2003), 28.

183. Joy Gordon, *Invisible War: The United States and the Iraq Sanctions* (Cambridge, MA: Harvard University Press, 2010), 22.

184. Al-Radi, *Baghdad Diaries*, 29.

185. Gordon, *Invisible War*, 22.

186. Al-Radi, *Baghdad Diaries*, 20; phone interview with S. by the author, July 8, 2020.

187. Secretary of Baghdad to the Ministry of Industry and Military Industrialization, "Running Purification Plants for Drinking Water in Baghdad," February 22, 1991, BRCC 01-3630-0003-0360; R. W. Apple Jr., "War in the Gulf: Combat; Raids Said to Badly Delay Baghdad Messages to Front," *New York Times*, February 11, 1991.

188. Al-Radi, *Baghdad Diaries*, 13, 15.

189. Al-Radi, *Baghdad Diaries*, 18.

190. Interview with Sabean-Mandean family by the author, Erbil, October 21, 2016.

191. Khoury, *Iraq in Wartime*, 39.

192. Torie Rose DeGhett, "The War Photo No One Would Publish," *The Atlantic* (August 8, 2014); Daniel Hallin, "TV's Clean Little War," *Bulletin of the Atomic Scientists* 47, no. 4 (1991): 16–19.

193. Khoury, *Iraq in Wartime*, 41–42.

194. Khoury, *Iraq in Wartime*, 133–34.

195. Interview S.4 in Baghdad, June 2016, and Interview S.7 in Baghdad, July 2016.

196. Party secretariat to president's office, "Headquarters Building," August 20, 1990, BRCC 01-3630-0003-0621; Party secretariat to president's office, "Headquarters Building," December 25, 1990, BRCC 01-3630-0003-0609.

197. Party secretariat to president's office, "Alternative Headquarters," January 28, 1991, BRCC 01-3630-0003-0560 to -0564.

198. Stephen Kinzer, "War in the Gulf: Baghdad Refuge; Hussein's Nuclear-Proof, Buried Fortress," *New York Times*, January 23, 1991.

199. Saddam Hussein to All Ministries, January 22, 1991, BRCC 01-3630-0003-0638.

200. President's Office to All Ministries, "Alternative Headquarters," January 23, 1991, BRCC 01-3630-0003-0571.

201. General Security Director to Security Chief of Baghdad, "Evaluation of the Evacuation Drill of Saddam City," December 29, 1990, CRRC SH-IDGS-D-001–431.

202. Patrick Tyler, "Standoff in the Gulf: Baghdad Mounts Mock Evacuation," *New York Times*, December 22, 1990.

203. "Saddam Hussein Reprimanding an Official," audio transcript, undated [December 1991], CRRC SH-SHTP-A-001–230. English translation provided by the CRRC; Party secretariat to Members of the Regional Leadership, "Civil Defense and Evacuation Plan," December 30, 1990, BRCC 01-3630-0003-0627.

204. Interviews with displaced Baghdadis by the author, Erbil, October 17, 2016; Interview S.5, Baghdad, July 2016; Interview S.7, Baghdad, July 2016.

205. Al-Radi, *Baghdad Diaries*, 20, 33–34.

206. Al-Radi, *Baghdad Diaries*, 36–37.

207. Youssef Abdul-Moati, ed., *A Diary of an Iraqi Soldier* (Kuwait: National Center for Documents of Iraqi Aggression on Kuwait, 1994), 18–19; Sassoon and Walter, "Diaries of Iraqi Soldiers: Views from Inside Saddam's Army": 192.

208. Party secretariat to Baghdad Organization, "Securing Elements," February 14, 1991, BRCC 028-1-4-0003.

209. Office of the President to Ministry of the Interior, "Al-Amiriyya Shelter," February 17, 1991, BRCC 028-1-4-0006.

210. "War in the Gulf: Baghdad Scene; Baghdad Rescuers Search for Life with Little Hope," *Associated Press*, February 14, 1991.

211. Party secretariat to president's office, "Information," February 22, 1991, BRCC 028-1-4-0014.

212. Party secretariat to president's office, "Information," February 23, 1991, BRCC 028-1-4-0020.

213. General Union of the Iraqi Workers' Unions to President of the Union, "Al-Amiriyya Shelter," October 19, 1991, BRCC 028-1-4-0062; Party secretariat to Central Office for Vocational and Popular Organizations, "Anniversary for the Victims of the al-Amiriyya Shelter," November 30, 1992, BRCC 028-1-4-0159.

214. Party secretariat to Military Office, "Record of the Mother of All Battles," May 12, 1993, BRCC 01-2214-0000-0368.

215. Al-Radi, *Baghdad Diaries*, 81.

216. Helfont, *Compulsion in Religion*, 121–27.

217. Khoury, *Iraq in Wartime*, 145–46.

218. Harith Hasan al-Qarawee, "Sectarian Identities, Narratives and Political Conflict in Baghdad," *Levantine Review* 4 (Winter 2015): 181.

219. Party secretariat to Leadership of Air Defense, "Information," May 20, 1999, BRCC 01-3219-0000-0424.

220. General Union of the Iraqi Workers' Unions to President of the Union, "Al-Amiriyya Shelter," October 19, 1991; BRCC 028-1-4-0062; Party secretariat to Central Office for Vocational and Popular Organizations, "Anniversary for the Victims of the al-Amiriyya Shelter," November 30, 1992, BRCC 028-1-4-0159.

221. Rashid Branch to party secretariat, "Report," September 4, 1996, BRCC file number withheld to protect identities.

222. Head of the president's office to party secretariat, "Al-Batawin Group," September 17, 1996, BRCC file number withheld to protect identities.

223. Kofman and Lebas, "Introduction: Lost in Transposition—Time, Space and the City," in *Writings on Cities*, 31.

224. Al-Radi, *Baghdad Diaries*, 20–21, 81.

Chapter 3

1. Richard Garfield, "Studies on Young Child Malnutrition in Iraq: Problems and Insights, 1990–1999," *Nutrition Reviews* 58 (2000): 269; Mustafa Koc et al., "Food Security and Food Sovereignty in Iraq," *Food, Culture, and Society* 10 (Summer 2007): 329.

2. Sassoon, *Saddam Hussein's Baʿth Party*, 238–39.

3. Garfield, "Studies on Young Child Malnutrition in Iraq," 270; Sarah Graham-Brown, *Sanctioning Saddam* (New York: I. B. Tauris, 1999), 70.

4. Abbas Alnasrawi, "Iraq: Economic Sanctions and Consequences, 1990–2000," *Third World Quarterly* 22, no. 2 (April 2001): 209.

5. Interview N.1, Baghdad, August 2016.

6. Al-Radi, *Baghdad Diaries*, 62, 68, 79, 115.

7. Yawmin Husein al-Jawaheri, *Women in Iraq: The Gender Impact of International Sanctions* (Boulder, CO: Lynn Rienner, 2008), 10–11.

8. Interview S.12, Baghdad, August 2016.

9. Interview S.3, Baghdad, June 2016.

10. Interview N.5, Baghdad, August 2016.

11. Party secretariat to Organizations of the North, South, Euphrates Region, and Center, "Distributing Food Resources," August 10, 1990, BRCC 005-3-5-0560.

12. Oversight of many aspects of the food rationing system was entrusted to the minister of trade at the time, Mohammed Mahdi Saleh al-Rawi, who wrote a memoir about this work: *Averting Famine in Iraq: My Memory for Years of U.N. Sanction 1990–2003* (by the author, 2023).

13. Al-Radi, *Baghdad Diaries*, 11.

14. Party secretariat to Organizational Offices in All of Iraq, "Inventory of the Families," September 20, 1990, BRCC 005-3-5-0376.

15. Party secretariat to Organizational Offices in all Iraq, "Cards," September 12, 1990, BRCC 005-3-5-0465.

16. Party secretariat to Organizational Offices in all of Iraq, "Inventory of the Families," August 26, 1990, BRCC 005-3-5-0501.

17. Party secretariat to Baghdad Organization, "Cards," August 31, 1990, BRCC 005-3-5-0484.

18. "Food Needs for Families according to the Number of Family Members for the Monthly Emergency Plan," August 1990, BRCC 005-3-5-0235; Ministry of Trade to party secretariat, "Inventory of the Families," August 22, 1990, BRCC 005-3-5-0518; Party secretariat to Organizational Offices in All of Iraq, "Inventory of the Families," August 23, 1990, BRCC 005-3-5-0522.

19. For example, Interview I.1, Baghdad, July 2016; Interview I.4, Baghdad, July 2016; Interview N.1, Baghdad, August 2016; Interview N.4, Baghdad, August 2016.

20. Interview S.7, Baghdad, July 2016; Interview I.3, Baghdad, July 2016.

21. Al-Jawaheri, *Women in Iraq*, 84.

22. Sassoon, *Saddam Hussein's Ba'th Party*, 243.

23. Frank Dikotter, *Mao's Great Famine* (New York: Walker, 2010), 333; Lizzie Collingham, *Taste of War: World War II and the Battle for Food* (London: Allen Lane, 2011), 329.

24. Gordon, *Invisible War*, 200.

25. "Saddam and Senior Ba'ath Party Officials Discussing UN Sanctions on Iraq," audio transcript, August 15, 1995, CRRC SH-SHTP-A-001–010. English translation provided by the CRRC and edited lightly for clarity.

26. Party secretariat to Organizational Offices in all Iraq, "Cards," September 12, 1990, BRCC 005-3-5-0465.

27. Interview S.5, Baghdad, June 2016.

28. Interview S.2, Baghdad, July 2016.

29. Ministry of Trade, Office of Minister to Party Secretariat, "Issuing an Opinion," August 30, 1992, BRCC 005-3-5-0059; General Company for Central Markets to Representatives of All Ministries, "Instructions," April 7, 1994, BRCC 01-3579-0003-0339.

30. Interview S.4, Baghdad, June 2016; Interview S.5, Baghdad, June 2016; Interview 4, Erbil, October 2016. See also Eckart Woertz, "Iraq under UN Embargo, 1990–2003: Food Security, Agriculture, and Regime Survival," *Middle East Journal* 73, no. 1 (Spring 2019): 104.

31. Party Secretariat to Comrade Vice Chair of the Country, September 3, 1990, BRCC 005-3-5-0396 to -0400.

32. Khoury, *Iraq in Wartime*, 153.

33. Ofra Bengio, "Iraq," in *Middle East Contemporary Survey*, vol. 10: *1986*, ed. Itamar Rabinovich and Haim Shaked (Tel Aviv: Dayan Center for Middle Eastern and African Studies, 1988), 374.

34. Party secretariat to Khalid bin al-Walid branch, "Information," December 30, 1995, *BRCC file number withheld to protect identities*.

35. Ministry of Trade to Presidential Diwan, "Recommendation," November 26, 1994, BRCC 01-3439-0001-0691.

36. Interview 9, Erbil, October 2016.

37. Party secretariat to Presidential Diwan, "Amount of Flour," September 7, 1991,

BRCC 005-3-5-0144; party secretariat to Presidential Diwan, "Popular Supervision," March 19, 1991, BRCC 01-2947-0002-0118. Also interview S.5, Baghdad, June 2016.

38. Party secretariat to Organizational Offices in All of Iraq, "Operation of Flour Mills," February 10, 1991, BRCC 005-3-5-0194; Ministry of Trade to Presidential Diwan, "Amount of Flour," September 16, 1991, BRCC 005-3-5-0143.

39. Interview S.7, Baghdad, July 2016; Interview S.5, Baghdad, June 2016. See also Woertz, "Iraq under UN Embargo," 104.

40. Interview S.12, Baghdad, August 2016.

41. Party secretariat to Organizational Offices in All of Iraq, "Operation of Flour Mills," February 10, 1991, BRCC 005-3-5-0194; Ministry of Trade to Presidential Diwan, "Amount of Flour," September 16, 1991, BRCC 005-3-5-0143.

42. Ministry of Trade to State Company for Processing Grains, "Delay in Processing Flour," August 19, 1992, BRCC 005-3-5-0074.

43. Ministry of Trade to party secretariat, "Response," August 10, 1994, BRCC 01-2968-0001-0013; Baghdad Organizations in Rusafa to party secretariat, "Study about Flour Mills," April 19, 1995, BRCC 01-3869-0003-0119.

44. Party secretariat to Presidential Diwan, "Amount of Flour," September 7, 1991, BRCC 005-3-5-0144; party secretariat to Presidential Diwan, "Popular Supervision," March 19, 1991, BRCC 01-2947-0002-0118.

45. Presidential Diwan to Ministry of Trade, "Food Agents," February 9, 1991, BRCC 005-3-5-0184; Party secretariat to Organizational Offices in All of Iraq, "Food Agents," February 15, 1991, BRCC 005-3-5-0189.

46. Ministry of Trade to Presidential Diwan, September 2, 1992, BRCC 005-3-5-0035.

47. Party secretariat to Furat Organizations, "Recommendation," September 25, 1992, BRCC 005-3-5-0023.

48. Al-Rawi, *Averting Famine on Iraq*, 55–77.

49. Party secretariat to Offices of the Northern, Southern, Furat, and Wasit Organizations, "Distributing Food Supplies," August 10, 1990, BRCC 005-3-5-0560.

50. Presidential Decree, "Popular Surveillance," October 11, 1990, BRCC 01-2947-0002-0044.

51. TNA, FCO 8/2538: Internal Affairs of Iraq, 1975, "The Arab Ba'ath Socialist Party in Iraq," p. 6; Faust, *Ba'thification of Iraq*, 65.

52. Rohde, "Echoes from Below?" 8–9.

53. For details about the responsibilities of popular committees, see RCC decree no. 25 from 1995.

54. Ministry of Trade to Party secretariat, "Loss of Ration Card," November 26, 1990, BRCC 005-3-5-0346 to -0347.

55. Party secretariat to Organizational Offices in All of Iraq, "Inventory of the Families," August 20, 1990, BRCC 005-3-5-0538.

56. Interview I.2, Baghdad, July 2016.

57. Katherine Verdery, "The 'Étatization' of Time in Ceausescu's Romania," in *What Was Socialism, and What Comes Next?* ed. Katherine Verdery (Princeton: Princeton University Press, 1996), 82–90; Paulina Bren and Mary Neuburger, "Introduction," in *Communism Unwrapped: Consumption in Cold War Eastern Europe*, ed. Paulina Bren and Mary Neuburger (New York: Oxford University Press, 2012), 13; Collingham, *Taste of War*, 330.

58. Interview S.4, Baghdad, June 2016; Jean Drèze and Haris Gazdar, "Hunger and Poverty in Iraq, 1991," *World Development* 20 (1992): 932.

59. Party secretariat to Ministry of Trade, "Information," November 29, 1992, BRCC *file number withheld to protect identities.*

60. Leaders of Baghdad Office, "Activities of the Economic Surveillance Committee for February 1991," BRCC *file number withheld to protect identities.*

61. General Interior Director to party secretariat, "People's Day," March 3, 2002, BRCC *file number withheld to protect identities.*

62. Party secretariat to Ministry of the Interior—Office for Combatting Economic Crimes, "Citizen Letter," December 15, 1991, BRCC *file number withheld to protect identities.*

63. Rashid branch to party secretariat, "Medical Report," June 27, 1999, BRCC *file number withheld to protect identities.*

64. Party secretariat to Organizational Offices in all of Iraq, "Popular Surveillance," February 10, 1991, BRCC 01-2947-0002-0036.

65. Head of Presidential Cabinet to party secretariat, "Situations of Exploitation," November 3, 1990, BRCC 01-2947-0002-0387.

66. Saddam Hussein, "Decision no. 365," September 5, 1990, BRCC 01-2947-0002-0182.

67. RCC decision no. 70, 1994. http://wiki.dorar-aliraq.net/iraqilaws/law/16026.html.

68. Saddam Hussein, "Decision no. 315," August 11, 1990, BRCC 01-2947-0002-0184 and 0186.

69. Makiya, *Republic of Fear*, xvi.

70. Party secretariat to Organizational Offices in All of Iraq, "Popular Supervision," February 10, 1991, BRCC 01-2947-0002-0036.

71. Party secretariat to Ministry of Trade, "Rations Agent," December 3, 1998, BRCC *file number withheld to protect identities*; Ministry of Trade to party secretariat, "Rations Agent," June 7, 1999, BRCC *file number withheld to protect identities.*

72. Migdal, *State in Society*, 17–18.

73. Khoury, *Iraq in Wartime*, 81.

74. Ninawa and Ta'mim branches to Council of Ministers, "Lentils," January 19, 2002, BRCC 01-2454-0002-0007; Party secretariat to Organizational Offices in All of Iraq, "Popular Surveillance," February 10, 1991, BRCC 01-2947-0002-0036.

75. Party secretariat to General Cooperative Union, "Information," January 2, 1992, BRCC *file number withheld to protect identities.*

76. Party secretariat to Organizational Offices in All of Iraq, "Inventory of the Families," November 4, 1990, BRCC 005-3-5-0423.

77. Musa al-Kadhim branch to party secretariat, "Information," May 13, 2002, BRCC *file number withheld to protect identities.*

78. Party secretariat to Special Security Apparatus, "Information," March 25, 1999, BRCC *file number withheld to protect identities.*

79. "Baʻth Revolutionary Command Meeting," audio transcript, December 21, 1991, CRRC SH-SHTP-A-001-461. English translation provided by the CRRC.

80. Ministry of Trade to party secretariat, "Announcement," June 8, 1991, BRCC 005-3-5-0164 and 0165.

81. Ministry of Trade to Presidential Diwan, "Recommendation," November 26, 1994, BRCC 01-3439-0001-0691.

82. Ministry of Trade to Presidential Diwan, "Recommendation," November 26, 1994, BRCC 01-3439-0001-0691.

83. Party secretariat to Leadership of All Party Branches, "Travel Outside of the Country," December 19, 1994, BRCC 01-3439-0001-0596.

84. Party secretariat to Karkh Organization in Baghdad, "Withholding Rations," February 1, 1995, BRCC *file number withheld to protect identities.*

85. Jabar, *Shiʻite Movement in Iraq*, 214–15. Examples from the archives of executions for membership in an opposition group include Baghdad Organization to party secretariat, "Incident," July 16, 1992, BRCC 01-3086-0001-0068.

86. Khoury, *Iraq in Wartime*, 102–3.

87. Original decree was in memo no. 19038, November 2, 1994. Cited in a memo from Abu Jaʻfar al-Mansur branch to party secretariat, "Breach," January 21, 1995, BRCC 01-3439-0001-0492.

88. Gordon, *Invisible War*, 38.

89. Jawaheri shares accounts of many formerly middle-class professionals who engaged in menial jobs during sanctions because those jobs paid slightly better. See *Women in Iraq*, 30–56.

90. Interview 9, Erbil, October 2016.

91. Collingham, *Taste of War*, 330.

92. Collingham, *Taste of War*, 11.

93. Decree no. 59 from 1994, "Severe Punishments for Those Who Commit Theft"; Decree no. 114 from 1994, "Modifying RCC Decree no. 59 from 1994 (Theft)"; Decree no. 109 from 1994, "Tattoo on the Forehead for any Person whose Hand was Cut Off as Punishment According to the Law for Cutting Hands"; Decree no. 117 from 1994, "Prohibition of Removing the Tattoo"; Decree no. 115 from 1994, "Punishment by Cutting Off the Outer Ear."

94. Khoury, *Iraq in Wartime*, 146–47, 154–55.

95. Council of Ministers to party secretariat, "Deserters," February 2, 1995, BRCC 01-3439-0001-0164.

96. Party secretariat to Ministry of Trade, "Death of a Deserter," April 6, 1995, BRCC 041-2-2-0254.

97. Senior Ministry Agent to party secretariat, "Displacement," June 3, 1995, BRCC 027-2-4-0258.

98. Khoury, *Iraq in Wartime*, 172–74.

99. Abu Ja'far al-Mansur Branch to party secretariat, "Breach," January 21, 1995, BRCC file number withheld to protect identities.

100. Saddam branch to party secretariat, "Issuing an Opinion," February 3, 1996, BRCC file number withheld to protect identities; Party secretariat to Saddam Branch, "Restoring Rations," April 3, 1996, BRCC file number withheld to protect identities.

101. Letter to party secretariat, undated [January 1995], BRCC file number withheld to protect identities; Party secretariat to Abu Ja'far al-Mansur branch, "Withholding Rations Card," January 23, 1995, BRCC file number withheld to protect identities.

102. Sassoon, *Saddam Hussein's Ba'th Party*, 246.

103. Party secretariat to Ministry of Trade, "Withholding Rations," February 19, 1995, BRCC 01-3439-0001-0456; Party Secretariat to All Party Branches, "Traveling Outside the Country," February 4, 1995, BRCC 01-3439-0001-0480.

104. Letter from an Iraqi woman to party secretariat, undated [January 1995], BRCC file number withheld to protect identities.

105. Letter from an Iraqi woman to party secretariat, January 26, 1995, BRCC file number withheld to protect identities.

106. Party secretariat to Ministry of the Interior, "Restoration," January 25, 1996, BRCC file number withheld to protect identities.

107. Party secretariat to President's Deputy, "Return of Exiled Family," May 25, 1995, BRCC file number withheld to protect identities.

108. Sa'd bin Abi Waqas Branch to party secretariat, "Arrest and Withholding Rations," March 18, 1995, BRCC file number withheld to protect identities.

109. Party secretariat to Rashid Branch, "Cutting Rations," June 11, 1995, BRCC file number withheld to protect identities.

110. Senior Ministry Agent to party secretariat, "Displacement," June 3, 1995, BRCC file number withheld to protect identities.

111. Party secretariat to Province of Baghdad—Mukhtar Affairs, "Exchanging Mukhtar," December 31, 1997, BRCC file number withheld to protect identities.

112. Interview S7, fifty-eight-year-old woman from Sadr City, January 6, 2023.

113. Saddam Branch to party secretariat, "Cutting Rations to the Families of Deserters," June 21, 1995, BRCC file number withheld to protect identities.

114. Abu Jaʿfar al-Mansur Brach to party secretariat, "Request," March 20, 1995, BRCC file number withheld to protect identities.

115. Khalid bin al-Walid Branch to party secretariat, "Restoring Rations," May 22, 1996, BRCC file number withheld to protect identities.

116. Undated letter [1995], BRCC file number withheld to protect identities.

117. Leadership of the Saʿd bin Abi Waqas Branch to party secretariat, "Cooperation of a Citizen," March 9, 1995, BRCC file number withheld to protect identities; Party secretariat to Assistant to the President, "Exceptional Families," March 15, 1995, BRCC file number withheld to protect identities.

118. Party secretariat to Saʿd bin Abi Waqas Branch, "Exceptional Families," March 22, 1995, BRCC file number withheld to protect identities.

119. Letter from a Baghdad man to party secretariat, undated [1994], BRCC file number withheld to protect identities.

120. Khalid bin al-Walid branch to party secretariat, "Issuing an Opinion," October 22, 1994, BRCC file number withheld to protect identities.

121. Party secretariat to Khalid bin al-Walid Branch, "Issuing an Opinion," October 16, 1994, BRCC file number withheld to protect identities.

122. Baram, *Saddam Husayn and Islam*, 10.

123. Special Advisor to Director of Central Intelligence, "Regime Intent," chap. 4 in *Comprehensive Report of the Special Advisor to the DCI on Iraq's WMD*, vol. 1 (Central Intelligence Agency, 2004).

124. Footage of this meeting, which took place on July 22, 1979, can be found online. See, for example, "Saddam Hussein's Very Public Purge," YouTube.com, uploaded November 2, 2015.

125. Saʿd bin Abi Waqas branch to party secretariat, "Dispute," February 15, 1992, BRCC file number withheld to protect identities.

126. Dina Khoury has written about this inconsistent approach to punishing and rewarding families in *Iraq in Wartime*, 172–78.

127. The Organizations of Babil and Karbala to party secretariat, "Recommendation," September 17, 1995, BRCC 01-3439-0001-0348.

128. The Organizations of Babil and Karbala to party secretariat, "Recommendation," September 17, 1995, BRCC 01-3439-0001-0348.

129. Party secretariat to Organizations of the Provinces of Babil and Karbala, "Recommendation," September 26, 1995, BRCC file number withheld to protect identities.

130. Official of Maysan and Wasit Organizations to Office of Assistant to the President, "Cutting Rations," November 2, 1995, BRCC 01-3439-0001-0353.

131. Ministry of Trade to party secretariat, Ministry of Defense, Ministry of the Interior, Ministry of Justice, and the intelligence and security organizations, "Ration Card Goods," February 12, 1996, BRCC 01-3439-0001-0408 through -0410.

132. Presidential Diwan to Ministry of Trade, "Rations," June 8, 1996, BRCC 01-3612-0001-0880.

133. Presidential Diwan to Ministry of Trade, "Rations," June 18, 1996, BRCC 01-3612-0001-0875.

134. Ministry of Trade to party secretariat, "Information," September 20, 1996, *BRCC file number withheld to protect identities*.

135. Maysan and Wasit Organization, "Cutting Rations," November 2, 1995, BRCC 01-3439-0001-0353.

136. Presidential Diwan to party secretariat, "Rations," June 2, 1996, BRCC 01-3439-0001-0352.

137. "Ba'ath Revolutionary Command Meeting 12/21/1991," audio transcript, December 21, 1991, CRRC SH-SHTP-A-001–461. English translation provided by the CRRC and edited lightly for clarity.

Chapter 4

Parts of Chapter 4 are developed from Alissa Walter, "Petitioning Saddam: Voices from the Iraqi Archives," published in Truth, Silence, and Violence in Emerging States, edited by Aidan Russell, 127–146. New York: Routledge, 2019. Used with permission of Taylor & Francis Informa UKLtd; permission conveyed through Copyright Clearance Center, Inc.

1. Regarding my methodology: I identified more than one hundred petitions in the Ba'th Party archives that were written by residents of Baghdad to regime officials between 1986 and 2002. Roughly half of these petitions were located in folders related to the celebration of People's Day, a Ba'th Party event that I describe later in the chapter. The other petitions were sprinkled throughout various archival boxfiles related to different Ba'th Party branches in Baghdad. Petitions in these boxfiles were tucked between bureaucratic memos and party correspondence about other matters. In other words, the relatively small sample size is due to the fact that petitions were not typically grouped together in the same boxfile, making them difficult to locate in the archives. Though the petitions I examine here span a period from 1986 to 2000, they disproportionately date from the 1990s and early 2000s, with only a few from the 1980s. It is unclear whether this reflects a genuine increase in petitioning activity in the 1990s or constitutes a quirk of the sample size that misrepresents actual trends and practices.

2. Dina Khoury, *Iraq in Wartime: Soldiering, Martyrdom, and Remembrance* (New York: Cambridge University Press, 2013), 146–47.

3. Letter from a woman in Baghdad, January 9, 1989, *BRCC file number withheld to protect identities*. The salary of 87 dinars was equivalent to $280 at the time. Exchange rate calculated from Economy Watch, "Dinar Exchange Rate," http://www.economywatch.com/exchange-rate/dinar.html.

4. Letter from a woman in Baghdad, January 9, 1989, BRCC file number withheld to protect identities.

5. Baghdad Organization to the Party Secretariat, "Issuing a Decision," February 13, 1989, BRCC file number withheld to protect identities.

6. Party Secretariat to the Baghdad Organization, "Confirmation," January 28, 1989, BRCC file number withheld to protect identities.

7. Joseph Sassoon, *Saddam Hussein's Ba'th Party: Inside an Authoritarian Regime* (New York: Cambridge University Press, 2012), 124.

8. Sassoon, *Saddam Hussein's Ba'th Party*, 124.

9. Yuval Ben-Bassat, *Petitioning the Sultan: Protests and Justice in Ottoman Palestine* (New York: I. B. Tauris, 2013), 2–4; Yigit Akin, "Reconsidering State, Party, and Society in Early Republican Turkey: Politics of Petitioning," *International Journal of Middle East Studies* 39, no. 3 (August 2007): 437.

10. Sassoon, *Saddam Hussein's Ba'th Party*, 178.

11. Party Secretary to President Saddam Hussein, December 31, 1989, BRCC file number withheld to protect identities.

12. Letter from a Ba'th Party official in Baghdad, December 1989, BRCC file number withheld to protect identities.

13. Head of the Presidential Diwan to [Name Withheld], January 20, 1990, BRCC file number withheld to protect identities.

14. Letter from a party member, May 12, 1997, BRCC file number withheld to protect identities.

15. Letter from a woman to Saddam, October 6, 1999, BRCC file number withheld to protect identities.

16. Aaron Faust, *The Ba'thification of Iraq: Saddam Hussein's Totalitarianism* (Austin: University of Texas Press, 2015), 4.

17. Samir 'Ulu, "Muhammad Muhammad al-'Alim: I Write Love Poetry with My Blood," *al-Qadisiyya*, November 29, 1993, BRCC 01-3607-0004-0013.

18. Party secretariat to Secretary of the President, "Oath Document," September 10, 1986, BRCC file number withheld to protect identities.

19. Letter from a citizen to the leader of the Abu Ja'far al-Mansur branch, "Donation," May 29, 2000, BRCC file number withheld to protect identities.

20. Letter from a man to Saddam, undated [December 2000], BRCC file number withheld to protect identities.

21. See, for example, Sarah Davies, "'Cult' of the *Vozhd*: Representations in Letters, 1934–1941," *Russian History* 24, nos. 1–2 (Spring–Summer 1997): 143; Joseph Sassoon, *Anatomy of Authoritarianism in the Arab Republics* (New York: Cambridge University Press, 2016), chap. 6.

22. Vesna Drapac and Gareth Pritchard, *Resistance and Collaboration in Hitler's Europe* (London: Palgrave Macmillan, 2017), 82–83.

23. *BRCC file numbers withheld to protect identities.* According to the UN Development Programme, Iraq's adult literacy rate in 2000 was 74.1 percent, though this may have been higher in Baghdad. There is no indication that Iraqis routinely hired professional petition writers or enlisted friends and relatives to write their petitions for them, except in these cases of adult illiteracy. This is a change from the early modern period: see Ben-Bassat's discussion of the role of professional scribes in writing Ottoman petitions in *Petitioning the Sultan*, 50–51.

24. Sheila Fitzpatrick, "Supplicants and Citizens: Public Letter-Writing in Soviet Russia in the 1930s," *Slavic Review* 55, no. 1 (Spring 1996): 80.

25. Sassoon, *Saddam Hussein's Baʻth Party*, 127.

26. Sheila Fitzpatrick, "Petitions and Denunciations in Russian and Soviet History," *Russian History* 24, nos. 1–2 (Spring–Summer 1997): 7.

27. Letter from a group of female medical students, undated [June 2002], *BRCC file number withheld to protect identities;* People's Day petition by four women, "Sewing Machines," June 2002, *BRCC file number withheld to protect identities.*

28. Rashid Branch to Party Secretariat, "Eviction Statement," April 23, 2001, *BRCC file number withheld to protect identities.*

29. Martin Dimitrov, "What the Party Wanted to Know: Citizen Complaints as a 'Barometer of Public Opinion,'" *East European Politics and Societies* 28, no. 2 (May 2014): 276.

30. Letter, April 15, 1995, *BRCC file number withheld to protect identities.*

31. Letter, January 1993, *BRCC file number withheld to protect identities.*

32. Hank Johnston, "Talking the Walk: Speech Acts and Resistance in Authoritarian Regimes," in *Repression and Mobilization,* ed. Christian Davenport, Hank Johnston, and Carol Mueller (Minneapolis: University of Minnesota Press, 2005), 108; Selçuk Aksin Somel, Christoph K. Neumann, and Amy Singer, "Re-Sounding Silent Voices," in *Untold Histories of the Middle East: Recovering Voices from the 19th and 20th Centuries,* ed. Amy Singer, Christoph K. Neumann, and Selçuk Aksin Somel (New York: Routledge, 2011), 1.

33. Achim Rohde, "Echoes from Below: Talking Democracy in Baʻthist Iraq," *Middle Eastern Studies* 53, no. 4 (2017): 552.

34. Kanan Makiya, *Republic of Fear: The Politics of Modern Iraq* (Berkeley: University of California Press, 1998), xi–xii; Faust, *Baʻthification of Iraq,* 58; Sassoon, *Saddam Hussein's Baʻth Party,* 124.

35. Letter from a male party member, January 1993, *BRCC file number withheld to protect identities.*

36. See, for example, Davies, "'Cult' of the Vozhd," 136–37; Fitzpatrick, "Supplicants and Citizens," 92.

37. J. E. Shaw, "Writing to the Prince: Supplications, Equity, and Absolutism in Sixteenth-Century Tuscany," *Past and Present* 215 (2012): 65, cited in Ben-Bassat, *Petitioning the Sultan,* 23.

38. Eyal Ginio, "Coping with the State's Agents 'from Below': Petitions, Legal Appeal, and the Sultan's Justice in Ottoman Legal Practice," in *Popular Protest and Political Participation in the Ottoman Empire*, ed. Eleni Gara, M. Erdem Kabadayi, and Christoph K. Neumann (Istanbul: Istanbul Bilgi Universitesi Yayinlari, 2011), 55; Ben-Bassat, *Petitioning the Sultan*, 4.

39. Petition from an Iraqi woman to Saddam Hussein, undated [February 1993], BRCC file number withheld to protect identities.

40. Khoury, *Iraq in Wartime*, 164–72.

41. Deniz Kandiyoti, "Bargaining with Patriarchy," *Gender and Society* 2, no. 3 (1988): 285.

42. Memo from party secretariat to Office of the President, February 17, 1993, BRCC file number withheld to protect identities.

43. Letter, April 15, 1995, BRCC file number withheld to protect identities. Emphasis added.

44. Letter, undated [June 1997], BRCC file number withheld to protect identities.

45. Petition from a man to party secretariat, undated [March 1995], BRCC file number withheld to protect identities.

46. See, for example, Soldier's petition to the Vice President of the Revolutionary Command Council, January 19, 1989, BRCC file number withheld to protect identities.

47. See, for example, Petition from a woman to the Vice President of the Revolutionary Command Council, undated [May 1995], BRCC file number withheld to protect identities.

48. Petition from a woman to Leaders of the Baghdad al-Jadida section, "Interview," December 10, 2001, BRCC file number withheld to protect identities.

49. Sassoon, *Anatomy of Authoritarianism*, 204. This kind of patriarchal language can be found in many other authoritarian regimes centered on a single male leader: Fitzpatrick, "Supplicants and Citizens," 91; Fitzpatrick, "Petitions and Denunciations," 5; Davies, "'Cult' of the Vohzd," 133.

50. Achim Rohde, *State-Society Relations in Ba'thist Iraq: Facing Dictatorship* (New York: Routledge, 2010), 75–118.

51. Fitzpatrick, "Supplicants and Citizens," 78–105.

52. Letter from a woman to the Vice Chair of the Revolutionary Command Council, November 22, 1988, BRCC file number withheld to protect identities.

53. Letter from a party member, "My Health Situation and Help from the Party," undated [March 1993], BRCC file number withheld to protect identities.

54. Letter from a party member, "My Health Situation and Help from the Party," undated [March 1993], BRCC file number withheld to protect identities.

55. Letter from a woman to the party secretariat, August 31, 1998, BRCC file number withheld to protect identities.

56. Party secretariat to Office of [Name Withheld]/Office of the President,

"Comrade Martyrs," March 23, 1999, BRCC *file number withheld to protect identities.*

57. This phrase borrows from the title of Kanan Makiya's influential *Republic of Fear*, which revealed to a broad audience Saddam Hussein's violent treatment of his own citizens. Since then, many scholars have noted that Saddam did not rely solely on repressive levels of violence to govern Iraq, but balanced violent terror with a system of lavish patronage and rewards. See, for example, Sassoon, *Saddam Hussein's Baʻth Party*, 193.

58. TNA, FCO 8/4126, Memo from British Embassy Baghdad, June 4, 1980; TNA, FCO 8/4126, "Annual Review for 1980," December 31, 1980.

59. Office of party secretariat to Leaders of All Party Branches, "Responsibility of State Administrations in Solving Citizens' Issues," September 12, 1993, BRCC 01-2214-0000-0259.

60. Martin Dimitrov and Joseph Sassoon, "State Security, Information, and Repression: A Comparison of Communist Bulgaria and Baʻthist Iraq," *Journal of Cold War Studies* 16, no. 2 (Spring 2014): 22–27.

61. Historians of Ottoman-era petitions have made similar arguments about the importance of petitions in the context of that empire. See Ginio, "Coping with the State's Agents," 41; Suraiya Faroqhi, "Political Activity among Ottoman Taxpayers and the Problem of Sultanic Legitimation," *Journal of the Economic and Social History of the Orient* 35 (1992): 1–39; Ben-Bassat, *Petitioning the Sultan*, 22.

62. Ben-Bassat makes a similar observation regarding Ottoman petitions in *Petitioning the Sultan*, 5–6, 23–24.

63. See, for example, Office of party secretariat to Ministry of Defense, "People's Day," September 10, 2002, BRCC 01-3389-0000-0233.

64. For comparisons to petitioning systems in the Soviet Union, China, and communist Bulgaria, see Dimitrov, "What the Party Wanted to Know," 277; Davies, "'Cult' of the Vozhd," 135; Keyuan Zou, "Granting or Refusing the Right to Petition: The Dilemma of China's *Xinfang* System," in *Socialist China, Capitalist China: Social Tension and Political Adaptation under Economic Globalization*, ed. Guoguang Wu and Helen Lansdowne (New York: Routledge, 2009), 125; Xi Chen, *Social Protests and Contentious Authoritarianism in China* (New York: Cambridge University Press, 2014), 100.

65. For more information about the Baʻth Party and Iraqi government structures, see Sassoon, *Saddam Hussein's Baʻth Party*, 34–56.

66. Sassoon, *Saddam Hussein's Baʻth Party*, 34–56.

67. Series of memos written between December 1992 and March 1993, BRCC *file number withheld to protect identities.*

68. Series of memos written in May 1995, BRCC *file number withheld to protect identities.*

69. Party secretariat to Abu Jaʻfar al-Mansur branch, "Withholding Rations Card," January 23, 1995, BRCC *file number withheld to protect identities.*

70. Letter from a woman to Baʿth Party officials for the Baghdad–Karkh organization, January 11, 1997, *BRCC file number withheld to protect identities*.

71. Abu Jaʿfar al-Mansur Branch to Party Secretariat, "Request," March 20, 1995, *BRCC file number withheld to protect identities*.

72. Leaders of Abu Jaʿfar al-Mansur branch to party secretariat, "Request," March 20, 1995, *BRCC file number withheld to protect identities*.

73. Rashid Branch to party secretariat, "Call for Help," August 23, 1999, *BRCC file number withheld to protect identities*.

74. Petition from a Baghdad Woman to President of the National Council, February 10, 1990, *BRCC file number withheld to protect identities*.

75. Baghdad Organization to party secretariat, "Interview," April 15, 1990, *BRCC file number withheld to protect identities*.

76. Party secretariat to Baghdad Organization, "Interview," April 22, 1990, *BRCC file number withheld to protect identities*.

77. Party secretariat to Office of the President, "Request," February 25, 1993, *BRCC file number withheld to protect identities*.

78. Letter from a retired police officer to Saddam, "Request for Help for a Family of a Martyr who had 8 Medals of Bravery," January 19, 1993, *BRCC file number withheld to protect identities*.

79. Party secretariat to Office of the President, "Request," February 25, 1993, *BRCC file number withheld to protect identities*.

80. Letter from a retired police officer to Saddam, "Request for Help for a Family of a Martyr who had 8 Medals of Bravery," January 19, 1993, *BRCC file number withheld to protect identities*.

81. Office of the President to party secretariat, "Request," March 15, 1993, *BRCC file number withheld to protect identities*.

82. Other requests by party members for financial assistance can be seen in the following petitions: Letter from a party member, "Report," September 14, 2002, *BRCC file number withheld to protect identities*; Letter from a Party Member to party secretariat, "Improving Life," May 12, 1997, *BRCC file number withheld to protect identities*.

83. Petition from a man to Secretary of the Council of Ministers, "Problem of an Iraqi Family," undated [February 1995], *BRCC file number withheld to protect identities*.

84. Leadership of Hamza Sayyid al-Shuhadaʾ branch to party secretariat, "Request of the Citizen [name]," February 26, 1995, *BRCC file number withheld to protect identities*.

85. Head of Presidential Diwan to Iskan *firqa* leadership, "Behavior," June 10, 1985, *BRCC file number withheld to protect identities*.

86. Khalid bin al-Walid Branch to Baghdad Organization, "Behavior," June 30, 1985, *BRCC file number withheld to protect identities*.

87. Baghdad Organization to Presidential Diwan, "Behavior," July 3, 1985, *BRCC file number withheld to protect identities*.

88. See examples: Office of the Vice Chair to party secretariat, "Request Referral," May 7, 1995, *BRCC file number withheld to protect identities*; Office of the Vice Chair to party secretariat, "Request Referral," August 17, 1996, *BRCC file number withheld to protect identities*; Office of the Vice Chair to party secretariat, "Request Referral," July 19,1997, *BRCC file number withheld to protect identities*.

89. See the full text of Saddam's speech given on the anniversary of the Gulf War on January 17, 1998: http://www.dhiqar.net/Merath/MK-M024.htm.

90. Chang-Tai Hsieh and Enrico Moretti, "Did Iraq Cheat the United Nations? Underpricing, Bribes, and the Oil for Food Program," Working Paper 11202, National Bureau of Economic Research, 2005, 23; Katerina Oskarsson, "Economic Sanctions on Authoritarian States: Lessons Learned," *Middle East Policy Council* 19 (Winter 2012): 88–102.

91. Joy Gordon, *Invisible War: The United States and the Iraq Sanctions* (Cambridge, MA: Harvard University Press, 2010), 94.

92. People's Day Pamphlet, 1998, BRCC 01-3866-0000-0430.

93. Party secretariat to Ministry of Health, "People's Day," January 3, 2002, BRCC 01-3389-0000-0063.

94. The pamphlet referenced above referred to a People's Day campaign in the municipality of Baghdad that lasted from January 12 to February 28, 1998. Judging from People's Day petitions in the archives, one party section appears to have held a People's Day event in both September and December 2001.

95. Amy Singer, *Charity in Islamic Societies* (New York: Cambridge University Press, 2008), 53. Most, though not all, of the People's Day petitions analyzed here were received during Ramadan, as referenced explicitly in some petitions.

96. Letter from a Retired Party Member to Saddam, undated [December 2002], *BRCC file number withheld to protect identities*; Baghdad–Rusafa Organization to party secretariat, "People's Day," December 17, 2002, *BRCC file number withheld to protect identities*.

97. Blank form for People's Day, Baghdad al-Jadida section, December 2001, BRCC 01-2170-0001-0041.

98. See, for example, Ministry of Labor and Social Affairs, "People's Day," February 13, 2002, *BRCC file number withheld to protect identities*; Ministry of Labor and Social Affairs, "People's Day," February 6, 2002, *BRCC file number withheld to protect identities*.

99. Based on exchange rates in 2001. At the time, 1 Iraqi dinar = $0.00050760 USD; http://www.economywatch.com/exchange-rate/dinar.html. Party secretariat to Rashid Branch, "People's Day," April 13, 2002, *BRCC file number withheld to protect identities*.

100. Letter from a retired public employee to Saddam, "Return to Employment," undated [January 2002], BRCC file number withheld to protect identities.

101. Foreign Ministry to party secretariat, "[Name withheld]," January 15, 2002, BRCC file number withheld to protect identities.

102. Khoury, *Iraq in Wartime*, 168.

103. Khoury, *Iraq in Wartime*, 168–69.

104. Letter from an Iraqi man to Director of the Administration of Ranks, "Request for Martyr Rights," undated [February 2001], BRCC file number withheld to protect identities; Ministry of Defense to party secretariat, "Martyr Rights," March 24, 2001, BRCC file number withheld to protect identities.

105. Fitzpatrick, "Supplicants and Citizens," 80–81.

Chapter 5

Parts of chapter 5 are developed from Alissa Walter, "Sex Crimes and Punishment in Baghdad," published in Religion, Violence, and the State in Iraq (2019): 10–16.

1. A significant increase in Iraq's divorce rate was apparent by the early years of the Iran-Iraq War, which one researcher attributed to the increase in women's education and employment, rather than to the stressors of war—though she pointedly did not mention this as a factor in her surveys. See: ʿAʾida Salim Muhammad Janabi, *Al-Mutaghayyirat al-Ijtimaʿiyya wa-l-Thaqafiyya li-Zahirat al-Talaq maʿ Dirasa Maydaniyya li-Zahirat al-Talaq fi Madinat Baghdad* [Social and Cultural Changes That Contributed to the Phenomenon of Divorce, with a Field Study for the Phenomenon of Divorce in the City of Baghdad] (Baghdad: Daʾirat al-Shuʾun al-Thaqafiyya wa-l-Nashr, 1983), 8.

2. V. Spike Peterson, "Gendering Informal Economies in Iraq," in *Women and War in the Middle East: Transnational Perspectives*, ed. Nicola Pratt and Nadje al-Ali (New York: Bloomsbury, 2009), 43.

3. Nuha Al-Radi, *Baghdad Diaries: A Woman's Chronicle of War and Exile* (New York: Vintage Books, 2003), 62, 80, 85, 52.

4. Party secretariat to Leadership of Air Defense, "Information," May 20, 1999, BRCC 01-3219-0000-0424.

5. That some people willingly choose sex work is, of course, not disputed. However, the increasing criminal penalties for sex work in the 1990s would have made this an extremely risky form of employment to enter into voluntarily. The hunger and economic destitution facing many Iraqis would undoubtedly have been a very strong push factor for any sex worker, raising questions about how "voluntary" such a choice would be for most in this specific context.

6. Achim Rohde, *State-Society Relations in Baʿthist Iraq: Facing Dictatorship* (New York: Routledge, 2010), 43, 100.

7. Isam Al-Khafaji, "War as a Vehicle for the Rise and Demise of a State-Con-

trolled Society: The Case of Ba'thist Iraq," in *War, Institutions, and Social Change in the Middle East*, ed. Steven Heydemann (Berkeley: University of California Press, 2000), 276.

8. Nuha Al-Radi, *Baghdad Diaries: A Woman's Chronicle of War and Exile* (New York: Vintage Books, 2003), 70.

9. Faleh A. Jabar, "The War Generation in Iraq: A Case of Failed Etatist Nationalism," In *Iran, Iraq, and the Legacies of War*, ed. Lawrence G. Potter and Gary G. Sick (New York: Palgrave Macmillan, 2004), 131–32; al-Khafaji, "War as a Vehicle," 275.

10. Rashid Branch to party secretariat, "Unnatural Behavior," March 5, 2002, *BRCC file number withheld to protect identities*.

11. 'Abbas ibn 'Abd al-Mutallib Branch to party secretariat, "Information," April 2, 2002, *BRCC file number withheld to protect identities*.

12. Report of an investigatory committee, December 27, 1992, *BRCC file number withheld to protect identities*.

13. Ministry of Interior to General Directorate of Police, "Information," October 6, 2002, *BRCC file number withheld to protect identities*.

14. NARA, "Narcotics Control Unit Established," American Embassy in Baghdad to Department of State, August 10, 1966, 1964/6/16 SOC-Social Conditions IRAQ, Box 3226, Subject-Numeric 1964–1966, RG 59.

15. "Information," party secretariat to Presidential Diwan, June 3, 2001, *BRCC file number withheld to protect identities*; "Information," Ministry of Health to party secretariat, November 5, 2002, *BRCC file number withheld to protect identities*.

16. "Analysis of Social Realities in the City of Baghdad and the Role of Party Organizations," BRCC 01-3751-0000-0401; party secretariat to General Directorate of Security, "Information," September 23, 1999, *BRCC file number withheld to protect identities*.

17. See, for example, "Arrest of a Gang," party secretariat to Ministry of Interior, June 30, 1999, *BRCC file number withheld to protect identities*.

18. "Iraq Marks World Day against Drug Abuse," *Baghdad Observer*, June 27, 1989, 2.

19. Party secretariat to Presidential Diwan, "Detention of a Hashish Smuggler," November 11, 2000, *BRCC file number withheld to protect identities*.

20. Sara Pursley, *Familiar Futures: Time, Selfhood, and Sovereignty in Iraq* (Stanford: Stanford University Press, 2019), 49.

21. Rohde, *State-Society Relations in Ba'thist Iraq*, 117.

22. "Saddam Hussein and Saddam City Tribal Leaders Talk," audio transcript, undated [1991], CRRC SH-SHTP-A-000–891. English translation provided by the CRRC and edited lightly for clarity.

23. "Saddam Hussein and Saddam City Tribal Leaders Talk," CRRC SH-

SHTP-A-000–891. English translation provided by the CRRC and edited lightly for clarity.

24. Hawraa al-Hassan, *Women, Writing, and the Iraqi Baʻthist State* (Edinburgh: Edinburgh University Press, 2020), 72.

25. Nicholas Krohley, *The Death of the Mehdi Army: The Rise, Fall, and Revival of Iraq's Most Powerful Militia* (New York: Oxford University Press, 2015), 125; Rania Abouzeid, "Out of Sight," *New Yorker*, September 28, 2015.

26. Amatzia Baram, *Saddam Husayn and Islam, 1968–2003: Baʻthi Iraq from Secularism to Faith* (Washington, DC: Woodrow Wilson Center Press, 2014), 52; Yasmin Husein Al-Jawaheri, *Women in Iraq: The Gender Impact of International Sanctions* (Boulder, CO: Lynne Rienner Publishers, 2008), 114.

27. Suzanne Goldenberg, "Uday: Career of Rape, Torture, and Murder," *The Guardian*, July 23, 2003.

28. Al-Jawaheri, *Women in Iraq*, 114.

29. Pursley, *Familiar Futures*, 119, 167.

30. For more on the Ghajar, see Ronen Zeidel, "Gypsies and Society in Iraq: Between Marginality, Folklore and Romanticism," *Middle East Journal* 50 (2014): 74–85; Marwan al-Absi and Eva Al-Absiová, "Gypsies in the Middle East in Past and Present Contexts," *Annual of Language and Politics and Politics of Identity* 8, no. 1 (2014): 79–92; Kristina Richardson, *Roma in the Medieval Islamic World: Literacy, Culture, and Migration* (New York: Bloomsbury Publishing, 2021).

31. Zeidel, "Gypsies and Society," 75, 77.

32. Party secretariat to Ministry of Interior, "Kidnapping of a Girl," March 14, 1999, BRCC *file number withheld to protect identities*.

33. Party secretariat to Rashid Branch, "Kidnapping of a Girl," July 1, 1999, BRCC *file number withheld to protect identities*.

34. See references to *sarifas* in Baghdad during the sanctions era in the following sources: Branch Leadership to party secretariat, "Settlement of Shepherds," June 8, 2002, BRCC 01-2083-0000-0181; party secretariat to Ministry of the Interior, "Information," June 19, 2002, BRCC 01-2083-0000-0228; Ministry of Trade to Saʻd Branch Rations Center, "Restoring Rations," May 17, 1995, BRCC *file number withheld to protect identities*.

35. Party secretariat to Ministry of Interior, "Information," June 19, 2002, BRCC *file number withheld to protect identities*.

36. Interview with Iraqi woman H. by the author, Alexandria, VA, May 2014.

37. Rural women have long been viewed by Iraq's elites as a particularly backward and difficult-to-reform segment of the population. For more on this, see Pursley, *Familiar Futures*, 167.

38. Bet-Shlimon, *City of Black Gold*, 37.

39. Liat Kozma, *Global Women, Colonial Ports* (Albany: SUNY Press, 2017), 53,

81. Paragraph 232 of the Baghdad criminal code passed in November 1918 explicitly outlawed prostitution, procurement, and the operation of brothels.

40. Jamal Haydar, *Baghdad: Malamih Madina fi Dhakirat al-Sitinat* [Baghdad: Features of a City in Memories of the 1960s] (Beirut: Al-Markaz al-Thaqafi al-ʿArabi, 2002), 22.

41. Memoirist Jamal Haydar blamed the creation of this red-light district on the arrival of the British in the early twentieth century: Haydar, *Baghdad: Malamih Madina*, 22. See also Al-Ashab, "The Urban Geography of Baghdad," 369–70; John Gulick, "Baghdad: Portrait of a City in Physical and Cultural Change," *Journal of the American Institute of Planners* 33, no. 4 (1967): 251.

42. "*Mukafahat al-Bighaʾ*" [Combatting Prostitution], Law no. 79, June 18, 1956; "*Mukafahat al-Bighaʾ*" [Combatting Prostitution], Law no. 54, November 1958.

43. Pursley, *Familiar Futures*, 164–65.

44. Party secretariat to President's Office, "Report," April 24, 1990, *BRCC file number withheld to protect identities*. The responsibility of popular committees to evict people accused of prostitution can be found in RCC decree no. 25 from 1995, paragraph 50.

45. "*Mukafahat al-Bighaʾ*" [Combatting Prostitution], Law no. 8 of 1988.

46. "*Mukafahat al-Bighaʾ*" [Combatting Prostitution], Law no. 8 of 1988.

47. "*Mukafahat al-Bighaʾ*" [Combatting Prostitution], Law no. 8 of 1988.

48. RCC no. 155 from 1993: "Regarding Combatting Indecency and Prostitution"; RCC no. 118 from 1994: "Decision to Punish by Execution Everyone Who Ran Pimping Operations...."

49. RCC Resolution no. 234 from 2001.

50. US Department of State, "Iraqi Women under Saddam's Regime: A Population Silenced," March 20, 2003; Al-Jawaheri, *Women in Iraq*, 114–15.

51. Khoury, *Iraq in Wartime*, 154–55.

52. Rohde, *State-Society Relations in Iraq*, 109–18.

53. Al-Jawaheri, *Women in Iraq*, 113; Rohde, *State-Society Relations*, 102–3.

54. Sarah Persinger, "On the Margins: Women, National Boundaries, and Conflict in Saddam's Iraq," in *Middle Eastern Belongings*, ed. Diane King (New York: Routledge, 2010), 14.

55. Party secretariat to Office of Students and Youth, "Information," January 11, 1992, *BRCC file number withheld to protect identities*.

56. Khalid bin al-Walid Branch to party secretariat, "Information," July 16, 1995, *BRCC file number withheld to protect identities*.

57. Yemen Section to Leadership of the Organization for Iraqis Abroad Branch, "Information," January 15, 1993, BRCC 033-4-2-0358, from Samuel Helfont, "Authoritarianism beyond Borders: The Iraqi Baʿth Party As a Transnational Actor," *Middle East Journal* 72, no. 2 (Spring 2018): 239.

58. Party secretariat to Ministry of Interior, "Request for Information," September 17, 1997, BRCC *file number withheld to protect identities.*

59. General Manager of the Interior to Directorate of the Police, "Brothels," June 7, 1999, BRCC *file number withheld to protect identities.*

60. Ministry of Interior to party secretariat, "Information," February 18, 2002, BRCC *file number withheld to protect identities.*

61. RCC no. 234 from 2001: "Regarding the Death Penalty for Anyone Who Commits Sodomy with a Male or a Female."

62. Collective petition, "Statement Proving the Practice of Pimping and Prostitution," 2001, BRCC *file number withheld to protect identities.*

63. Assistant Director of party secretariat to Khalid bin al-Walid Branch, "Information," May 28, 2001, BRCC *file number withheld to protect identities.*

64. Khoury, *Iraq in Wartime*, 154–55.

65. The regime explicitly lays out this strategy in CRRC SH-IDHS-D-000-370, Security Brigadier General to Coordination and Tracking Director, "Clans—Required Role," c. 1991–92.

66. Rashid Branch to party secretariat, "Information," August 25, 1999, BRCC *file number withheld to protect identities.* This kind of persecution and violent attacks on Iraqi Ghajars increased after the fall of the Baʻthist government in 2003. "Gypsies Call for Greater Rights," *IRIN* March 3, 2005.

67. Letter to Special Security Apparatus, undated [1998], BRCC *file number withheld to protect identities;* party secretariat to Leadership of Rashid Branch, "Assault Incident," May 17, 1998, BRCC *file number withheld to protect identities.*

68. For more on changing Baʻth Party positions on ʻurfi marriage, see Rohde, *State-Society Relations*, 113.

69. Rashid Branch leadership to party secretariat, "Assault Incident," May 28, 1998, BRCC *file number withheld to protect identities.*

70. Haytham Bahoora, "The Figure of the Prostitute, *Tajdid*, and Masculinity in Anticolonial Literature of Iraq," *Journal of Middle East Women's Studies* 11, no. 1 (2015): 43.

71. Rohde, *State-Society Relations*, 110–11, 116.

72. "A Dispatch by Saddam Hussein Discussing the Effects of Sanctions after the Mother of All Battles," undated, CRRC SH-MISC-D-001-055. English translation provided by the CRRC and edited lightly for clarity.

73. Al-Jawaheri, *Women in Iraq*, 116–17; Rohde, *State-Society Relations*, 111. The Baʻth Party archives do contain investigations into criminal gangs like these. See Party Secretariat to Ministry of Interior, "Arrest of Gang," June 30, 1999, BRCC *file number withheld to protect identities.*

74. Al-Radi, *Baghdad Diaries*, 80.

75. Al-Radi, *Baghdad Diaries*, 102.

76. Interviews by the author, Erbil, October 2016. See also Nadje al-Ali, "Sexual Violence in Iraq: Challenges for Transnational Feminist Politics," *European Journal of Women's Studies* 25, no. 1 (2018): 16; Persinger, "On the Margins," 29; Goldenberg, "Uday."

77. Al-Jawaheri, *Women in Iraq*, 116–18.

78. Al-Ali, *Women and Gender in Iraq*, 113.

79. Al-Jawaheri, *Women in Iraq*, 16, 28; Bassam Yousif, *Human Development in Iraq: 1950–1990* (New York: Routledge, 2013), 127; Nadje al-Ali, "Reconstructing Gender: Iraqi Women between Dictatorship, War, Sanctions and Occupation," *Third World Quarterly* 26, nos. 4–5 (2005): 744.

80. The promotion of state feminist policies in the 1970s has been discussed by Al-Jawaheri, *Women in Iraq*, 16, 28; Yousif, *Human Development in Iraq*, 127; Al-Ali, "Reconstructing Gender," 744; Jeff Reger, "Ba'thist State Feminism: The General Federation of Iraqi Women in the Global 1970s," *Journal of Women's History* 32, no. 4 (Winter 2020): 48–50; Ali, *Women and Gender in Iraq*, 88–96.

81. Al-Jawaheri, *Women in Iraq*, 22; Rohde, *State-Society Relations*, 93; Ali, *Women and Gender in Iraq*, 101.

82. Pursley, *Familiar Futures*, 119, 164–65.

83. Baghdad Organization to party secretariat, "Suggestions for the Campaign to Raise Awareness about Reducing Dowers and Encouraging Early Marriage," April 5, 1988, BRCC 01-2383-0004-0297.

84. Certain authorities had to ask for official permission to marry in Saddam's Iraq: military officers and Ba'th Party officials were among them. See Sassoon, *Saddam Hussein's Ba'th Party*, 43, 144. Zahra Ali also describes women agreeing to being a second wife as an economic survival strategy in the sanctions era: *Women and Gender in Iraq*, 111–12.

85. CADN 54PO/B/6, "Monthly Summary from April–May 10," May 17, 1986; Sassoon, *Saddam Hussein's Ba'th Party*, 254–55; al-Jawaheri, *Women in Iraq*, 22.

86. Hussein, *Al-Usra wa-l-Numuww al-Sukkani*, 5.

87. Bengio, "Iraq," in *Middle East Contemporary Survey*, vol. 10: *1986*, ed. Itamar Rabinovich and Haim Shaked (Tel Aviv: Dayan Center for Middle Eastern and African Studies, 1988), 371.

88. Persinger, "On the Margins," 27.

89. Quoted in Persinger, "On the Margins," 27.

90. "A Dispatch by Saddam Hussein Discussing the Effects of Sanctions after the Mother of All Battles," undated, CRRC SH-MISC-D-001–055.

91. Al-Ali, *Iraqi Women*, 148.

92. "A Dispatch by Saddam Hussein Discussing the Effects of Sanctions after the Mother of All Battles," undated, CRRC SH-MISC-D-001–055. English translation provided by the CRRC and edited lightly for clarity.

93. "A Dispatch by Saddam Hussein Discussing the Effects of Sanctions after

the Mother of All Battles," undated, CRRC SH-MISC-D-001–055. English translation provided by the CRRC and edited lightly for clarity.

94. Al-Jawaheri, *Women in Iraq*, 36–37.

95. Al-Jawaheri, *Women in Iraq*, 55.

Chapter 6

1. Michael O'Hanlon and Ian Livingston, "Iraq Index: Tracking Variables of Reconstruction and Security in Post-Saddam Iraq" (Washington, DC: Brookings Institution, November 30, 2011), 23.

2. Rajiv Chandrasekaran, "Fueling Anger in Iraq," *Washington Post*, December 9, 2003.

3. O'Hanlon and Livingston, "Iraq Index," 25; "The World Bank in Iraq," World bank.org, accessed March 2024.

4. Khulud Qamar et al., "The Rise of Cholera in Iraq: A Rising Concern," *Annals of Medicine and Surgery* 81 (September 2022): 1–2.

5. Interview F1 (fifty-eight-year-old man) with the author's research team, Fadhil, January 8, 2023.

6. From 2019 to 2022, I interviewed more than a dozen Iraqis and Americans regarding their involvement in a US–created local council system. These interviews took place over the phone and in person in Baghdad. Other interviews quoted in this chapter were carried out in collaboration with Dr. Ali Taher al-Hammood, a sociologist currently holding faculty positions at Baghdad University and al-Bayan University in Iraq. In 2022, we together developed a structured interview questionnaire for sixty residents in four different neighborhoods: the affluent Sunni district of ʿAdhamiyya, the historic Shiʿi shrine district of Kadhimiyya, the low-income Sunni neighborhood of Fadhil, and the large, low-income Shiʿi district of Sadr City. Ali and his students conducted the interviews, and we analyzed their findings together. Additional insights from our research are published in our co-authored article, "The Politics of Memory in Contemporary Baghdad: A Comparative Neighborhood Study," *International Journal of Middle East Studies* 55, no. 2 (2023): 353–61. I thank Ali for his excellent contributions to our research collaboration and for his permission to share qualitative data from our interviews in my book.

7. Interview A8 (sixty-six-year-old man) with the author's research team, ʿAdhamiyya, January 3, 2023.

8. Interview F3 (fifty-six-year-old man) with the author's research team, Fadhil, January 8, 2023.

9. Interview A5 (sixty-two-year-old woman) with the author's research team, ʿAdhamiyya, January 3, 2023.

10. Interview F1 (fifty-eight-year-old man) with the author's research team, Fadhil, January 8, 2023.

11. Interview F9 (fifty-two-year-old man) with the author's research team, Fadhil, January 12, 2023.

12. David Siddartha Patel, *Order Out of Chaos: Islam, Information, and the Rise and Fall of Social Orders in Iraq* (Ithaca, NY: Cornell University Press, 2022), 2–3.

13. Patrick Cockburn, *Muqtada al-Sadr and the Shia Insurgency in Iraq* (London: Faber & Faber, 2008), 107–14.

14. Cockburn, *Muqtada al-Sadr and the Shia Insurgency in Iraq*, 124–33.

15. Observations by LTC Joe Rice, "Center for Army Lessons Learned to Multi-National Corps—Iraq," journal notes, visit to Karrada District Council, 14 November 2005, p. 1. Document provided to the author.

16. Christoph Wilcke, "Castles Built of Sand: US Governance and Exit Strategies in Iraq," *MERIP* 232 (Fall 2004).

17. Wilcke, "Castles Built of Sand."

18. Derick Brinkerhoff and Samuel Taddesse, "Creating Representative Councils in Baghdad," *RTI International Lessons Learned Brief*, Brief No. 6, May 2005, 2.

19. Interview with H. by the author, Baghdad, March 20, 2022.

20. Theola Labbe, "Death of a Civil Servant," *Tampa Bay Times*, November 2, 2003.

21. Interview with Joe Rice by the author, August 29, 2019; email correspondence with Joe Rice by the author, February 25, 2024.

22. Phone interview with Ron Johnson by the author, October 22, 2019.

23. Phone interview with Derick Brinkerhoff by the author, August 26, 2019.

24. Denise Dauphinais, interview by Larry Lesser, United States Institute of Peace, Iraq Experience Project, July 27, 2004, 18–19.

25. Joe Rice, interview by Bernard Engel, United States Institute of Peace, Iraq Experience Project, July 31, 2004, 13.

26. Rice, interview by Bernard Engel, United States Institute of Peace, Iraq Experience Project, July 31, 2004, 8.

27. P. J. Dermer, interview by Arma Jane Karaer, United States Institute of Peace, Iraq Experience Project, August 22, 2004, 8.

28. Phone interview with Ron Johnson by the author, October 22, 2019.

29. *Implementation of the Baghdad Citizen Advisory Council System*, updated version from June 7, 2003 [original version from May 24, 2003], p. 2, original emphasis.

30. Dermer, interview by Arma Jane Karaer, United States Institute of Peace, Iraq Experience Project, August 22, 2004, 6–7.

31. Quoted in Herbert Docena, "Silent Battalions of Democracy," *MERIP* 232 (Fall 2004).

32. International Crisis Group, *Iraq: Can Local Governance Save Central Government?* October 27, 2004, 19. The council structure originally included a city council, but because this was dissolved after a few years, I am focusing instead on the role of neighborhood and district advisory councils.

33. Leslie A. "Cap" Dean, interview by Haven North, United States Institute of Peace, Iraq Experience Project, October 28, 2004, 18; Eric Bauer, interview by Barbara Nielsen, United States Institute of Peace, Iraq Experience Project, October 21, 2004, 5.

34. Rice, interview by Bernard Engel, United States Institute of Peace, Iraq Experience Project, July 31, 2004, 2–3.

35. *The Baghdad Citizen Advisory Council Handbook*, 3rd ed., November 7, 2003, p. 3; phone interview with S. by the author, July 8, 2020; phone interview with George Phelan by the author, August 24, 2020.

36. Phone interview with H. by the author, October 29, 2020.

37. Dermer, interview by Arma Jane Karaer, United States Institute of Peace, Iraq Experience Project, August 22, 2004, 7; Rice, interview by Bernard Engel, United States Institute of Peace, Iraq Experience Project, July 31, 2004, 9.

38. Dermer, interview by Arma Jane Karaer, United States Institute of Peace, Iraq Experience Project, August 22, 2004, 11–12. Though the bomb shelters had been questionably adequate to protect city residents during the Iran-Iraq and Gulf Wars, as discussed in chapter 2, they evidently had stood the test of time quite well. Colonel Dermer remarked that Sadr City's bomb shelters, built in the 1980s, were still in 2003 "masterpieces of architectural construction, phenomenal."

39. Rice, interview by Bernard Engel, United States Institute of Peace, Iraq Experience Project, July 31, 2004, 16.

40. Phone interview with H. by the author, October 29, 2020.

41. Phone interview with Jeff Neumann by the author, September 11, 2020.

42. Dan Murphy, "Baghdad's Tale of Two Councils," *Christian Science Monitor*, October 29, 2003.

43. *Implementation of the Baghdad Citizen Advisory Council System*, updated version from June 7, 2003 [original version from May 24, 2003], p. 2, copy provided to the author.

44. Rice, interview by Bernard Engel, United States Institute of Peace, Iraq Experience Project, July 31, 2004, 11.

45. Dermer, interview by Arma Jane Karaer, United States Institute of Peace, Iraq Experience Project, August 22, 2004, 18.

46. Dermer, interview by Arma Jane Karaer, United States Institute of Peace, Iraq Experience Project, August 22, 2004, 7.

47. Joel Brinkley, "The Struggle for Iraq: Building Democracy; Iraqis Learn Bureaucracy at Town Hall Meetings," *New York Times*, November 30, 2003.

48. Interview with H. by the author, Baghdad, March 20, 2022.

49. "The Baghdad Council Addresses the Parliament to Find a Mechanism to Complete the Projects Implemented by the Municipal Councils," *'Ayn al-'Iraq News*, October 31, 2019.

50. Email from "Cap" Leslie Dean, Regional Coordinator for Baghdad 2003–4,

to LTC Joe Rice, Subject: "Re: Comments on Notes," January 6, 2006; included in Joe Rice's "Center for Army Lessons Learned to Multi-National Corps—Iraq," journal notes, pp. 51–55. Document provided to the author.

51. Phone interview with Ron Johnson by the author, October 22, 2019.

52. Donald Wright and Col. Timothy Reese, *On Point II: Transition to the New Campaign* (Fort Leavenworth, Ks: Combined Studies Institute Press, 2008), 411.

53. *Baghdad Citizen Handbook*, 6.

54. Wright and Reese, *On Point II*; Brinkley, "The Struggle for Iraq."

55. Phone interview with Rick Burns by the author, September 11, 2019.

56. ICG, *Can Local Governance Save Central Government?* 9.

57. Wright and Reese, *On Point II*.

58. Brinkley, "The Struggle for Iraq."

59. Phone interview with Michael Cole by the author, September 4, 2020.

60. ICG, *Can Local Governance Save Central Government?* 8.

61. *Baghdad Citizen Handbook*, 20; Bauer, interview by Barbara Nielsen, United States Institute of Peace, Iraq Experience Project, October 21, 2004, 6.

62. *Baghdad Citizen Handbook*, 22.

63. "Report Paints Grim Picture of Iraqi Life," *CNN*, May 12, 2005.

64. Interview with neighborhood council member A. by the author, Baghdad, March 21, 2022.

65. Interview K10 (sixty-one-year-old man) with author's research team, Kadhimiyya, January 7, 2023.

66. Phone interview with George Phelan by the author, August 3, 2020.

67. Phone interview with Michael Cole by the author, September 4, 2020.

68. Local Council for al-Risala Neighborhood, Facebook photo album "Opening a Sports Field," June 18, 2011, https://www.facebook.com/media/set/?vanity=205073576199849&set=a.217134841660389; Local Council for Risala Neighborhood, Facebook photo album "Charitable Market in Council Headquarters," May 27, 2011, https://www.facebook.com/media/set/?vanity=205073576199849&set=a.205347752839098; Local Council for al-Risala Neighborhood, Facebook photo album "Following Up on Services," April 30, 2011, https://www.facebook.com/media/set/?vanity=205073576199849&set=a.205348389505701.

69. CPA Funding Request, "Southern Rashid Dirt Road Improvement Project," March 12, 2004. Document provided to author.

70. Interview with a councilmember A. by the author, Baghdad, March 21, 2022.

71. Interview A1 (sixty-year-old man) with the author's research team, 'Adhamiyya, January 2, 2023.

72. Interview A1 (sixty-year-old man) with the author's research team, 'Adhamiyya, January 2, 2023; interview with a councilmember A. by the author, Baghdad, March 21, 2022.

73. Local Council for Risala Neighborhood, Facebook photo album "Following

Up on Citizens' Complaints," June 18, 2011, https://www.facebook.com/media/set/?vanity=205073576199849&set=a.217137178326822.

74. Interview K4 (fifty-six-year-old woman) with author's research team, Kadhimiyya, January 2, 2023.

75. Interview K8 (forty-one-year-old woman) with author's research team, Kadhimiyya, December 20, 2022.

76. Interview K6 (seventy-year-old man) with author's research team, Kadhimiyya, December 20, 2022.

77. Interview A10 (fifty-three-year-old man) with the author's research team, 'Adhamiyya, January 4, 2023.

78. Interview F2 (seventy-year-old man) with the author's research team, Fadhil, January 8, 2023.

79. Interview K4 (fifty-six-year-old woman) with author's research team, Kadhimiyya, January 2, 2023.

80. Interview A3 (sixty-three-year-old woman) with the author's research team, 'Adhamiyya, January 2, 2023.

81. Interview S4 (forty-five-year-old man) with the author's research team, Sadr City, January 6, 2023.

82. Paraphrased observations by CPT Sheila Matthews after Karrada District Advisory Council meeting, "Center for Army Lessons Learned to Multi-National Corps—Iraq," journal notes, January 30, 2006, p. 88. Document provided to the author.

83. Paraphrased remarks made by CPT Todd Olsen, Civilian Affairs Team Leader in 9 Nissan, to LTC Joe Rice, "Center for Army Lessons Learned to Multi-National Corps—Iraq," journal notes, December 20, 2005, pp. 39–40. Document provided to the author.

84. Paraphrased remarks made by CPT Todd Olsen, Civilian Affairs Team Leader in 9 Nissan, to LTC Joe Rice, "Center for Army Lessons Learned to Multi-National Corps—Iraq," journal notes, December 20, 2005, pp. 39–40. Document provided to the author.

85. Phone interview with a Sadr City district council member S. by the author, July 8, 2020.

86. Phone interview with H. by the author, October 29, 2020.

87. Phone interview with Michael Cole by the author, August 7, 2020.

88. Phone interview with Michael Cole by the author, August 7, 2020; email correspondence with Michael Cole, January 17, 2021.

89. *My Country, My Country*, dir. Laura Poitras (Independent Television Service and POV/American Documentary, 2006).

90. Interview A4 (sixty-seven-year-old man) with the author's research team, 'Adhamiyya, January 3, 2023.

91. Interview F3 (fifty-six-year-old man) with the author's research team, Fadhil, January 8, 2023.

92. Dean, interview by Haven North, United States Institute of Peace, Iraq Experience Project, October 28, 2004, 23; Sabrina Tavernise and David Rohde, "Few Iraqis Reach U.S. Havens Despite Program," *New York Times*, August 29, 2007.

93. Phone interview with S. by the author, July 8, 2020.

94. Ali, *Women and Gender in Iraq*, 184.

95. ICG, *Can Local Governance Save Central Government?* 14; Nicholas Krohley, *The Death of the Mehdi Army* (New York: Oxford University Press, 2015), 72.

96. Damien Cave and Stephen Farrell, "At the Street Level, Unmet Goals of Troop Buildup," *New York Times*, September 9, 2007.

97. Christiana Parreira, "Power Politics: Armed Non-State Actors and the Capture of Public Electricity in Post-Invasion Baghdad," *Journal of Peace Research* 20, no. 10 (2020): 2.

98. Peter Munson, *Iraq in Transition* (Washington, DC: Potomac Books, 2009), 208.

99. John Hagan et al., "Neighborhood Sectarian Displacement and the Battle for Baghdad: A Self-Fulfilling Prophecy of Fear and Crimes against Humanity in Iraq," *Sociological Forum* 30, no. 3 (September 2015): 678.

100. Interview S3 (fifty-nine-year-old man) with the author's research team, Sadr City, January 6, 2023.

101. Interview S3 (fifty-nine-year-old man) with the author's research team, Sadr City, January 6, 2023.

102. Interview S10 (fifty-two-year-old man) with the author's research team, Sadr City, January 3, 2023.

103. Interview S7 (fifty-eight-year-old woman) with the author's research team, Sadr City, January 6, 2023.

104. Interview S7 (fifty-eight-year-old woman) with the author's research team, Sadr City, January 6, 2023.

105. Interview S4 (forty-five-year-old man) with the author's research team, Sadr City, January 6, 2023.

106. Interview S5 (fifty-three-year-old woman) with the author's research team, Sadr City, January 5, 2023.

107. Parreira, "Power Politics," 2.

108. Munson, *Iraq in Transition*, 208.

109. Interview S8 (forty-eight-year-old woman) with the author's research team, Sadr City, December 26, 2022; Interview S9 (sixty-three-year-old man) with the author's research team, Sadr City, January 4, 2023; and interview S10 (fifty-two-year-old man) with the author's research team, Sadr City, January 3, 2023.

110. Amir Taha, "Turning Ex-Combatants into Sadris: Explaining the Emergence of the Mahdi Army," *Middle Eastern Studies* 55, no. 3 (February 2019): 365.

111. Phone interview with Joe Rice by the author, July 31, 2020; Yaroslav Trofimov, "In Baghdad Slum, A Tense Standoff over Democracy," *Wall Street Journal*, October 20, 2003.

112. Dan Murphy, "Baghdad's Tale of Two Councils," *Christian Science Monitor*, October 29, 2003.

113. Trofimov, "Tense Standoff over Democracy."

114. Trofimov, "Tense Standoff over Democracy."

115. Murphy, "Baghdad's Tale of Two Councils."

116. Rice, interview by Bernard Engel, United States Institute of Peace, Iraq Experience Project, July 31, 2004, 29.

117. Krohley, *Death of the Mehdi Army*, 66, 72–73.

118. Paraphrased observations made by Sadr City District Advisory Council Chair [name withheld] to LTC Joe Rice, "Center for Army Lessons Learned to Multi-National Corps—Iraq," journal notes, November 19, 2005, pp. 11–12. Document provided to the author.

119. Paraphrased observations made by Major Kurt Anderson, stationed in Sadr City, to LTC Joe Rice, "Center for Army Lessons Learned to Multi-National Corps—Iraq," journal notes, November 24, 2005, p. 11. Document provided to the author.

120. Paraphrased remarks made by a member of the Sadr City District Advisory Council and of the Baghdad City Council [name withheld] to LTC Joe Rice, "Center for Army Lessons Learned to Multi-National Corps—Iraq," journal notes, February 2, 2006, pp. 89–90.

121. Mehiyar Kathem, "New Imperialism in Iraq: How the US Occupation Helped Establish But Then Cannibalised the Sadr District Council," *Peacebuilding* (June 2019): 10.

122. "Coalition Apologizes to Family of Shiite Community Leader Killed by US Soldier," *Voice of America News*, November 14, 2003; phone interview with Joe Rice by the author, July 31, 2020.

123. Kathem, "New Imperialism in Iraq," 10.

124. Kathem, "New Imperialism in Iraq," 6–7.

125. Phone interview with Joe Rice by the author, July 31, 2020.

126. Kathem, "New Imperialism in Iraq," 6–7.

127. "U.S. Says Kills 30 in Sadr City Air Strike," *Reuters*, August 8, 2007; Sattar Raheem and Aseel Kami, "U.S. Military Says Kills 49 in Baghdad Raid," *Reuters*, October 20, 2007.

128. David E. Johnson, M. Wade Markel, and Brian Shannon, "The 2008 Battle of Sadr City," Rand Arroyo Center Occasional Paper, 2011; John Spencer, "Stealing the Enemy's Urban Advantage: The Battle of Sadr City," *Modern War Institute*, January 31, 2019.

129. Krohley, *Death of the Mehdi Army*, 1–3.

130. Spencer, "Stealing the Enemy's Urban Advantage."

131. Johnson, Markel, and Shannon, "The 2008 Battle of Sadr City."

132. Spencer, "Stealing the Enemy's Urban Advantage."

133. Krohley, *Death of the Mehdi Army*, 2–3; Johnson, Markel, and Shannon, "The 2008 Battle of Sadr City," 17.

134. Kathem, "New Imperialism in Iraq," 14.

135. Kathem, "New Imperialism in Iraq," 14.

136. Interview F4 (sixty-year-old man) with the author's research team, Fadhil, January 8, 2023.

137. Interview K5 (forty-five-year-old man) with the author's research team, Kadhimiyya, January 2, 2023.

138. Interview A6 (fifty-five-year-old man) with the author's research team, ʿAdhamiyya, January 3, 2023.

139. Interview S3 (fifty-nine-year-old man) with the author's research team, Sadr City, January 6, 2023.

140. Interview S7 (fifty-eight-year-old woman) with the author's research team, Sadr City, January 6, 2023.

141. Congressional Budget Office, "Paying for Iraq's Reconstruction," January 2004, 5.

142. Curt Tarnoff, *Iraq: Reconstruction Assistance*, Congressional Research Service, August 7, 2009, 1; Special Inspector General for Iraq Reconstruction, *Final Report to the United States Congress*, September 9, 2013, 1.

143. Congressional Budget Office, "Paying for Iraq's Reconstruction," January 2004, 5.

144. Interview A7 (forty-two-year-old man) with the author's research team, ʿAdhamiyya, January 3, 2023.

145. Interview S1 (eighty-four-year-old man) with the author's research team, Sadr City, December 26, 2022.

146. Jane Arraf, "15 Years after U.S. Invasion, Some Iraqis Are Nostalgic for Saddam Hussein Era," *NPR*, April 30, 2018.

Conclusion

1. To name just a few of many: Saʿid al-Daywachi, *Tarikh al-Mawsul* [History of Mosul] (Baghdad: al-Majmaʿ al-ʿIlmi al-ʿIraqi, 2002); Mahdi Muhammad Qadi, *Dirasat fi Tarikh Arbil al-Muʿasir* [Studies in the Modern History of Erbil] (Erbil: Maktab al-Tafsir lil-Tabaʿ wa-l-Nashr, 2019); Caecilia Pieri, *Bagdad: La Construction d'une Capitale Moderne (1914–1960)* (Beirut: Presses de l'IFPO, 2015).

2. Arbella Bet-Shlimon, "Beyond Baghdad: Writing a History from the Iraqi Periphery," in Mona Damluji et al., "Roundtable: Perspectives on Researching Iraq Today," *Arab Studies Journal* 23, no. 1 (2015): 239–40.

3. Farah al-Nakib, *Kuwait Transformed: A History of Oil and Urban Life* (Stanford: Stanford University Press, 2016), 99.

4. CRU Report June 2020; Samir Sumai'dae April 2021, https://www.wilsoncenter.org/article/hijacking-democracy-role-political-parties-iraq.

5. Fanar Haddad, "From Existential Struggle to Political Banality: The Politics of Sect in Post-2003 Iraq," *Review of Faith and International Affairs* 18, no. 1 (2020): 75; Toby Dodge, "Beyond Structure and Agency: Rethinking Political Identities in Iraq after 2003," *Nations and Nationalism* 26 (2020): 114, 116.

6. Toby Dodge et al., "Iraq Synthesis Paper: Understanding the Drivers of Conflict in Iraq," *Conflict Research Programme* (2018): 4.

7. Maxime Agator, "Iraq: Overview of Corruption and Anti-Corruption," Transparency International, April 2013.

8. Toby Dodge et al, "Iraq Synthesis Paper: Understanding the Drivers of Conflict in Iraq," *Conflict Research Programme* (2018): 12.

9. Zahra Ali, "Iraqis Demand a Country," *MERIP* 292, no. 3 (Fall–Winter 2019).

10. Mona Damluji, "Securing Democracy in Iraq," 76–78.

11. Karin Brulliard, "'Gated Communities' for the War-Ravaged," *Washington Post*, April 23, 2007.

12. Mohammed K. Al-Hasani, "Urban Space Transformation in Old City of Baghdad: Integration and Management," *Megaron* 7 (2012): 83; Sana Murrani, "Baghdad's Thirdspace: Between Liminality, Anti-Structures and Territorial Mappings," *Cultural Dynamics* 28, no. 2 (2016): 3.

13. Caecilia Pieri, "Can T-Wall Murals Really Beautify the Fragmented Baghdad?" *Jadaliyya*, May 18, 2014.

14. Michael M. R. Izady, "Urban Unplanning: How Violence, Walls, and Segregation Destroyed the Urban Fabric of Baghdad," *Journal of Planning History* 19, no. 1 (2020): 64; Damluji, "Securing Democracy in Iraq"; Murrani, "Baghdad's Thirdspace": 189–210; Pieri, "Can T-Wall Murals Really Beautify?"

15. Fanar Haddad, "Perpetual Protest and the Failure of the Post-2003 Iraqi State," *MERIP* 306 (March 22, 2023).

16. Haddad, "Perpetual Protest."

17. Omar Sirri, "Seeing the Political in Baghdad's Shopping Malls," London School of Economics blog, January 9, 2020.

18. Sirri, "Seeing the Political in Baghdad's Shopping Malls."

19. Jane Arraf and Yasmine Mosimann, "Baghdad Loses Green Space to Real Estate Boom," *New York Times*, January 30, 2023.

20. Hannah Allam, "Iraq's Date Palms Also Damaged by War," *Seattle Times*, July 10, 2020.

21. Sirri, "Seeing the Political in Baghdad's Shopping Malls."

22. Arraf and Mosimann, "Baghdad Loses Green Space to Real Estate Boom."

23. Interview K6 (seventy-year-old man), Kadhimiyya, December 20, 2022.

24. Hadi Mizban, "Iraq's Years of Carnage Still Engrained in Baghdad's Streets," *Associated Press*, April 19, 2023.

BIBLIOGRAPHY

Archival Sources

BRCC Iraqi Baʿth Party Archives, Boxfiles of the Regional Command Center (Hoover Institution, Stanford, CA, USA)

CADN Centre des Archives Diplomatiques de Nantes (Nantes, France)

CRRC Conflict Records Research Center, Saddam Hussein Collection (Washington, DC, USA)

DAA Doxiadis Associates Archives (Athens, Greece)

INLA Iraq National Library and Archives (Baghdad, Iraq)

KDS Kuwait Dataset of the Iraqi Baʿth Party Archives (Hoover Institution, Stanford, CA, USA)

NARA National Archives and Records Administration (College Park, MD, USA)

TNA The National Archives (Kew, UK), including the collections of the Foreign Office (FO) and the Foreign and Commonwealth Offices (FCO)

Published Sources

ʿAbd al-Rusul, Salima. *Al-Mabani al-Turathiyya fi Baghdad* [Historic Buildings in Baghdad]. Baghdad: Ministry of Culture and Media, 1987.

Abdul-Moati, Youssef, ed. *Diary of an Iraqi Soldier*. Kuwait: National Center for Documents on Iraqi Aggression on Kuwait, 1992.

Al-Absi, Marwan, and Eva Al-Absiová. "Gypsies in the Middle East in Past and Present Contexts." *Annual of Language and Politics and Politics of Identity* 8, no. 1 (2014): 79–92.

Ahmad, Sabin ʿAbd al-Munʿim. "Al-Aathar al-Ijtimaʿiyya lil-Hijra al-Dakhiliyya ila Manatiq al-Sinaʿa fi Madinat Baghdad maʿ Dirasa Tatbiqiyya li-Usar baʿd al-'Ummal al-Muhajirin" [The Social Effects of Internal Migration to Industrial Areas in the City of Baghdad, with an Applied Study with the Families of Some of the Migrant Workers]. MA thesis, Cairo University, 1969.

Akin, Yigit. "Reconsidering State, Party, and Society in Early Republican Turkey: Politics of Petitioning." *International Journal of Middle East Studies* 39, no. 3 (August 2007): 435–57.

Aksin, Selçuk Somel, Christoph K. Neumann, and Amy Singer. "Re-Sounding Silent Voices." In *Untold Histories of the Middle East: Recovering Voices from the 19th and 20th Centuries*, edited by Amy Singer, Christoph K. Neumann, and Selçuk Aksin Somel, 1–22. New York: Routledge, 2011.

Alahmed, Nida. "Illuminating a State: State-Building and Electricity in Occupied Iraq." *Humanity: An International Journal of Human Rights, Humanitarianism, and Development* 8, no. 2 (Summer 2017): 335–53.

Alansari, Bassim. "Althawra, Quartier de Bagdad" [Al-Thawra: Baghdad District]. PhD diss., École des Hautes Études en Sciences Sociales, 1979.

Alger, Andrew. "The Construction of Urban Space in Iraq, 1921–1963." PhD diss., City University of New York, 2020.

Ali, Hassan Mohammed. *Land Reclamation and Settlement in Iraq*. Baghdad: Baghdad Printing Press, 1955.

al-Ali, Nadje Sadiq. *Iraqi Women: Untold Stories from 1948 to the Present*. London: Zed Books, 2007.

———. "Reconstructing Gender: Iraqi Women between Dictatorship, War, Sanctions and Occupation." *Third World Quarterly* 26, nos. 4–5 (2005): 739–58.

———. "Sexual Violence in Iraq: Challenges for Transnational Feminist Politics," *European Journal of Women's Studies* 25, no. 1 (2018).

al-Ali, Nadje Sadiq, and Nicola Pratt. *What Kind of Liberation? Women and the Occupation of Iraq*. Berkeley: University of California Press, 2009.

Ali, Zahra. "Iraqis Demand a Country." *MERIP* 292, no. 3 (Fall/Winter 2019).

———. *Women and Gender in Iraq: Between Nation-Building and Fragmentation*. New York: Cambridge University Press, 2018.

Ali, Zahra. and Safaa Khalaf. "Southern Discontent Spurs an Iraqi Protest Movement." *Current History* 117, no. 803 (December 2018): 338–43.

al-Ali, Zaid. *The Struggle for Iraq's Future: How Corruption, Incompetence and Sectarianism Have Undermined Democracy*. New Haven: Yale University Press, 2014.

Alkazaz, Aziz. "The Distribution of National Income in Iraq, with Particular Reference to the Development of Policies Applied by the State." In *Iraq: Power and Society*, edited by Derek Hopwood, Habib Ishow, and Thomas Koszinowski, 193–257. Reading, UK: Ithaca Press, 1993.

Alnasrawi, Abbas. *The Economy of Iraq: Oil, War, Destruction of Development and Prospects, 1950–2010*. Westport, CT: Greenwood Press, 1994.

———. "Iraq: Economic Sanctions and Consequences, 1990–2000." *Third World Quarterly* 22, no. 2 (April 2001): 205–18.
al-'Alwachi, 'Abd al-Hamid. *Min Turathina al-Sha'bi* [From our Popular Heritage]. Baghdad: Ministry of Culture and Guidance, 1966.
al-'Ani, Khattab. *Jughrafiyyat al-'Iraq al-Zira'iyya* [Iraq's Agricultural Geography]. Cairo: Arab League Press, 1972.
al-Ansari, Fadil. *Sukkan al-'Iraq: Dirasa Dimughrafiyya-Jiyughrafiyya Muqarina* [Iraq's Population: A Demographic-Geographic Comparative Study]. Damascus: Maktabat Atlas, 1970.
Architects Collaborative. *Urban Design Study: Khulafa Development Project.* Cambridge, MA: 1982.
Arthur Erickson Architects. *Amanat al Assima: Abu Nuwas Conservation/Development Project.* Vancouver: Arthur Erickson Architects, 1981.
al-Ashab, Khalis H. "The Urban Geography of Baghdad." Vol. 1. PhD diss., University of Newcastle upon Tyne, 1974.
Awni, Muhammad Hussein. "Urban Case Studies: Baghdad, Iraq: Low Income Dwelling Surveys and a Site and Services Proposal." MA thesis, Massachusetts Institute of Technology, May 1979.
Babakhan, Ali. "The Deportation of Shi'is during the Iran-Iraq War: Causes and Consequences." In *Ayatollahs, Sufis and Ideologues*, edited by Faleh Abdul-Jabar, 183–210. London: Saqi Books, 2002.
The Baghdad Citizen Advisory Council Handbook. 3rd ed. Iraq, November 7, 2003.
Baghdadi, 'Abbas. *Baghdad fi al-'Ishrinat* [Baghdad in the 1920s]. Baghdad: Dar al-Shu'un al-Thaqafiyya al-'Amma, 2000.
Bahoora, Haytham. "The Figure of the Prostitute, *Tajdid*, and Masculinity in Anticolonial Literature of Iraq." *Journal of Middle East Women's Studies* 11, no. 1 (2015).
Baram, Amatzia. "Neo-Tribalism in Iraq: Saddam Hussein's Tribal Policies 1991–96." *International Journal of Middle East Studies* 29, no. 1 (February 1997): 1–31.
———. *Saddam Husayn and Islam, 1968–2003: Ba'thi Iraq from Secularism to Faith.* Washington, DC: Woodrow Wilson Center Press, 2014.
Bashkin, Orit. *New Babylonians: A History of Jews in Modern Iraq.* Stanford: Stanford University Press, 2012.
———. *The Other Iraq: Pluralism and Culture in Hashemite Iraq.* Stanford: Stanford University Press, 2008.
———. "Representations of Women in the Writings of the Intelligentsia in Hashemite Iraq, 1921–1958." *Journal of Middle East Women's Studies* 4, no. 1 (Winter 2008): 53–82.
Batatu, Hanna. *The Old Social Classes and the Revolutionary Movements of Iraq: A Study of Iraq's Old Landed and Commercial Classes and of Its Communists, Bathists and Free Officers.* London: Saqi, 2012.

Bauer, Eric. Interview by Barbara Nielson. United States Institute of Peace, Iraq Experience Project, October 21, 2004.

Ben-Bassat, Yuval. *Petitioning the Sultan: Protests and Justice in Ottoman Palestine.* New York: I. B. Tauris, 2013.

Bengio, Ofra. "Iraq." In *Middle East Contemporary Survey*, vol. 5: *1980–1981*, edited by Colin Legum, Haim Shaked, and Daniel Dishon, 578–99. New York: Holmes & Meier Publishers, 1982.

———. "Iraq." In *Middle East Contemporary Survey*, vol. 7: *1982–1983*, edited by Colin Legum, Haim Shaked, and Daniel Dishon, 560–91. (New York: Holmes & Meier Publishers, 1985).

———. "Iraq." In *Middle East Contemporary Survey*, vol. 8, *1983–1984*, edited by Haim Shaked and Daniel Dishon, 465–93. Tel Aviv: Dayan Center for Middle Eastern and African Studies, 1986.

———. "Iraq." In *Middle East Contemporary Survey*, vol. 10: *1986*, edited by Itamar Rabinovich and Haim Shaked, 361–96. Tel Aviv: Dayan Center for Middle Eastern and African Studies, 1988.

———. "Iraq." In *Middle East Contemporary Survey*, vol. 12, *1988*, edited by Ami Ayalon and Haim Shaked, 500–538. Boulder, CO: Westview Press, 1990.

———. "Iraq." In *Middle East Contemporary Survey*, vol. 13, *1989*, edited by Ami Ayalon, 372–413. Boulder, CO: Westview Press, 1990.

Bernhardsson, Magnus. "Visions of Iraq: Modernizing the Past in 1950s Baghdad." In *Modernism and the Middle East: Architecture and Politics in the Twentieth Century*, edited by Sandy Isenstadt and Kishwar Rizvi, 81–96. Seattle: University of Washington Press, 2008.

Bet-Shlimon, Arbella. *City of Black Gold: Oil, Ethnicity, and the Making of Modern Kirkuk.* Stanford: Stanford University Press, 2019.

———. "Kirkuk, 1968–1968: Oil and the Politics of Identity in an Iraqi City." PhD diss., Harvard University, 2012.

———. "State-Society Relations in the Urban Spheres of Baghdad and Kirkuk, 1920–58." In *State and Society in Iraq: Citizenship under Occupation, Dictatorship and Democratisation*, edited by Benjamin Isakhan, Shamiran Mako, and Fadi Dawood, 50–68. New York: I. B. Tauris, 2017.

Bier, Lara. *Revolutionary Womanhood: Feminisms, Modernity, and the State in Nasser's Egypt.* Stanford: Stanford University Press, 2011.

Blaydes, Lisa. *State of Repression: Iraq under Saddam.* Princeton: Princeton University Press, 2018.

Bowen, Stuart, Jr., ed. *Hard Lessons: The Iraq Reconstruction Experience.* Washington, DC: US Independent Agencies and Commissions, 2009.

Bren, Paulina, and Mary Neuburger. "Introduction." In *Communism Unwrapped: Consumption in Cold War Eastern Europe*, edited by Paulina Bren and Mary Neuburger, 3–19. New York: Oxford University Press, 2012.

Brinkerhoff, Derick, and Samuel Taddesse. "Creating Representative Councils in Baghdad." *RTI International Lessons Learned Brief.* Brief No. 6, May 2005.

Carpenter, Ami C. *Community Resilience to Sectarian Violence in Baghdad.* New York: Springer, 2014.

———. "Havens in a Firestorm: Perspectives from Baghdad on Resilience to Sectarian Violence." *Civil Wars* 14, no. 2 (June 2012): 182–204.

Carroll, Katherine Blue. "Tribal Law and Reconciliation in the New Iraq." *Middle East Journal* 65, no. 1 (Winter 2011): 11–29.

Caswell, Michelle. "'Thank You Very Much, Now Give Them Back': Cultural Property and the Fight over the Iraqi Baath Party Records." *American Archivist* 74, no. 1 (Spring/Summer 2011): 211–40.

Chalabi, Muhsin K. "Low Income Housing in Iraq." MA thesis, University of New Mexico, 1975.

Chen, Xi. *Social Protests and Contentious Authoritarianism in China.* New York: Cambridge University Press, 2014.

Chubin, Shahram, and Charles Tripp. *Iran and Iraq at War.* Boulder, CO: Westview Press, 1988.

Cochrane, Marisa. *The Fragmentation of the Sadrist Movement.* Iraq Report No. 12. Washington, DC: Institute for the Study of War, 2009.

Cockburn, Patrick. *Muqtada al-Sadr and the Shia Insurgency in Iraq.* London: Faber & Faber, 2008.

Collingham, Lizzie. *Taste of War: World War II and the Battle for Food.* London: Allen Lane, 2011.

Cordesman, Anthony, and Ahmed Hashim. *Iraq: Sanctions and Beyond.* Washington, DC: CSIS, 1997.

Damluji, Mona. "'Securing Democracy in Iraq': Sectarian Politics and Segregation in Baghdad, 2003–2007." *Traditional Dwellings and Settlements Review* (2010): 71–87.

Damluji, Mona, et al. "Roundtable: Perspectives on Researching Iraq Today." *Arab Studies Journal* 23, no. 1 (2015): 236–65.

al-Darbandi, 'Abd al-Rahman Sulayman. *Al-Mar'a al-'Iraqiyya al-Mu'asira* [The Modern Iraqi Woman], vol. 2. Baghdad: Wazirat al-Tarbiya wa-l-Ta'lim, 1968.

Dauphinais, Denis. Interview by Larry Lester. United States Institute of Peace, Iraq Experience Project, July 27, 2004.

Davies, Sarah. "'Cult' of the Vozhd: Representations in Letters, 1934–1941." *Russian History* 24, nos. 1–2 (Spring/Summer 1997): 131–47.

Davis, Eric. *Memories of State: Politics, History, and Collective Identity in Modern Iraq.* Berkeley: University of California Press, 2005.

Dean, Leslie A. "Cap." Interview by Haven North. United States Institute of Peace, Iraq Experience Project, October 28, 2004.

Dermer, P. J. Interview by Arma Jane Karaer. United States Institute of Peace, Iraq Experience Project, August 22, 2004.

Dewachi, Omar. *Ungovernable Life: Mandatory Medicine and Statecraft in Iraq*. Stanford: Stanford University Press, 2017.

Dikotter, Frank. *Mao's Great Famine: The History of China's Most Devastating Catastrophe, 1958–1962*. New York: Walker, 2010.

Dimitrov, Martin. "What the Party Wanted to Know: Citizen Complaints as a 'Barometer of Public Opinion.'" *East European Politics and Societies* 28, no. 2 (May 2014): 271–95.

Dimitrov, Martin, and Joseph Sassoon. "State Security, Information, and Repression: A Comparison of Communist Bulgaria and Baʻthist Iraq." *Journal of Cold War Studies* 16, no. 2 (Spring 2014): 3–31.

Docena, Herbert. "Silent Battalions of Democracy." *MERIP* 232 (Fall 2004).

Drapac, Vesna, and Gareth Pritchard. *Resistance and Collaboration in Hitler's Europe*. London: Palgrave Macmillan, 2017.

Drèze, Jean, and Haris Gazdar. "Hunger and Poverty in Iraq, 1991." *World Development* 20 (1992): 921–45.

Efrati, Noga. "Productive or Reproductive? The Roles of Iraqi Women during the Iraq-Iran War." *Middle Eastern Studies* 35, no. 2 (April 1999): 27–44.

———. *Women in Iraq: Past Meets Present*. New York: Columbia University Press, 2012.

Faroqhi, Suraiya. "Political Activity among Ottoman Taxpayers and the Problem of Sultanic Legitimation (1570–1650)." *Journal of the Economic and Social History of the Orient* 35 (1992): 1–39.

Farouk-Sluglett, Marion, and Peter Sluglett. *Iraq since 1958: From Revolution to Dictatorship*. New York: I. B. Tauris, 2001.

———. "The Transformation of Land Tenure and Rural Social Structure in Central and Southern Iraq, c. 1870–1958." *International Journal of Middle East Studies* 15, no. 4 (1983): 491–505.

Faust, Aaron. *The Baʻthification of Iraq: Saddam Hussein's Totalitarianism*. Austin: University of Texas Press, 2015.

Fawaz, Mona. "The State and the Production of Illegal Housing: Public Practices in Hayy el Sellom, Beirut-Lebanon." In *Comparing Cities: Middle East and South Asia*, edited by Kamran Asdar Ali and Martina Rieker, 197–220. New York: Oxford University Press, 2009.

Feldman, Ilana. *Governing Gaza: Bureaucracy, Authority, and the Work of Rule, 1917–1967*. Durham, NC: Duke University Press, 2008.

Fitzpatrick, Sheila. *Everyday Stalinism: Ordinary Life in Extraordinary Times: Soviet Russia in the 1930s*. New York: Oxford University Press, 1999.

———. "Petitions and Denunciations in Russian and Soviet History." *Russian History* 24, nos. 1–2 (Spring/Summer 1997): 1–9.

———. "Supplicants and Citizens: Public Letter-Writing in Soviet Russia in the 1930s." *Slavic Review* 55, no. 1 (Spring 1996): 78–105.

Franzen, Johan. "Development vs. Reform: Attempts at Modernisation during the Twilight of British Influence in Iraq, 1946–58." *Journal of Imperial and Commonwealth History* 37, no. 1 (2009): 77–98.

———. *Red Star over Iraq: Iraqi Communism before Saddam*. London: Hurst & Co., 2011.

Fuccaro, Nelida. "Introduction: Histories of Oil and Urban Modernity in the Middle East." *Comparative Studies of South Asia, Africa and the Middle East* 33, no. 1 (2013): 1–6.

Garfield, Richard. "Morbidity and Mortality among Iraqi Children from 1990 through 1998: Assessing the Impact of the Gulf War and Economic Sanctions." Campaign against Sanctions in Iraq, March 1999.

———. "Studies on Young Child Malnutrition in Iraq: Problems and Insights, 1990–1999." *Nutrition Reviews* 58 (2000): 269–77.

Ginio, Eyal. "Coping with the State's Agents 'from Below': Petitions, Legal Appeal, and the Sultan's Justice in Ottoman Legal Practice." In *Popular Protest and Political Participation in the Ottoman Empire*, edited by Eleni Gara, M. Erdem Kabadayi, and Christoph K. Neumann, 41–56. Istanbul: Istanbul Bilgi Universitesi Yayinlari, 2011.

Gordon, Joy. *Invisible War: The United States and the Iraq Sanctions*. Cambridge, MA: Harvard University Press, 2010.

Government of Iraq, Ministry of Economics, Principal Bureau of Statistics. *Report on the Housing Census of Iraq for 1956*. Baghdad: Ar-Rabita Press, 1956.

Graham-Brown, Sarah. *Sanctioning Saddam: The Politics of Intervention in Iraq*. New York: I. B. Tauris, 1999.

Gregory, Derek. "The Biopolitics of Baghdad: Counterinsurgency and the Counter-City." *Human Geography* 1, no. 1 (March 2008): 5–8.

Gulick, John. "Baghdad: Portrait of a City in Physical and Cultural Change." *Journal of the American Institute of Planners* 33, no. 4 (1967): 246–55.

Haddad, Fanar. *Sectarianism in Iraq: Antagonistic Visions of Unity*. London: Hurst & Co., 2011.

Hagan, John, et al. "Neighborhood Sectarian Displacement and the Battle for Baghdad: A Self-Fulfilling Prophecy of Fear and Crimes against Humanity in Iraq." *Sociological Forum* 30, no. 3 (September 2015): 675–97.

al-Hajjiyya, 'Aziz Jasim. *Baghdadiyyat: Taswir lil-Haya al-Ijtima 'iyya wa al- 'Adat al-Baghdadiyya khilal Mi'a 'Amm* [Baghdadiyyat: Pictures of Social Life and Baghdad Customs Over One Hundred Years], vol 5. Baghdad: Ministry of Culture and Media, 1985.

Hakim, Besim Selim. "Co-Op Housing: Baghdad, Iraq." MA thesis, Harvard University, 1971.

Hallin, Daniel. "TV's Clean Little War." *Bulletin of the Atomic Scientists* 47, no. 4 (1991): 16–19.

Hammudi, Basim 'Abd al- Hamid. *'Adat wa Taqalid al-Haya al-Sha'biyya al-'Iraqiyya* [Customs and Traditions from Everyday Iraqi Life]. Baghdad: Dar al-Shu'un al-Thaqafiyya al-'Amma, 1986.
al-Hasani, Mohammed K. "Urban Space Transformation in Old City of Baghdad—Integration and Management." *Megaron* 7 (2012): 79–90.
Hass, Richard. "Economic Sanctions: Too Much of a Bad Thing." Brookings Policy Brief No. 34, June 1, 1998.
al-Hassan, Hawraa. *Women, Writing, and the Iraqi Ba'thist State: Contending Discourses of Resistance and Collaboration, 1968–2003*. Edinburgh: Edinburgh University Press, 2020.
Haydar, Jamal. *Baghdad: Malamih Madina fi Dhakirat al-Sitinat* [Baghdad: Features of a City in Memories of the 1960s]. Beirut: Al-Markaz al-Thaqafi al-'Arabi, 2002.
Helfont, Samuel. *Compulsion in Religion: Saddam Hussein, Islam, and the Roots of Insurgencies in Iraq*. New York: Oxford University Press, 2018.
Hilmi, Waleed Abbas. "Internal Migration and Regional Policy in Iraq." Vol. 2. PhD diss., University of Sheffield, 1978.
Hiro, Dilip. *The Longest War: The Iran-Iraq Military Conflict*. New York: Routledge, 1991.
Hsieh, Chang-Tai, and Enrico Moretti. "Did Iraq Cheat the United Nations? Underpricing, Bribes, and the Oil for Food Program." Working Paper 11202. National Bureau of Economic Research, 2005.
Husayn, 'Abd al-Razzaq 'Abbas. *Nasha'at Mudun al-'Iraq wa Tatawwurha* [Growth and Development of Iraq's Cities]. Baghdad: Ma'had al-Buhuth wa-l-Dirasat al-'Iraq, 1973.
Hussein, Saddam. *Al-Usra wa-l-Numuww al-Sukkani fi Ahadith al-Ra'is al-Qa'id Saddam Hussein* [Family and Population Growth in the Speeches of President Leader Saddam Hussein]. Baghdad: Dar al-Shu'un al-Thaqafiyya al-'Amma, 1988.
International Crisis Group. *Iraq: Can Local Governance Save Central Government?* October 27, 2004.
Iraq: A Pictorial Record. Cologne-Deutz, Germany: In Cooperation with the Iraqi Commissariat of the World Exhibition, Brussels, 1958.
Ismael, Jacqueline S., and Shereen T. Ismael. "Gender and State in Iraq." In *Gender and Citizenship in the Middle East*, edited by Suad Joseph, 185–211. Syracuse, NY: Syracuse University Press, 2000.
Ismael, Tareq. *The Rise and Fall of the Communist Party of Iraq*. New York: Cambridge University Press, 2008.
Izady, Michael M. R. "Urban Unplanning: How Violence, Walls, and Segregation Destroyed the Urban Fabric of Baghdad," *Journal of Planning History* 19, no. 1 (2020): 52–68.

Jabar, Faleh A. *The Shi'ite Movement in Iraq.* London: Saqi Books, 2003.

———. "Sheikhs and Ideologues: Deconstruction and Reconstruction of Tribes under Patrimonial Totalitarianism, 1968–1998." In *Tribes and Power: Nationalism and Ethnicity in the Middle East*, edited by Faleh Abdul-Jabar and Hosham Dawod, 69–109. London: Saqi Books, 2003.

———. "The War Generation in Iraq: A Case of Failed Etatist Nationalism." In *Iran, Iraq, and the Legacies of War*, edited by Lawrence G. Potter and Gary G. Sick, 121–41. New York: Palgrave Macmillan, 2004.

———. "The Worldly Roots of Religiosity in Post-Saddam Iraq." *MERIP* 227 (Summer 2003).

al-Jabburi, 'Adnan Rashid. *Al-Wathiqa al-Tarikhiyya fi al-Niza' al-'Iraqiyya al-Iraniyya* [Historical Documents in the Iraqi-Iranian Conflict]. Baghdad: Dar al-Shu'un al-Thaqafiyya al-'Amma, 1995.

Jabiri, Muhsin Muhammad Hasan. *Mukhtaru Baghdad* [The Neighborhood Leaders of Baghdad]. Baghdad: Matba'at Ufsit Hassam, 1985.

Janabi, A'ida Salim Muhammad. *Al-Mutaghayyirat al-Ijtima'iyya wa-l-Thaqafiyya li-Zahirat al-Talaq ma' Dirasa Maydaniyya li-Zahirat al-Talaq fi Madinat Baghdad* [Social and Cultural Changes that Contributed to the Phenomenon of Divorce, with a Field Study for the Phenomenon of Divorce in the City of Baghdad]. Baghdad: Da'irat al-Shu'un al-Thaqafiyya wa-l-Nashr, 1983.

al-Jassar, Saad Salim. "Social Indicators and Housing Policy in Baghdad, Iraq." MA thesis, University of Washington, 1977.

al-Jawaheri, Yasmin Husein. *Women in Iraq: The Gender Impact of International Sanctions.* Boulder, CO: Lynne Rienner Publishers, 2008.

Jawwad, Naji. *Baghdad: Sira wa Madina* [Baghdad: A Life and a City]. Beirut: al-Mu'assasa al-'Arabiyya lil-Dirasat wa-l-Nashr, 2000.

Johnson, David E., M. Wade Markel, and Brian Shannon. "The 2008 Battle of Sadr City." Rand Arroyo Center Occasional Paper, 2011.

Johnson, Ian M. "The Impact on Libraries and Archives in Iraq of War and Looting in 2003: A Preliminary Assessment of the Damage and Subsequent Reconstruction Efforts." *International Information and Library Review* 37, no. 3 (2005): 209–71.

Johnston, Hank. "Talking the Walk: Speech Acts and Resistance in Authoritarian Regimes." In *Repression and Mobilization*, edited by Christian Davenport, Hank Johnston, and Carol Mueller, 108–37. Minneapolis: University of Minnesota Press, 2005.

Joseph, Suad. "Elite Strategies for State-Building: Women, Family, Religion and State in Iraq and Lebanon." In *Women, Islam and the State*, edited by Deniz Kandiyoti, 176–200. Philadelphia: Temple University Press, 1991.

Kandiyoti, Deniz. "Bargaining with Patriarchy." *Gender and Society* 2, no. 3 (September 1988): 274–90.

Kathem, Mehiyar. "New Imperialism in Iraq: How the US Occupation Helped Establish But Then Cannibalised the Sadr District Council." *Peacebuilding* (June 2019): 363–78.

Katzman, Kenneth. "Iraq: Politics, Elections, and Benchmarks." Congressional Research Service, March 1, 2011.

Khadduri, Majid, and Edmund Ghareeb. *War in the Gulf, 1990–1991: The Iraq-Kuwait Conflict and Its Implications.* New York: Oxford University Press, 1997.

al-Khafaji, Isam. "War as a Vehicle for the Rise and Demise of a State-Controlled Society: The Case of Baʿthist Iraq." In *War, Institutions, and Social Change in the Middle East,* edited by Steven Heydemann, 258–91. Berkeley: University of California Press, 2000.

Khajehpour, Bijan, Reza Marashi, and Trita Parsi. "The Trouble with Sanctions." *Cairo Review of Global Affairs,* July 21, 2013.

al-Khalil, Samir. [Pseudonym: see also Kanan Makiya.] *The Monument: Art, Vulgarity and Responsibility in Iraq.* Berkeley: University of California Press, 1991.

Khan, Geoffrey. "The Historical Development of Medieval Arabic Petitions." *Bulletin of the School of Oriental and African Studies* 53 (1990): 8–30.

Khoury, Dina. *Iraq in Wartime: Soldiering, Martyrdom, and Remembrance.* New York: Cambridge University Press, 2013.

———. "Violence and Spatial Politics between the Local and Imperial: Baghdad, 1778–1810." In *The Spaces of the Modern City: Imaginaries, Politics, and Everyday Life,* edited by Gyan Prakash and Kevin M. Kruse, 181–213. Princeton: Princeton University Press, 2008.

Khudayyir, Muhammad. *Basrayatha: The Story of a City.* New York: Verso, 2008.

Koc, Mustafa, et al. "Food Security and Food Sovereignty in Iraq." *Food, Culture, and Society* 10 (Summer 2007): 317–48.

Kofman, Eleonore, and Elizabeth Lebas. "Introduction: Lost in Transposition—Time, Space and the City." In *Writings on Cities,* translated and edited by Eleonore Kofman and Elizabeth Lebas, 3–62. Malden, MA: Blackwell Publishers, 2000.

Kozma, Liat. *Global Women, Colonial Ports: Prostitution in the Interwar Middle East.* Albany: SUNY Press, 2017.

Krohley, Nicholas. *The Death of the Mehdi Army: The Rise, Fall, and Revival of Iraq's Most Powerful Militia.* New York: Oxford University Press, 2015.

Lefebvre, Henri. "Levels of Reality and Analysis." In *Writings on Cities,* translated and edited by Eleonore Kofman and Elizabeth Lebas, 111–18. Malden, MA: Blackwell Publishers, 2000.

———. *Production of Space.* Oxford: Blackwell, 1974.

———. *Rhythmanalysis: Space, Time and Everyday Life.* Translated by Stuart Elden and Gerald Moore. New York: Continuum, 2004.

———. "The Right to the City." In *Writings on Cities*, edited and translated by Eleonore Kofman and Elizabeth Lebas, 147–59. Malden, MA: Blackwell Publishers, 2000.

———. "Spectral Analysis." In *Writings on Cities*, edited and translated by Eleonore Kofman and Elizabeth Lebas, 139–46. Malden, MA: Blackwell Publishers, 2000.

Limbert, Mandana E. *In the Time of Oil: Piety, Memory, and Social Life in an Omani Town*. Stanford: Stanford University Press, 2010.

Makiya, Kanan. [See also Samir al-Khalil, pseudonym.] *Republic of Fear: The Politics of Modern Iraq*. Berkeley: University of California Press, 1998.

Makiya, Muhammad. "Baghdad al-Sitiniyyat" [1960s Baghdad]. In *Baghdad*, edited by Muhamad Makiya, 95–99. London: AlWarrak Publishing, 2005.

———. "Al-Dur al-Baghdadiyya wa-l-Turath al-Sakani" [Baghdadi Houses and Residential Heritage]. In *Baghdad*, edited by Muhammad Makiya, 278–80. London: AlWarrak Publishing, 2005.

———. "Al-Mahallat al-Baghdadiyya" [Baghdad's Neighborhoods]. In *Baghdad*, edited by Muhammad Makiya, 267–78. London: AlWarrak Publishing, 2005.

Marozzi, Justin. *Baghdad: City of Blood, City of Peace*. New York: Allen Lane, 2014.

Marr, Phebe. *The Modern History of Iraq*. Boulder, CO: Westview Press, 1985.

Massicard, Elise. *Street-Level Governing: Negotiating the State in Urban Turkey*. Stanford: Stanford University Press, 2022.

McDowall, David. *A Modern History of the Kurds*. New York: I. B. Tauris, 2004.

Ménoret, Pascal. "Development, Planning and Urban Unrest in Saudi Arabia." *Muslim World* 101, no. 2 (April 2011): 269–85.

———. *Joyriding in Riyadh: Oil, Urbanism, and Road Revolt*. New York: Cambridge University Press, 2014.

Migdal, Joel. *State in Society: Studying How States and Societies Transform and Constitute One Another*. New York: Cambridge University Press, 2001.

Mitchell, Timothy. *Colonising Egypt*. Berkeley: University of California Press, 1988.

———. *Rule of Experts: Egypt, Techno-Politics, Modernity*. Berkeley: University of California Press, 2002.

Montgomery, Bruce. "Immortality in the Secret Police Files: The Iraq Memory Foundation and the Baath Party Archive." *International Journal of Cultural Property* 18, no. 3 (August 2011): 309–36.

———. "US Seizure, Exploitation, and Restitution of Saddam Hussein's Archive of Atrocity." *Journal of American Studies* 48, no. 2 (May 2014): 559–93.

Moreh, Shmuel, and Zvi Yehuda, eds. *Al-Farhud: The 1941 Pogram in Iraq*. Jerusalem: Hebrew University Magnes Press, 2010.

Mumayyiz, Amin. *Baghdad Kama 'Ariftuha* [Baghdad As I Knew It]. Baghdad: Afaq 'Arabiyya, 1985.

Munson, Peter. *Iraq in Transition: The Legacy of Dictatorship and the Prospects for Democracy*. Washington, DC: Potomac Books, 2009.

Murrani, Sana. "Baghdad's Thirdspace: Between Liminality, Anti-Structures and Territorial Mappings." *Cultural Dynamics* 28, no. 2 (2016): 189–210.

Murray, Williamson, and Kevin M. Woods. *The Iran-Iraq War: A Military and Strategic History*. Cambridge: Cambridge University Press, 2014.

Najm, Nuri. *Fi al-Harb wa-l-Salam* [In War and Peace]. Baghdad: Dar al-Hurriyya lil-Tibaʻa, 1986.

Nakash, Yitzhak. *The Shiʻis of Iraq*. Princeton: Princeton University Press, 2003.

Al-Nakib, Farah. *Kuwait Transformed: A History of Oil and Urban Life*. Stanford: Stanford University Press, 2016.

———. "Revisiting *Hadar* and *Badu* in Kuwait: Citizenship, Housing, and the Construction of a Dichotomy." *International Journal of Middle East Studies* 46, no. 1 (2014): 5–30.

Al-Nasiri, Anwar ʻAbd al-Hamid. *Suq al-Jadid: Mahalla Mudiʼa min al-Janib al-Gharbi bi-Baghdad* [Suq al-Jadid: A Luminous Neighborhood in Western Baghdad]. Vol. 2. Baghdad: Dar al-Shuʼun al-Thaqafiyya al-ʻAmma, 1997.

Natali, Denise. *The Kurdish Quasi-State: Development and Dependency in Post–Gulf War Iraq*. Syracuse, NY: Syracuse University Press, 2010.

O'Hanlon, Michael, and Ian Livingston. "Iraq Index: Tracking Variables of Reconstruction and Security in Post-Saddam Iraq." Washington, DC: Brookings Institution, November 30, 2011.

Oskarsson, Katerina. "Economic Sanctions on Authoritarian States: Lessons Learned." *Middle East Policy Council* 19 (Winter 2012): 88–102.

Packer, George. *Assassin's Gate: America in Iraq*. New York: Farrar, Straus & Giroux, 2005.

Parreira, Christiana. "Power Politics: Armed Non-State Actors and the Capture of Public Electricity in Post-Invasion Baghdad." *Journal of Peace Research* 20, no. 10 (2020): 1–14.

Patel, David Siddartha. *Order Out of Chaos: Islam, Information, and the Rise and Fall of Social Orders in Iraq*. Ithaca, NY: Cornell University Press, 2022.

Persinger, Sarah. "On the Margins: Women, National Boundaries, and Conflict in Saddam's Iraq." In *Middle Eastern Belongings,* edited by Diane King, 13–38. New York: Routledge, 2010.

Peterson, V. Spike. "Gendering Informal Economies in Iraq." In *Women and War in the Middle East: Transnational Perspectives*, edited by Nicola Pratt and Nadje al-Ali, 35–64. New York: Bloomsbury, 2009.

Pieri, Caecilia. "Baghdad Architecture 1921–1958: Reflections on History as a 'Strategy of Vigilance.'" *Bulletin of the Royal Inter-Faith Studies* 8, nos. 1–2 (2006): 69–93.

———. *Bagdad: Construction d'une Capitale Moderne (1914–1960)*. Beirut: Presses de l'Ifpo, 2015.

———. "Urbanism in Bagdad before the Planning: A Codification between the Fates of the Arbitrary and Urgent Needs (1920–1950)." DC Papers. *Revista de crítica y teoría de la arquitectura* 1 (2008): 266–71.

———. "Walling Strategy: Can T-Wall Murals Really Beautify the Fragmented Baghdad?" Ibraaz.org, June 2014.

Podeh, Elie. *The Politics of National Celebrations in the Arab Middle East*. New York: Cambridge University Press, 2011.

Poitras, Laura, dir. *My Country, My Country*. Documentary film. Independent Television Service and POV/American Documentary, 2006.

Prakash, Gyan. "Introduction." In *The Spaces of the Modern City: Imaginaries, Politics, and Everyday Life*, edited by Gyan Prakash and Kevin M. Kruse, 1–18. Princeton: Princeton University Press, 2008.

———. "The Impossibility of Subaltern History." *Nepantla: Views from the South* 1, no. 2 (2000): 287–94.

———. "Subaltern Studies as Postcolonial Criticism." *American Historical Review* 99, no. 5 (1994): 1475–90.

Pursley, Sara. *Familiar Futures: Time, Selfhood, and Sovereignty in Iraq*. Stanford: Stanford University Press, 2019.

Pyla, Panayiota. "Back to the Future: Doxiadis's Plans for Baghdad." *Journal of Planning History* 7, no. 1 (February 2008): 3–19.

Qamar, Khulud, et al. "The Rise of Cholera in Iraq: A Rising Concern." *Annals of Medicine and Surgery* 81 (September 2022).

al-Qarawee, Harith Hasan. "Sectarian Identities, Narratives and Political Conflict in Baghdad." *Levantine Review* 4 (Winter 2015): 177–200.

al-Radi, Nuha. *Baghdad Diaries: A Woman's Chronicle of War and Exile*. New York: Vintage Books, 2003.

Ra'uf, 'Imad 'Abd al-Salam. *Al-Usul al-Tarikhiyya li-Mahallat Baghdad* [The Historic Origins of Baghdad Neighborhoods]. Baghdad: al-Muthanna, 2004.

al-Rawi, Mohammed Mahdi Saleh. *Averting Famine on Iraq: My Memories for Years of U.N. Sanction, 1990–2003*. By the author, 2023.

Razoux, Pierre. *The Iran-Iraq War*. Translated by Nicholas Elliott. Cambridge, MA: Belknap Press of Harvard University Press, 2015.

Reger, Jeff. "Ba'thist State Feminism: The General Federation of Iraqi Women in the Global 1970s." *Journal of Women's History* 32, no. 4 (Winter 2020): 38–62.

Rice, Joe. Interview by Bernard Engel. United States Institute of Peace, Iraq Experience Project, July 31, 2004.

Richardson, Kristina. *Roma in the Medieval Islamic World: Literacy, Culture, and Migration*. New York: Bloomsbury Publishing, 2021.

Rohde, Achim. "Echoes from Below: Talking Democracy in Baʿthist Iraq." *Middle Eastern Studies* 53, no. 4 (2017): 551–70.

———. "Opportunities for Masculinity and Love: Cultural Production in Baʿthist Iraq during the 1980s." In *Islamic Masculinities (Global Masculinities)*, edited by Lahoucine Ouzgane, 184–201. New York: Palgrave Macmillan, 2006.

———. *State-Society Relations in Baʿthist Iraq: Facing Dictatorship*. New York: Routledge, 2010.

Rubin, Avi. *Ottoman Nizamiye Courts: Law and Modernity*. New York: Palgrave Macmillan, 2011.

Saeed, Mahmoud. *Saddam City*. London: Saqi Books, 2004.

Said, Edward. "Foreword." In *Selected Subaltern Studies*, edited by Ranajit Guha and Chakravorty Spivak, i–x. New York: Oxford University Press, 1988.

Saleh, Zainab. "On Iraqi Nationality: Law, Citizenship, and Exclusion." *Arab Studies Journal* 21, no. 1 (2013): 48–78.

Salim, Bakr Mustafa. *Al-Sara'if fi Baghdad* [Sarifas in Baghdad]. Baghdad: Shatri, 2005.

Salim, Kamal Latif. *Suwwar Baghdadiyya* [Baghdad Photos]. Baghdad: Maktabat al-Nadha, 1985.

Sassoon, Joseph. *Anatomy of Authoritarianism in the Arab Republics*. New York: Cambridge University Press, 2016.

———. *Economic Policy in Iraq, 1932–1950*. New York: Routledge, 1987.

———. "The Iraqi Baʿth Party Preparatory School and the 'Cultural' Courses of the Branches," *Middle Eastern Studies* 50, no. 1 (2014): 27–42.

———. *Saddam Hussein's Baʿth Party: Inside an Authoritarian Regime*. New York: Cambridge University Press, 2012.

Sassoon, Joseph, and Alissa Walter. "Diaries of Iraqi Soldiers: Views from Inside Saddam's Army." *International Journal of Contemporary Iraqi Studies* 12, no. 2 (2018): 183–98.

———. "The Iraqi Occupation of Kuwait: New Historical Perspectives." *Middle East Journal* 71, no. 4 (Fall 2017): 607–28.

Scott, James C. *Domination and the Arts of Resistance: Hidden Transcripts*. New Haven: Yale University Press, 1990.

———. *Seeing Like a State: How Certain Schemes to Improve the Human Condition Have Failed*. New Haven: Yale University Press, 1998.

———. *Weapons of the Weak: Everyday Forms of Peasant Resistance*. New Haven: Yale University Press, 1985.

Shaw, J. E. "Writing to the Prince: Supplications, Equity, and Absolutism in Sixteenth-Century Tuscany." *Past and Present* 215, no. 1 (2012): 51–83.

Shiblak, Abbas. *Iraqi Jews: A History*. London: Saqi Books, 2005.

Shukri, Fahmi Mahmud. *Bab al-Shaykh wa-l-Shaykhliyya ʿAbr al-Tarikh* [The Bab al-Shaykh and Shaykhliyya Neighborhoods throughout History]. Amman, 2007.

Singer, Amy. *Charity in Islamic Societies.* New York: Cambridge University Press, 2008.

Singerman, Diane. *Avenues of Participation: Family, Politics, and Networks in Urban Quarters of Cairo.* Princeton: Princeton University Press, 1996.

Sluglett, Peter. *Britain in Iraq: Contriving King and Country.* London: I. B. Tauris, 2007.

Somel, Selçuk Aksin, Christoph K. Neumann, and Amy Singer. "Re-Sounding Silent Voices." In *Untold Histories of the Middle East: Recovering Voices from the 19th and 20th Centuries,* edited by Amy Singer, Christoph K. Neumann, and Selçuk Aksin Somel, 1–22. New York: Routledge, 2011.

Sontag, Susan. *Regarding the Pain of Others.* New York: Picador, 2003.

Spencer, John. "Stealing the Enemy's Urban Advantage: The Battle of Sadr City." *Modern War Institute,* January 31, 2019.

Spivak, Gayatri Chakravorty. "Subaltern Studies: Deconstructing Historiography." In *Selected Subaltern Studies,* edited by Ranajit Guha and Gayatri Chakravorty Spivak, 3–34. New York: Oxford University Press, 1988.

Stoler, Ann Laura. *Along the Archival Grain: Anxieties and Colonial Common Sense.* Princeton: Princeton University Press, 2009.

Stone, Blake. "Blind Ambition: Lessons Learned and Not Learned in an Embedded PRT." *Prism* 1, no. 4 (2010): 147–58.

Sulayman, Sabah. *Adwa' 'ala al-Harb al-'Iraqiyya al-Iraniyya* [Shedding Light on the Iraq-Iran War]. Baghdad: al-Maktaba al-Wataniyya bi-Baghdad, 1981.

Susa, Ahmad. "Rayy Baghdad Qadiman wa Hadithan" [Baghdad Irrigation, Past and Present]. In *Baghdad,* edited by Muhammad Makiya, 99–147. London: Al-Warrak Publishing, 2005.

Taha, Amir. "Turning Ex-Combatants into Sadris: Explaining the Emergence of the Mahdi Army." *Middle Eastern Studies* 55, no. 3 (February 2019): 357–73.

Tejel, Jordi. "'Dangerous Liaisons' between 'Abd al-Karim Qasim and the Student Body during the First Iraqi Republic, 1958–1963." In *State and Society in Iraq: Citizenship under Occupation, Dictatorship and Democratisation,* edited by Benjamin Isakhan, Shamiran Mako, and Fadi Dawood, 133–55. New York: I. B. Tauris, 2017.

Theodosis, Lefteris. "'Containing' Baghdad: Constantinos Doxiadis' Program for a Developing Nation." *Revista de Crítica y Teoría de la Arquitectura* 1 (2008): 167–72.

Tripp, Charles. *A History of Iraq.* Cambridge: Cambridge University Press, 2007.

———. "The Iran-Iraq War and the Iraqi State." In *Iraq: Power and Society,* edited by Derek Hopwood, Habib Ishow, and Thomas Koszinowski, 91–116. Reading, UK: Ithaca Press, 1993.

Ursinus, Michael. *Grievance Administration (Sikayet) in an Ottoman Province*. New York: Routledge Curzon, 2005.

Verdery, Katherine. "The 'Étatization' of Time in Ceausescu's Romania." In *What Was Socialism, and What Comes Next?* edited by Katherine Verdery, 82–90. Princeton: Princeton University Press, 1996.

Volcker, Paul, Richard J. Goldstone, and Mark Pieth. *Manipulation of the Oil-for-Food Programme by the Iraqi Regime*. Independent Inquiry Committee into the United Nations Oil-for Food Programme, October 27, 2005.

van Voss, Lex Heerma. "Introduction." In *Petitions in Social History*, edited by Lex Heerma van Voss, 1–10. New York: International Review of Social History and Internationaal Instituut voor Sociale Geschiendenis, 2001.

Wali, Najim. *Baghdad: Sirat Madina* [Baghdad: Biography of a City]. Beirut: Dar al-Saqi, 2015.

Walter, Alissa. "The Repatriation of Iraqi Ba'th Party Archives: Ethical and Practical Considerations." *Journal of Contemporary Iraq and the Arab World* 16, nos. 1–2 (2022): 117–36.

Walter, Alissa, and Ali Taher al-Hammood. "The Politics of Memory in Contemporary Baghdad: A Comparative Neighborhood Study." *International Journal of Middle East Studies* 55, no. 2 (2023): 353–61.

Weld, Kristen. *Paper Cadavers: The Archives of Dictatorship in Guatemala*. Durham, NC: Duke University Press, 2014.

Whiting, Rebecca Abby. "Living and Dying on Record: 'Atrocity Archives' as Sacred Remains." *Journal of Contemporary Iraq and the Arab World* 16, nos. 1–2 (2022): 137–50.

Wilcke, Christoph. "Castles Built of Sand: US Governance and Exit Strategies in Iraq." *MERIP* 232 (Fall 2004).

Woertz, Eckart. "Iraq under UN Embargo, 1990–2003: Food Security, Agriculture, and Regime Survival." *Middle East Journal* 73, no. 1 (Spring 2019): 92–111.

Workman, W. Thom. *Social Origins of the Iran-Iraq War*. Boulder, CO: Lynne Rienner Publishers, 1994.

Wright, Donald, and Col. Timothy Reese. *On Point II: Transition to the New Campaign*. Leavenworth, KS: Combined Studies Institute Press, 2008.

Yang, Dali L. *Calamity and Reform in China: State, Rural Society, and Institutional Change since the Great Leap Famine*. Stanford: Stanford University Press, 1996.

Yousif, Bassam. *Human Development in Iraq: 1950–1990*. New York: Routledge, 2013.

Zaidi, Sarah. "Child Mortality in Iraq." *The Lancet* 350, no. 9084 (October 11, 1997): 1105.

Zangana, Haifa. "Walling in Iraq: The Impact on Baghdadi Women." *International Journal of Contemporary Iraqi Studies* 4, nos. 1–2 (2010): 41–58.

Zeidel, Ronen. "Gypsies and Society in Iraq: Between Marginality, Folklore and Romanticism." *Middle East Journal* 50, no. 1 (2014): 74–85.

Zou, Keyuan. "Granting or Refusing the Right to Petition: The Dilemma of China's *Xinfang* System." In *Socialist China, Capitalist China: Social Tension and Political Adaptation under Economic Globalization*, edited by Guoguang Wu and Helen Lansdowne, 124–37. New York: Routledge, 2009.

INDEX

Abadan, 69
ʿabaya, 176
Abbasid Empire, 23, 229
absenteeism, 79, 116–18
Abu Ghraib prison, 208
Abu Hanifa, 25
Abu Nuwas Street, 26, 64
al-Adhadh, Riyadh, 64
ʿAdhamiyya district, 13, 25, 51, 127, 189, 204–6, 208, 220; ʿAdhamiyya District Advisory Council, 208
Ahwaz, 69
Air Force Intelligence Office, 68
air strikes, 68–71, 88, 92–93, 96
al-ʿAlwiya social club, 26
ʿAmara province, 28
ʿAmil neighborhood, 119
Amiriyya neighborhood, 92–94; Amiriyya shelter bombing, 92–93
Anfal campaign, 62
Arab nationalism, 4
Arabs, 12, 74–75
ʿArif, ʿAbd al-Rahman, 4, 41, 45
ʿArif, ʿAbd al-Salam, 4, 40–41

Army Canal, 42, 44–45, 51, 58; Army Canal Highway, 51
Army Day 93
al-ʿAsima. *See* Sadr City
assassination, 39, 41, 68, 116, 192, 194, 199, 209, 215
austerity, 67, 81
ʿAziz, Tariq, 67–68, 75

Bab al-Muadhim neighborhood, 168
Babil province, 127
Babil (newspaper), 176
Baghdad Central Office, 194–203, 207, 213, 215
Baghdad Citizen Advisory Council Handbook, 198, 201
Baghdad Observer (newspaper), 14, 163
Baghdad province, 146, 197–98
Baghdad University, 31, 44, 171
Baker, James, 97
al-Bakr, Ahmad Hassan, 4, 64
Basra, 61, 67, 70, 86, 89, 191, 193, 213, 216
Batawin neighborhood, 28, 95, 166
bayʿa, 83

303

Baʻth Party, 1, 4, 6–8, 10, 12, 14–20, 38, 40–42, 44–45, 47–50, 55, 58–59, 61–62, 67, 71, 73–76, 78–80, 82, 84, 89–92, 94, 97, 103–4, 106, 108–10, 115–16, 120, 122–27, 129–30, 133–35, 137, 139–43, 145–54, 160–64, 167–75, 177–78, 181–82, 187, 193, 202, 207, 221–24; abuses by Party militias, 41, 47; administration of February–November 1963; archives, 12, 14–20, 61, 71, 110, 126–27, 140, 154, 161–62, 172, 174, 223; effects of 1991 *intifada* on, 89–93, 160; ethnic cleansing by, 62; *faraʻ*, 6–8, 102, 147, 197; *firqa*, 8, 102–3, 122, 124–25, 149–50, 152–53, 155, 174–75, 193, 202, 207, 221, 224; and housing, 55; internal communication, 17, 58–59, 71, 106, 126; militarization of society, 74; Office of the Secretariat, 104, 119–20, 126, 146–48, 149–50, 153; officials of, 1, 6–8, 59, 103–4, 106, 123, 125–27, 133–35, 148–52, 160, 162–3, 173–75, 178, overthrow of ʻArif regime (1968), 45; and petitions, 132–58, Regional Command, 15–16; and rationing, 106–15; response to internal criticism, 127–30; Revolutionary Command Council (RCC), 1, 82, 111–12, 114, 117, 133; Saddam's purge of members (1979), 126–7; *shuʻba*, 7–8, 103, 122, 124–25, 147, 151, 193, 197, 221
Bet-Shlimon, Arbella, 19, 223
black markets, 10, 82, 108–9, 111, 113–15, 159, 163, 179, 182
blast walls, 11, 226–27
bombing, 68–69, 88, 91–93, 95–96, 130, 215, 217
Bremer III, L. Paul, 187, 193–96, 213

bridges, 3, 24, 26, 64, 88
Britain 12, 23, 26–27, 36, 42, 49, 65, 67, 83, 144, 164, 177; cooperation with Hashemites, 26–27, 49, 177; occupation of Iraq during World War I, 26; British Empire, 168
bureaucrats, 2, 8, 18, 51, 71, 96, 119, 155, 194, 221–22, 224, 228
Burns, Lt. Col. Rick, 202
buses, 4, 34–36, 44–45
Bush (George W.) administration, 15, 194

Cairo, 14, 23
Camp Rashid, 9
children, 1, 33, 54, 78, 80, 83–84, 86, 95–96, 101–2, 105, 110–11, 125, 128–29, 133, 135, 141, 143, 148–51, 157, 161, 164, 166, 177–80; as victims of war, 71, 96; child care, 80, 207; fertility campaign, 71, 86, 178–9; humanitarian situation of, 101, 110–11, 151, 157, 161, 166; labor of, 102; petitions regarding, 125, 133, 135, 141–43, 148–49
China, 105, 108
cholera, 33, 188
Christians, 3, 12, 226
CIA, 126
Civil Affairs (US), 194, 198
Coalition Provisional Authority (CPA), 4, 187, 194–95, 197–99, 201–4, 208, 213, 222
Cockburn, Patrick, 64–65
Cold War, 31
collective punishment, 115, 117–21, 127–31, 170
Commanders Emergency Response Program (CERP), 203, 217
communists, 12, 41, 46, 58, 73, 137; coup

attempt by, 41–42; crackdown
against, 40–41;
Iraqi Communist Party, 10, 38, 41, 46,
80, 116
Congress (US), 219
conscription, 77–79, 82, 86–87, 89
corruption, 97, 109, 111–12, 114, 152, 160,
164, 176, 206, 217, 220, 225–29
coups, 4, 33, 38–39, 64, 83, 168;
attempted, 41–42
COVID-19, 12
crime, 10, 15–16, 18, 20, 37, 73, 81, 111–13,
115–17, 133, 142, 159–61, 162–66,
167–71, 173–74, 176–77, 180–83, 188.
See also punishment *and* collective
punishment *and* law

Damascus, 23
Dauphinais, Denise, 194
Daʿudi neighborhood, 51
Daʿwa Party, 10, 58, 62, 67–69, 73–75,
116, 142
death squads, 11, 188, 226
Defense Intelligence Agency (US), 15, 195
Department of Defense (US), 14–15
Dermer, Col. P. J., 195–96, 200, 213
Desert Shield, 87. *See also* Gulf War
Desert Storm, 60, 88, 90, 93, 96, 106. *See also* Gulf War
deserters, 55, 79, 102–3, 115–16, 118–19,
122–23, 128–29, 160, 162–65, 170, 173,
177
development, 11, 13, 49–51, 60, 62, 86,
167, 193, 216, 220, 224, 227–28; and
corruption, 97, 206; impact of
sanctions on, 96, 101, 127, 154, 156,
158; modernization, 10, 27, 30, 34, 56,
60, 64, 224; urban, 7, 10–11, 13–14,
23–24, 26–32, 36–37, 42–43, 53–54,
56, 60, 62, 64–67, 73, 86, 227

Development Board, 27–32, 37, 49
Dewachi, Omar, 46
Dezful, 69
Dimitrov, Martin, 137
diplomats, 63, 70, 73, 83
Directorate General of Health, 48
Directorate of Civilian Defense, 1
Directorate of Cooperative Unions, 50
Directorate of the Police, 148
disabled people, 69, 111, 157
District Advisory Councils, 192–94,
197–98, 200, 202, 204, 206, 212
Diyala province, 121
Doctors' and Pharmacists' Union, 49,
54
Dora district, 45, 64, 228
Doxiadis, Constantinos, 13, 29, 31,
34–35, 37–38, 42–23, 46, 49–50,
54–56, 224
al-Duri, ʿIzzat Ibrahim, 114, 130, 133,
141, 145–46, 148–49, 152–53, 155

Economic Surveillance Committees,
82, 109, 112
Egypt, 11
elderly people, 78, 95, 111, 141, 149, 153,
157
electricity, 6, 30, 33, 48, 91, 96, 130,
188–89, 191, 205–6, 210–11, 218, 220
embargo. *See* sanctions
emigration, 119–20
Erbil, 12, 223
execution, 17, 62, 111–12, 116–17, 161, 170,
172, 182

Fadhil neighborhood, 13, 189–90, 205,
208
Faisal I. *See* al-Hashemi, Faisal bin
al-Husayn
Faisal II, 168

faraʿ. *See* Baʿth Party.
farmers, 28, 79, 96, 153
Faust, Aaron, 83
Faw, 63, 86
Feldman, Ilana, 10
Fidaʿiyyu Saddam militia, 170
firqa. *See* Baʿth Party
Fitzpatrick, Sheila, 141
food rationing. *See* rationing
food shortages, 101, 108
France, 11
fraud, 104, 109–10, 113–15, 163
Freedom Monument, 226

al-Gaylani, Rashid ʿAli, 168
Gaza, 10
gender. *See* masculinity *and* women
General Federation of Iraqi Women. *See* women
Ghajar, 167–68, 174–75, 177, 181, 183
Ghazaliyya neighborhood, 138, 200
Glendale, CO, 198
Greece, 11–13
Green Zone, 15, 194, 213, 216
Gropius, Walter, 31
Gulf States, 224
Gulf War (1990–91), 20, 60–61, 70, 86–89, 93–96, 108, 124, 128, 130, 159, 162, 167, 177; "highway of death", 89. *See also* Desert Storm *and* Desert Shield

Haidar, Salih, 27, 121
Haifa Street, 64, 229
al-Hakim family, 68
al-Hammood, Ali Taher, 13
Hanafi school, 25
Harthiyya neighborhood, 30, 106
al-Hashemi, Faisal bin al-Husayn (Faisal I), 3, 27

Hashemite monarchy, 3–4, 23, 26–28, 31–32, 36–38, 40, 49, 55–56, 168, 177
al-Hassan, Hawraa, 165
Haydar, Jamal, 23
Helfont, Samuel, 85, 94, 171
highways, 3, 28–29, 42, 57, 226
hijab, 176
honor killing, 170–71
Hoover Institution, 14–16, 18, 137
housing, 6, 10–11, 14, 20, 23–24, 28–32, 36–40, 43, 45, 47, 49–58, 62, 64, 67, 76, 86, 95–96, 133–34, 142, 149–50, 153, 158; lotteries for, 50, 54, 134; designs, 54–56, informal, 30, 33, 35, 40, 48. *See also sarifas*, slums.
human rights, 18
Hussein, Saddam, 1, 4–5, 7–9, 11, 14–15, 17, 27, 33, 55, 61–70, 72–75, 77–78, 80–85, 87–91, 93–97, 101–3, 105–6, 108–18, 121, 123–24, 126–35, 137–41, 144–47, 149–55, 157–62, 164–67, 170–71, 174, 176–79, 182, 187, 189, 191–94, 198, 207–9, 220; cult of personality, 72–74, 78, 83–85, 93–94, 134–5, 141; political career, 7–8, 64, 103, 187; and war, 61–70, 77–78, 87–91, 101, 187; and religion 73–75, 84–85; and food rations 101–31; policies towards women 78–79, 81, 140–41, 169–70, 175–76, 177–81; views on masculinity 141, 161–66, 179, 181–82; Office of the President, 128, 140, 144, 150. *See also* Baʿth Party
Hussein, ʿUday, 135, 166, 170, 176

iftar, 85
imaginary geographies, 11, 57–59, 226–29
India, 67, 167

inflation, 80–81, 86, 153
informants, 17, 82, 136, 138, 145, 174
internally displaced persons, 210
International Crisis Group, 202
intifada: 1952, 36; 1991: 9, 87, 89–90, 94–95, 103, 108, 129–30, 139, 160, 162, 164
Iran, 2, 8, 55, 61–72, 74–78, 85–86, 88, 90, 96, 107, 119, 133, 142, 163, 224
Iran-Iraq War (1980–88), 13, 20, 24, 57, 60–63, 65, 70, 72, 74–75, 78, 80, 82, 84–86, 88, 91, 94, 97, 107, 109, 116, 124, 128, 133, 139–40, 160–61, 167, 169, 177–78, 199, 224; monuments to, 72–74, petitions relating to, 120, 123–245, 139–41, 156; War of the Cities, 62, 69–70. *See also* deserters
Iranian Revolution (1979), 63
Iraq Memory Foundation, 15
Iraq National Bank, 27
Iraq National Library and Archives, 14
Iraq Petroleum Company, 26–27
Iraqi Communist Party. *See* communists
Iraqi Development Board. *See* Development Board
Iraqi Governing Council, 199
Iraqi National Museum, 229
Iraqi Revolution (1958), 4, 38–39, 128
Isfahan, 69
Islam, 94, 165; political, 85
Islamic Courts, 3

Jamila neighborhood, 44–45, 150
al-Jawad, Imam Muhammad ibn 'Ali, 25
al-Jawaheri, Yasmin Husein, 104, 176, 180
Jews, 3, 28
al-Jibara, 'Abd al-Hassan, 217
Jihad neighborhood, 119, 151

Johnson, Ron, 195, 201
Jordan, 120, 160

al-Ka'abi, Muhannad, 215
al-Kadhim, Imam Musa ibn Ja'far, 25
Kadhimiyya district, 5, 13, 25, 33, 35–36, 45, 204–6, 223, 229; Kadhimiyya District Council, 204
Kamaliyya neighborhood, 166
Karbala, 70, 84, 127, 223
Karkh district, 5, 24–26, 36, 45, 58, 64
Karrada district, 5, 33, 45, 202; Karrada District Advisory Council, 202
Kathem, Mehiyar, 215
Khadra' neighborhood, 6
Khomeini, Ayatollah Ruhollah, 63, 69, 85
Khoury, Dina, 17, 19, 61, 74, 77, 85, 94, 113, 117, 156, 170
Khulafa' Street, 64
killing, extrajudicial, 41, 62, 67, 89–90, 150, 160–62, 200, 212, 215, 218, 226
Kirkuk, 168
Kurds, 12, 62; Kurdistan, 12, 90, 226; Kurdistan Regional Government, 90
Kuwait, 2, 8, 58, 66, 87–89, 92–94, 101, 103, 130, 162, 224; Iraqi invasion of, 93–94

law, 7, 10, 24, 28, 40, 42, 50, 111–12, 114, 117, 122, 143–44, 155–56, 161, 166, 168–74, 176, 182, 198, 213, 218, 228; against crime related to food rationing, 111, 114; against desertion, 116–18, 129, 170, 173; against prostitution, 161, 168–69, 170, 172–73; against sodomy, 182; housing, 50. *See also* punishment *and* collective punishment *and* crime

Le Corbusier, 31
LeFebvre, Henri, 33, 61, 96, 181
al-liwat. See sodomy
Local Governance Program, 193–94
looting, 14–15, 187–88, 218, 229

mahalla, 3–4, 6, 8, 53
Mahdi Army, 210–16, 219
Maidan neighborhood, 168
Makiya, Kanan, 15
Makiya, Muhammad, 30
malaria, 33
al-Maliki, Nouri, 203, 215–17
Mansur district, 5–6, 30, 36, 45, 83
marriage, 80, 86, 119, 166, 175, 177–80, 182; *zawaj 'urfi*, 175
Marsh Arabs, 40
martyrs, 55, 62, 72, 76–77, 84, 93, 95, 128, 139, 143, 147, 150, 156
Martyrs' Day, 84, 93
Martyrs' Monument, 72
masculinity, 141, 161–66, 179, 181–82
Maysan province, 128
Mecca, 84
Medical City, 65
migration, 3, 40, 48, 167
Military Directorate, 67
militias, 77–78, 170, 190–91, 207, 209–12, 214–16
Ministry of Agriculture, 51
Ministry of Defense, 148, 151, 157, 225
Ministry of Development, 31
Ministry of Finance, 51
Ministry of Housing and Construction, 86
Ministry of Labor and Social Affairs, 169
Ministry of Oil, 225
Ministry of Planning, 14, 67
Ministry of Social Affairs, 31

Ministry of the Interior, 225
Ministry of Trade, 105, 108, 110, 112–13, 118–19, 122–23, 129
Ministry of Transportation, 150
Minoprio, Spencely, MacFarlane, 56, 224
modernization, 11, 27, 30, 34, 56, 60, 64, 224
Mosul, 70, 223
Mother of All Battles Mosque, 94
Muhammad (prophet), 83
muhasasa, 225–26, 228
mukhtars, 3, 6, 7, 120, 122–23, 131, 189, 202, 207, 211, 221, 224
Mustansariyya University, 67
Mutanabbi Street, 229
Muthanna airbase, 71
My Country, My Country, 208

Nahrain University, 73
Najaf, 70, 223
Najm, Nuri, 66
al-Nakib, Farah, 58
Narcotics Control Unit, 163
Neighborhood Advisory Councils, 197, 201, 204–5
New Baghdad district, 5, 154, 163, 206
NGOs, 204, 216
Nigeria, 224
Non-Aligned Movement, 64, 66–67

Office of Reconstruction and Humanitarian Assistance, 187
Office of the Vice Chair of Iraq's Revolutionary Command Council, 148, 152
Officers' City neighborhood, 39
Officers' Neighborhood, 39
oil, 2, 11, 20, 24, 26–27, 30–31, 49, 55, 57, 60, 66, 69, 81, 87, 96, 101–2, 104–5,

129–30, 152, 188, 206, 220, 224–25; oil boom, 20, 24, 26, 30, 49, 57; oil revenues, 2, 11, 26–27, 31, 49, 55, 60, 66, 101, 220, 224
Oil-for-Food Program, 104, 129, 152
OPEC, 27
Ottoman Empire, 3, 23, 30, 32, 75–76, 97, 134, 222, 229

Pahlavi, Muhammad Reza, 63
Pakistan, 120
Parliament, 200, 207, 210
parties (political), 190, 210, 212, 214, 218, 222, 224–25, 228
party officials, 1, 6, 7–9, 17, 59, 76, 83, 90–91, 93, 95, 97, 102–4, 106, 113, 115, 118–20, 122–23, 125–31, 133–35, 146, 148–55, 157, 160, 162–63, 171, 173–75, 178. *See also* Ba'th Party
Patel, David Siddhartha, 191
People's Day, 152–57
Persian Empire, 74
Persian Gulf, 224
Persians, 74–75
Persinger, Sarah, 179
petitions, 2, 16, 18, 20, 96, 112, 118, 120, 123, 125, 132–58, 204, 210, 221
Pieri, Caecilia, 227
police, 6, 17, 33, 42, 46–47, 51–54, 104, 109, 120, 122, 124, 138, 148, 150, 160, 163, 165–66, 168, 171–72, 188, 214, 216
Ponti, Gio, 31
Popular Army, 9, 67, 69, 77–79, 87, 147, 151
popular committees, 6–7, 109, 112–13, 131, 169, 178, 202
prices, 27–28, 38, 50–51, 82, 86–87, 106, 114, 127, 158, 179, 229
prison, 17, 41, 44, 111, 124, 169–70, 172–73, 182, 227. *See also* Abu Ghraib prison
prostitution, 16, 96, 113, 137, 159, 161, 163, 165–73, 175–77, 179, 181–83; brothels, 166, 169, 172–75; pimping (*samsara*), 167, 169–70, 172–73
protests, 9, 36, 63, 89–90, 95, 127, 162, 196, 225–27
punishment, 2, 10, 74, 79, 102, 111–12, 115–23, 125–32, 143, 161, 163, 168, 170–73, 182. *See also* collective punishment *and* crime *and* law
Pursley, Sara, 61

Qadisiyya, Battle of (637 CE), 75, 178
Qadisiyyat Saddam. *See* Iran-Iraq War
al-Qaeda in Iraq, 190
Qajar dynasty, 75–76
al-Qarawee, Harith, 94
Qasim, 'Abd al-Karim, 4, 33, 38–41, 49–51, 168–69
Qom, 69

radio, 138
al-Radi, Nuha, 88, 93, 96, 159, 162
Radwaniyya Neighborhood Advisory Council, 204
Ramadan, 84–85, 104, 139, 153
Ramadan, Taha, 106
Rashid district, 112, 122, 172
Rashid Street, 28, 36
rationing (food), 10, 12, 16, 20, 96, 101–31, 149, 151, 158, 163, 170, 179, 207, 210, 221
Regional Command Council (RCC), 68, 145, 148, 173
rent, 30, 38–40, 50, 55, 81, 148, 151
Republican Guards, 114, 150
Republican Palace, 15, 194
Research Triangle International, 193

Retirement Department, 148
Revolution City. *See* Sadr City
Revolutionary Command Council (RCC). *See* Baʻth Party
Rice, Col. Joe, 198, 215
Risala neighborhood, 204–5
Risala Neighborhood Advisory Council, 205
Riyadh, 38
Robert's Rules of Order 198, 208
Rohde, Achim, 164, 170, 176
Rusafa district, 5, 24–26, 29, 36, 45, 58, 189
Russia, 69, 141

Sabean-Mandeans, 12
Saddam City. *See* Sadr City
Saddam Hussein Day, 83
Saddam University, 73
Sadr Bureau, 210–12, 214, 218–19
Sadr City (al-ʻAsima/Revolution City/al-Thawra/Saddam City), 5, 11, 13, 33, 38–49, 57–58, 64, 68, 72–74, 80, 91, 96, 114, 118, 123, 164, 182, 192–93, 204, 206, 209, 211–17, 219–20, 223; design, 42, 47; forced displacement to, 41–42, 44, 47; surveillance of, 42, 48, 57; opposition groups in, 41–42, 46, 58, 73; services in, 45–46, 48, 210–12, 214, 218–19; Sadr City District Advisory Council, 204, 213–17
al-Sadr, Grand Ayatollah Muhammad Baqir, execution of, 68
al-Sadr, Grand Ayatollah Muhammad Sadiq, 192
al-Sadr, Muqtada, 20, 191–93, 209–10, 216–19
al-Saʻid, Nuri, 27, 38
al-Saʻidi, Lt.-Gen. ʻAbd al-Wahhab, 225
Salam neighborhood, 4, 40–41, 125

Saleem, Jawad, 226
Salter, Lord Arthur, 31
same-sex activity (male), 164–66. *See also* sodomy
samsara. *See* prostitution
sanctions, 9, 12, 27, 82, 87, 90, 93–97, 101–4, 106–68, 111, 114, 116, 119, 122, 126, 129, 131, 149–50, 152, 154, 156, 158–64, 166–67, 170–71, 176, 178–81, 187, 218, 224–25; and corruption, 225; effect on regime, 114, 119, 131, 160, 162–63, 171; humanitarian impact of, 2, 20, 62, 95–97, 102, 106–7, 113, 120–21, 127, 130, 133, 143, 151, 159, 179; impact on infrastructure, 218; impact on oil sector, 224; petitions relating to, 154, 156, 158; effects on women, 166, 179–81; terms of, 101, 108, 160, 162–63
sarifas, 28–29, 32–44, 46–49, 52, 55, 57–58, 73, 167–68, 193
Sasanian Empire, 75
Saudi Arabia, 3, 66, 87, 224
Saydiyya Neighborhood Advisory Council, 204
Saʻdun neighborhood, 28–29
Scud missiles, 69
Sectarian violence (2005–2009), 97, 188, 190, 205, 209–12, 214, 218, 222, 226–27
Security Council (UN), 101
Security Directorate, 67
services (public), 6, 9–10, 13, 17, 20, 33, 46, 48, 65, 90, 107, 116, 129–30, 195, 197, 199, 201–7, 209–15, 217–20, 222, 224–27; construction of, 33, 46, 65; effects of war on, 130, 187–91, 205–6, 209, 224
sewers, 33, 89, 190
sex work. *See* prostitution

Shah. *See* Pahlavi, Muhammad Reza
Shakriyya neighborhood, 33, 35–36, 45
Shama, Hassan, 217
Shatt al-ʿArab, 61, 63
Shawra wa Umm Jidr neighborhood, 44
Shiʿa, 10, 12–13, 20, 25, 58, 62–63, 67–68, 70, 73–75, 84–85, 89, 94, 116, 190–92, 196, 204, 210–12, 214, 216, 218–19, 225–26, 229; Shiʿa-majority neighborhoods, 33, 46, 190, 193, 204, 210–11, 214, 219, 223, 226, 229; persecution of, 68, 74–77, 94, 116; role in government, 225. *See also* Daʿwa Party
shuʿba. See Baʿth Party
Shuʿla neighborhood, 41–42, 44, 46, 193, 210
al-Sistani, Ayatollah ʿAli, 196
Sirri, Omar, 228
slums, 23, 25, 27–29, 31–33, 35, 37, 39, 41, 45, 47, 49, 51, 53, 55, 57, 59
smuggling, 10, 113, 159, 162–63, 179
Social Solidarity Fund, 140, 156
sodomy, 161–62, 164, 166, 168–70, 172, 181. *See also* same-sex activity
Soviet Union, 105, 108, 116, 136, 141, 157
Stanford University, 14–16, 18
State Company for Foodstuff Trading, 108, 115
State Company for Grain Processing, 108
students, 11, 14, 44, 68, 75, 78–79, 136–37, 171, 226
Sunnis, 3–4, 12–13, 25, 94, 190, 200, 205, 210, 212, 214, 219, 225–26
Syria, 66

Tahrir Square, 226–28
Tal Muhammad neighborhood, 33, 35
tanzim, 7

Tawhid wa-l-Jihad. *See* al-Qaeda in Iraq
Tehran, 69
terrorism, 62, 67, 225
Tharthar dam, 26, 32
al-Thawra (newspaper), 70, 86, 176
al-Thawra. *See* Sadr City
theft, 15, 113, 117, 159, 162–63, 212
Tigris River, 5, 24, 26, 36, 45, 57, 89, 229
Tikrit, 70
Tishrin protests, 225, 229
torture, 17, 161
tribal groups, 47, 164–65, 175, 182, 190, 198, 207–8, 218–19
Turkey, 163
television, 68, 84, 138, 173

United Nations (UN), 2, 20, 36, 87–88, 90, 96, 101, 106–7, 129, 152, 160, 162, 193
UN Resolution no. 678, 88
unemployment, 48, 153, 157, 159, 160–62, 177, 182, 203, 207, 219, 226
unions, 38–39, 50–51, 56–57
United Arab Emirates, 224
United Kingdom. *See* Britain
United States, 4, 12, 14–15, 18–19, 87–88, 90–91, 101, 105, 134, 187, 196, 216, 220, 225
University neighborhood, 53
Unknown Soldier Monument, 72
uprisings, 90, 93, 102–3, 130, 135, 150, 164
US Agency for International Development (USAID), 193–95, 205
US invasion (2003), 2, 4, 14–15, 96–97, 187–88, 190, 192–93, 202–5, 209–10, 218–20, 222, 225; US occupation of Iraq (2003–2011), 13, 188–89, 192, 195, 209–10
US military, 11, 13, 200, 202–3, 210, 213–17, 226, 228

Victory Arches, 72
violence, 13, 15, 17, 41, 67–68, 86, 90, 97, 112, 121, 143, 151, 158, 166, 171, 173–75, 177, 181–82, 190, 209–10, 218, 227, 229
vocational neighborhoods, 53–56

War of the Cities. *See* Iran-Iraq War
Washash neighborhood, 33, 36, 41–42, 45
Washington, DC, 14, 16, 18
Wasit province, 128
wasta, 225
water, 6, 41, 46, 64, 71, 86, 88–89, 91–92, 101, 130, 187–89, 191, 205, 218
water buffalo, 33, 40, 47
Wathba (1948), 36
Western Baghdad neighborhood, 39, 54–55.

Whiting, Rebecca, 17–18
women, 12, 33, 47, 62, 71, 77–80, 86–88, 95, 110, 113, 136, 140–41, 160, 162, 164–72, 175–83, 200–1, 204; General Federation of Iraqi Women, 79–80, 178; Saddam Hussein's policies towards, 78–79, 81, 140–41, 169–70, 175–76, 177–81; violence towards, 151–52, 170, 176
World War I, 3, 26, 75
World War II, 24, 28, 56, 116
Wright, Frank Lloyd, 31

Yarmuk neighborhood, 45, 51, 58
Yemen, 171

Zafraniyya neighborhood, 64
zawaj 'urfi. *See* marriage
Zayuna neighborhood, 51

The authorized representative in the EU for product safety and compliance is:
Mare Nostrum Group B.V.
Mauritskade 21D
1091 GC Amsterdam
The Netherlands
Email address: gpsr@mare-nostrum.co.uk

KVK chamber of commerce number: 96249943

The authorized representative in the EU for product safety and compliance is:
Mare Nostrum Group
B.V Doelen 72
4831 GR Breda
The Netherlands

www.ingramcontent.com/pod-product-compliance
Lightning Source LLC
Chambersburg PA
CBHW032134250426
43661CB00077B/1873